A Pictorial Biography of

A PICTORIAL BIOGRAPHY OF

Jack London

by Russ Kingman
Foreword by Irving Stone

FOR

JACK LONDON RESEARCH CENTER

PUBLISHED BY

DAVID REJL   **CALIFORNIA**

Library of Congress Cataloging in Publication Data

Kingman, Russ.
    A pictorial life of Jack London.

    Includes index.
    1. London, Jack, 1876–1916—Iconography. 2. Authors,
American—20th century—Biography. I. Title.
PS3523.046Z665 1979   818'.5'209 [B]   79–17998
ISBN: 0–517–531631 (cloth)
          0–517–540932 (paper)

10 9 8 7 6 5 4 3

TO
WINIFRED KINGMAN
MY WIFE AND COLLABORATOR

Jack London had his mate—
Charmian. Winnie is mine
and we have shared everything,
including this book, for fifty-two years.

Acknowledgments

I owe much to the merchants and restauranteurs of Jack London Square in Oakland, who in 1968 asked me to be Executive Director of the Jack London Square Association. At that time I had very little knowledge of Jack London. It was obvious that if I were going to handle the promotion of Jack London Square I had best know much more about the man. I opened his books. Then I began to open books about him. When I finished *Sailor on Horseback* by Irving Stone, I knew I would never be satisfied until I had learned everything possible about the man and his works. From that day to this I have read everything I have been able to find.

While at Jack London Square I shared my office for a few years with that unsurpassed Jack London scholar, Jim Sisson. Whenever I ran into a dead end I called on him and invariably he had the answer or was able to tell me where I could find it. Sisson has been researching Jack London for over thirty years and Jack London scholarship owes more to him than any person I know. Only when Jim returned a copy of my manuscript with his approval did I send it to the publisher.

During the past ten years I have talked with everyone I could locate who had known Jack London. On this trail I found facts and inspiration to go on with my research. In every instance these people had nothing but fond memories. Lee Kynock, who worked on the ranch, said, "My job was to take care of the horses. Whenever Jack returned to the ranch he handed the reins to me. I never saw him when he had had too much to drink. He was a wonderful man."

Jack's daughters, Joan and Bess, have both shared every memory they could bring to mind about their father. Our years of close friendship have made me feel like one of the family.

Elsie Martinez is the daughter of Jim Whitaker and the wife of Xavier Martinez and, therefore, was often with Jack. The endless hours we have spent talking about Jack and the "crowd" have made me feel that I was there with them hunting abalone in Carmel or on a picnic at the old Dingee place in Oakland.

Carrie Burlingame drew vivid pictures of her many visits to the ranch. Arthur Wiget told me how angry his brother Werner became when people called Jack a drunk and how he always told them, "I have been Jack London's foreman on the ranch since 1906, and I have never seen him drunk or even with too much to drink."

The most golden of all hours were those spent listening to Irving Shepard talk about his Uncle Jack. He lived on the Jack London ranch from the age of ten until he died sixty-six years later. He was a treasure trove of information and, in his modest way, always willing to share what he had learned through the years.

And how can I adequately thank that master of the biographical novel, Irving Stone, for all the encouragement he has given me. He gave me unrestricted use of his own research material for *Sailor on Horseback.* How I envy him when I read his interviews with so many of Jack's closest friends who had passed on many years before my research on Jack began. To be sure, these people contributed every mistake in Stone's book, but they also gave him the inspiration he needed to bring out the charisma of Jack London in a way that will probably never be duplicated.

I was also able to review the Jack London materials at the University of California at Berkeley, the University of California at Los Angeles, Utah State University, Stanford University, the University of Southern California, the Jack London State Historical Park in Glen Ellen, and—especially—the Henry E. Huntington Library. The expertise and willingness of the Huntington staff made it possible for me to scan thousands of items in months instead of years. I am especially indebted to David Mike Hamilton and Allan Jutzi for their assistance "far beyond the call of duty." To the Huntington I owe much of the material in this book. In addition, a large portion of it was authenticated from originals I was allowed to see there. Most Jack London scholars are genuinely appreciative of Charmian London's foresight in placing the majority of Jack's material in the safe and competent hands of Huntington.

I have had excellent cooperation from everyone I turned to for information. For instance, Frank M. Festa, Superintendent of the Erie County Correctional Facility in Alden, New York, and Kristin Keough and Walter S. Dunn, Jr., of the Buffalo and Erie County Historical Society, went out of their way to provide pictures and information concerning Jack's incarceration in the Erie County Penitentiary in 1894.

It would take another volume to list the many friends who have encouraged me and helped me along the way. To Bill and Irene Purcell, Katherine Littell, Sal Noto, Clarice Stasz, Dale Walker, Andrew Flink, Franklin Walker, Joseph MacDonald, Waring Jones, Carl Bernatovech, David Schlottmann, and hundreds of our customers at the Jack London Bookstore I can only say thanks!

To Milo Shepard, Executor of the Jack London Estate, I am indebted for the unlimited use of pictures in Jack London's nearly one hundred photograph albums, unrestricted access to everything concerning Jack London under his control, and for his willingness to hunt for obscure items still re-

maining at the ranch. This book could never have been produced without him.

I have reserved for last the ones who have contributed enough to this book to be considered collaborators. On completion of the first draft, I sent one copy of the manuscript to Richard Weiderman, publisher of Wolf House Books, and another copy to Earle Labor, author of *Jack London* and a leading Jack London scholar. These copies were returned with corrections and suggestions for improvement of the work. Armed with their ideas, I rewrote the manuscript in its entirety. Any excellence this work has is mainly due to these two London scholars—any inaccuracies or flaws in the manuscript are mine.

Finally, I would like to acknowledge the assistance of my editor at Crown Publishers, Jake Goldberg, whose guidance and suggestions were invaluable.

Foreword by Irving Stone

The love of reading is the background for the love of writing. By the age of nine, I had read my way through the children's section of the neighborhood library in San Francisco, which prompted me to start writing my own stories. However, it was not until I came across Jack London's superb and autobiographical novel, *Martin Eden*, at the age of thirteen or fourteen, that I understood that I could and would spend my entire life writing books.

Mine is not a unique experience. I have met authors in almost every country in the world who confided that they owed their impetus and original strength to become book writers from reading *Martin Eden* and others of Jack London's compelling novels, such as *The Sea Wolf* and *The Valley of the Moon*, as well as his superb short stories, and his socioeconomic masterpieces, *The Iron Heel* and *The People of the Abyss*.

Jack London was the most widely read and beloved author in America for some fifteen years after the turn of the century. But the American reading public is fickle, dropping an author immediately after his death, perhaps a protest against anyone who appears immortal yet proves to be only too mortal in the end. Herman Melville went unread for decades, until rediscovered by a literary critic.

Jack London's many fine and moving books, with the exception of *The Call of the Wild*, plunged into as deep an abyss as the Atlantic or Pacific oceans. In 1938 when I wrote my biography of Jack London, *Sailor on Horseback*, he was regarded as a writer of wild adventure stories and children's yarns.

And Jack London had been dead for only twenty-two years!

At long last, the tide is turning. In 1977 two biographies of Jack London were published. *Sailor on Horseback* was updated. There was considerable press coverage of the books and discussions on the air, most of them enthusiastic about Jack London and his literary contributions.

The revival is off and running. Russ Kingman's pictorial biography will add new fuel and excitement. For after all, Jack London was an authentic American genius and a writer of worldwide significance.

Preface

In *Jack London and the Klondike*, Franklin Walker pointed out that London always wrote best when he drew his material from the stuff of his own life. A vast amount of his output, both fiction and non-fiction, was eminently autobiographical, which gave his work the ring of truth.

In this biography I am dealing openly and directly with a number of controversial and little-understood facets of Jack's life, especially such facets as his birth, his attitudes toward capitalism and socialism, and the causes of his death.

There will always be controversy over London's birth. Who was his father? Was it W. H. Chaney, John London, or some unknown party? Jack's nephew, Irving Shepard, honestly convinced that John London was Jack's real father, told me, "I have seen a letter from Jack London to George Sterling in which he told George that he was thoroughly convinced that John London was his father."

Irving Shepard's sincerity notwithstanding, after many years of in-depth research, the preponderance of evidence leads me to conclude that W. H. Chaney and Flora Wellman were married June 12, 1874. Chaney denied that he was married to Flora because he had never bothered to divorce his three wives. But we cannot verify this because all record in San Francisco were destroyed by the 1906 earthquake and fire.

Capitalists in this work is a general term used in Jack's own context. He was never at war with individual capitalists who were not exploiting their workers—those who shared the profits in a reasonable proportion with the workers who were responsible for the added value of the product. However, he hated the capitalistic system with a white-hot passion in his early years because of the hopeless, pathetic position in which it put the masses of people. Luxury in those days was limited to the lucky few who inherited their position in life, with little or no effort or ability of their own, in most cases, and to the few strong ones who had donned nail-studded boots and ruthlessly climbed over their fellow workers to become exploiters themselves.

You will note as the book unfolds that Jack's socialism declined in almost direct proportion to the gradual takeover of socialist reform measures by the other political parties. In 1904 the socialists with whom Jack associated were struggling for abolition of child labor, better working conditions, some form of job insurance, community ownership of public utilities and transportation, government ownership or control of all essential industry, etc. Many of these goals began to filter into the platforms of the two major parties and caused the socialist vote to decline, until by 1916, when Jack resigned from the Socialist Party, it had little power and practically no political influence.

Another controversy that will probably never be settled concerns the cause of Jack's death. A few biographers have been guilty of coming to published conclusions without having done adequate research—or, in some cases, without having had access to vital information in the hands of the Jack London Estate or in the extensive collections of London material at the Huntington Library in San Marino, California and the Utah State University Library at Logan, Utah. My own research leads me to believe that Jack London could not have committed suicide. I have no doubt that, had he wanted to do so, he would have. He always believed that a man had that right. However, the manner in which some suggest Jack died would have been completely out of character for him. Had they said, "He inadvertently took an overdose of morphine, which in combination with his uremic condition triggered a coma and subsequent death," we would have to admit to that possibility, since no one was present at the time. The fact that his own physician, Dr. William S. Porter, head of Merritt Hospital in Oakland, was with him at the time of his death and that three other doctors who were there agreed with his diagnosis carries significant weight. I have chosen to accept the medical judgment of the four competent doctors who were present at the time of death.

While nearly ten years of extensive research has been done in an effort to give a true picture of Jack London to the same general audience he has captivated all these years, this biography lays no claim to being either definitive or scholarly. My most difficult problem has been in deciding what should be omitted, since to do justice to Jack London would require at least three volumes of six hundred pages each.

Jack had nearly one hundred photograph albums, and his scrapbooks required two full reels of microfilm. We have selected the most representative pictures and articles available to make this book more enjoyable.

World War I was the most devastating force in Jack's life. It destroyed his foreign market, slowed his American market to a trickle, caused a deadly wedge to form in the International Socialist movement, made Jack resign from the Socialist Party, and ruined his greatest contribution to American literature—*The Star Rover*. The latter book was published in 1915 when World War I was uppermost in the minds of the reading public. The publisher, therefore, did very little promotion and one of the best novels ever written in this country received little attention and has been overlooked by literary critics ever since.

Though the Industrial Workers of the World were far too fanatical for Jack, in some ways he was much closer to them than to the namby-pamby Socialist Labor Party to which he had belonged. But Jack's sympathies were with the Allies in the war against Germany. The I.W.W. and the Socialist Party were pacifists in the struggle. This was the final reason for Jack's resignation from the party.

Jack had been thoroughly misunderstood. The majority of his socialist comrades couldn't understand his building Wolf House, his use of servants, and his life, as they thought, as a landed aristocrat. Everything had been blown out of proportion. They failed to realize that many members of the party lived in much finer homes than his ranch cottage and that his ranch was small in comparison with ones owned by many socialists across the land.

Mark Twain made a silly statement to the press: "It would serve this man London right to have the working class get control of things. He would have to call out the militia to collect his royalties." Twain's humor was superior to his knowledge and understanding of Jack London. He didn't know that Jack would have been overjoyed to have his royalties go to the cause. He would have been happy to live the simple life he loved under a socialist-run government based upon equality for all people.

Jack never believed in the idea of putting all wealth into one great pie to be divided equally. His idea of government was one under which all men would have equal opportunity, but with ample rewards for incentive. Jack sincerely believed in the right of any man to better himself financially through his own efforts. He lived in a system of capitalism, and he saw nothing wrong in his enjoyment of the benefits he had earned under this system. When socialism took over the reins of government, he would gladly relinquish whatever was necessary to be a part of it. He felt the benefits would be far greater than the sacrifices. He realized, however, that the cooperative commonwealth was a long way in the future. In the meantime, he would go on demonstrating how such a society could exist by the way he operated his ranch in the Valley of the Moon.

Jack London must be recognized as a major figure in American literature. During his writing years he was the most popular and highest-paid author in America. His name was a household word around the world, and no other author before or since has had the astonishing amount of newspaper coverage he has had.

He was published in every leading magazine of his day: The *Atlantic, Century, Harper's, McClure's, Collier's, Cosmopolitan, Saturday Evening Post,* etc., and received top dollar for his work. From 1899 to 1916 he wrote a thousand words a day and sold every word he wrote. He produced over fifty books in seventeen years on an extremely diversified range of subjects. In addition to his books, he wrote over a thousand separately published items.

Documentation has been purposely omitted in this book. However, I will be happy to supply the exact references for any material used to any London scholar on request. A full set of source references and other extensive biographical information is also available through the Jack London Educational Research Foundation, Box 337, Glen Ellen, CA 95442.

Jack London was and is a literary giant. Critics today have a difficult time with Jack and tend to criticize his work in relation to their contemporaries instead of his. While he was a portrayer of his times, his writing was far ahead of his day. A comparison of the writing of Jack London in the early years of the twentieth century with other writers of that period tells us why a suffering public turned en masse to the freshness and vitality with which Jack kicked open the literary gates of a new century.

Jack's knowledge of philosophy and psychology furnished him with many themes. His rich, unusual experiences gave reality to his plots. A fine sense of drama, a thorough knowledge of his craft, and the ability to keep out of the literary mold of his day made his writing effective, enjoyable, powerful, and readable. He was a true storyteller, and his tales, which have lived for over sixty years, will continue to live as long as there is ink and paper in the world to print them.

This biography is presented as a tribute to those wonderful tales as well as to the man himself.

Russ Kingman
Glen Ellen, California
1979

It was wedding day for Flora Wellman Chaney and John London on September 7, 1876. Flora's eight-month-old son, John Griffith Chaney, was present. From that moment he knew real father-love, but never knew who his real father was. For about fourteen years he used the name John London—Johnny at home—but after that he was known to the world as Jack London.

Despite the close and warm relationship with John London, Jack always lived under a cloud of doubt as to the identity of his real father. He must have seen his mother's wedding certificate in the plain wooden box where she kept her keepsakes. Yet Frank Atherton, Jack's childhood chum, never mentioned Jack's concern about his paternity in his unpublished manuscript, *Jack London in Boyhood Adventures,* so it is possible Jack did not know that he was not a London until 1897, when he was twenty-one.

Jack London's nature compelled him to search for his real father, but Flora's personality made it impossible for Jack to ask her. His logical mind led him across the Bay to the San Francisco Library to dig through old newspaper files for records of his birth.

Under births in the *Chronicle* he looked for the name Flora Wellman Chaney, since that was his mother's name on the marriage certificate when she married John London. Thumbing back to January 13, 1876, he read this announcement:

BIRTHS
CHANEY—In this city, January 12, the wife of
W. H. Chaney, of a son.

There it was in print. No denying it. He thumbed back several more months hunting for further clues. He was dumbfounded when he saw this article in the *Chronicle* of June 4, 1875:

A DISCARDED WIFE
WHY MRS. CHANEY TWICE
ATTEMPTED SUICIDE

Driven from Home for Refusing to Destroy her Unborn Infant—A Chapter of Heartlessness and Domestic Misery
Day before yesterday Mrs. Chaney, wife of "Professor" W. H. Chaney, the astrologer, attempted suicide by taking laudanum. Failing in the effort she yesterday shot herself with a pistol in the forehead. The ball glanced off, inflicting only a flesh wound, and friends interfered before she could accomplish her suicidal purpose.

THE INCENTIVE TO THE TERRIBLE ACT
was domestic infelicity. Husband and wife have been known for a year past as the center of a little band of extreme Spiritualists, most of whom professed, if they did not practice, the offensive free-love doctrines of the ·licentious Woodhull. To do Mr. Chaney justice, he has persistently denied the holding of such broad tenets. He has been several times married before this last fiasco of the hearthstone, but it is supposed that all his former wives have been duly laid away to rest, and now repose, like Polonius, in rural churchyards,

At their hearts a grass-green turf
At their backs a stone

The last marriage took place about a year ago. Mrs. Chaney, formerly Miss Flora Wellman, is a native of Ohio. She came to this coast about the

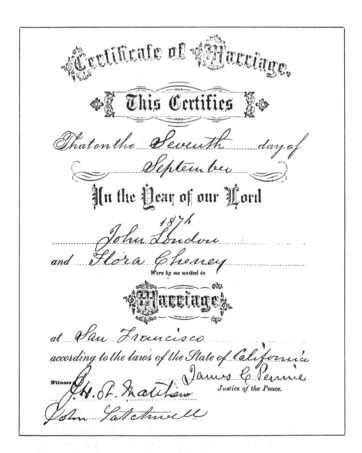

Certificate of marriage for Flora Chaney and John London

time the Professor took the journey overland through the romantic sagebrush, and for awhile supported herself by teaching music. It is hard to see what attracted her toward this man, to whom she was united after a short acquaintance. The union seems to have been the result of a mania like, and yet unlike, that which drew Desdemona toward the sooty Moor.

THE MARRIED LIFE OF THE COUPLE

is said to have been full of self-denial and devoted affection on the part of the wife, and of harsh words and unkind treatment on the part of the husband. He practiced astrology, calculated horoscopes for a consideration, lectured on chemistry and astronomy, blasphemed the Christian religion, published a journal of hybrid doctrines, called the *Philomathean,* and pretended to calculate "cheap nativities" on the transit of the planets for $10 each, for all of which he obtained but slender pecuniary recompense. Astrological knowledge is, of course, highly valuable, but the supply in San Francisco seems to be slightly in excess of the demand, and no matter how much Professor Chaney lectured, scattered circulars, watched the movements of the planets, and cast nativities, his exchequer continued painfully bare and his larder nearly empty. Sometimes he almost

PINED AGAIN FOR THE CONFINEMENT OF THE TOMBS Prison, within those massive walls and gloomy shadows his rigorous assertion of personal freedom is once said to have brought him. The wife assisted him in the details of business, darned his hose, drudged at the wash-tub, took care of other people's children for hire, and generously gave him whatever money she earned and could spare beyond her actual expenses. She never told her sorrow, nor since her recent great trouble had she communicated them, except to intimate friends. She says that about three weeks ago she discovered, with a natural feeling of maternal pleasure, that she was *enceinte.* She told her husband, and asked to be relieved for two or three months of the care of the children by means of which she had been contributing to their material support. He refused to accede to the request and some angry words followed.

DRIVEN FROM HOME

Then he told her she had better destroy her unborn babe. This she indignantly declined to do, and on last Thursday morning he said to her,

Flora Wellman Chaney

"Flora, I want you to pack up and leave this house." She replied, "I have no money and nowhere to go." He said, "Neither have I any to give you." A woman in the house offered her $25, but she flung it from her in a burst of anguish, saying, "What do I care for this? It will be of no use to me without my husband's love." This show of sincere affection had no effect on the flinty-headed calculator of other people's nativities. He told the poor woman that he had sold the furnishings (for which she had helped to pay) and it was useless to think of her remaining there any longer.

THE WIFE'S DESPAIR AND ATTEMPTED SUICIDE

He then left her, and shortly afterwards she made her first attempt at suicide, following it by the effort to kill herself with a pistol on the following morning, as already stated. Failing in both endeavors, Mrs. Chaney was removed in a half-insane condition from Dr. Ruttley's on Mis-

Professor William H. Chaney

Professor Chaney's astrological work

sion Street to the house of a friend, where she still remains, somewhat pacified and in a mental condition indicating that she will not again attempt self-destruction. The story given here is the lady's own, as filtered through her near associates.

JACK'S CORRESPONDENCE WITH CHANEY

Finding Chaney was no problem for Jack. Chaney was well known in his field, and after a brief search Jack got his Chicago address from one of his fellow astrologers. To keep his mother from knowing, he used his friend Ted Applegarth's address for a reply and wrote to Chaney on May 28, 1897, asking what kind of woman his mother was and whether Chaney was his father. A few days later Jack received this reply:

June 4, 1897
Prof. W. H. Chaney
College of Astrology
2829 Calumet Avenue
Chicago

Dear Sir:

Yours of the 28th ultimo 1st inst. received. I shall comply with your wish to observe silence and secrecy.

I was never married to Flora Wellman, of Springfield, Ohio, but she lived with me from June 11th 1874 till June 3rd 1875. I was impotent at that time, the result of hardship, priva-

Chaney replies to Jack London about his parenthood

tion & too much brain-work. Therefore I cannot be your father, nor am I sure who your father is.

A young man whom Flora knew in Springfield had a lodging room in my house in the Spring of 1875. The weather was warm & windows were open. I went to my office early in the morning & he slept late. The neighbors gossiped & talked scandal, but I know nothing of my own knowledge.

A very fine gentleman, a broker, employed me to write a $20 nativity for him. When done Flora asked the privilege of taking it to him, to which I assented. A rumor reached me later that she frequently met him afterwards. His wife & daughter, a young lady, were then in Europe. I was told that Flora demanded ten thousand dollars hush money from him. He was then greatly embarrassed financially having stocks that required margins. I know of his embarrassment for he told me all about his affairs in Dec. 1875, just before I started for Portland, Oregon, but made no mention of Flora. A month or two later I read in a San Francisco paper that he had shot himself, financial troubles being the alleged cause. Subsequently, when his estate was settled, it was found that his stocks had appreciated & he was worth sixty thousand dollars.

I cannot remember the name of the gentleman from Springfield, nor of the broker, but both were fine men. I do not know as either was your father, nor do I know who is. I know nothing of my own knowledge regarding any indiscretion on the part of Flora, but give what I have been told. What I state on my own knowledge is true.

There was a time when I had a very tender affection for Flora; but there came a time when I hated her with all the intensity of my intense nature, & even thought of killing her & myself. As many a man has under similar circumstances. Time, however, has healed the wounds & I feel no unkindness towards her, while for you I feel a warm sympathy, for I can imagine what my emotions would be were I in your place.

It is not my province to advise, but I think it better for you & for Flora that you never mention the subject to her. If, however, you think otherwise, you had better begin by simply handing her this letter to read.

That trouble blighted ten years of my life, for the San Francisco *Chronicle* published that I was in the habit of whipping her, that I compelled her to take in washing for my support (I even hired the washing of her own garments to be done) & that I turned her out of doors because she would not submit to an abortion. This was copied & sent broadcast over the country. My sisters in Maine read it & two of them became my enemies. One died believing I was in the wrong. Another may be dead, I have not heard from her these many years. All others of my kindred, except one sister in Portland, Oregon are still my enemies & denounce me as a disgrace to them. I published a pamphlet at the time containing a report from a Detective, given me by Timothy G. Cockerill, Chief of Police, showing that many of the slanders against me were false, but neither the *Chronicle* nor any of the papers that had defamed me would correct the false statements. Then I gave up defending myself & for years life was a burden. But reaction finally came and now I have a few friends who think me respectable. I am past 76 & quite poor. But on 15th inst. I am going to Michigan for a vacation, the first in 13 years. One of my students has offered me a home during summer in return for teaching her. My letters will be forwarded. My name may be in the papers there, & if so I will send you copies to Jack London, 402 Plymouth Ave.

Yours truly,
W. H. Chaney

Thinking that Chaney knew more than he related, Jack wrote another appeal for information. Chaney wrote one last letter in which he still denied being Jack's father. The letter was again sent to Ted Applegarth's address:

June 14, 1897
PROF. W. H. CHANEY
College of Astrology
2829 Calumet Avenue
Chicago

Dear Sir:

Yours of 8th inst. came to hand this morning. We have everything packed for storing & leave for Ceresco, Mich. tomorrow. I am in a hurry & must be brief.

Flora had lived with Lee Smith of Seattle, as his wife, for a month, with a Mrs. Upstone, whose husband was a blacksmith. They may still be in San Francisco. Lee Smith's wife had left him to live with another man whose name was Pat Healey, or Pat was a particular friend, I forget which.

Flora was known as my wife, in the same lodging house, Mrs. Upstone's, where she had passed as the wife of Lee Smith & we stayed there a

month. It was a very respectable place, & one day when I came home I found all the lodgers moving away & great excitement throughout the house. As soon as I entered our room Flora locked the door, fell on her knees before me & between sobs begged me to forgive her. I said I had nothing to forgive. Finally, after much delay & pleading she confessed about Lee Smith & said the lodgers were leaving on account of her being known as "Miss Wellman," "Mrs. Smith" & "Mrs. Chaney," all at nearly the same time.

Had I followed my first impression, I should have left her then, & it would have saved years of misery. But my own life had been a broken one, & on reflection I forgave her.

Mrs. Upstone was all broken up & moved to another house. She may still be in San Francisco. She was a large, fleshy woman & then had two little girls, under ten years old, and Flora was teaching them music for her room & board. If Upstones are still living there you can find them from these descriptions. Perhaps Healey's name was "TIM," at any rate he was Irish. I cannot remember anyone else, now living who knew about it. Mrs. Upstone knew more than all the others.

The cause of our separation began because Flora one day said to me:

"You know that motherhood is the great great desire of my life, & as you are too old—now some time when I find a good, nice man are you not willing for me to have a child by him?"

I said yes, only he must support her. No, she must always live with me & be the wife of "Prof. Chaney." A month or so later she said she was pregnant by me. I thought she was only trying me & did not think she was pregnant. So I made a great fuss thinking to warn her not to make the attempt. This brought on a wrangle that lasted all day & all night. After daylight, I got up & told her she could never be a wife to me again. She was humbled in a moment, for she knew I was in earnest. Then she crawled on her knees to me, sobbing, & begged my forgiveness. But I would not forgive her, although I still thought she was merely pretending to be in a family way. But her temper was a great trial, & I had often thought before that time that I must leave her on account of it, & not for loose morals, for I did not ever suspect her up to that time. But after she was gone, every busybody had a story to tell about her, & I think some of them were lies.

When she left she went to Dr. Ruttley's house; went out to the back yard, soon returned, a pistol (double barrel) in one hand & a box of cartridges in the other, a wound on the left side of her forehead & the blood running over her face. In reply to Mrs. Ruttley she said:

"This little woman has been trying to kill herself & made a bad job of it."

A great excitement followed. A mob of 150 gathered, swearing to hang me to the nearest lamp-post. Mrs. Upstone went to see her & give her $5, believing her story of my cruelty & that I had turned her out of doors, pennyless, because she would not submit to an abortion.

T. G. Cockerill put a detective on the case who reported:

The pistol was second-hand & had not been discharged since being oiled. It smelled of oil & had no smell of gun powder. A carpenter within 20 feet of her at the time heard no report of a pistol. Some boys on the other side of the fence heard no report. Her face would have been filled with powder had she shot as she said, but there was no mark of powder about her, etc.

Wm. H. Slocumb, formerly a writer on the *Chronicle,* later, publisher of a Spiritual paper called *Common Sense,* took Flora into his house & kept her for a long time. I think till after your birth. He afterwards separated from his wife & married a young girl.

A man named McKinney, or some such name, lived in the house with me at the time that Flora left. His wife, "Kittie" has since died. He was connected with the publication of the *Stock Report* & also the *San Francisco Directory,* in partnership with his brother, & may be yet.

An old man & his son, whose names I forget, were at that time the house doctors for Leland Stanford, then Governor. They had a room in my house before the young man from Springfield, Ohio. A man & his wife were also rooming there. One night he caught the son in bed with his wife & there was a hell of a time. Next day I cleared the house of the four.

After I had been in Oregon a year or two that "Son" came there & called on me. He told me that Flora had taken up with a widower who had some little children & was keeping a house of assignation. I did not believe it and asked him how he knew. He said she told him so, & besides, he had taken a woman there—I forget whether it was the wife of the man who caught him or some other woman. At any rate, he said he had got that fellow's wife away from him. I do not fully credit him because he acted as though seeking revenge because I turned him out of doors, while

he said Flora & I were as bad as he & that woman.

A very loose condition of society was fashionable at San Francisco at the time & it was not thought disgraceful for two to live together without marriage. I mean the Spiritualists & those who claimed to be reformers. Todd, formerly a Methodist preacher; Stowe of San Jose, whose wife was a medium & loose character; & Morse were leaders. Todd is dead, but his widow, "Marion" was living when last I heard of her. A lawyer named "Lewis," who lived in Oakland, but was a clerk, was for a time very intimate with the great medium Ada Foy, now in Chicago, but she threw him over for another man & then he joined me in public debate against those who opposed marriage. A dozen or more speakers were against us. He debated for months at Spiritual Conference. Lewis was highly educated & we were more than a match for our opponents, as shown by their getting angry & attacking us personally. Telling lies about us, etc. An old sea captain who told a scandalous lie about me made me so angry I called him a "liar & coward," offering to fight him. The audience interfered & he ran away, saying that he was not "heeled." I said, "Heel yourself for I will shoot you on sight." This broke up our debate. If Lewis is there you could learn much from him, although he was not personally acqainted with Flora. In fact, any of the Spiritualists then living, & still alive could tell you many things.

So far as I know of my own knowledge, Flora was not spoken of publicly as a loose character up to the time I left San Francisco in Dec. 1875. I cannot think of any additional clues to give you. It was well known among Spiritualists that we were not married, but not by the public till she told in a lecture she gave in Charter Oak Hall, after the separation, when she publicly denounced me in awful language, accusing me of diseasing her in Seattle & again in San Francisco. Lee Smith told that she diseased him & that was why he left her. But I think he lied, for she did not disease me nor was I diseased when I first met her at the house of Mrs. Yesler, in Seattle. They were from Springfield, Ohio, and said Flora belonged to a very respectable family & hinted that she had done wrong in some way. Flora was boarding with the Yeslers who were my warm friends, but both are dead. I never suspected anyone as being your father. In my anger & hatred I never cared nor gave it a thought. I cared only for the disgrace to myself.

Fitzgibbons, or some such name, was proprietor of Charter Oaks Hall where Flora lectured. Strange how the names come back to me as I review the events.

My own life has been a very sad one, more so than I think yours will be. Still, I feel a sympathy for you & will aid you in any way possible.

Yours truly,
W. H. Chaney

There is no record of any other correspondence between the two, and there is no evidence that Jack ever pursued the question further. Evidently he was satisfied that Chaney was his father, or he lost interest in the search.

Despite Chaney's denials, he probably was Jack's father. He had been married several times before he met Flora and had lived with other women after he left her. Considering this evidence, his claim of being impotent has a hollow ring. He enjoyed living with Flora, but the prospect of being a father at age fifty-five terrified him. In addition, he probably had no intention of making his relationship with Flora permanent. At this point, a child could have made things much too complicated. It is also possible that he believed himself incapable of being a father, since none of his former wives or girl friends had become pregnant. If the thought of his own sterility occurred to him, he may have sincerely believed that he was not Jack's father.

When Chaney received Jack's inquiry in 1897, it is understandable that he would take the stand he did. The long years of suffering caused by his relationship with Flora were still strong in his memory. The whole sordid mess was in the past, and he determined to keep it there. He wanted no involvement with Flora's son.

William H. Chaney was born in a log cabin near Chesterville, Maine on January 13, 1821. His father died when William was nine, and the fortunes of the family were radically changed. There was no one to farm his mother's land, and the family broke up, each going his own way. William was bound out to a harsh farmer in the area. He refused to submit to cruel treatment and ran away. By the time he was sixteen, seven farmers had used him as a "work beast."

Fulmer Mood, in *An Astrologer from Down East,* said, "He worked for awhile in a sawmill, and tried his hand at the carpenter's bench, but always in a surly spirit, for he hated the manual labor that kept him from study and books.

"His conduct was misunderstood by the farmers and sawyers of the community. His own kinsmen gave him dark looks, and rated him as a black sheep. An elderly deacon, the censor of this backwoods society, flatly told him that he was the devil's unaccountable. Small wonder, then, that under such stress his nature soured and that he came to nourish a great detestation for mankind. The gangster had not yet entered society, but river pirates still lingered on in the Southwest, more of a plague than a romantic memory. Chaney made up his mind to join their company. But preparation was necessary. Quite seriously he set about to obtain it. A good knowledge of seamanship and navigation was essential for one who had ambitions to copy Captain Kidd's model. Accordingly, young Chaney shipped on a Yankee fishing schooner to learn something of the way of the sea. He spent two years in this mode of life, and next thought to round out his term of preparation by service in the Navy. He enlisted but remained with the colors only nine months, deserting the *Columbus,* a receiving ship, as she lay at Boston in July 1840.

"He aimed now to reach the Gulf Coast—the haunt of pirates—as quickly as possible. In the Gulf and on the Mississippi he expected to find kindred spirits and Byronic opportunities. Travelling only at night, sleeping by day, and with a price on his head, the deserter made his way Westward. At Portsmouth on the Ohio the adventurer had just signed on as a member of the crew of a flat boat that was making for New Orleans when he fell sick of an attack of chills and fever. The Captain discharged him, and Chaney, from the bank, watched his raft float off. Penniless but resourceful, his affairs were soon in good shape. So kindly did the farmers of the countryside round about treat him, with an outfit of old clothes, a show of sympathy and kindness, and the offer of a post as school teacher, that soon love of humanity rather than misanthropy came to possess his heart. There was no more talk of a pirate's career."

In the ensuing years Chaney was deeply involved in politics, journalism, and law. His was a restless spirit and no job held him for long. In his *Primer of Astrology and Urania* Chaney wrote, "School teachers disliked me because I repudiated so much of science and philosophy that they believed true. Lawyers disliked me because I would not run in the old rut of 'precedents', unjust laws, etc., but more especially because if employed to prosecute one of them I did not spare him any more than I would a common thief.... In 1857 ... I lost everything I possessed, all my books went for rent, I could not find employment of any kind (this was after I had been editor and had been practicing law for ten years), and when my last penny was gone, sooner than beg or steal, I walked the streets of Boston for three days without tasting food. On another occasion I hired to work in a match factory at $4 a week and board myself—cheap food, but the salary kept me alive and paid for lodging."

Nothing is known of Chaney's life during the next nine years. In 1866 he comes to light again in New York City when he became acquainted with Dr. Luke Broughton, astrologer. Almost immediately Broughton gained a disciple with special talents in writing and lecturing, and Chaney began a new career. He said, "Astrology is the most precious science ever made known to man" and in October published this declaration: "I shall now devote my life to Astrology."

Soon after the railroad to the West was completed in 1869 Chaney was on his way to California. His wife remained behind in New York since he was just making a short visit. It lasted seventeen years.

In 1871 and 1872 he lived in Salem, Oregon. "While in Oregon," he wrote, "I enjoyed the friendship, 'in private,' of U.S. Senators, Congressmen, Governors, Judges of the Supreme and lower courts, etc., but they were timid about recognizing me in public, except to salute me pleasantly. I helped many a one to his position, working in secret, but they dare not reward me openly, although in private they were my best and truest friends." It was probably during this period that he became a friend of Mayor Yesler and his wife, at whose home in Seattle he met Flora.

Chaney went to San Francisco in October 1873 to purchase a ticket for New York City. A pickpocket got to his wallet before he got to the station. He was penniless, but as Chaney explained, "A gentleman advanced money to hire Dashaway Hall and pay advertising for a course of eight lectures on Astro-theology, on condition that I would share the profits equally with him. This gave me a start again.

"I spent the winter in San Jose, lecturing, teaching and practicing Astrology, and had an eight-days debate with Elder Miles Grant, the great Second Adventist of Boston. By May, 1874, I had saved money enough to return East, but just before starting, received an anonymous letter from my wife ... stating that she was divorced and could marry again, but if I ever married again she would have me imprisoned.

"This aroused my ire and on June 11th, 1874 ... three weeks later ... I took another wife. We lived together till June 3d, 1875 ... almost a year ... and then separated."

During this year Chaney and Flora had a flourishing business. Though he was not enamored with Flora's spiritualism, he never interfered with her seances and lectures on the subject. She in turn sold tickets for his lectures on astrology, astronomy, and astro-theology. Flora also gave piano lessons to bring in a little extra money. Spiritualism and astrology were much in vogue in the San Francisco of the 1870s, so the Chaneys were well respected and popular. It was a very pleasant arrangement until Flora announced her pregnancy.

Chaney found it impossible to continue working in San Francisco after all the adverse publicity. A few weeks before Jack's birth he fled to the Northwest. Flora moved in with friends, Bill and Amanda Slocum, and continued her seances and lectures until Jack's birth. The publicity had done her no harm. Her business increased steadily, as did her outlook on life.

Moving in with the Slocums had been a lucky move for Flora. The Slocums were well known in San Francisco and lived in what was probably an elegant home at 615 Third Street. In 1875 Amanda Slocum was listed in the San Francisco Directory as Superintendent of the Women's Publishing Company and advertising manager for *Common Sense,* the paper for which her husband, William Slocum, was managing editor and to which Prof. Chaney had been a regular contributor.

Flora Wellman was born August 17, 1843, in Massillon, Ohio, the youngest child in a family of five. Her father, Marshall Wellman, was one of the wealthiest men in the area. Her mother, Eleanor Garrett Jones, was born in Brookfield, Ohio in 1810, the daughter of "Priest Jones," a devout circuit-rider of Welsh extraction. Flora's mother died when she was a baby, and when she was four her stepmother, Julia Frederica Hurxthal Wellman, joined the family. Flora resented her and never allowed her to become a mother to her.

Little Flora was deluged with culture, taught elocution, music, and manners. She was showered with anything money could buy and spoiled beyond belief. But at a young age she came down with a terrible fever that ruined her beauty forever. Her growth was so stunted that she never came close to reaching five feet; her hair was so badly damaged that she had to wear a wig the rest of her life. In her adult years, she wore a size-twelve child's shoe. Most significantly, the fever affected her mind, causing instability and melancholia.

At sixteen she left home to stay with her married sisters—until she wandered off on her own. Her family in Massillon never heard from her again. Nothing is known of her life from the time she left Massillon until she appears as a boarder in the home of Mayor Yesler and his wife in Seattle. It was in the Yesler home that she met Chaney.

The thought of San Francisco life was a great temptation and certainly played a major role in her decision to move in with Chaney. She loved excitement and San Francisco was full of that. Even the horsecars that ran up Market Street toward Twin Peaks seemed to be more exciting than the ones in Seattle. San Francisco was a fun city and life was evident everywhere. Even death was exciting. Where else would a funeral procession be headed by a band? Parades were common. Few people worried about morals. It was a carnival atmosphere.

An Englishman, Joshua Norton, quietly built a fortune through his real estate office on Montgomery street in the gold-mad town. Just as quietly he lost his fortune, went mad and thought he was an emperor—Norton The First, Emperor of the United States, Mexico, and China.

The earliest known picture of Flora Wellman

He was one of the city's pet diversions and nearly everybody accepted his bogus money as genuine. Why should they put him in a mental institution? As long as he wanted to be Emperor they would be his subjects. Gold was still king, and rumors of new bonanzas were common in 1874. The rich, especially the new rich, were building massive, showy homes on Nob Hill.

Flora looked out across the city and pronounced all this splendor good. Life here with Chaney would be fun, and the free spirit of the citizenry would be a real asset to their business.

Pregnancy shattered all of Flora's dreams. Jack was her "badge of shame" and always remained so. He was never to experience a moment of love from his mother, but he was expected to contribute to the family budget as soon as he was old enough to carry a newspaper. By the time he was ten years old he was a work beast.

Flora was not strong and birth was difficult. She had been through a lot and had little desire to live and little strength to sustain life for herself or her baby. The doctor advised a wet nurse and suggested Mrs. Alonzo Prentiss—probably one of his patients—who had recently lost her baby in childbirth. Jack was taken to Mrs. Prentiss's home at 15 Priest Street on Nob Hill. Here was real love, and Aunt Jennie never failed to love her little white child. That love was returned fully by Jack, who loved his black mother far more than his own.

Jennie Prentiss was a proud woman and especially proud of being black. Jack's mother taught him that all other races were inferior. In later years his love for Kipling led him to believe in the "white man's burden" and to have an inordinate pride in his Anglo-Saxon heritage. Aunt Jennie thought the black race was superior. Jack thought everybody should be equally proud of his own race. It was this belief that caused him to become a racial purist. Whether right or wrong, he always believed that both races were weakened by interracial marriages. In Kipling's *Beyond the Pale,* Jack had read, "A man should, whatever happens, keep to his own caste, race and breed." In Jack's own *A Daughter of the Snows,* Corliss says, "It's a common characteristic of all peoples to consider themselves superior races—a naive, natural egoism, very healthy and very good,

but none the less manifestly untrue." While Jack must be considered an advocate of racial purism, it is incorrect to call him a racist in the modern sense. In many of his short stories he demonstrated his sympathy for an understanding of the oppressed of all races. In "The Mexican," "The League of the Old Men," "The Chinago," etc., he reveals his own race as brutal oppressors and portrays minorities with sympathy and understanding.

Now that the burden of the baby had been shifted to Jennie Prentiss, Flora grew stronger. Her health improved rapidly, and she was able to start giving piano lessons again. In addition to her other skills, she was an expert seamstress. Because she had no money to pay for Jack's care, Flora made some shirts for Mrs. Prentiss's husband in appreciation. This outpouring of generosity and appreciation paid double dividends—it earned Flora the heartfelt thanks of the Prentisses as well as a new husband. Mr. Prentiss worked for John London as a carpenter and told him about the wonderful shirts Flora made for him. John wanted to buy some and asked for Flora's address. Flora was an interesting woman and John was a lonely man. Flora needed a home for her baby and John needed a home for his two girls. It seemed quite natural that they should get married.

JOHN LONDON

John London was born January 11, 1828, in Clearfield County, Pennsylvania, and grew to manhood on a farm. He obtained the same meager education as most farm kids in those days.

Little is known of his early days. At nineteen, while working as section boss on the railroad, he fell in love with his boss's daughter and married her. Seven children later, John enlisted in the army during the Civil War. At the close of the war, minus the use of one lung, the result of a combination of pneumonia and smallpox, he moved with his family to the town of Moscow, Muscatine County, Iowa.

One daughter, Eliza, destined to be a major influence in the life of her stepbrother, Jack, was born

in Moscow. Not long after the birth of another daughter, Ida, John's wife, Mary Jane, died. He was left with nine children. His son, Charles, was injured in the chest playing baseball. The doctor advised that the boy's only hope for recovery was to be taken to California. Hurried preparations provided care for the other children, and John sped West with Eliza, Ida, and Charles. Little Charles died eleven days after they arrived.

Deciding to live in California, John sold his Iowa farm and worked as a carpenter in San Francisco. Eliza and Ida were placed in the Protestant Orphan Asylum until he could establish a home for them.

It was only a short time until he met Flora. He

found in her more than the ability to sew fine shirts and decided that she would make an excellent mother for Ida and Eliza. The two girls were amazed when they discovered their new mother to be about their own height and not very pretty. But they welcomed the chance for a home again, and Eliza promptly became a substitute mother for Flora's little Johnny. For the next several years Jack was raised by his stepsister. Flora was delighted because she could spend that much more time with her spiritualism, and not be bothered by Johnny.

John London was a kind, gentle, hard-working man—a person of very high morals and stability. Many attempts have been made to prove that John London was Jack London's real father. This is highly unlikely for several reasons. His high moral character would have prevented his having relations with another man's wife. Flora told Joan, Jack's daughter, how she had first met John London because of the shirts she had made for Alonzo Prentiss, implying that she was first acquainted with John only after her son was born. Joan was thoroughly convinced that her grandfather was W. H. Chaney. On several occasions, she said, her father had insisted that his daughter know the facts regarding his birth. Furthermore, on April 12, 1875, about the time of Jack's conception, John London had signed a receipt in the Treasurer's office in Muscatine County, Iowa, indicating that he could scarcely have been in San Francisco.

It is apparent that John London was not what he would have given anything to be—Jack's real father. He loved Jack as his own son, and Jack loved him as a father. They enjoyed a very close relation-

Jack's stepfather, John London

ship, often being thrown together as refugees from Flora and her seances or temper tantrums. His concern for Jack was such that it is hard to believe that he would have kept the truth from him if he had been Jack's actual father.

JACK'S EARLY YEARS

Jack was returned to the family after about eight months with the Prentisses. By this time the Londons had moved from their small flat south of Market Street to Bernal Heights. John, his health seriously impaired since the Civil War, was unable to cope with the severe competition of the contracting game and was barely making a living selling sewing machines from door to door.

A constant succession of rented and mortgaged houses during Jack's early years attested to the family's poverty and misfortune. From Bernal Heights they moved to a roomy two-story house at 920 Natoma Street and then to a six-room flat on Folsom Street. While living here, Jack and Eliza came down with diptheria and both nearly died. Their doctor recommended they get out of the city. Accordingly, John moved his family across the Bay to Oakland. John managed to get a few acres of ground near the present Emeryville and started a truck garden. It was an instant success, and he be-

N. Clark & Sons' Pottery in Alameda, built on the old Davenport place. The house at left is probably where the Londons lived when John worked the place in 1882.

came known for the fine produce he grew. He sold to the local produce market until an opportunity came to run his own store at Seventh and Campbell Street. It seemed that every time John was doing well Flora wanted to go faster. At her suggestion John brought G. H. Stowell into the operation for expansion. Flora, John, and the children moved in with the Stowells at Wood and Seward streets.

We have no way of knowing what happened, but Stowell ended up with the store and John London moved his family to Alameda, where he worked a twenty-acre tract of land for Matthew Davenport. The family lived in the old Weckerlee home at 221 Pacific Avenue near the present Naval Air Station.

Jack attended his first school here, the West End School. His primary teacher was Mrs. Mary Burge. Eliza and Ida also attended West End. Eliza was graduated from the eighth grade at the time Johnny started his education. Even at this age, Eliza remembered Jack as always having a book to read. When he needed love most, it had to come from his beloved stepsister, who took over the job of mothering him, a job she never shirked. Jack never forgot her devotion.

Flora became restless and she could see the grass shining green and bright across the fence. They had a chance to work a farm down the coast and she just knew this was their big chance. As usual John went along with her plans. On Jack's seventh birthday, January 12, 1883, as he put it later, "We had horses and farm wagon, and onto that we piled all our household belongings, all hands climbing up on the top of the load, and with the cow tied behind, we moved 'bag and baggage' to the coast in San Mateo County, six miles beyond Colma."

Jack's first bout with "John Barleycorn" came just prior to the move to the San Mateo County potato ranch. His father was in the habit of drinking a small bucket of beer in the afternoon. One day as he was bringing the bucket out to the field where his dad was plowing, Jack decided he would have a sample. It must be good, if his father liked it. The pail was too full anyway, so he drank some. It tasted like medicine. Were adults wrong? He tried a little more. By the time the pail was delivered he was drunk and sick. Beer never appealed to him again.

But now they were on their way to a brand-new venture. John would work hard, as usual, and Flora would be sure to come up with some new schemes. Maybe this time the ranch would be a huge success and Flora could again be a "lady." John was content with raising the finest potatoes possible.

It was a wild, primitive countryside on the bleak, sad coast of San Mateo County south of San Francisco. The months on the potato ranch were mostly drudgery for Jack and the school he attended was as primitive as the land. Only two things stood out in his memory. He remembered a party at the neighboring ranch and how he was forced to drink large quantities of wine for the merriment of the other guests. He was sick for days afterward and hardly needed his mother's injunction to avoid John Barleycorn in the future.

Earliest known picture of Jack London

The other memorable event was his discovery of the poor man's club of his day, the saloon. His father delivered potatoes to the city, and sitting on the heavy potato wagon, Jack listened to the sounds made by the horses as they plodded along the deep road through the sandhills. One bright vision shortened the tedium of the trip—the saloon at Colma, where his father, or whoever drove, always stopped for a drink.

Jack would get out to warm himself by the great stove and eat a soda cracker. Just one soda cracker, but to him it was a fabulous luxury. Back on the wagon again, he made that cracker last as long as possible. Saloons were wonderful places. Jack especially liked the San Francisco saloons because they served many delicious dainties free—various breads and crackers, cheeses, sausages, sardines— foods that he had never seen on their meager table at home. And once a barkeeper gave him a temperance drink of syrup and water. Jack never forgot this kindness.

John London was successful enough on the potato ranch to buy an eighty-seven-acre ranch in Livermore. The family was on the move again. Jack did the chores while his father planted olive trees, put in vineyards, planted an orchard, and cultivated the fields. Once again the produce sheds in Oakland were selling John London's produce and people were asking for "J. L." corn. John always culled his produce and gave the culls to the poor, selling only the very best.

Being the chore boy was not Jack's idea of fun,

but there were compensations. The Livermore school was vastly superior, and the Valley was a beautiful and warm place to live. There was plenty of food on the table now and his father was happy and contented. His mother even got Jack some store-bought underwear.

It was here that Jack London discovered the world of books. His teacher loaned him a copy of Irving's *Tales of the Alhambra*. From the bricks of an old chimney he built his own model of the Alhambra; towers, terraces, and all were complete, and chalk inscriptions marked the different sections. His other reading matter at that time consisted mainly of dime novels and newspapers in which he read of the adventures of poor but virtuous working girls. This kind of reading material was ridiculously romanticized, but being very lonely, he read everything that came his way, and was greatly impressed by Ouida's story, *Signa*, which he devoured regularly for a couple of years. He never knew the finish until he grew up, for the closing chapters were missing from his copy. His work on the ranch at that time was to watch the bees, and as he sat under a tree from sunrise until late in the afternoon, waiting for them to swarm, he had plenty of time to read and dream.

When he returned *The Alhambra* to his teacher, he hoped she would lend him another book. Because she didn't, he cried all the way home on the three-mile trek to the ranch. Time after time he was at the point of asking her for another, but never quite found enough nerve.

Irving Stone in *Sailor on Horseback* has said, "Jack writes that reading *Signa* pushed back his narrow hill-horizon, and all the world was made possible if he would dare it. Eliza reports him saying at the time, 'you know, Lize, I'm not going to get married until I'm forty years old. I'm going to have a big house, and one room is going to be filled with books.' By the time he was forty he had the big house, and several rooms filled with books. . . ."

Even though the ranch was growing and everything was better than ever with the Londons, their home was not happy or pleasant. Flora was the dominant one and her instability kept the place in a state of turmoil. She continued to hold seances and "Plume," her medium from the other world, was almost like a member of the family, though quite unwelcome to the rest. Whenever Flora failed to get her way, she could always count on her fre-

An early school picture

quently staged heart attacks to regain her position.

Eliza was still taking care of her brother. Flora was never mean to Jack but bestowed little love. Eliza gladly provided the affection he needed in addition to her tasks of cooking and keeping house.

As usual, the money was not coming in as fast as Flora wanted, so she arranged to board Captain Shepard, a middle-aged Civil War veteran who had been widowed with three children. Now Eliza had the added responsibility of caring for them. To Flora London, Shepard meant a few dollars to add to the budget, but to sixteen-year-old Eliza he was a romantic figure, even though old enough to be her father. Besides, he soon became the means of

escaping ranch drudgery. In 1884 Eliza and Captain Shepard were married and moved to Oakland. This came as a severe blow to Flora, who now had to do her own work as well as losing the extra board money.

Eliza and her husband had barely left when an epidemic devastated John's chicken flocks and there was no money to pay the interest on the mortgage. John's dream was gone—a blow from which he never fully recovered. His spirit went with the ranch. Once more the old potato wagon was piled high with all their belongings and the horses were pointed toward Oakland.

OAKLAND

In 1885 Oakland opened up a new world to Jack London. His home was only two blocks from his sister Eliza, making life worthwhile again. The Londons settled into a small cottage across from

the new four-room Garfield School on Twenty-third Avenue between Sixteenth and Seventeenth streets. Here Jack not only continued to work on the three *R*'s but also learned the fine art of fight-

The Oakland area about the time Jack was growing up

ing. Being a tough, wiry, little guy, he surprised many a bully who had sized him up as easy prey because of his fair complexion, sensitive mouth, curly hair, and light blue eyes. He looked more like a cherub than a fighter.

Jack was still a very shy youngster. His mother was known as a weird lady whose seances and obsession with the spirit world had led to many embarrassing experiences for him. Jack had had few companions and his life had been overwhelmed with drudgery. The only stabilizing influences he had known were his sister Eliza and his father.

John London had been passive and tolerant through all of Flora's neurotic demands. He put up with her pseudo heart attacks and frequent elocution demonstrations. He even went along with her schemes to get rich. They were now embarked on her latest scheme—they would board the young girls who had been imported from Scotland to work in the California cotton mills. They mortgaged the lot next door and built another cottage for additional rooms. All went well until Flora lost interest in the project. Her interest in getting rich even more quickly through a local lottery probably

took the money that was being saved for the mortgage. In any event, they lost both houses, and the family was once again ready for the old potato wagon, except that they no longer owned it.

Young Jack was not concerned with exactly where the family lived at this point. He had discovered the Oakland Public Library. Here were thousands of books, and he could borrow as many as he wanted. His first ventures were a little strange. He remembered being impressed by the title *The Adventures of Peregrine Pickle*. He filled out the application blank and the librarian handed him the collected and entirely unexpurgated works of Smollett in one huge volume. He read everything he could lay his hands on, principally history and adventure, and all the old travels and voyages. He read mornings, afternoons, and nights. He read in bed, he read at the table, he read as he walked to and from school, and he read at recess while the other boys were playing.

At the library he found another friend whose influence was to affect him deeply, Ina Coolbrith. She soon gathered Jack under her wing and guided him along a much more orderly literary path. Jack

The old Cameron house, East Seventeenth Street between Twenty-second and Twenty-third avenues, Oakland, California

The Londons lived for a short while in an apartment in the Remillard Building on San Pablo Avenue near Eighteenth Street as they were forced for financial reasons to move from East Oakland to the less affluent West End.

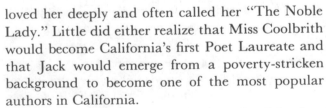

The house John London built next to the Cameron house.

loved her deeply and often called her "The Noble Lady." Little did either realize that Miss Coolbrith would become California's first Poet Laureate and that Jack would emerge from a poverty-stricken background to become one of the most popular authors in California.

Jack had progressed to the Franklin School at Eleventh Avenue and Fifteenth Street when his time for reading was abruptly shortened by the family's change of fortune. After living for a very brief time in an upper apartment in the Remillard Building on San Pablo Street in downtown Oakland, Flora was unable to come up with a scheme to stop their move to one of the poorest sections of the city, in West Oakland. Her pride was shattered

by her lowered social status and life became even more intolerable in their home.

John tried desperately to find work, but times were bad and jobs were scarce even for healthy young workers. He was getting old, tired, and sick, but there was no such thing as retirement for the poor. He just kept hunting until he found a job as a night watchman. The last years of his life were spent in irregular hours as special constable, special policeman, or night watchman. The hours were bad and the pay was small, but at least it allowed him to pay the rent and feed his family.

Jack was now working as a newsboy or whatever else a boy his age could do to make a few cents. He had no time to read. He was too busy working,

The Londons lived here at 1455 Linden Street in 1886.

Jack went to Oakland and had this picture taken to give to his sister Eliza. He was between nine and ten years of age.

The Londons also lived in this house on Seventh Street, near Adeline, in 1886.

learning how to fight, and in general becoming a brash street kid. He had a lively imagination and curiosity about all things, not least among them the saloon. And he was in and out of many. Saloons ran from corner to corner in those days on the east side of Broadway between Sixth and Seventh.

Life in the saloon was different. Men talked big and laughed heartily, and there was always an atmosphere of greatness. Here was something seemingly more than the common everyday world where nothing happened. Here life was vivid, and sometimes even lurid. Blows were struck, blood was shed, and the police came rushing in. These were great moments for Jack, whose head was full of the wild and violent fighting in the stories he had read. There were no big moments when he trudged along the streets throwing papers in at doors. But in the saloon, even the drunks sprawling across the tables or in the sawdust were objects of mystery and wonder.

Little did Jack realize that what these men sought was forgetfulness and relief from drudgery and exploitation. But he was learning and would soon learn more about the ways of the exploited and the tragedies of work beasts who were caught in the inescapable "trap" of poverty and exploitation.

When Jack was eleven, the family was living at 944 Thirty-sixth Street, and his father was working fairly steadily as a deputy constable. His sister Ida was a laundress in the Contra Costa Laundry; and Jack was still delivering papers, working as boy helper on an ice wagon, setting up pins in a bowling alley, sweeping out saloons at Sunday picnic grounds, and working hard on his books at Cole Grammar School in West Oakland. His paper route paid twelve dollars a month, all of which went to Flora on payday. From then until he was sixteen he had a thousand and one different occupations.

Life at Cole Grammar School was more fun. He had found a chum in Frank Atherton, and developed a relationship with him that lasted all their lives. Frank in *Jack London in Boyhood Adventures* tells of the time Mike Panella, leader of the Cole hoodlums, noticed Jack's penchant for books and decided the "sissy" should be straightened out:

"Hey kid, why don'cha ever play with the rest of us. Ain't you had 'nough books widout readin' at recess like a sissy?"

Jack glanced at him and resumed reading. But Mike, itching for a fight, kept on.

"Think yer somebody, doncha! Well try this on." Mike grabbed the book out of Jack's hand and threw it across the playground. With the agility of a cat, Jack was on his feet. "I'll make you pay for that, you dirty low-down dago." There ensued a battle royal like Cole had never seen before until Jack landed a little fist on the point of Mike's chin, followed by a stronger one in the very center of his nose. Mike lay in the dust cursing, and Jack stood over him with bloody knuckles. About this time Miss

944 Thirty-sixth Street, east of San Pablo Avenue

McDonald arrived on the scene, and both boys were soon guests of Mr. Garlick, the principal.

Mr. Garlick suggested that if they would hug each other he would suspend punishment. Mike grabbed at the chance, but Jack determined that he would not be a hypocrite, nor would he humiliate himself to escape punishment.

"I'll take the licking, Mr. Garlick," Jack said. "I know I was in the right, and I'll do it again if I have to."

This early incident is indicative of Jack's character. Frank Atherton went on to say, "He loved a clean fight and always wanted to win whether boxing, fencing, swimming, debating or writing. But he never took advantage of an opponent and always fought fair and square. When he won, his pride was evident, but it was a manly pride, without a hint of boast or conceit."

One of Jack's few pleasures at this time was the collecting of picture cards. Very seldom able to buy any for his collection, he became a shrewd trader. Anything of value he could get his hands on was bartered for more and more cards until he had

The Cole Grammar School in West Oakland

accumulated one of the finest collections in West Oakland.

One day Frank asked him how much money he had saved from his paper route. Jack replied:

Why I can't save a penny. I give every cent of it to my folks to buy food. My father is only a Special Officer and his salary is real small. By the time we pay rent and buy food there is nothing left to buy clothes, let alone saving anything. Once in a while I work on Sunday at the Bowling Alley, so I earn a little extra, but most of that has to be turned in too. Sometimes I buy a little candy, but that's all.

A real treat would occur when his dad could go fishing with him on the wharf or the rock wall that ran out opposite the Alameda Mole. A few times John would even rent a rowboat.

Frank and Jack became pals and spent a lot of time in each other's homes. Frank said, of his first visit to Jack's house, "I was strongly impressed by the contrast between Mr. and Mrs. London. He was so tall and stalwart, while she was extremely short and stout. They reminded me of a dwarf and a giant I had once seen in a side show."

In his book Frank provides a rare glimpse of the London home at 807 Pine Street:

Supper was served in the kitchen. While Mr. London carved the beefsteak and cut the bread, I glanced about the room. The furnishings were plain, but serviceable: a wood and coal stove, portable cupboard, bare wooden chairs and a drop leaf table at which we sat. The floor was bare but clean from frequent scrubbing.

On the stove, I observed the iron skillet used for beefsteak and potatoes. From one side a large section was missing, evidently having been broken sometime in the past. I wondered if they were too poor to buy a new one. Afterward, however, I learned they had a new skillet, but Mrs. London preferred the broken one. She claimed the steak cooked in it had a superior flavor. Our meal consisted of beefsteak, fried potatoes, bread and butter, and coffee. There was plenty for all. There was no dessert, neither was there any pretense of style, newspapers being used in lieu of a table cloth, which also indicated poor circumstances.

Flora never served pastries or dessert of any kind, preferring to use the money saved to buy better cuts of meat. She fried the meat in a dry but heavily salted pan and gained a sort of fame for her recipe.

On another occasion Frank visited the home during one of Flora's seances:

"Hi, Frank, come set on the porch, but don't talk too loud."
"Is someone sick?"
"No, they are having a seance," Jack said.
"What's that?"

The Cole Grammar School class, 1887. Jack London is second from the right in the second row. Frank Atherton is third from the left in the third row.

807 Pine Street, West Oakland

Jack was laughing so hard he had trouble explaining, "A seance is a meeting of spiritualists trying to talk to dead people. My mother is a medium, and once in awhile her followers come here to communicate with the spirits. My mother believes she is guided by the spirit of an Indian Chief named 'Plume.' When she holds a seance, she goes into a trance. Her eyes roll around and she mumbles something to the big chief. I guess nobody understands what she is saying. And then the fun begins; her followers imagine they can see spirits, and they begin to moan a chant like a bunch of ignorant savages in a war dance. Gosh, Frank, it's just like a comedy; I wish you could see how foolish they act. I don't believe in spirits and ghosts; it's all nonsense. When a person dies, that's the end so far as he is concerned."

A few weeks in the summer of 1889 was the most carefree period in Jack's entire boyhood. Frank's family had moved to Auburn, and he invited Jack to spend the summer with him. It was a fabulous vacation with no responsibilities. He and Frank did everything two normal country kids could be expected to do. They had their favorite swimming holes and spent days roaming and having wild adventures in the hills.

Graduation from Cole Grammar School only meant hunting for a job, and jobs were scarce. Hickmott's Cannery would be opening soon so he would wait. Frank's family had moved to San Jose, so Jack went down for a short visit before starting work in the cannery. He had thought he was already a work beast, but he soon discovered what a real work beast was.

The capitalists had taken over the country and had found it necessary to have a surplus army of laborers. If the workers decided to go on strike they could always find men from this surplus army to work in their place. No one seemed to care about the hardships a man faced while he was unem-

971 West Street, West Oakland

ployed. Jack discovered that the masses of working people were caught in this surplus army, with little hope of ever getting into the regular ranks of the employed. Regular employment wasn't much better, but a man could make enough to pay rent and buy food. He had no future, but at least he had some hope for the present, and by working long, extra hours he could even provide a few small luxuries for his family.

Hickmott's Cannery, housed in a converted stable, was a very unpleasant place to work. Jack's usual day was twelve hours, but often he worked eighteen. The pay was ten cents an hour and every hour was pure slavery. He recalled the times when, with his head filled with the tales of the old voyagers and visions of tropical isles and far-off places, he had sailed his father's little centerboard skiff around San Francisco Bay and on the Oakland Estuary. Now he was in another world, the world of the work beasts, who could only work and sleep and then go to work again without time to even see the world around them.

It was dark when he went to work, and it was dark when he arrived home. All he experienced was the monotony of stuffing pickles into jars hour after hour. Little children of six and seven were doing the same work. Life held little hope for any of them. They didn't even look like children any more, but more like little work beasts. He saw men of twenty-five who looked sixty. There was no

gleam left in their eyes, no spring in their step as they shuffled from place to place. No horse in Oakland worked longer hours.

Workers had half an hour for dinner and half an hour for supper; they worked every night until ten, eleven, or twelve o'clock. Jack's wages were small, but he worked such long hours that he sometimes made as much as fifty dollars a month. It all went to Flora. It was his duty, and duty was a religion with him. He worked in that cannery for thirty-six hours straight one time and he was only a child of fourteen.

He was trying to save the money to buy a skiff that cost eight dollars. All that summer he saved and scrimped. In the fall he had five dollars as a result of doing without all the pleasures. His mother came to the machine where he worked and demanded it. It was a cruel blow, after a year of hell, to have that pitiful little hoard taken away. The loss of his boat was not nearly as affecting as the heartlessness of his mother.

Jack realized that something was wrong with society. He brooded over a system that would let six- and seven-year-old kids work in coal mines and canneries so the owners could buy beautiful mansions and silver-trimmed, rubber-tired carriages. The owners' sons went to colleges and their daughters to finishing schools, while their workers lived in shacks and starved.

When French Frank wanted to sell his sloop, the *Razzle Dazzle,* Jack rushed to Aunt Jennie to borrow the money. She was more prosperous than his own parents. She worked as a nurse at a good weekly wage. Would she lend her "white child" the money? What she had was his, but she was appalled at the thought of his becoming an oyster pirate.

"But Jack, those Oyster Pirates are thieves and you could go to jail."

"What have I to lose?" he replied. "Suppose I am caught. The prisoners in San Quentin are better off. They work fewer hours than I do and eat better. When I am through at night, I am too tired to go anywhere anyway. I may as well be in jail!

"Aunt Jennie," he continued, "this is my only hope of escaping. I feel myself dying inside. Please loan me the money, and I'll pay you back real soon. I know I'm only fifteen, but I am strong and as tough as any of the Oyster Pirates."

Jack ran as fast as he could to find French Frank and buy his boat. He even forgot to haggle for a lower price. In the morning they met at Johnny Heinold's First and Last Chance Saloon at the foot of Webster Street. Jack handed over Aunt Jennie's shiny twenty-dollar gold pieces. The deal was sealed with a man-sized shot of whiskey, and Jack was off to high adventure. Free at last! Now he would show everyone. The "trap" was behind him and the whole bright world was just ahead.

Jennie Prentiss standing in the doorway of her home in Alameda

Johnny Heinold behind the bar. Jack is wearing an ice delivery apron.

Without a moment's hesitation, Jack climbed aboard, hauled in the anchor, set sails, and tacked his way out into San Francisco Bay. He loved every minute of sailing and never lost his zeal. There were to be many periods of depression, but they always disappeared once he was on the water.

Early the next morning Jack and his one-man crew, Spider Healy, were off to the oyster beds. Jack knew the danger, but he wanted to be in the thick of it, raiding oyster beds, fighting at night on the shoals, and going to the markets in the morning in Oakland where people came down to the docks to buy. Every raid on an oyster bed was a felony. The penalty was state imprisonment, the stripes, and the lockstep, but being an oyster pirate or a convict was far more romantic than being a machine slave.

For many years Pacific oysters were brought in from Washington, but were considered inferior to Eastern oysters by Californians. As soon as the railroad arrived in the West, yearling oysters were brought in and bedded in the tidelands off San Mateo. These were government lands that had been usurped by the Southern Pacific Railroad and leased to the oyster growers. Before long a group of waterfront hoodlums realized that these beds were vulnerable. Because the owners had a monopoly, prices were very high, and so the inevitable came to pass—oyster pirates. The people were on the side of

the oyster pirates because they hated the Southern Pacific. The police felt the same way and had to be forced to do anything about the situation.

In 1899, his first year as a professional writer, Jack told Cloudesley Johns that he had made more money in one week as an oyster pirate than he was making at that time in a year. It was said on the waterfront that Jack had taken on a mistress when he bought the *Razzle Dazzle*. Evidently Jack believed the myth himself at times, for he later stated that he had done just that. It is possible that it actually happened, but not probable. Jack met Mamie aboard the *Razzle Dazzle* when he first approached French Frank about its purchase. Mamie was aboard on a visit with her sister Tess and her chaperone, Mrs. Hadley. It hardly seems likely that someone who required a chaperone on Saturday would move aboard as mistress on Monday. The fact that her uncle, Spider Healy, lived aboard, and that the sloop only had one small cabin, has to be considered also.

One biographer has said that Jack got his title "Prince of the Oyster Pirates" because he became Mamie's boyfriend. It is true that the oyster pirates had crowned her "Queen of the Pirates," but Jack's title was earned. His daring, camaraderie, skill, and charisma caused his fellow pirates to bestow it on him.

The oyster pirates got their money easily and

Johnny Heinold, owner of the "First and Last Chance" saloon, was always there when Jack needed a few dollars or a sympathetic ear.

him extremely well for his associations, but not for the taste of him. All the time I was striving to be a man amongst men, and all the time I nursed secret and shameful desires for candy. But I would have died before I'd let anybody guess it. I used to indulge in lonely debauches, on nights when I knew my crew was going to sleep ashore. I would go up to the Free Library, exchange my books, buy a quarter's worth of all sorts of candy that chewed and lasted, sneak aboard the *Razzle Dazzle,* lock myself in the cabin, go to bed, and lie there long hours of bliss, reading and chewing candy." Money spent across the bar could only buy acceptance by his companions, but books were a window through which he could see the world.

After several months of this kind of life, the *Razzle Dazzle*'s mainsail burned and Jack lost his crew. "Young Scratch" Nelson's *Reindeer* had also suffered damage about the same time, but it was repairable. Jack and Nelson had been pals and both were now broke, so they became partners. They borrowed money for an outfit of grub from Johnny Heinold, filled their water barrels, and sailed away toward the oyster beds. Jack was thirsting for adventure, and in the next few months with "Young Scratch" he got plenty of it.

Jack London never regretted his days with the oyster pirates, nor the fact that he spent money as fast as he got it. He had shown the pirates he could spend with the rest. It may have been a reaction to his childhood poverty and the excessive toil, or, as he put it, "possibly my inchoate thought was: Better to reign among booze-fighters, a prince, than to toil twelve hours a day at a machine for ten cents an hour. There are no purple passages in machine toil. But if the spending of one hundred and eighty dollars in twelve hours isn't a purple passage, then I'd like to know what is."

spent it the same way. They were a rough lot. Jack was barely sixteen, and though his years running around with the Boo Gang in Oakland had given him experience, he now had to earn acceptance from the roughest gang of all. He outdrank, outsailed, and outyarned the entire gang. To be a man among men he drank heavily and swaggered with the rest. But this was not the real Jack London. He much preferred a different life.

In *John Barleycorn,* Jack wrote, "Drink as I would, I couldn't come to like John Barleycorn. I valued

THE CALIFORNIA FISH PATROL

The world was opening up for Jack. Already he knew several hundred miles of California waterways, as well as the towns and cities and fishing haunts along the shores. The desire to range farther became strong. This, however, was too much for Nelson, who pined for his beloved Oakland water-

front, and when he elected to return to it, he and Jack separated in all friendliness.

One day in the Oakland Library Jack read a story in the November, 1884, *St. Nicholas Magazine* entitled "The Cruise of the Pirate-Ship 'Moon Raker,'" by F. Marshall White. In the story, Harry

Bronson fell under the evil influence of trashy juvenile fiction, which led him to run away from home. He became the leader of a gang of "wharf-rats" and cruised about New York harbor on a captured yacht. His semipiratical adventures came to an end when the *Moon Raker* was overhauled by a police patrol tug.

Jack saw himself in the story and began to have second thoughts about how his career of piracy might end. Charley LeGrant of the California Fish Patrol had offered him a job as his deputy. As a deputy Fish Patrolman he would receive no salary but would get half of the fines levied on those fishermen he arrested. The next day Jack headed toward Benicia and went to work.

The old town of Benicia, on the Carquinez Straits, was now home. In a cluster of fishermen's arks, moored in the tules on the waterfront, dwelt a congenial crowd of drinkers and vagabonds. He joined them. The small amount of money earned was a long way from those fat oyster pirating days, but it was honest work, and he was now on the side of law and order. Besides, he could still be a sailor, and no man ever loved to sail more than Jack London.

One of the most traumatic episodes of his life occurred shortly after he started wearing the badge of the Fish Patrol. He had discovered that his new companions drank more than the pirates, and one night after a prodigious binge, he staggered aboard a sloop at the end of the wharf for a bit of sleep. He stumbled overboard into the fast-moving waters of Carquinez Straits and was borne away by the current. He was not startled. He thought the misadventure delightful. A strange thought of going out with the tide suddenly obsessed him. Thoughts of suicide had never entered his head but now it seemed to make sense. It would be a good way to end his short career. Underneath the constant drunkenness in which he had lived for months, there lurked in his own mind a sense of wrongdoing. In a flash he saw the worthlessness of it all. He remembered all the broken-down bums and loafers he had bought drinks for and saw himself as they were.

It was a long night, and before daylight the chill of the water and the passage of the hours had sobered him enough to make him realize he didn't in the least want to drown. Then he was scared. He found scores of reasons for living, but the more reasons he discovered, the more likely it seemed that he was going to drown anyway.

After he had been in the water for four hours, he found himself fighting the hazardous riptides off Mare Island light. He was beginning to swallow salt water when a Greek fisherman running in for Vallejo saw him and dragged him into his boat more dead than alive.

His many death-defying adventures in the next few months are set down in his exciting collection of short stories, *Tales of the Fish Patrol.* Some are based on Jack's own experiences and the rest on those of his fellow deputies, but all are real.

The waters of San Francisco Bay contained all manner of fishing boats manned by all manner of fishermen. To protect the fish from this motley floating population many wise laws had been passed, and the fish patrol enforced them. Wildest among the fishermen were the Chinese shrimp catchers.

One instance worth mention was the time Jack and George, his cowardly crew member, were taking a group of Chinese fishermen, who had been caught using illegal shrimp nets, to San Rafael on the *Reindeer.* George had a revolver, but Jack was unarmed. When the prisoners threatened to overpower their captors, Jack asked George to hold them off with his gun. But between the threatening Chinese and the rising water in their leaky boat, George was beside himself with fright. Here is the story as Jack told it in his short story "White and Yellow":

"It's sink or float together," I said. "And if you'll give me your revolver, I'll have the *Reindeer* bailed out in a jiffy."

"They're too many for us," he whimpered. "We can't fight them all."

I turned my back on him in disgust. The salmon boat had long since passed from sight behind a little archipelago known as the Marin Islands, so no help could be looked for from that quarter. Yellow Handkerchief came up to me in a familiar manner, the water in the cockpit slushing against his legs. I did not like his looks. I felt that beneath that pleasant smile he was trying to put on his face there was an ill purpose. I ordered him back, and so sharply that he obeyed.

"Now keep your distance," I commanded, "and don't you come closer!"

"Wha'fo?" he demanded indignantly. "I t'ink—

um talkee talkee heap good."

"Talkee talkee," I answered bitterly, for I knew now that he had understood all that had passed between George and me. "What for talkee talkee? You no sabbe talkee talkee."

He grinned in a sickly fashion. "Yep, I sabbe velly much. I honest Chinaman."

"All right," I answered. "You sabee talkee talkee, then you bail water plenty plenty. After that we talkee talkee."

He shook his head, at the same time pointing over his shoulder to his comrades. "No can do. Velly bad Chinamen, heap velly bad. I t'ink um—"

"Stand back!" I shouted, for I had noticed his hand disappear beneath his blouse and his body prepare for a spring.

Disconcerted, he went back into the cabin, to hold a council, apparently, from the way the jibbering broke forth. The *Reindeer* was very deep in the water, and her movements had grown quite loggy. In a rough sea she would have inevitably swamped; but the wind, when it did blow, was off the land, and scarcely a ripple disturbed the surface of the bay.

"I think you'd better head for the beach," George said abruptly, in a manner that told me his fear had forced him to make up his mind to some course of action.

"I think not," I answered shortly.

"I command you," he said in a bullying tone.

"I was commanded to bring these prisoners into San Rafael," was my reply.

Our voices were raised, and the sound of the altercation brought the Chinese out of the cabin.

"Now will you head for the beach?"

This from George, and I found myself looking into the muzzle of his revolver—of the revolver he dared to use on me, but was too cowardly to use on the prisoners.

My brain seemed smitten with a dazzling brightness. The whole situation, in all its bearings, was focused sharply before me—the shame of losing the prisoners, the worthlessness and cowardice of George, the meeting with LeGrant and the other patrolmen and the lame explanation; and then there was the fight I had fought so hard, victory wrenched from me just as I thought it within my grasp, and out of the tail of my eye I could see the Chinese crowding together by the cabin doors and leering triumphantly. It would never do.

I threw my hand up and my head down. The first act elevated the muzzle, and the second removed my head from the path of the bullet which went whistling past. One hand closed on George's wrist, the other on the revolver. Yellow Handkerchief and his gang sprang toward me. It was now or never. Putting all my strength into a sudden effort, I swung George's body forward to meet them. Then I pulled back with equal suddenness, ripping the revolver out of his fingers and jerking him off his feet. He fell against Yellow Handkerchief's knees, who stumbled over him, and the pair wallowed in the bailing hole where the cockpit floor was torn open. The next instant I was covering them with my revolver, and the wild shrimp-catchers were cowering and cringing.

The Fish Patrol offered a lot of excitement, and the danger was an added inducement for Jack Where else could he get paid to have all this fun. There were two problems, however. One was that he found himself drinking more heavily with the Fish Patrol than he ever had drunk with the pirates. The other was that the world was out there somewhere and he was itching to see it. Finally the time came when he decided to leave. He said good-bye to Charley LeGrant and his wife and his Benicia friends, and in the fall of 1892 headed back to Oakland.

BACK IN OAKLAND

Back in Oakland Jack was left with time on his hands and no work. He drifted into the only social life he knew, that of the waterfront. Life was very dull here. He had lived with the fearless Fish Patrolmen, the reckless and carefree oyster pirates, stevedores, bay sailors, and the hardy men of the scow-schooners. Now where was he to go? The deep-water sailors he met had roamed the world, and Jack listened to every word as they told him of their adventures. He looked with yearning beyond the Golden Gate toward China, Japan, and hundreds of other fabulous ports he had read about in books. It was only a matter of time and opportunity before he would be off on another great adventure, and he was only sixteen.

It was also a time to study the inner workings of

society. Foundations were being built for his later beliefs in socialism and prohibition. His hatred for the exploitation of the poor by the capitalists grew and was to be the key factor in understanding the real Jack London.

Jack noted that the doors of the saloon, the poor man's club, were always open and a warm welcome waited within. He could go into the saloon and wash up, brush his clothes, and comb his hair. He couldn't go into the dwellings of strangers that way. And saloons were always so damnably convenient. They were everywhere.

He had hardly known men of conventional morals and conventional lives. And from what he did know, he was not attracted to them. There was no glamor about them, no romance, no adventuresome spirit. They were the sort to whom things never happened. They would live and die in Oakland. They were dull and incapable of camaraderie. Jack wanted friends who had a little life in them and who, on occasion, could swagger a little. It was this kind of person, Jack noted, that alcohol grabbed—the fellows with fire and go in them. It quenched their spirit and killed their vitality, and twisted them into the derelicts, drunks, and bums he had been rubbing elbows with for over a year.

Jack turned away from the average run of men— the ones cold of heart and cold of spirit who didn't smoke, or swear, or do much of anything else that was different from their lackluster kind. One didn't meet these in saloons, or flaming along the paths of adventure, or loving as God's own mad lovers. They were too busy keeping their feet dry, conserving their energy, and making of life a well of mediocrity.

Much of London's time was spent with "Young Scratch" Nelson, who was now on shore and living more madly than ever. Jack occasionally went for cruises of several days on the bay to help out the shorthanded scow-schooners. He practically lived in saloons, and had become a barroom loafer. The tragedy was that too many people in Oakland remembered the Jack London of this period instead of the person he was to become.

Late in 1892 the worst experience Jack ever had with alcohol occurred. One night he was sitting in the Overland House in Oakland. It was early in the evening and the only reason he was there was that he was broke. It was election time and local politicians made the rounds of the saloons, hunting votes.

Joe Goose, an old oyster pirate friend, entered and said,

"Come on fellows—free booze—all you want of it."

"Where?"

"Come on—I'll tell you as we go along. It's the Hancock Fire Brigade. All you have to do is wear a red shirt and a helmet, and carry a torch. They're going down on a special train to Haywards to parade. The politicians who run it are short of torch-bearers."

The politicians had bought out the saloons and the booze was free. Extra barkeepers couldn't keep up with the crowd. Jack and his gang grabbed bottles, went outside, and drank themselves into oblivion. Jack hadn't learned discretion with straight whiskey. He believed in drinking all he could get as long as it was free. He hated the stuff, but drank it anyway.

The politicians were too wise to leave Haywards filled with drunks from the waterfronts of Oakland. They rounded everybody up to put them on the train home. Jack tried to walk, but his coordination broke down, his legs tottered under him, his head was swimming, his heart pounding, his lungs panting for air. Realizing he would never make it by following the crowd, he left the ranks and ran along a row of trees. Every time he fell, roars of laughter went up from the other drunks. They didn't know he was struggling for breath. He finally fell unconscious, and "Young Scratch" Nelson carried him aboard the train.

By the time Jack got to his seat, he was fighting for air so badly that Nelson knew he was in a bad way. Jack said later, "I often think that was the nearest to death I have ever been. I was scorching up, burning alive internally, in an agony of fire and suffocation, and I wanted air—I madly wanted air. My efforts to raise a window were vain, for all the windows in the car were screwed down. Nelson had seen drink-crazed men, and thought I wanted to throw myself out. He tried to restrain me, but I fought on. I seized some man's torch and smashed the glass."

The breaking of the glass started a free-for-all, and Jack was the first to be knocked out. Being knocked cold and motionless was perhaps the best thing that could have happened to him. His violent struggles had only sped up his already dangerously accelerated heart and increased the need for oxygen in his suffocating lungs.

Later he recorded, "Heavens! That was twenty years ago and I am still very much and wisely alive; **and I have seen much, done much, lived much, in** the intervening score of years; and I shudder when I think how close a shave I ran, how near I was to missing that splendid fifth of a century that has been mine since."

Everywhere he saw men doing drunk what they would never dream of doing sober. Under the spell of alcohol, men did the most frightful things—things that even shocked Jack's hardened soul. He saw his friends marched off to jail. He considered his situation and realized that he was sinking into a bad way of living. Living this way brought death too quickly to suit him.

THE *SOPHIA SUTHERLAND*

The sealing fleet was wintering in San Francisco Bay, and in the saloons Jack met skippers, mates, hunters, boat-pullers, and boat-steerers. He became friendly with one of the seal-hunters, Pete Holt, and agreed to be his boat-puller and to sign on any schooner that Pete signed on. Jack was afraid something would happen to him before sailing day, which was set for some time in January. He lived more circumspectly, drank less, and went home more frequently. When drinking grew too wild, he got out.

On the twelfth of January, 1893, Jack turned seventeen. Eight days later he stood before the shipping commissioner and signed the articles of the *Sophia Sutherland,* a three-masted sealing schooner bound on a voyage to the coast of Japan. At last Jack was to see the other side of the Golden Gate. It was an exhilarating experience. The ship's course was along the Southern passage to take advantage of northeast trade winds. They passed so close to Hawaii that Jack could see the volcanoes. They reached the Bonin Islands in fifty-one days.

The first few weeks on the *Sophia Sutherland* were the toughest for Jack. There were twelve men in the forecastle, ten of whom were hardened, experienced seamen. His shipmates were men who had gone through the hard school of the merchant service of Europe. As boys, they performed their ship's duty, and, in addition, by immemorial sea custom, they were slaves of the ordinary and able-bodied seamen. When they became ordinary seamen themselves they were still slaves of the able-bodied seamen.

Jack's problem was quite apparent. He was a boy, even though he had a man's body, who had never been to sea before. However, he was a good sailor and knew his business. It was a case of hold-ing his own with the other men or of going under. He had signed on as an equal, and as an equal he had to maintain himself, or else endure seven months of hell at their hands. It was this very equality they resented. By what right was he an equal? He had not earned that high privilege. He had not endured the miseries they had endured as maltreated boys or bullied ordinaries. Worse than that, he was a landlubber making his first voyage. And yet, by the injustice of fate, according to the ship's articles he was their equal.

Jack resolved to do his work so well that no man would be called upon to do it for him. He never malingered when pulling on a rope, for he knew the eagle eyes of his mates were on him every minute. He made it a point to be among the first of the watch going on deck, among the last going below, never leaving a sheet or a tackle for someone else to coil over a pin. He ran eagerly aloft for the shifting of topsail sheets and tacks, or for the setting or taking in of topsails; and always did more than his share.

Jack's parents were living in this house at Badger Park when he shipped out on the Sophia Sutherland.

The Sophia Sutherland

Furthermore, Jack had a volatile temper himself. He knew better than to accept any abuse or the slightest patronizing. At the first hint of such he exploded. He might be beaten in the subsequent fight, but he left the impression that he was a wild-cat and that he would just as willingly fight again. He let it be known that the man who imposed on him would have a fight on his hands. The innate sense of justice of the men, coupled with their wholesome dislike for a clawing and rending ruckus, soon led them to quit their heckling. He was soon accepted as an equal. From then on, the voyage was a happy one.

It took Jack no more than a few minutes to learn the names and uses of the few new ropes. After all, he was an able seaman. He had graduated from the right school. From the time he was twelve he had listened to the lure of the sea. When he was fifteen he was captain and owner of an oyster pirate sloop. By the time he was sixteen he was sailing in scow-schooners, fishing salmon with the Greeks up the Sacramento River, and serving as a sailor with the California Fish Patrol.

It was simple. As a small-boat sailor, he had learned to reason out and know the why of every-thing. It is true he had to learn how to steer by compass, but when it came to steering "full-and-by" and "close-and-by," he could beat many of his shipmates because that was the way he had always sailed. In fifteen minutes he could box the compass around and back again. And there was little else to learn during that seven-month cruise, except fancy rope tying.

After an interview with Jack, Ninetta Eames in her *Overland Monthly* article, "Jack London," published May, 1900, described one incident that oc-curred before his full acceptance by the crew:

Our sailor man one day sat on his bunk weav-ing a mat of rope-yarn when he was gruffly ac-costed by a burly Swede (big red John) taking his turn at "peggy-day" (a fo'castle term signify-ing a sailor's day for cleaning off the meals, washing up the dishes, and filling the slush lamps), a part of which disagreeable tasks the man evidently hoped to bulldoze the green hand into doing for him.

"Here, you landlubber," he bawled with an oath, "fill up the molasses. You eat the most of it!"

"Big Red" John, Jack's shipmate on the Sophia Sutherland.

Jack, usually the most amiable of the hands, bristled at the roughness; besides, he had vivid memories of his first and only attempt to eat the black, viscous stuff booked "molasses" on the fo'castle bill of fare, and so indignantly denied the charge.

"I never taste it. T'aint fit for a hog. It's your day to grub, so do it yourself."

Not a messmate within hearing of the alterca-tion but pictured disaster to the beardless, un-dersized boy.

Jack's defiant glance again dropped to his mat, and he quietly went on twisting the yarn. At this the sailor, both arms heaped with dishes, swore the harder and threatened blood-curdling consequences if he was not obeyed, but Jack kept silent, his supple hands nimbly intent on the rope strands. Through the tail of his eye he took note of his enemy.

Another threat, met by exasperating indiffer-ence, and the incensed Swede dropped the cof-fee-pot to give a back-handed slap on the boy's curled mouth. The instant after, iron-hand knuckles struck squarely between the sailor's eyes, followed by the crash of crockery. The Swede, choking with rage, made a lunge at Jack with a sledge-hammer fist, but the latter dodged, and like a flash vaulted to the ruffian's back, his fingers knitting in the fellow's throat-pipes. He bellowed and charged like a mad bull, and with every frenzied jump, Jack's head was a battering ram against the deck beams. Down crashed the slush lamp and the lookers-on drew up their feet in the bunks to make room for the show; they saw what the Swede did not—that Jack was getting the worst of it. His eyes bulged horribly and his face streamed blood, but he only dug his fingers deeper into that flesh-padded larynx and yelled through his shut teeth, "Will you promise to let me alone? Eh—will you promise?"

The Swede, tortured and purple in the face, gurgled an assent, and when that viselike grip on his throat lessened, reeled and stumbled to his knees like a felled bullock. The sailors, jamming their way through a wild clutter of food and broken dishes, crowded around the jubilant hero of the hour with friendly offers of assistance and a noticeable increase of respect in their tone and manner.

Jack, age seventeen, in Yokohama while on the voyage of the Sophia Sutherland

In the Bonin Islands, the rendezvous of the Canadian and American sealing fleets, they filled their water barrels and made necessary repairs before starting on the hundred days' hunting of the seal herd along the northern coasts of Japan to the Bering Sea.

In frosty, wintry weather they pursued the elusive seals and then sailed south to Yokohama and then to California by a northerly course. One particular event on this voyage, a typhoon encountered off the coast of Japan, changed the whole course of Jack London's life.

The wind was slowly rising, and by three o'clock, with a dozen seals in their boat, they were deliberating whether to go on or turn back, the recall flag was run up at the schooner's mizzen.

The sea became wild and turbulent. The wind was blowing half a gale, and the captain ordered the topsails made fast. The flying jib was run down and furled. The roar of the wind whistled through the rigging and the sea crashed over the weather bow and seemed to be tearing the ship apart. The creaking and groaning of the timbers, stanchions,

and bulkheads grew louder every minute. It was almost impossible to move on the heaving decks or to breathe as the fierce gusts came by. They were forced to run before the gale under a single reefed jib. The wind created such a tremendous sea that it was impossible to heave her to. The steersman changed course rapidly to starboard, then to port, as the enormous seas struck the schooner astern and nearly broached her to.

All hands had been on deck most of the night. Jack was called from his bunk at seven in the morning to take the wheel. Not a stitch of canvas was set. The ship was running before the storm under her bare poles, yet she tore along. The schooner was almost unmanageable, rolling to starboard and to port, veering and yawing anywhere between southeast and southwest, and constantly threatening to broach to. Had she broached to, she would eventually have been reported lost with all hands.

Jack took the wheel. The sailing-master watched him. He was afraid of Jack's youth, afraid he lacked the strength, but when he saw him successfully wrestle the schooner through several bouts, he went below to breakfast. Fore and aft, all hands were below decks. For forty minutes he stood there alone at the wheel, in his hands the wildly careening schooner and the lives of twenty-two men. At the end of the hour, sweating and played out, Jack was relieved. But he had done it. With his own hand he had done his trick at the wheel, driving a hundred tons of wood and iron through a million tons of foam-capped waves.

Heady adventure for a seventeen-year-old lad, but it was the capping climax to many such he had experienced on the *Sophia Sutherland.*

On August 26, 1893, the *Sophia Sutherland* dropped anchor in San Francisco Bay, and Jack headed for home in Oakland. He found John and Flora in debt as usual. After buying a secondhand hat, some forty-cent shirts, two fifty-cent suits of underwear, a secondhand coat and vest, and seventy-cents worth of drinks, he emptied the rest of his money into Flora's apron and went to look for work.

THE SOCIAL AND INTELLECTUAL CLIMATE

Jack was born in the midst of a great intellectual revolution. Evolutionary concepts were challenging traditional beliefs. The new thinkers and old idealists were at war. Science was arrayed against the metaphysicians, and Jack read every word he could find on the subject. He was to plunge deep, but the tragedy was that he had little guidance. As a result, his philosophy was to be a curious mixture of **Kant, Nietzsche, Darwin, Spencer, Schopenhauer, Haeckel, and Marx**, tempered with reverence for **Christ and Abraham Lincoln.** Matter, Force, and Motion were to become gods of the Universe to him. The *Origin of the Species* was to provide the basis for his ideas on social Darwinism; Herbert Spencer's *Synthetic Philosophy* would establish evolution as a science and philosophy; Karl Marx's *Communist Manifesto* challenged capitalism; and Nietzsche introduced the "superman" theory in an unforgettable way.

Being inquisitive and intelligent, Jack London soon realized that society was badly put together and that he and others like him were caught in the "trap." In later years his writing, thinking, and lectures reflected this idea. A country as rich and progressive as the United States should produce a better way of life for everybody. Jack watched the machinery work. He watched the wheels of the social machine go around, and he learned that the dignity of manual labor wasn't what he had been told it was by teachers, preachers, and politicians. The men without trades were helpless cattle. If one learned a trade, he was compelled to belong to a union in order to work at his trade. And his union was compelled to slug it out with the employers in order to hold up wages or hold down hours.

The employers likewise bullied and slugged. Jack couldn't see any dignity at all. And when a workman got old, or had an accident, he was thrown onto the scrapheap like any wornout machine.

He was about to study the "trap" from the inside. He had already had a taste of working-class life in the cannery as a youngster. Now he was a man, though he was only eighteen, and he would soon know what it meant to be "exploited," to be a work beast in the full sense of the words. He would know the agony of long hours and the misery of poverty. He would see the loved ones of his fellow workers dying because they couldn't afford a doctor or medicine, while the employers were smoking one-dollar cigars.

Jack found himself facing the same deplorable labor conditions that his father had been struggling against for years. It was estimated that over two million men were out of work and that at least sixty thousand were riding the rails in search of work.

One of the biggest causes of social and political discontent in the 1890s was related to the mismanagement of the currency. The decrease in the gold supply and the increase in silver was causing a serious variation in the quantity of money in circulation. The purchasing power of the dollar was unstable, and the people were apprehensive of the government's ability to do anything about it. Between 1865 and 1900 the population increased faster than the supply of gold. To pay for the Civil War, the government issued more dollars. By 1865 the number of dollars in circulation had doubled, but the amount of gold had not. There were more dollars, but each one had less purchasing power. Much of the new money was paper, and the people recognized that paper money was merely a promise by the government to pay. Because the average person was afraid of this new currency, it usually was worth half that of the dollar. Simply put, the increased currency during and after the Civil War brought inflation. After the Civil War, the government tried to return to the gold-backed dollar. Because of the diminished supply of gold, the government had to drastically decrease the currency in circulation, which brought deflation.

In 1876, at the time of Jack London's birth, John London found it twice as hard to get his hands on a dollar as he had in 1864. Because bad money always drives good money out of circulation, the uncertain dollars drove gold and silver into the hands of hoarders. Prices were based on the depreciated currency. Thus if John London had paid five thousand dollars for a farm in 1865, he could only sell it for two thousand dollars in 1879. Those on the lower rungs of society found themselves unable to earn enough dollars to pay their debts, and most owed more on their homes than they could sell them for.

Western mine owners clamored for silver coinage and political groups seeking increased currency joined them. The indigent Western farmer who needed more dollars and the rich Western silver mine owners joined hands. The capitalist in the East fought to stay on a limited gold standard. In 1878 the Bland-Allison Act put the country on a bimetal basis. Hundreds of millions of dollars in silver and silver certificates were issued and immediately the hoarders grabbed the gold and stored it away. By 1892 the government's vaults could back only a fraction of the money in circulation. The Eastern creditors were demanding payment in gold. The silver groups were gaining in power and demanded unlimited silver coinage. Creditors began to panic as they could see debts being paid by new, cheaper silver. Mortgages were foreclosed on any excuse, and securities were sold at discount. In 1893 India stopped its unlimited coinage of silver and the American silver dollar dropped in value, plunging the United States into the worst depression in its history up to that time.

The country was in chaos. Speculation and enterprise were dead, or at least dormant. The railroads brought a new emphasis on greed and monopoly power. Common ownership of railroad and manufacturing gave unfair advantage, since the railroad set much higher freight rates for their competitors and drove them into bankruptcy. There was no Interstate Commerce Commission until 1887, and no effective regulation of the railroads until 1906. The railroad tycoons used their power ruthlessly. Individual businesses were destroyed, bankruptcies were common, workmen were forced out of work, families were dislocated, and whole communities were destroyed.

Men of the 1890s saw the railroad as having more power over them than the government, and they knew that somewhere behind it all some remote capitalist was pulling the strings. A report to Congress in 1899 by the Interstate Commerce Commission summed it up: "No one thing does so much to force out the small operator, and to build up those trusts and monopolies against which law and public opinion alike beat in vain, as discrimination in freight rates."

Oakland was the western terminus for the railroad and had been having a running battle for years with the Southern Pacific over ownership of the waterfront. In 1892 and again in 1893 the battle nearly erupted in armed conflict. The period 1893–1894 was a year of strikes, lockouts, and riots. In Oakland ten cents an hour was good pay for able-bodied men. Things were equally bad across the Bay. San Francisco had a roadbuilding program in Golden Gate Park to provide jobs. The pay was ten cents an hour and thousands of men stood in line all night to get work.

THE JUTE MILL

It was not an auspicious time for Jack London to start looking for work. He finally landed a job at the jute mill—a ten-hour-day at ten cents an hour. He was receiving no more than when he worked in the cannery several years before. But there was a promise of a raise to a dollar and a quarter a day after a few months. The jute mill was a miserable place to work and Jack hated every minute of it.

He would take his place at one of the many machines, and before him, above a bin filled with small bobbins, were large bobbins revolving rapidly. Upon these he would wind the jute-twine from the small bobbins. The work was simple; all that was required was speed. There were no idle moments.

There was only one bright spot in his memory of those dismal months in the jute mill. The *San Francisco Morning Call* was conducting a contest for the best piece of descriptive writing by any young person under twenty-two years of age. Evidently Flora saw a chance for another twenty-five dollars. Expenses were higher now that the family had moved back to East Oakland. Johnny had not stopped talking about that typhoon when he was on the *Sophia Sutherland*. Now was a good time to write about it, and she begged him to write the story. Finally he relented and, very tired and sleepy, knowing he had to be up at half-past five, he began writing at midnight, working straight on until he had written two thousand words, the limit of the article. His idea was only half worked out, however. The next night, under the same conditions, he continued, adding another two thousand words before he had finished. The third night he spent in cutting out the excess so as to bring the article within the conditions of the contest.

The *Morning Call* for Sunday morning, November 12, 1893, announced the winners of the contest and printed their pictures and their entries. Jack was awarded the first prize of twenty-five dollars for his "Story of a Typhoon Off the Coast of Japan." The second prize of fifteen dollars went to Jessie A. Ryan of Stanford University, and Beatrice Reynolds of Berkeley walked off with the ten-dollar third prize. Not bad for a lad who had never gone beyond grammar school. Jack thought he had arrived and wrote some gush, as Jack called it, for the *Call* that was promptly rejected. He settled back into the work-beast atmosphere of the jute mill.

Those ten hours a day in the jute mill were humdrum machine toil. He wanted a more interesting life than operating a machine for ten cents an hour. He wanted something new. He strayed into the Young Men's Christian Association. Life there was healthful and athletic, but too juvenile. For Jack it was too late. He was no longer a boy, despite his paucity of years. He had travelled with big men, and he had known mysterious and violent things. He was from the wrong side of the tracks so far as concerned the young men he encountered at the YMCA. He spoke another language, possessed a sadder and more terrible wisdom. He realized that he had never had a boyhood. At any rate, the YMCA young men were too juvenile for him, too unsophisticated. Their meager physical and intellectual experiences outweighed their wholesome morality and healthful sports. All the clean, splendid young life that was theirs was denied him. He knew too much too young.

JACK'S FIRST LOVE

Late in 1893 Jack met Louis Shattuck and they became chums. Louis was an innocently devilish young fellow who was quite convinced that he was a sophisticated man-about-town. He was handsome and graceful, and filled with love for the girls. With him it was an all-absorbing pursuit. Jack knew nothing about girls. Here was an entirely new phase of existence that had escaped him. Jack decided that he, too, wanted to play the game.

This was more difficult than it sounded. Louis had never been entertained in any girl's home. And, of course, neither had Jack. They were unable to go to dancing schools or public dances—good places for getting acquainted—because they didn't have the money. Louis was a blacksmith's apprentice, and was earning only slightly more than Jack. Both lived at home and paid their way. After necessities they had between seventy cents and a dollar left for the week, which they shared. Curiously, Jack didn't mind the poverty. The disregard for money he had learned from the oyster pirates had never left him.

Despite all this, it wasn't long before Jack learned about women. His first girl friend was Haydee. She was between fifteen and sixteen. Her skirt reached the top of her little shoes. They met at a

Salvation Army meeting. They sat next to each other, but they did not speak. For half an hour they glanced shyly at each other. She had a slender oval face and brown eyes. She wore a tam-o'-shanter, and he thought her brown hair the prettiest shade of brown he had ever seen. From that single experience of half an hour, Jack was always convinced of the reality of love at first sight. They never went anywhere, not even to a matinee. But he knew she loved him, and he was certain that he loved her. He dreamed of her for a year or more. He never forgot her.

THE POWER PLANT

Because the owners of the jute mill failed to raise his pay, Jack quit. He wanted to settle down. One thing was clear—unskilled labor didn't pay. He decided that electricity would be a good trade. He didn't have the money to go to a technical school or university. Besides, he didn't think much of schools. As a young man he believed in the old myths that were the heritage of his day. "A canal boy could become president. Any boy who took employment with any firm, could, by thrift, energy, and sobriety learn the business and rise from position to position until he was taken in as a junior partner. After that the senior partnership was only a matter of time."

Jack went out to the power plant of the Oakland, San Leandro, and Haywards Electric Railway. He saw the superintendent himself and told him that he was unafraid of work and wanted to become a practical electrician. After a lengthy talk in which the superintendent outlined a rosy future that of necessity must begin at the bottom, Jack agreed to go to work in the morning as a coal heaver. He was to work a ten-hour day, every day of the month including Sundays and holidays, with one day off each month, for a salary of thirty dollars a month. Earnings were about the same as at the jute mill, but here he felt he was learning a trade.

Jack suddenly found that he didn't know the first thing about real work. He had to pass coal for the day and night shifts, and, despite working through the noon hour, he never finished his task before eight at night. He was working a twelve- to thirteen-hour day with no overtime. Finally one of the firemen told Jack the truth. The superintendent had hired him to displace two men who had been paid forty dollars a month each. Jack was killing himself and saving the railway fifty dollars a

The power plant of the Oakland, San Leandro & Haywards Electric Railway

month. Once more he quit. The effect of the work orgy in the boiler room sickened Jack. The very thought of work became repulsive. He went home, and proceeded to sleep the clock around.

Back in the cannery, he had watched the owner's daughter drive up in her beautiful carriage drawn by high-spirited horses in their trappings of silver. He and the little kids working with him had provided the wealth to buy all of this luxury, but would never have a chance to enjoy any of it. The workers lived in hovels and the owner lived on Nob Hill in San Francisco.

Jack realized as never before that there was something wrong in the way society was structured. He never expected the owners to lose money. They deserved a just profit, but not the excess profits they demanded, especially when their workers were in such pitiful circumstances. He learned by experience that "excess profits were unpaid wages." The jute mill had been as bad as the cannery, and the power plant was worse than either.

It was a lot better to roam and frolic over the world in the way he had previously done. Therefore he decided to take the path of adventure again, where he could escape the merciless exploitation of his muscles. Besides, he wondered if the conditions were as bad in the rest of the United States as they were in Oakland. Maybe it was only in Oakland that exploitation was so bad. Coxey's Army was a way he could satisfy his wanderlust and study social conditions in other places. It also was a chance to get out of the "trap" again.

COXEY'S INDUSTRIAL ARMY

In the "heart-breaking nineties" corn was selling for ten to fifteen cents a bushel in Kansas and the tenant farmer in the South found it impossible to pay his debts with cotton selling for five cents a pound. Hard times, mortgage foreclosures, business failures, and labor turmoil were everyday occurrences.

In 1892 Jacob S. Coxey was able to get his Good Roads bill introduced in Congress. The basic purpose of the bill was to enable the Secretary of the Treasury to issue five hundred million dollars in legal tender notes to construct good roads throughout the country. This would provide employment for those who needed it and put more money into circulation.

Unable to get his ideas accepted, Coxey decided to march an army of the unemployed to Washington—a living petition in favor of his plan to provide money, good roads, and jobs for the unemployed. Coxey's scheme aroused interest all over the country and soon "industrial armies" from the Far West joined the movement. In San Francisco "General" Charles T. Kelly became the leader of the West Coast contingent. The Mayor of San Francisco paid the ferry passage for six hundred men across the Bay to Oakland. They were marched to the Mills Tabernacle where they were to stay until transportation was arranged.

The City of Oakland was incensed over having San Francisco's unemployed dumped on it, but the citizens responded to their needs and fed them. They also raised two hundred dollars to pay their transportation to Sacramento, but lost patience when the army refused to ride in boxcars. The city authorities demanded that they leave.

At 2 A.M. the general fire alarm brought out the fire department and a large group of citizens, most of whom were deputized on the spot. The Chief of Police and the Sheriff had their forces surround the tabernacle and demanded that Kelly march his men immediately. When he refused, he was arrested and taken to jail. The army agreed to leave when Kelly was returned. When he arrived, they marched to the railroad station and were soon en route to Sacramento.

Kelly and his army appeared at a very opportune time. Here was Jack's chance to get away. He had been thinking for a long time of a tramping trip. It had started in Oakland when he was sixteen. There was nothing doing in oysters just then, so he decided to run up to Benicia, to get his blankets. Since he was running past Port Costa anyway, he decided to return a stolen boat belonging to his friend Dinny McCrea. The fact that the boat was in the hands of the constable made it a little difficult, but he could use the ten-dollar reward offered by Dinny. The constable was going to charge at least twenty-five dollars in fees for having captured the boat and taking care of it—his particular form of graft.

Jack turned to his companion, Nicky the Greek, and said, "With the low water on the river it's the best time of the year to make Sacramento."

After grabbing Dinny's boat, they cast off and were under way. In Sacramento they fell in with a gang of "road kids" having a swim. These kids had been all over the country and had developed their own language. "Their wanderings," said Jack, "made my oyster piracy look like thirty cents." A new world was calling—a world of "rods and gunnels," "blind baggages," and "side-door pullmans," "bulls" and "shacks," "floppings" and "chewins," "get-aways," "strongarms," "bindle-stiffs," "punks," and "profesh." And each new word spelled adventure.

After the swim they dressed and went to town. Jack tagged along. The kids began "battering" the "main-stem" for "light pieces," or, in other words, begging for money on the main street. Jack had never begged in his life, and this was the hardest thing for him to do when he first went on the road. He had strong feelings about begging. His philosophy, up to that time, was that it was better to steal than to beg; and that robbery was even better because the risk and the penalty were proportionately greater. As an oyster pirate, he had already earned convictions at the hands of justice that could have sent him to state's prison. To rob was manly, to beg was sordid and despicable. But in the days to come he learned to look upon begging as a "joyous prank, a game of wits, a nerve exerciser."

No kid was a road kid until he had tramped his way by train over "the hill"—such was the law of the road he heard expounded in Sacramento. All right, he'd go over the hill and matriculate. The hill was the Sierra Nevadas. The whole gang was going over the hill on a jaunt and Jack went along. The gang gave him the "moniker" of "Sailor Kid," later to be changed to "Frisco Kid," when he had put the Rockies between him and his native state.

Jack learned a lot of other things—how to roll a drunk or gang up on a lonely pedestrian. "Bindle-stiffs" were their favorite prey. A bindle-stiff was a working tramp. He took his name from the roll of blankets he carried, which was known as a bindle. Because he worked, a bindle-stiff usually had some small change on him and it was that small change the road kids were after.

In a short time Jack acquired the unmistakable airs of the "blowed-in-the-glass" profesh. The profesh were the aristocracy of the road. They were the lords and masters, the aggressive men, the primordial noblemen, the blond beasts so beloved of Nietzsche.

When he came back over the hill from Nevada, he discovered that some river pirate had stolen Dinny McCrea's boat. With the loss of Dinny's boat, Jack was pledged to the road. He once said, "The road had gripped me and would not let me go, and later, when I had voyaged to sea and done one thing and another, I returned to the road to make longer flights, to be a comet and a profesh, and to plump into the bath that wet me to the skin."

Jack and his friend Frank Davis had been reading and hearing all the news about the Industrial Army and made plans to join as soon as it left Oakland. Their experiences with the road kids in Sacramento had whetted their desire for adventure. Not knowing about the army's early departure from Oakland, they slept through the whole thing and were left behind. Jack's sister Eliza had pressed a ten-dollar gold piece into his hand before he left. They bought tickets to Sacramento and left Oakland at 4:30 P.M. the same day. Upon arrival they found the army had left for Ogden. After supper at the Mississippi Kitchen, the two boys caught the 10 P.M. Overland bound east.

They arrived in Truckee at 7 A.M., where the first order of business was to send their suitcases back to Oakland by Wells Fargo. Tramping and suitcases were incompatible. Somehow their signals got mixed and Frank caught the 8 P.M. Overland. Jack didn't. Since they had agreed to meet in Wadsworth, Jack caught a freight at 11 P.M. and was sidetracked in Reno. He woke up at 3:30 A.M. nearly frozen. He finally grabbed an evening freight to Wadsworth. Frank had already gone but left a postcard saying that he would meet him in Winnemucca, so Jack climbed aboard the 10:45 for the ride across the desert: From Humboldt he rode the bumpers of an orange special to Winnemucca.

On April 11 Frank decided the road was not for him and returned to Oakland. Jack worked his way to Carlin shoveling coal for the fireman. Finally he caught up with the Reno detachment of the Industrial Army on April 17.

General Kelly had managed to get transportation for his army to the Missouri River. From there to Des Moines they walked. By the 23rd of April Jack's feet were so sore he had to ride in the surgeon's wagon. On the 24th he walked six miserable miles into Walnut. An old soldier, feeling sorry for the kid, harnessed his horse and drove him into Atlantic. He managed to get rides until the 28th, when he sorefooted the eleven miles through Dexter to Earlham. Here he played on the sympathy of the locals, who bought him a ticket to Van Meter. On the 29th he mustered up his courage and walked on eight blisters the four miles to Booneville. April 30 he stumbled another fifteen miles to Des Moines and vowed he would never walk again.

The next week was spent in Des Moines. Unable to get rail transportation, General Kelly decided to go by boat. The army would build one hundred and fifty flat boats ten feet by six feet and go down the Des Moines River to the Mississippi, down to Cairo, and then up the Ohio to Wheeling, West Virginia, within three hundred miles of Washington.

Jack was now in his own element. You didn't need feet to operate a boat and he had an enjoyable trip from Des Moines to Hannibal, Missouri. The night of his arrival in Hannibal he wrote in his diary, "We went supperless to bed. Am going to pull out in the morning. I can't stand starvation." The goals of Coxey's Army were just not the same as his. Their Holy Grail was the front lawn of the White House; he was on the path to adventure, seeking answers to his questions about how society was put together.

It was the same everywhere. The rich were getting richer and the poor were still in the same abyss of poverty. The "trap" was everywhere and exploitation was not limited to Oakland.

The following day he abandoned the army and caught the Cannon Ball out of Fell Creek at 2:11 A.M. He was on his way to Chicago. On arrival on May 29 he picked up a letter from home containing four dollars. With this fortune Jack headed for South Clark Street and, after much haggling, bought an overcoat, hat, pants, and shirt. He went to the theater in the evening, and then found a luxurious—or so it seemed—fifteen-cent bed at the Salvation Army—the first bed he had seen since leaving Oakland.

In Chicago he visited the grounds where the World's Fair had been held and then took the steamer across Lake Michigan to St. Joseph for a visit with his Aunt Mary Everhard. While there he met his cousin Ernest Everhard, whose name he immortalized a few years later in *The Iron Heel.* After a short visit he headed for Niagara Falls.

He rode into Niagara Falls in a "side-door Pullman," or, in common parlance, a boxcar. He arrived in the afternoon and headed straight from the freight train to the falls. Once his eyes were filled with that vision of down-rushing water, he was captivated. He could not tear himself away long enough to "batter" the homes for his supper. Night came on, a beautiful moonlit night, and he lingered by the falls until after eleven. Then he hunted for a place to eat.

Somehow he had a hunch that Niagara Falls was a bad town for hoboes, so he headed out into the country, climbed a fence, and flopped in a field. It was a balmy night and he slept until dawn. But when he awoke at the first gray daylight, he remembered the wonderful falls. He climbed the fence and started down the road to have another look.

The town was asleep when he arrived. As he walked along a quiet street, he saw three men coming toward him along the sidewalk, walking abreast. Hoboes, he decided, like himself, who had got up early. The men on each side were hoboes all right, but the man in the middle wasn't. He was a "fly-cop" and the two hoboes were his prisoners. John Law was up and out after the early worm. Jack was the worm.

"What hotel are you stopping at?" he queried.

Jack was had. He didn't know the name of a hotel in the place. He said, "I just arrived."

"Well, you turn around and walk in front of me, and not too far in front, there's somebody wants to see you."

Jack had been pinched. He knew who wanted to see him and led the way to the city jail. There he was searched and his name was registered.

Later he said, "I have forgotten, now, under which name I was registered. I gave the name of Jack Drake, but when they searched me, they found letters addressed to Jack London. This caused trouble and required explanation, all of which has passed from my mind, and to this day I do not know whether I was pinched as Jack Drake or Jack London. But one or the other it should be there today in the prison register of Niagara Falls."

Jack, in the lower right corner, with Kelly's Army

From the office they were led to an iron cage where minor offenders were confined. At last, when they totaled sixteen, they were led upstairs into the courtroom. It was there that Jack received a shock from which he never fully recovered.

In the courtroom were the sixteen prisoners, the judge, and two bailiffs. The judge acted as his own clerk. There were no witnesses. There were no citizens of Niagara Falls present to look on and see how justice was administered in their community. The judge glanced at the list of cases before him and called out a name. A hobo stood up. The judge glanced at a bailiff. "Vagrancy, your Honor," said the bailiff. "Thirty days," said his Honor. The hobo sat down, and the judge was calling another name and another hobo was rising to his feet.

The trial of that hobo had taken just about fifteen seconds. The trial of the next hobo came off with equal speed. The bailiff said, "Vagrancy, your Honor," and his Honor said, "Thirty days." Thus it went like clockwork, fifteen seconds to a hobo—and thirty days.

Jack was disgusted. Behind him were the many generations of his American ancestry. One of the liberties those ancestors of his had fought and died

for was the right of trial by jury. This was his heritage, and he would demand a jury trial.

"He got to me. My name, whatever it was, was called, and I stood up. The bailiff said, 'Vagrancy, your Honor,' and I began to talk. But the judge began talking at the same time, and he said, 'Thirty days.' I started to protest, but at that moment his Honor was calling the name of the next hobo on the list. His Honor paused long enough to say to me, 'Shut up!' The bailiff forced me to sit down. And the next moment that next hobo had received thirty days and the succeeding hobo was just in process of getting his."

They were taken below, locked up, and given breakfast. It was a pretty good breakfast, as jail breakfasts go, and it was the best he was to get for a month to come.

Jack was dazed. "Here am I, under sentence, after a farce of a trial wherein I was denied not only my right of trial by jury, but my right to plead guilty or not guilty." He asked for a lawyer and they laughed at him. And this was a full-fledged penitentiary he was headed for.

Here was a plucky, happy, easygoing youngster in search of knowledge of the social system heading

Jack London's railroad ticket was good for any line in America. He crawled under a freight car, put the groove of this piece of wood on a rail, and sat down and rode to his next stop.

for prison because Erie County needed men for their rock pile. It was a lesson that he was never to forget, and one that destined him to become an outstanding propagandist in later years in socialism's battle to right the wrongs of society.

Jack had learned a lot during this period. He had learned to "throw his feet" (beg) for meals and was as good as the next in "slamming a gate" (approaching a private home) for a "set down" (eating at the table), or hitting for a "light piece" (money) on the street. Tramping or sailing, playing or working, reading or writing, or whatever, Jack London always gave it his best shot. He had won his moni-

ker "Sailor Kid" when with the road kids, and now he had won the respect of his new companions who looked upon him as a true "profesh" (highest honor in the tramp world).

Tramping had taken him all over the United States. He had met men with good educations and ability eating stew along the tracks because they could find no work. He had seen men with families back home who were riding the rods in hopes of finding a job so they could feed and clothe their children. And all of this in the richest country in the world.

DOING TIME

The small chain gang marched through the streets of Niagara Falls to the railroad station. With much rattling and clanking they sat down, two by two, in the seats of the smoking car. Jack was indignant, but too practical to lose his head. Thirty days of mystery and unusual adventure were before him.

He believed that his sense of survival and the knowledge gained on the road would enable him to leave prison with no permanent scars. He looked about for someone who knew the ropes and picked a squat, heavily built man out of the group. He was a brute beast but there was humor in the corner of his eyes. Now Jack had to determine one thing for sure. Prison was like the road in that there were few

women around, leading to problems of homosexuality. Having no such tendencies himself, latent or otherwise, Jack had been thoroughly disgusted with the problem and at times had to prove his point with his ready and able fists. After talking with his new friend for a while, he was certain he had chosen wisely. As they became chummy, this man cautioned Jack to follow his lead when they got to the prison.

They were marched into the barbershop and ordered to strip and bathe, each man to scrub his neighbor's back—a futile precaution, for the prison swarmed with vermin. The men lathered themselves, and the barbers shaved them at the rate of a

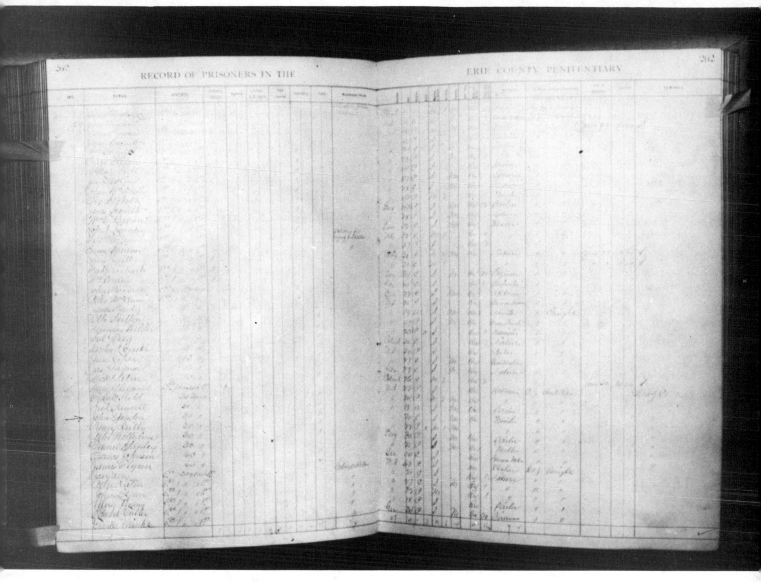

Page 262 of the Erie County Penitentiary Records at Buffalo, on which John Lunden (sic) was entered in 1894

man a minute. A haircut took a trifle longer. In three minutes the down of eighteen years was scraped from Jack's face, and his head was as smooth as a billiard ball.

Then came the lineup, forty or fifty naked men to be vaccinated by medical students. After his vaccination Jack put on his badge of shame, a stout prison shirt along with coat and trousers conspicuously striped. Leaving the reception area, Jack got his first taste of marching the lockstep.

Hardly had they been in their cell when a convict sauntered down the gallery and looked in. It was Jack's friend. He had the freedom of the hall, he explained, and was unlocked at six in the morning and not locked up again until nine at night. He was in with the "push" in that hall, and had been promptly appointed a trustee of the kind technically known as "hall man." Jack's pal informed him that newcomers had to stay in their cells for

the rest of the day, and the next morning they would be put to hard labor in the prison yard.

Dinner consisted of two hunks of dry bread and some hot water called soup. A lonely drop of grease and a little salt saved it from being just hot water. The rest of the meals were the same. A ration of bread was about the size of one's two fists, and each prisoner received three rations a day. They got plenty of water. In the morning it was called "coffee," at noon it was called "soup," and at night it was masqueraded as "tea." The prisoners called it "water bewitched." In the morning it was black, the color resulting from boiling it with burnt bread crusts. At noon it was served minus the color with salt and a little grease added. At night it was served with a purplish-auburn hue that defied speculation; it was poor tea, but it was dandy hot water.

After two days of working in the yard Jack was made a trustee, a hall man, thanks to his new friend. It was a brutal job, but far better than hard labor in the yard—and the graft that came with the job made life easier. There were thirteen hall men over about five hundred fellow prisoners. It was up to them to keep order, and the guards didn't care how they did it.

It was a living hell, and it was up to the thirteen to rule. It was impossible, considering the nature of the prisoners, for them to rule by kindness. They ruled by fear. When a man got out of line, they had a guard open his cell, and the hall men went inside to work him over.

It wasn't all bad, though. Jack had fun with the system of barter that prevailed. There was plenty of money in circulation—sometimes smuggled in, but more frequently coming from the barbershop, where the newcomers were robbed of their meager possessions. Most of it, however, flowed from the cells of the longtimers. Jack never found out how they got the money.

The hall men grafted the general population, and the first hall man was the head grafter and grafted on the rest of the hall men, who held their particular grafts by his permission and had to pay for that right.

Once a week the men who worked in the yard received a five-cent plug of chewing tobacco. This tobacco was the coin of the realm. The hall men controlled the food supply and they made sure that at each feeding the prisoners received a little less than their full allotment. In this way the hall men's stock in trade was kept in full supply. They peddled the bread; two or three rations for a plug was the exchange. Jack knew it was like taking candy from a baby, but what could he do? He went along with the system that prevailed.

When he found a man with a pair of suspenders, Jack exchanged half a dozen rations of bread for them. Then he traded the suspenders for meat. Meat was what Jack wanted most. Once in a while he was able to trade for a worn paperback novel which, in the penitentiary, was considered a real treasure. He read the novel and then traded it to the bakers for cake, or to the cooks for meat and vegetables, or to the firemen for decent coffee, or to someone else for a newspaper that occasionally filtered in.

In *The Road,* Jack tells about many other forms of graft, but little about the horrors that prevailed. Had society been more permissive in 1907, he

The Yard, Erie County Penitentiary, Buffalo, New York

A cell block, Erie County Penitentiary, Buffalo, New York

would have curled our hair with his descriptions of what actually went on in the Erie County Pen in 1894.

A few minutes after his release on July 29, Jack grabbed the first train and headed for Pennsylvania. He wanted to put as many miles as possible between himself and Buffalo's Erie County Penitentiary. For all his hatred of Buffalo, it is ironic that one of his first essays ("From Dawson to the Sea") was sold to *The Illustrated Buffalo Express* (June 4, 1899).

BACK ON THE ROAD AGAIN

Jack was traveling south on board a Western New York and Pennsylvania freight train. As the train sped through New York toward Pittsburgh, he tried to forget his recent ordeal, but he couldn't. Lying in a boxcar, listening to the music of the wheels, Jack remembered his cell block, filled with the dregs of society—degenerates, wrecks, lunatics, addled minds, epileptics, weaklings—in short, a very nightmare of humanity.

In the twilight of the freight car, with the smell of coal smoke and dust in his nostrils, the injustice of the whole thing festered in his brain. The law and the penal authorities had perpetrated this whole sordid affair—he expected no better. Long ago he had learned that the man behind the key was often worse than the man behind the lock. This was just one more proof. And it wasn't that the people of New York didn't know what was being done in their name. The thing that bothered Jack was that the politicians and the citzens just didn't care what happened to tramps, the poor, and the exploited. Few judges ever listened to the tramps who, when apprehended, were automatically guilty of whatever crime the constable charged them with. Society was willing to turn its back on the brutality and bestiality of the police to their prisoners as long as the "law" kept the vagrants off the streets. As these thoughts went through his head, Jack determined that he wouldn't get caught again. In future entanglements with the police, his memories of Buffalo would give speed to his feet.

Jack often recalled those tramp days. He loved to tell about his experience in Harrisburg when he was invited to a "set down" with two maiden ladies, who took him not to their kitchen but to their dining-room. They ate eggs, out of eggcups! It was the first time he had ever seen or heard of eggcups. He confessed that he was a bit awkward, but he was hungry and unabashed. He mastered the eggcup, and he mastered the eggs in a way that delighted those two maiden ladies.

Before leaving Harrisburg, Jack went swimming in the Susquehanna near the tracks. As he was dressing he discovered he had been robbed. Penniless, he beat his way to Washington, D.C., where he found a job as janitor in a stable for bed and board. During his time off he took in all the sights, enjoying the White House and Federal buildings like a paying tourist.

En route to New York he stopped in Baltimore's Druid Hill Park, where he sat enthralled, listening to intellectual debates and lectures of the educated tramps and other soapbox orators. In New York he missed very few of the sights, but foremost in his memory was the haunting sight of the poor on the Bowery—a picture he never forgot and an experience for which he never forgave the city. However, New Yorkers did have a better side—they loved to give a handout. Much of his time was spent reading in the little green square near City Hall. Milk was one cent a glass, and Jack managed to "get away with from five to ten glasses each afternoon."

Catching a freight out of Harlem, Jack headed for Boston. Because Boston jails were notoriously unclean, he elected to brave the cold fall winds and sleep on a park bench. He wandered until he finally saw a comfortable-looking bench on the Boston Common. All was well until about 2 A.M., when a policeman tapped him on the feet.

"Always placate the policeman," he had learned. "He is at once the dispenser and obfuscator of life, liberty, and the pursuit of happiness. He shapes the destinies of lesser creatures, and free air or dungeon lurk in his gruff 'move on,' or 'come on.' "

There was no way his feet could get him out of this encounter—he would have to resort to his gift for telling stories. He pretended to be half-asleep and started to mumble.

"What did you say?" the officer demanded.

"Oh, never mind. I wasn't awake yet and was dreaming about Ueno Park."

"Where's that?"

"Japan," Jack replied. Then he proceeded to take the policeman on a tour of Japan. For two hours he led him through the streets of Yokohama and Tokyo, or Fujiyama, through teahouses and temples. Desperately remembering what he had seen when he was in Japan in 1893, he added a few items about places he had only visited in travel brochures. The policeman hadn't been there, so Jack threw in bazaars and marketplaces that even the Japanese had never seen, until his listener forgot that he was a policeman. Jack said, "At the end of that time he discovered that my teeth were chattering, said he was sorry he hadn't any whiskey about him, gave me a silver quarter instead, and departed—he and his club." Breathing a huge sigh of relief, Jack made haste in translating the gift into a juicy steak and a cup of "java."

With winter coming on, Jack beat his way to Ottawa, carefully avoiding the bulls in Rutland, Vermont, who he was told recruited tramps the hard way for the local marble quarries. From Ottawa he made a mad dash across Canada to Vancouver. Over one thousand miles of this westward trip were spent in a coalcar reflecting on his tramping experiences. The year 1894 had been a year of learning. His experiences on the road were his Harvard and his Yale—profound lessons in the ways of society. From them Jack learned that the story was the same everywhere. The poor had little hope and the rich were indifferent. The exploited in one town were as helpless as in the next. According to him, the only people who found anything good in capitalism were the politicians and the capitalists who controlled it.

His prison experience was the most instructive of all. He had been imprisoned without due process in the United States of America, where a man was supposed to be innocent until proven guilty. It was a miracle that he didn't chuck all his ideals and turn to crime, but he had studied that route too well and knew where it led.

On the road he listened to stories from laboring men who were fired when their muscles were no longer strong, and he saw men who were let go when they lost an arm or leg in an unprotected machine. He met others who were well educated but who couldn't find a place in society because they challenged the accepted concepts of their day. Few teaching positions were available for the men who sought to change things rather than accept the things that were.

The "class struggle" was no longer a meaningless lecture delivered by a vagrant socialist on a soapbox—it was now a sheer, naked reality, the implications of which he was beginning to understand, for he had seen the wage slaves in the crowded labor ghettoes of the East struggling to wrest a more equitable share of the profits, derived from the products of their labor, from the grasp of their capitalist masters.

On the long road home Jack wondered if the masters of society could be beaten. At various times during the last few months he had observed the struggle of the working class. Their overwhelming numbers gave them a powerful edge at the ballot box—as long as they were allowed to vote. He also discovered Karl Marx and Friedrich Engels, who taught working men class consciousness and urged them to overthrow the present archaic, exploitative, and inefficient economic system. Workers alone, they argued, could usher in the classless society where the products of man's labor would be used for the benefit of all.

When Jack left Oakland, he was still a believer in Kipling's work ethic. He had believed the teachers and preachers who proclaimed the honor of work. Now he could see that hard labor was not as honorable as he had been told. It was also clear that even his young muscles brought no money either. His young muscles were strong, but they could earn only a pittance. It was plain that he had a future only as long as they remained so. As soon as they lost their strength, he would be thrown out on the scrap heap of society. The vaunted dignity of labor was pure nonsense. Men without trades had no hope. Those with trades were utterly dependent upon the whims of the labor market.

Reasoning thus, he decided that there would be no life of crime for him. There would be no working life either. His only hope of ever escaping the "trap" was to sell brains, and to do that he must get an education. He would "open the books."

In that old coalcar traveling across Canada, Jack remembered the men he had worked with shoulder to shoulder—sailors, soldiers, laborers, the educated, and the ignorant. Some were stronger and some were weaker than he. Some had been born in the "trap" and some were there because of bad luck

The S.S. Umatilla

or accidents. These castaways were men as good as himself. This knowledge had confirmed his reasons for going back to school. It was either that or surrender to the dismal, miserable life of a work beast.

When Jack's freight finally pulled into Vancouver, he was anxious to head home and enter Oakland High School. But it took him several days to find a ship on which he could work his way to San Francisco—he had had enough of the road. Those days of waiting proved enjoyable, however. He received "set downs" more often than "handouts." In fact, he was only refused twice. This was because both times he arrived after dinner. But even then he was given two bits to make up for the refusal. Vancouver was a perfect ending for Jack's life as a tramp and would always be a fond memory.

Finally after several failures he managed to work his way home as a coal stoker on the S.S. *Umatilla*.

OPENING THE BOOKS

When Jack returned home, his father was earning a little money as a special policeman, and his mother was giving piano lessons. He hunted for part-time jobs to help pay the rent and put food on the table. With a free conscience and the approval of his parents, he entered Oakland High School with the winter class of '97.

Flora fixed up a combination bedroom and den in their tiny cottage at 1639 Twenty-second Avenue. Jack knew his mother well enough to know that he would have a good bed and enough steak and vegetables to keep him healthy. There would be no desserts and no frills, but he was used to that. Eliza would always be there when he needed her; she was the most stabilizing influence in his life. She rushed out and bought him a table large enough for his books and other study needs. He kept his meager wardrobe in an old dresser. A small chair and a bedside stand to hold the lamp completed the furnishings. It was from this little room that the world-renowned author would emerge, but only after many hundreds of agonizing hours of study and work.

Work and smoke. Smoke and work. The air was always blue with smoke. His only relaxation was an occasional visit with Eliza, who lived just around the corner and loved to have Jack over for breakfast. He would ride there on his bicycle. Eliza described his first attempts to ride the old "bone shaker" this way: "At first he was most of the time sprawled about the ground, and he'd come over to my house for breakfast—bruised, dripping wet and red in the face, his curls all tousled, fighting mad, and explaining carefully what slow work it was getting the best of that 'infernal machine!' Then he'd burst out laughing at the idea of how he must look when he tangled up and went down in a heap with it." It is probable that Jack learned more cuss words using that old bicycle than in the eight months on the *Sophia Sutherland*.

It was about forty blocks from his house to the school at Twelfth and Jefferson. Eliza came to the rescue again and bought him a new "safety" wheel for the daily trek.

On the road Jack had chewed tobacco to keep his bad teeth from aching. His sister agreed to buy him a set of uppers and have the rest of his teeth fixed on condition that he quit chewing. "Well," Jack remarked when the job was completed, "here I am with my first store teeth and the first toothbrush I ever bought." He got them both at the same time, at nineteen years of age.

Jack wasted no time in getting acquainted with the Aegis Publishing Company—the most popular student organization in the school. More students belonged to it than all the rest of the school organizations combined. Jack couldn't belong since to be eligible a student must have completed his low junior term. The company issued a thousand shares of stock with a par value of fifty cents. Each member could buy only one share. Though Jack was never a member, he was well respected for his writing ability and became a close friend of the staff.

Only a few weeks after enrolling in school, Jack saw his two-part article on the "Bonin Islands" published in *The High School Aegis* of January 18, 1895, and February 1, 1895. Irving Stone said of this article, "It is written with verve, with a freshness and vitality that keeps it enjoyable even at this distance. The pictures of the sealing fleet and the

Jack lived here at 1639 Twenty-second Avenue in East Oakland when he attended Oakland High School in 1895.

Jack London during his high school year

islands are vivid, the characters are warmly human and lovable, and above all the prose has a music of words."

During his year at Oakland High, Jack submitted eight more articles and short stories, which were promptly published. The stories were varied in content and all were well received by the student body, even though his socialist article, "Pessimism, Optimism, and Patriotism," March 1, 1895, raised a lot of eyebrows—especially those of Mr. McChesney, the principal. In this last article, Jack charged capitalism, "The powers that be," with creating a program of "long hours, sweating systems and steadily decreasing wages" leading "to naught but social and moral degradation." The closing sentence shocked the conservative principal: "Arise, ye Americans, patriots and optimists! Awake! Seize the reins of a corrupted government and educate your masses!"

The last story published in *The Aegis,* December 18, 1895, was "One More Unfortunate." This story tells of a young musician who, inspired by Ouida's *Signa,* goes out to conquer the musical world but settles for an obscure life as a fiddler in a rundown nightclub. Realizing how he has desecrated his early ambitions, he goes down to the docks just before dawn, and plunges into the cold gray waters. "A plunge, a bubble and no more." This story was based on an evening spent with Frank Atherton, when he had come up from San Jose to attend a concert with Jack in San Francisco. After the concert Jack took Frank down to the Barbary Coast to see the sights. One particularly vile place was the Bella Union Theatre, but since it was cheap, they went there. Jack was especially interested in the violinist, who had an excellent gift for music. The

violinist never achieved any fame, but was immortalized in "One More Unfortunate."

No one remembers when the students of Cole Grammar School started the Henry Clay Club, but Jack London and Edward Applegarth were charter members. The club was active during Jack's high school days and was extremely beneficial. Many of the members were from better families and Jack was fully accepted by them. They didn't frown on his shabby clothes, nor did they care that his family was poor. Since one of the main activities of the club was debate, the members welcomed and admired Jack's natural abilities in this area. They also loved to listen to Jack's yarns. His quick wit, keen sense of humor, and remarkable ability to describe past experiences at sea and on the road held them spellbound. They would rather listen to Jack spin a yarn than debate.

"Ted" Applegarth, whose cultured English family had moved to the area a few years back, became his closest friend, accepting Jack for what he was and for the potential he could see in him. At this time Ted, Eliza, and John London were the only ones who fully realized that Jack was destined for greatness. Few others could understand him. Georgia Loring Bamford, for example, another of Jack's classmates, said that on one occasion he would look like a cherub and the next a waterfront hoodlum. She was puzzled by his supreme self-confidence mixed with a definite sense of inferiority due to his family's poverty. He was shy and unassuming and yet commanding and forceful. These traits were always a part of him.

One day Ted Applegarth took Jack home and introduced him to his family. When Jack met Ted's sister, Mabel, he promptly forgot Haydee, the Salvation Army girl. Mabel was a student at the University. Conscious of her own superiority, she cheerfully accepted the challenge of polishing this young bundle of energy and excitement. Under her guidance, his grammar and manners constantly improved.

No puppy love was greater or sweeter than Jack's utter surrender to Mabel and all she represented. She was three years older and her education was a constant amazement to him. She had read all the great classics and could quote poetry beautifully. Her fragile, ethereal beauty enslaved him.

The Applegarths lived in another world, a world remote from the one Jack had been raised in. Refined, cultured, full of books and book talk—he had read about people like them but had never aspired to be included. They possessed a security he had never known. They were free of the worries of rent and food that had dogged his days. Theirs was a new and better world, and Mabel was its most prized attraction. He was not in love with a girl—he was in love with a dream. Such was Jack's initial vision of Mabel. He would later come to believe that the vision was a mirage inspired by her frailty and lack of vitality.

In the Applegarth home Jack increased his appreciation for music. His mother had exposed him to music through her piano lessons. As youngsters, Jack and a cousin played at least one piano duet for a local church. Throughout his life he loved fine music, especially opera.

As school dragged on Jack became impatient with his studies and then disgusted with them. He tired of sitting at a desk transferring the teacher's notes to his own pad. The only stimulus to his intellect were the books he borrowed and discussed with members of the Henry Clay Club. Earle La-

bor, the noted London scholar, has expressed the importance of this stimulation in these words:

He began meeting other young intellectuals with whom he could exchange ideas and begin to articulate his growing awareness of the world of thought. He was by now reading widely, not merely books of romance, travel, and fiction, but heavier stuff: Charles Darwin's *Origin of the Species,* Adam Smith's *The Wealth of Nations,* Immanuel Kant's *Critique of Pure Reason,* Benjamin Kidd's *Social Evolution,* and—most important—Herbert Spencer's *Philosophy of Style,* to which he subsequently attributed his own mastery of style, and *First Principles,* which he claimed would do more for mankind through the ages than a thousand books like Dickens' *Nicholas Nickleby* and Harriet Beecher Stowe's *Uncle Tom's Cabin* (Letters, 51). Spencer's audacious synthesis of the laws of biology, physics, and sociology; his emphasis on the necessity of progress and the perfectability of man; his survival-of-the-fittest ethic; and his advocacy of the individual over society—these were exactly what Jack's voracious intellectual appetite had been craving, and to the god who had provided them he would remain faithful for the rest of his life, long after the great Spencerian fad which swept America had declined.

When he wasn't at school, or with the Henry Clay fellows, he was working—for Flora depended on him now that his father was seldom able to work. It was necessary for Jack to pick up odd jobs in addition to his janitorial work at the high school. In a letter to Mabel dated November 30, 1898, he records the extremity of his situation at that time: "How often as I swept the rooms at high school, had my father come to me at my work and got half a dollar, or two dollars? And you know I had a place to put every bit of it myself. Aye, I have had my father come there, when I did not have a cent, and went to the *Aegis* fellows and borrowed it—mortgaged my next month's wages."

Jack spent part of the summer vacation with the Applegarths in Yosemite, where they had taken Mabel to recuperate from a serious illness. The rest of the summer was spent as usual in the pursuit of money for rent and food. He was sorely tempted not to go back to school in the fall. As the time drew near, he looked wistfully in the direction of his former cronies on the waterfront, but his "holy grail" was shining too brightly. He was after that

City Hall Plaza, Oakland, where Jack was inspired to join the Socialist Labor Party by soapbox orators

Oakland City Hall. The Oakland Public Library is on the left.

"university sheepskin," that vital key to the future in the 1890s. To be a "college man" was the key that unlocked the door to success and social acceptance. Above all, it was absolutely essential for a literary career.

When school opened in the fall, Jack was back with his class of December '97, but not for long. His old impatience with his studies and teachers returned; he began to believe he could master the material faster on his own. All the books he needed

were there on the shelves in the public library. He would forego the help of teachers—he was a natural student. And, besides, he knew that Mr. Bamford, a new friend he had discovered at the library, was very able and always willing to help.

On his way to the library Jack would ride through City Hall Plaza, where he often stopped to listen to the knot of wordy socialists and working-class philosophers on their soapboxes. Each time he tore himself away reluctantly from these men whom he found to be serious and dignified. The stuff of their thoughts was so vital, their arguments so stimulating, their ideas so alive.

On several of these visits Jack heard Herbert Spencer quoted, and his ideas particularly appealed to him. On one occasion Frank Strawn-Hamilton, a disciple of Spencer, appeared; he held Jack's attention for over an hour. Strawn-Hamilton's mind was subtle, and his arguments profound and so eloquently presented that they dazzled Jack's mind. Leaving the park, he rushed to the library and drew out *First Principles*.

Once before he had tried Spencer, and choosing the *Principles of Psychology* to begin with, had failed. There was no understanding the book, and he had returned it undigested. But this night after algebra and physics, and an attempt at a sonnet, he got into bed and opened *First Principles*. Morning found him still reading. It was impossible to sleep. Nor did he write or study that day. He lay on the bed till his body grew tired. Then he tried the hard floor, reading on his back, the book held in the air above him, or changing from side to side. He slept that night and did his studying next morning, and then the book tempted him and he yielded, reading all afternoon, oblivious to everything.

Jack London was mastered by curiosity all his days. He wanted to know, and it was this desire that had sent him adventuring to the Bering Sea and across the United States and back through Canada. But he was learning from Spencer what he had never known, and what he never could have known, and he continued his sailing and wandering forever. He had merely skimmed over the surface of things, observing detached phenomena, accumulating fragments of facts, and making superficial little generalities. The mechanism of the flight of birds he had watched and reasoned about with understanding; but it had never entered his head to try to explain the process whereby birds, as organic flying mechanisms, had been developed. He had never dreamed there was such a process. How birds had come to be was unguessed. They always had been. They just happened.

As it was with birds, so it had been with everything. His unprepared attempts at philosophy had been fruitless. The medieval metaphysics of Kant had given him the key to nothing, and had served the sole purpose of making him doubt his own intellectual powers. His study of evolution had been confined to hopelessly technical volumes. He had

understood nothing. Now he learned that evolution was no mere theory but an accepted process of development; that scientists no longer disagreed about it, their only differences being over the method of evolution.

And here was Spencer, organizing all knowledge for him, reducing everything to unity, elaborating ultimate realities, and presenting to his startled gaze a universe so concrete that it was like the model of a ship such as sailors make and put in glass bottles. There was no caprice, no chance. All was law. All things were related to all other things, from the farthermost star in the wastes of space to the myriads of atoms in the grain of sand under one's foot. This new concept was a perpetual amazement to Jack, and he found himself engaged continually in tracing the relationship between all things under the sun. He drew up lists of the most incongruous things and was unhappy until he succeeded in establishing kinship between them all—kinship between love, poetry, earthquakes, fire, rattlesnakes, rainbows, sunsets, the roaring of lions, cannibalism, beauty, and murder. He unified his universe and looked at it not as a terrified traveler in the thick of mysteries, but observing and charting and becoming familiar with all there was to know. And the more he knew, the more passionately he admired the universe, and life, and his own life in the midst of it.

Jack plunged into the Oakland Public Library with a determination to prepare for fall exams at Berkeley. His friend Fred Jacobs and Fred's fiancée, Bess Maddern, helped him in his studies. When not studying, Jack was working at every odd job he could find, for his father was growing increasingly feeble and contributing less and less to the family income.

Somewhere in his busy schedule Jack found time to continue his study of socialism, gaining a degree of notoriety in the Bay Area as he did so. On February 16, 1896, the *San Francisco Chronicle* published a story about the boy socialist from Oakland:

Jack London, who is known as the boy socialist in Oakland, is holding forth nightly to the crowds that throng City Hall Park. There are other speakers in plenty, but London always gets the biggest crowd and the most respectful attention.

London is young, scarcely 20, but he has seen many sides of the world and has travelled extensively. He was born in San Francisco in the Centennial year, and went through the California grammar schools before he started out in the world. . . . He is a high school boy, and supports himself as a janitor in the institution. At present he is fitting himself for a course at the University of California, where he will make a specialty of social questions.

The young man is a pleasant speaker, more earnest than eloquent, and while he is a broad socialist in every way, he is not an Anarchist. He says on the subject, when asked for a definition of socialism, "It is an all-embracing term—communists, nationalists, collectionists, idealists, utopians, altrurians, are all socialists, but it cannot be said that socialism is any of these—it is all."

Any man, in the opinion of London, is a socialist who strives for a better form of government than the one he is living under.

THE UNIVERSITY ACADEMY

Fred Jacobs and Ted Applegarth were both preparing for the University of California at the University Academy in Alameda. Recognizing the need for professional guidance, Jack decided to join them. The Academy was geared to wealthy students and was expensive, but once more his sister Eliza came up with the money. He was put in the senior class, which was scheduled to graduate right into the University of California in four months. A prodigious orgy of study brought him apace with his advanced classmates.

This was intellectual heaven. The professors at Anderson's "Cramming Academy" were a dedicated group and actually wanted to teach and see their pupils learn as fast as their abilities allowed.

As he studied night and day, Jack grew more and more confident that his goal would be achieved. He was so busy with his studies that he failed to notice the resentment of his classmates. They were jealous of his ability and their "blue blood" couldn't tolerate this poorly dressed "socialist rebel." Why should an ex-oyster pirate and tramp be allowed to do in four months what they had taken two years to do?

Dissatisfaction grew rapidly until one day Mr. Anderson called Jack into his office and told him that he would have to leave. "It wasn't because of the students' reactions," Jack wrote, "but he was afraid the University would cancel their accreditation if they allowed a student to compress the two-year curriculum into four months." Anderson added that Jack's money would be refunded in full. It is more probable that he was afraid of losing his wealthy clientele in a row over one threadbare student from the East End of Oakland.

Jack was aghast. His enrollment had been ap-

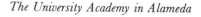
The University Academy in Alameda

proved by Mr. Anderson and his progress had been satisfactory to the school. He had met every standard. It was the same old story. Justice was for the rich and not for the poor. In a sense this was as bad as the treatment he had received in the courthouse at Niagara Falls.

THE JACK LONDON "CRAMMING ACADEMY"

Jack was more determined than ever to be a member of the class of 1900 at the University. Eliza was paid back with his refund and he opened his own "cramming joint" at 1639 Twenty-second Avenue. He shut himself in his room and crammed for nineteen hours a day. Mabel helped him with English, Fred Jacobs helped him with chemistry and physics, which Jack mastered without a laboratory, and Bess Maddern led him over the hurdles of advanced mathematics. He clawed his way through chemical formulas, simultaneous equations, geometric problems, historical studies, and everything else that he found on the sample examinations he used as his study guides. He hoped to gain enough points to enter the university as a special student. So he studied nineteen hours a day for twelve weeks, a killing pace, but one from which he never wavered. His body and mind grew weary, but he stayed with it. Toward the last, he got a bit addled, believing he had discovered the formula for squaring a circle.

On August 10, 1896, Jack rode his bicycle to Berkeley and started the three-day exams. They were much tougher than the samples he had studied. Later he discovered that the school had far more applicants than it could handle, so the examinations were toughened to weed people out. When he turned in his last examination paper, his brain was completely worn out. He never wanted to see a book again.

There was but one prescription for such a condition, and he wrote it himself—the path of adventure. Not waiting to learn the results of the examination, he stowed a roll of blankets and some cold food into a borrowed Whitehall boat and set sail. Out of the Oakland Estuary he drifted on the last of an early morning ebb, and raced along with a spanking breeze.

Benicia showed before him. He sailed along abreast of the clustering fishermen's boats where in the old days he had lived and drunk.

He sailed in to shore, made everything fast, and hurried up among the arks. Charley LeGrant and his wife, Lizzie, gave him an enthusiastic welcome. Billy Murphy and Joe Lloyd joined other survivors of the old guard in another rousing reception. Charley seized the can and started for Jorgensen's saloon across the railroad tracks. That meant beer. Jack wanted whiskey, so he called after Charley to bring it. This was the first drinking spree Jack had been on for months—he decided he had earned a good one. More old friends dropped in, fishermen, Greeks, Russians, and Frenchmen. They took turns treating. They came and went, but Jack stayed and drank with them all.

Jacks friends wanted him to stay over, but he decided to cruise upriver by himself. Charley LeGrant shifted Jack's outfit into a big Columbia River salmon boat. Jack cruised for nearly a week, and returned ready to enter the University. If he passed, and he was sure he had, he would at last be a college man.

THE CLASS OF '00

Entering the University of California in the fall term with the "Naughty-Naughts" was an exciting experience. The class of '00 was energetic and full of pranks. At first the campus foolishness intrigued Jack, but he soon grew tired of its adolescence and turned his attention to his socialist friends.

Jack never felt at home on the Berkeley campus. Most of his friends never graduated from high school. He had entered an adolescent world dominated by the sons and daughters of the leisure class. He was amazed at their general stupidity and lack of goals. Mediocrity of mind and ambition abounded in students and professors.

The novelist and short story writer Jimmy Hopper has left us a picture of Jack during his University days. Greeting Jack that fall at Berkeley, Hopper remembers that:

The dominating quality of Jack London's character was bigness ... he met my advance with open frankness that was like a flood of sunshine. Sunshine—the word leaps of itself to the end of my pen. ... He had a curly mop of hair which seemed spun of its gold; his strong neck, with a loose, low soft shirt, was bronzed with it; and his eyes were like a sunlit sea. His clothes were floppy and careless; the forecastle had left a suspicion of a roll in his broad shoulders; he was a strange combination of Scandinavian sailor and Greek god, made all together boyish and lovable by the lack of two front teeth, lost cheerfully somewhere in a fight.

He was full of gigantic plans—just as, indeed I was to find him always whenever I came upon him later in life. ... He was going to take all the courses in English, all of them, nothing less. Also, of course, he meant to take most of the courses in the natural sciences, many in history, and bite a respectable chunk out of the philosophies.

There is no record that Jack ever wrote for student publications as he had in high school. Perhaps he was too busy with his small group of friends, his increased activity with the Oakland Socialists after joining the American section of the Socialist Labor Party in April, and his various jobs.

He became increasingly disillusioned with the University. The classes were routine and monotonous. The professors were academic drudges. Jack had hoped to find the University seething with thought, alive to ideas and the bright stinging things of the spirit. Instead he found no vitality, no awareness of life, and the entire campus was oblivious of the inequities in the social structure.

It began to dawn on Jack that he could make faster progress studying on his own, as he had done before. There were many fine libraries near him. He could use them and learn everything a college could teach and learn it faster and more directly. Indeed, he had already demonstrated his ability to chase an idea through the stacks at the University library when he went there to do his homework. Jimmy Hopper remembered seeing him there and remarked that "Jack's brain was like a dry sponge—impossible of saturation in its many folds. He was never satisfied by the instruction he received and rushed to the library to read and study more about the idea. Nobody ever read as much collateral reading before or since."

Despite his discontent, Jack returned for the second term. He knew he could go faster on his own, but he also realized that the world only recognized the diploma, and cared little about how it was obtained. Maybe some financial miracle would allow him to stay until he had earned his degree. He would take the regular courses to satisfy his professors, but would take on all the extra work he could cram in. The miracle never happened and financial circumstances forced him to leave the University with an honorary dismissal on February 4, 1897. When he left, it was with the hope that he could return as soon as he could get his finances straight, but Jack was never able to return to Berkeley.

WRITING FLURRY

Leaving the University, Jack buried his frustrations in a frenzy of socialist activity and writing. He continued his reading of Marx and other socialist thinkers. He attended section meetings and study groups. And he continued gathering crowds in the park near Tenth and Broadway, a feat that surprised Jack as much as it did his comrades, who were mild Fabians.

Gathering these crowds was in violation of Oakland City Ordinance No. 1676, which declared that it was unlawful for any person to conduct or take part in any public meeting held on any public street situated within the fire limits of the City of Oakland unless permission to hold such a public meeting had been first obtained in writing from the Mayor of the city.

Several socialist lecturers had been forced to leave the park because of this ordinance, which they believed was a direct violation of the right of free speech and public assembly guaranteed by the Constitution of the United States. As Lincoln's birthday approached, the Oakland chapter of the Socialist Labor Party decided to challenge the despised ordinance. When a volunteer was requested, Jack responded. Since Abraham Lincoln was one of his two heroes (Jesus Christ was the other), this was an ideal time for him to voice the section's protest. And Jack was an excellent choice. He was young, he was already known as the "boy socialist," and his letters on socialism had been published in the *Oakland Times* and *The Item*.

Jack mounted the soapbox on February 10, 1897, and began haranguing the crowd in grand style. The police promptly arrested him and took him to jail. He demanded a jury trial, which was held on February 18 in the City of Oakland Police Court, Judge Samuels presiding (the same judge who in 1910 became involved with Jack in the *Muldowney* case). Speaking in his own defense, Jack managed to convince all but one of the jury to vote for acquittal. On February 26 the city dropped the case.

All the press coverage of the arrest and trial was so much free publicity for the Oakland Socialists. In order to attract as much attention as possible, the section nominated Jack London as their candidate for the Oakland School Board in an upcoming election.

In addition to being a student of working-class philosophy, Jack also wanted to be a worker. But he couldn't find work, and this at a time when his family desperately needed money. His father's income was limited to commissions obtained from peddling pictures door to door in Alameda County. Flora added to this meager sum with the money from her piano students. With the family in desperate straits, Jack decided to launch his writing career, hoping to make more with his pen than he did with the shovel at the street railway company.

Fiction writing was not Jack's preference. Given his choice, he would have preferred music, poetry, or the writing of philosophical, economic, and political essays. Eliminating music as impossible, he settled down in his bedroom and tackled his second, third, and fourth choices simultaneously. "Heavens, how I wrote!" he later confessed. "Never was there a creative fervor such as mine from which the patient escaped fatal results. The way I worked was enough to soften my brain and send me to a mad-house."

He wrote everything—ponderous essays, both scientific and sociological, short stories, humorous verse, verse of all sorts from triolets and sonnets to blank verse tragedy and elephantine epics in Spenserian stanzas. On occasion he composed steadily, day after day, for fifteen hours a day. At times he forgot to eat, or refused to tear himself away from his passionate outpouring.

Only Jack could tell about that infernal typing machine: "And then there was the matter of typewriting. My brother-in-law owned a machine which he used in the daytime. In the night I was free to use it. That machine was a wonder. I could weep now as I recollect my wrestlings with it. It must have been a first model in the year one of the typewriter era. Its alphabet was all capitals. It was informed with an evil spirit. It obeyed no law of physics, and overthrew the hoary axiom that like things performed to like things produce like results. I'll swear that machine never did the same thing in the same way twice. Again and again it demonstrated that like actions produce unlike results.

"How my back used to ache with it. Prior to that experience, my back had been good for every violent strain put upon it in a none too gentle career. But that typewriter proved to me that I had a pipestem for a back. Also it made me doubt my shoulders. They ached as with rheumatism after every bout. The keys of that machine had to be hit so hard that to one outside the house it sounded like distant thunder or someone breaking up the furniture. I had to hit the keys so hard that I strained my first fingers to the elbows, while the ends of my fingers were blisters burst and blistered again. Had it been my machine I'd have operated it with a carpenter's hammer."

He composed thousands of words each day and typed them laboriously for the waiting editors. All his waking hours, except those with the infernal typewriter, were spent in a creative frenzy. But the waiting editors elected to keep on waiting. His manuscripts made amazing roundtrip records between the Pacific and the Atlantic. He never knew whether it was the weirdness of the typewriting or his writing that kept them from buying even one little offering. But then the stuff he wrote was also weird. Failing to make any money writing, he sold his hard-bought schoolbooks for ridiculous sums to secondhand bookmen. He borrowed small sums of money whenever he could, and suffered his old father to feed him with the meager returns of his failing strength.

This writing flurry was short lived, lasting only a few weeks, when he had to surrender and go to work. He was not defeated. His career was only retarded. He knew he needed further preparation. His waking hours, and most of the hours he should have used for sleep, were spent studying.

BELMONT ACADEMY LAUNDRY

Eliza's stepson, Herbert Shepard, needed a helper at the Belmont Academy Laundry and she suggested Jack. Jack went down to the Peninsula and went to work. All the way down from Oakland he was thinking about what an opportunity this was. It was still only thirty dollars a month, but this time he got room and board. He could send cash to his family, he would have time to read, and he could do a ton of writing with someone else paying the bills.

It didn't work out as Jack imagined. Instead, he was more viciously exploited than ever before. The owner had bought modern machinery and quickly determined that two strong men could do the work instead of four. Once more he was doing the work of two for the pay of one.

Herbert and Jack sorted, washed, and ironed the clothing of the professors and their wives. They worked like tigers, especially as summer came on and the academy boys started wearing duck trousers. It consumed a dreadful amount of time to iron one pair of duck trousers. And there were so many pairs of them. They sweated their way through long sizzling weeks at a task that was never completed; and many a night, while the students snored in bed, Jack and Herbert toiled on under the electric lights at the steam mangle or ironing board.

Jack found himself a work beast again, toiling longer hours than horses toil, thinking scarcely more thoughts than horses think. The books remained closed. He brought a trunkful to the laundry but found himself unable to read them. He fell asleep the moment he tried to read, and if he did manage to keep his eyes open for several pages, he couldn't remember the contents of those pages. He gave up attempts to study jurisprudence, political economy, and biology, and tried what he thought would be lighter stuff, such as history. Still he fell asleep. He tried literature, and fell asleep. And finally, when he fell asleep over lively novels, he gave up. He never succeeded in reading one book in all the time he spent in the laundry.

The only fun Jack and Herbert got out of the whole brutal experience was when they overstarched their clients' dainty linen, secure in the knowledge that the hidebound modesties of these Victorian ladies would seal their lips from complaint. "Lord, Lord," Jack exploded later with a wicked giggle, "I thought about the boards we made of those garments!" Jack was still giggling in the Klondike months later, as was Herbert, who was stationed in the Philippines during the Spanish-American War.

In June the Academy closed for the summer and the agony was over. Jack packed his things and went back to Oakland.

KLONDIKE ADVENTURES

On July 14, 1897, the S.S. *Excelsior* entered the Golden Gate and tied up in San Francisco. A few unkempt men fresh from the Klondike went ashore with their golden riches. In only a few hours the United States and the rest of the world knew about the Klondike gold discoveries. In a few days the Klondike Gold Rush became a madness. Those who could chucked their jobs and headed North. Those who were unable to go grubstaked somebody who could. It was a case of national lunacy. With-

Leaving San Francisco for the Klondike

out thought or reason, men by the thousands got caught up in the mania—"Klondicitis," as some newspapers called it.

Jack came down with the gold fever. Now that the Academy was closed, he had no job and he wanted to join the gold rush. His old problem asserted itself: lack of money. He tried everything he could think of to raise cash. He tried, without success, to get a local newpaper to send him to the Klondike as their reporter. He rushed up to get advice from the world-famous California poet, Joaquin Miller, but discovered the "Sweet Singer of the Sierras" was already singing his way North.

Unexpectedly Jack's brother-in-law, Captain Shepard, caught Klondicitis. Shepard offered to grubstake Jack if he would take him along and do all the heavy work that Shepard's weak heart couldn't stand. Jack was skeptical. The old man was not well and the trip would be too arduous. Jack tried to point this out to his brother-in-law. "Each man," he said, "has to take a year's supplies in with him. There'll be such a jam that the Indian packers won't be able to handle it. We will have to pack our outfits across ourselves." Captain Shepard knew Jack was right, but the Klondike was several thousand miles away and his old cavalry blood was beginning to surge. Jack bowed to the inevitable. Eliza put a hefty mortgage on their home and the next few days were spent obtaining outfits.

Charmian London describes this spending spree in the *Book of Jack London:*

Such a buying jamboree Jack had never enjoyed. Eliza's hundreds flowed like water: fur-lined coats, fur caps, heavy high boots, thick mittens; and red-flannel shirts and underdrawers of the warmest quality—so warm that Jack had to shed his outer garments packing over Chilcoot Pass. . . . The average outfit of the Klondike also must include a year's supply of grub, mining implements, tents, blankets, Klondike stoves, everything requisite to maintain life, build boats and cabins. Jack's dunnage alone weighed nearly 2000 pounds.

With his usual thoroughness, Jack had borrowed a copy of Miner Bruce's *Alaska.* It was his AAA guide to the Klondike. It told him what to take with him, how to get there, and what to do when he arrived. It was the single most important item in his outfit and was consulted over and over again in the following weeks.

The day following the buying spree, July 25, 1897, the S.S. *Umatilla* departed two hours late, carrying Jack and Captain Shepard through the Golden Gate headed for the Golden North.

Though the crowds at the wharves were cheerful, Jack's departure from home was sad; he knew he was bidding a final farewell to his bedridden father, who died on October 15, 1897, shortly after Jack arrived at Split-Up Island.

The *Umatilla,* crack steamship of the Pacific Steamship Company, was licensed to carry 290 passengers, but managed to carry 471 as far as Port Townsend. The fare was twenty-five dollars from San Francisco to Juneau. At Port Townsend Jack and the rest of the eager argonauts transferred to the *City of Topeka* for the rest of the trip, arriving in Juneau on August 2.

On the trip north the miners got acquainted and formed partnerships. Jack and Shepard threw in their lot with Ira Merritt Sloper, a forty-year-old man fresh from adventures in South America, "Big Jim" Goodman, and Fred C. Thompson, who kept a diary of the trip.

Jack and his party spent two rainy days in Juneau. At eleven o'clock on the morning of August 5 they left Juneau in seventy-foot canoes. The rented canoes were paddled by their Indian owners up the Lynn Canal to Dyea. On August 8 Jack wrote a letter to Mabel from Dyea:

We lay several days in Juneau, then hired canoes and paddled 100 miles to our present quarters. The Indians with us brought along their squaws, papooses & dogs. Had a pleasant time. The 100 miles lay between mountains which formed a Yosemite Valley the whole length, & in many places the heights were stupendous. Glaciers & waterfalls on every side. Yesterday a snow slide occurred & the rumble & roar extended for fully a minute.

I expect to carry 1000 lbs. 100 lbs. to the load on good trail & on the worst, 75 lbs. That is, for every mile to the Lakes, I will have to travel from 20 to 30 miles. I have 1000 lbs. in my outfit. I have to divide it into from 10 to 15 loads according to the trail. I take a load a mile & come back empty. That makes two miles. 10 loads means 19 miles, for I do not have to come back

The newspapers and magazines were loaded with "Klondike Fever" items.

after the 11th load for there is none. If I have 15 loads it means 29 miles. Am certain we will reach the lake in 30 days. Including Indians there are about 2000 people here & half as many at Skagway Bay, 5 miles from here.

Dyea was located at the mouth of the Dyea River. Its beach boasted thirty-foot tides and no wharves. Most ships anchored out several hundred feet, and gold seekers scrambled madly to rent space on a boat to get their goods ashore. Everybody was in somebody's way and they were all shouting. Hundreds of prospectors were fighting to get their outfits ashore before the tide went out. Donkey-engines on board the ships dumped outfits into boats of every description. Outfits were hopelessly entangled. So were tempers. Now and then a gun settled the arguments.

If the scene on the water was confusion, that on shore was confusion compounded. The tents and outfits of over 1500 gold seekers were everywhere. There was no semblance of order.

Jack and his partners were anxious to get on the trail. It was six miles up Dyea River, eight miles up the canyon, and three-quarters of a mile to the top of the Chilcoot Pass. From there it would be much easier.

Prices for packing had risen from eight cents to forty cents a pound. This rate was too expensive for Jack and his partners. They bought an old boat and moved their goods to the head of navigation on the Dyea River.

The view here was superb. Snow peaks in all

A packer's home at the foot of the canyon along Dyea Trail

their splendor rose majestically on either side. Spruce, birch, and elder trees grew abundantly alongside the streams. Beautiful grayling and trout sported in the river. But the men had eyes only for the trail. The Indians went back and forth in stoic silence. It was their way. But sheer, total exhaustion made the newcomers equally stoic.

Men struggled under the weight of their outfits, picked themselves up when they fell, and trudged on. Lured on by the lust for gold, the argonauts also struggled against the advance of winter and inevitable freezeup, which heralded the death of their hopes.

The rugged trail was too much for Captain Shepard, who lasted only two days before sensibly heading for home. A Mr. Tarwater, whom Jack later immortalized in "Like Argus of the Ancient Times," replaced him.

By August 21 Jack and his partners had managed to cross the rubble-covered flats to Sheep Camp. Glacial rocks of every size and description made the footing difficult. They had crossed and recrossed the Dyea River six or seven times in the trip from Dyea. Fording the icy currents had been a miserable ordeal.

Sheep Camp was the jumping-off place—the point of no return. Hikers either rested here before

going on or gave up in despair and went back down the trail. Some simply could take neither the trail nor the thought of failure, and either went mad or pointed a gun at a vulnerable spot and pulled the trigger. It was a busy place filled with tents, gamblers, canvas restaurants, and misery. Many were busy buying, trading, or selling outfits. A few just sat and stared off into the distance.

For three days it rained as they pushed on to the Scales, a stopping place on the trail where the Indian packers weighed their loads. It was like wading through a cold muddy sea. By August 25, this portion of the trail had been conquered, and they made camp at Stone House, another stop on the trail where there was a huge boulder that looked like a house.

Now above the timberline, they fought boulders bigger than they were. The trail was steep and rugged. There was no wood for fires and no poles for tents. Huddled under overhanging glaciers, they caught what sleep they could.

Jack could never forget the horses. He loved animals in a primitive way. On this tragic trail they suffered terribly. They were forced to carry excessive loads without proper food and fell by the trail, starved and exhausted, and were piled in heaps in all directions. They drowned in icy streams and

Packers on trail near sheep camp

sometimes in a fit of Klondike insanity their owners beat them to death with hammers. Such was the trail.

As Jack and his friends came closer to the mountain, the trail became steeper and steeper. Finally on August 27 they dumped their final load at the Scales and took a look up at the famous Chilcoot Pass. It was all they expected it to be. They had climbed to the Scales, but the rest of the trip to the summit looked like it was straight up. By the time they reached the top they were sure of it.

There is no way to adequately describe the Chilcoot Pass. Any miner who crossed it would agree that it was literal torture. It took hours to bring each load to the top. The climb up was a nightmare and the scramble back down empty-handed was nearly as bad. Jack tried every way possible to make the packing easier. He adjusted the straps

and figured ways to pad his shoulders until he was able to outpack most of the white men and many of the Indians. Each load weighed from seventy-five to one hundred fifty pounds and sat like a demon on his broad shoulders.

From the summit to Happy Camp to Long Lake, from Long Lake to Deep Lake, and from Deep Lake up over the enormous hogback and down to Linderman, the man-killing race against winter kept on. Men broke their hearts and backs and wept beside the trail. But winter never faltered. The fall gales blew colder and colder, and amid bitter soaking rains and ever increasing snow flurries Jack and his friends jubilantly stacked the first of their supplies on the beach of Lake Linderman on September 8, exactly as Jack had predicted to Mabel.

DOWN THE WATERWAYS

There was no time for rest. Early the next morning Jack and Sloper went across the lake where, about five miles upriver, above a roaring torrent, they located a patch of spruce and set up their

boat-building site. Tarwater and Goodman packed the rest of the outfit in and set up camp at Linderman.

By this time Jack's group had become friendly

with another party. They decided to work together on their boats. Jack's group would build the *Yukon Belle,* while Charles Rand, Dave Sullivan, and William Odette built the *Belle of the Yukon.* Together they built a saw-pit and, by hand, with an inadequate whipsaw, sawed the spruce trunks into lumber. Night and day they worked, and as the green planks came down, Sloper's crew built the boats.

The days grew shorter. The wind shifted into the north and blew in an unending gale. In the morning the weary men crawled from their blankets and thawed out their frozen shoes by the fire Tarwater always had burning.

The boats were finally completed, and rowed across the south end of Lake Linderman in the thick of a fall blizzard. Next morning they would load and start their perilous traverse of five hundred miles of lakes, rapids, box canyons, and rivers.

They fought their way north. There was no doubt that the freezeup was imminent. A delay now could be very dangerous. Jack decided to shoot the rapid stream connecting Linderman to Lake Bennett in their fully loaded boat. It was customary to haul the empty boat down by line and to portage the cargoes across. Even then, many empty boats had been wrecked. Time simply precluded such precautions.

A shift of the gale to the south gave them a fair wind down Lake Bennett, and Jack's homemade sail went to work. They entered Caribou Crossing, sailing down the connecting link to Lakes Tagish and Marsh. In the stormy twilight they crossed the dangerous Windy Arm while they witnessed two other boatloads of gold-rushers capsize and drown. Fred Thompson insisted they beach for the night, but Jack kept on, steering down Tagish by the sound of the surf on the shoals and by sighting the occasional shore fires of more timid travelers.

The 50 Mile River flows out of Marsh Lake with a varying width of from an eighth to a quarter of a mile. The current is deep and swift. Suddenly it narrows to one hundred yards, rounds a bend where a landing may be made in an eddy, and dashes between towering rock walls about eighty feet apart. This is the dreaded Box Canyon. Here the enormous volume of water contracts to a narrow passageway and attains terrific speed. The waves rise like huge walls. By some peculiar action or pressure against the rocky sides, the center of the rapids forms a backbone varying from six to eight feet in height. This is the "Ridge."

Tying up the *Yukon Belle* in the eddy above the Box, Jack and his three comrades walked ahead to investigate. Hundreds were portaging their outfits on their backs. This meant two days of severe toil, while if they ran through, it would take only two minutes. They unanimously agreed to take the chance and run through.

Lashing the steering oar so it couldn't possibly be lost, Jack placed his crew, for he had been elected captain. He put Merrit Sloper in the bow with a paddle. Thompson and Goodman were stationed side by side at the oars. Jack told Tarwater to walk around. It would be a tough shot; their twenty-seven-foot boat was dangerously overloaded and had little buoyancy left. With little freeboard the boat was deep in the water and sluggish.

"Be sure to keep on the Ridge," cried the men on the bank as they cast off. The water, though swift, had a slick, oily appearance until they ran madly into the very jaws of the Box, where it instantly took on every attribute of chaos. Fearing the rowers might catch a crab or make some other disastrous mistake, Jack called the oars in.

They met it on the fly. Jack caught a glimpse of the spectators along the brink of the cliffs above, and another glimpse of the rock walls dashing by like twin express trains. Then his whole energy was concentrated in keeping to the Ridge, which the boat, dead with weight, had trouble mounting, being forced to jab her nose through at every lunge. For all the danger, Jack caught himself smiling at the ridiculous capers cut by Sloper perched in the bow and working like mad. Just as he would let his paddle drive for a tremendous stroke, the stern would fall in a trough, jerking the bow clear up, and he would miss the water completely. At the next stroke, perhaps, the bow would dive clean under, almost sweeping him away. But never did he lose his presence of mind. Once he turned and cried some warning at the top of his lungs, but it was drowned in the pandemonium of sound. The next instant they fell off the Ridge. The water came aboard in all directions, and the boat, caught in a transverse current, threatened to twist broadside. That would mean destruction. Jack threw himself against the steering oar until he could hear it cracking. At the same time, Sloper up in the bow broke his paddle in two.

Miles Canyon

And all the time they were flying through the water less than two yards from the wall. Several times it seemed all would be up with them; but finally, mounting the Ridge almost sidewise, they took a header through a tremendous comber and shot into the whirlpool in the center of the canyon.

Jack ordered the oars out for better steerage-way, and keeping a close eye on the split currents, he caught one quick breath before they flew into the second half of the canyon. Though they crossed the Ridge from left to right and back again, it was merely a repetition of the first half. A few moments later the *Yukon Belle* reached quiet water. They had run the mile of canyon in exactly two minutes.

Sloper and Jack walked back by way of the portage and ran a boat through for the Retts—a family with whom they had become friends at Lake Linderman. This was more ticklish, for the little craft was but twenty-two feet over all and proportionately more heavily loaded than the *Yukon Belle.* After this second successful passage they bailed out their own boat and went on for two miles before reaching the famed White Horse Rapids.

The White Horse Rapids were actually more dangerous than the Box Canyon—only few had run it in previous years. It was customary to portage everything around; even the boats were skidded along on spruce trunks. But Jack and his party were in a hurry and enthusiastic over their previous good luck.

The dangerous point in these rapids was at the tail, called the "Mane of the Horse," because of a succession of foamy, mountainous waves. Extending three-quarters of the way across, a rocky reef threw the whole river against the right bank, and it was thrown back to the left, forming another whirlpool, more risky by far than that of the Box.

When it struck the "Mane," the *Yukon Belle* forgot her heavy load, taking a series of leaps almost clear of the water, alternating with as many burials in the troughs. Jack lost control! A crosscurrent caught the stern, and the boat began to swing broadside into the whirlpool. Sloper snapped a second paddle and received another ducking. From every quarter the water came aboard, threatening to swamp the boat, which headed directly for the jagged left bank. And though Jack was up against

the steering sweep till it cracked, he couldn't turn her nose downstream. Onlookers from the shore tried to take snapshots, but their efforts were only rewarded with pictures of angry waters and flying foam, for the boat was already out of range.

The boat was still running wild and alarmingly close to the bank. In a flash Jack realized he was trying to buck the whirlpool. Immediately he bore down on the opposite side of the steering oar. The boat answered, at the same time following the movement of the whirlpool and heading upstream. Sloper, certain of destruction, leaped to the top of a rock. Then on seeing they had missed by a couple of inches, he scrambled back aboard.

Though still caught in the rushing waters of the whirlpool, they breathed easier. Abruptly completing the circle, they were thrown into the "Mane," which they ran a second time, landing in quiet water below the rapids. They walked back and repeated the performance with the Retts' boat.

By the time they reached Lake LeBarge the land was covered with snow. At the entrance of Lake LeBarge they found a hundred stormbound boats. Out of the north, across the wide expanse of the great lake, blew a steady wintry gale. Three mornings they put out and fought it. The cresting seas turned to ice as they splashed aboard and forced them back to shelter. The delay irritated them since it was obvious that it was but a matter of days before LeBarge would freeze up. Beyond, the rapid rivers would continue to run for days; but unless they got past the lake, and immediately, they would be iced in for the long Yukon winter. On September 28 Jack announced, "Today we go through or spend the winter here with the rest. We will turn back for nothing."

By nightfall they were halfway across the lake and by running all night they finally reached the 30 Mile River. As day broke clear and cold they entered the river and left behind them a sea of ice. The rest of the trip was relatively uneventful. Night and day, not daring to stop for fear of the freezeup, they ran on until they tied up at Split-Up Island at 3:00 P.M. October 9. The *Belle of the Yukon,* their sister craft, stopped long enough to pick up Mr. Tarwater and kept on going to Dawson.

Split-Up Island, also called Upper Island, was situated between the Stewart River and Henderson Creek about eighty miles from Dawson City. Jack and his friends moved into an old cabin abandoned by the Alaska Commercial Company. Discouraged prospectors heading for Dyea and home had spread the word along the way that Dawson City was due for a terrific famine because of its mushrooming population and lack of supplies. These men also warned that there were no claims left to stake. Sifting through the many reports, Jack decided his only hope of finding gold was on Henderson Creek, which was about the only unstaked area left in the Yukon Territory.

On October 10 London's party piled all their belongings in the cabin. Early the next morning Jim Goodman made a quick trip to Henderson Creek. He returned with glowing reports of the area and displayed small grains of gold he had found. Jack smiled and decided Miner Bruce was right.

Bright and early on the morning of the 12th, according to Fred Thompson's diary, Jack and Jim, accompanied by two other gold seekers (Thompson called them Charles and Elma—they were probably Charlie Borg and Emil Jensen) set out for Henderson Creek, where they spent three days prospecting.

Thompson recorded on the 15th: "Boys got back from Henderson, staked 8 claims." The next day Jack, Thompson, Charles, and Elma (or Emil) boarded the *Yukon Belle* and drifted down to Dawson to record claims. Taking grub to last about three weeks, tent, and blankets, they went to get news, mail, and to find out what was going on. They stopped for the night at the old station at Sixtymile where they filled their boat with wood to use in Dawson. On October 18 they camped three miles from Dawson City. Jack and the rest crossed the Klondike River by ferry to Dawson. They met Marshall and Louis Bond in one of the saloons and were invited to pitch their tent on a vacant spot next to their cabin.

Evidently Jack wasn't worried that anybody would jump his claim, since he didn't bother to record it until November 5. At that time he recorded Claim No. 54, "more particularly described as placer mining Claim No. 54 on the Left Fork ascending Henderson Creek in the aforesaid Mining Division." He solemnly swore before the Gold Commissioner in Dawson that he had discovered therein a deposit of gold. Thompson later claimed that Jack found only mica. This story is discredited by the presence of Jim Goodman, who was an experienced miner.

Little is known of Jack's stay in Dawson City. What is known comes from Marshall and Louis Bond, Yale-educated sons of a prominent Santa Clara, California judge. It was their dog Jack who was immortalized as Buck in London's great American classic, *The Call of the Wild,* six years later. Marshall Bond writes:

One of these men was of medium height, with very square broad shoulders. His face was masked by a thick stubby beard. A cap pulled down low on his forehead was the one touch necessary to the complete concealment of head and features, so that that part of the anatomy one looks to for an index of character was covered with beard and cap. He looked as tough and as uninviting as we doubtless looked to him.

On a box, out of the circle of light from the lamp, he sat in silence one night, a confused blur of cap, mackinaw, and moccasins. Conversation turned to the subject of socialism. Some of those present confused it with anarchism. One of our number, who at least knew more of the subject than the rest of us, clarified it somewhat with his greater knowledge, but this was soon exhausted. Then from out of the shadow of the lamp, from the blur of beard and cap, came a quick-speaking, sympathetic voice. He took up the subject from its earliest history, carried it on through a rapid survey of its most important points and held us thrilled by the hypnotic effect which a profound knowledge of a subject expounded by an exalted believer always exerts. Intellectually he was incomparably the most alert man in the room, and we felt it. Some of us had minds as dull as putty, and some of us had been educated and drilled into a goose step of conventionalism. Here was a man whose life and thoughts were his own. He was refreshing. This was my first introduction to Jack London.

On December 3, 1897, Jack left Dawson City on the hazardous trek back to Split-Up Island. Charmian says Thompson was with him, but her source for this information has evidently been lost. The river froze later than usual, so the ice was thin in spots, making river travel difficult and dangerous. Hiking was equally difficult, since there was no trail packed down yet. Later in the winter the dog toboggans would leave a surface much like a concrete sidewalk, but this snow was not like the snow in the United States. It was hard, fine, and dry like frost.

The winter on Split-Up Island was a busy one. The cabin on Henderson Creek was about eighteen miles from the main camp at Split-Up. The long, bitter-cold nights seemed endless. Jack described living in a Yukon cabin as "forty days in a refrigerator." Most of the time was spent in bunks, since the floors were too cold to stand on. Frozen food was stored on lower shelves in the cabin without fear that they would thaw.

A letter to Charmian from a member of the Split-Up group written after Jack's death provides another glimpse of Jack in the Klondike. W. B. Hargraves said in the letter:

It was in October of 1897 that I first met him.... No other man has left so indelible an impression upon my memory as Jack London. He was but a boy then, in years.... But he possessed the mental equipment of a mature man and I have never thought of him as a boy except in the heart of him ... the clean, joyous, tender unembittered heart of youth. His personality would challenge attention anywhere. Not only in his beauty—for he was a handsome lad—but there was about him that indefinable something that distinguishes genius from mediocrity, he displayed none of the insolent egotism of youth; he was an idealist who went after the attainable, a dreamer who was a man among strong men; a man who faced life with superb assurance and who could face death serenely imperturbable. These were my first impressions which months of companionship only confirmed.

... I have met men who were worthwhile; but Jack was the one man whom I have come in personal contact who possessed the qualities of heart and mind that made him one of the world's overshadowing geniuses.

He was intrinsically kind and irrationally generous ... with an innate refinement, a gentleness that had survived the roughest of associations. Sometimes he would become silent and reflective, but he was never morose or sullen. His silence was an attentive silence.... He was always

good-natured; he was more—he was charmingly cheerful.

These are the words of a man who was cooped up with Jack for the long winter of 1897–1898, and any old Klondiker will verify that by spring one knew a man better than he knew himself.

We know that on January 27, 1898, Jack was staying in the Henderson Creek cabin, because he wrote his name on a log high on the back wall of C. M. Taylor's cabin situated on Claim No. 151 some distance above his own claim. We also know that by this time he had resumed thinking of his writing career because after his name he added "Miner/Author." In 1969 an expedition went to the Klondike to make final authentication of this cabin. When its authenticity was established, both Canadian and United States agencies cooperated in a project to dismantle and move the cabin so that for the first time in history two nations might have identical monuments with half of the original cabin in each. Each part of the cabin was reassembled using logs from the original and from trees felled at the site. The building with the lower half of the original cabin was set up in Dawson City, Yukon Territory; and the one with the original upper half was placed at Jack London Square in Oakland, California. The latter cabin is located a few feet from Heinold's First and Last Chance Saloon.

In May Jack developed scurvy from lack of fresh vegetables and fruit. This was a common disease of those living on the three "Bs" menu—Bread, Beans, and Bacon. He could no longer travel the trail to his claim or hunt for tobacco or a stray book. His gums began to swell and bleed and his teeth rattled, the dread symptoms of the "Klondike plague." When he pushed dents into his skin, they remained. All hope of working his claim vanished. Since there was no cure for scurvy in the camp he would have to go home or occupy a cold grave in the Yukon. Dr. B. F. Harvey, sharing the cabin, urged a hasty withdrawal.

Now it was a deadly race between the worsening of his scurvy and the opening of the Yukon River so he could leave. The ice flow began at five in the morning early in May, and already the days were so long that Jack and Doc. Harvey were able to watch the spectacle with awe. The ice tore by, great cakes of it caroming against the banks, uprooting trees, and gouging out earth by the hundreds of tons. All about them the land shook from the shock of those tremendous collisions. At the end of an hour the run stopped. Somewhere below it was blocked by a jam. Then the river began to rise, lifting the ice until it was higher than the bank. From upstream ever more water bore down, and more tons of ice added their weight to the congestion. The pressures and stresses became terrific. When the jam broke, the noise of grinding and smashing grew louder. After nearly an hour the river began to recede. But the huge walls of ice that extended out of the water to the tops of the bank remained.

After the ice had passed, Jack saw open water for the first time in over six months. He knew that a lot of ice still remained in the upper areas of the Stewart River, and that it could break loose any time. But his need for medical help was too desperate for him to linger.

Having already torn their cabin down and constructed a raft with the logs, Jack and Dr. Harvey, with the help of many friends, managed to ease their clumsy raft into the open waters and float down the Yukon to Dawson City. On arrival they sold the logs from the raft for six hundred dollars. Jack needed the money for food and medicine. He moved in with Emil Jensen, but most of his last days in Dawson were spent at Father Judge's hospital.

Father Judge advised Jack to leave as soon as possible. By this time his scurvy was so advanced that Jack required little urging. He planned to return, however, if his partners reported his claim was worth working.

Emil Jensen, who had been with London most of the winter at Split-Up Island, gives us another glimpse of him in his unpublished manuscript, *Jack London at Stewart River:*

Monotony found no place in Jack London's make-up. The little as well as the big things in our daily life held for him, always, a stimulus that made his every waking hour worth living. To him, there was in all things something new, something alluring, something worthwhile, be it a game of whist, an argument, or the sun at noonday glowing cold and brilliant above the hills to the south. He was ever on tiptoe with expectancy, whether silent with wondering awe, as on a night when we saw the snows aflame beneath a weird, bewildering sky or in the throes of a frenzied excitement while we watched a mighty river at flood-tide.

I never tired of his companionship. It was refreshing, stimulating, helpful, and always he was consistent. A fair weather friend? No; nor one who stopped to count the cost, or dream of profits to come. He stood ever ready, were it a foraging trip among the camps for reading matter, to give a helping hand on a woodsled or to undertake a two day's hike for a plug of tobacco when he saw us restless and grumpy for the want of a smoke. Whether the service was big or little, asked or unasked, it was all one to him, and he gave not only himself, but his private belongings, even to his store of whiskey—the only quart within a radius of seventy-five miles—when one of our number (my partner) lay at death's door and only an operation could save him.

Thanks to the benumbing effect of that whiskey, my partner survived the butchering, for butchering it was, as cruel as it was necessary, and our skillful old "Thousand and One Nights" sickened as he completed his surgical job.

Previous to the operation, a friend had started out for the camps below us on a hunt for anaesthetics, or for anything that would dull or deaden pain. He came from the search as several of us were discussing my partner's case in Jack's cabin. "No luck," he reported, but went on to tell of a doctor's outfit that he had run across in a cabin near the mouth of the Henderson. "The man in charge of the cabin," he said, "refuses to rummage among things that do not belong to him."

Here Fred Thompson, who, as I have heretofore mentioned, was a gentleman although inclined sometimes to be pompous and offish, rose from where he was sitting and took charge as becomes the head of a house. "A very unreasonable man," said he, in his slow and deliberate way, and turning to Jack he continued: "This is what we must do. We must organize a small but well-armed party and interview this stubborn being once more. I have not the slightest doubt but that we can induce him to listen to reason."

So the party was formed, and the stubborn, overscrupulous man when accosted listened to reason and to what was good for him; but the search was in vain, as the doctor's outfit contained neither chloroform nor ether. The man mentioned that whiskey might help if the stuff could be found. In a second Jack was on his feet. In another, a jug of whiskey was on the table. "Take it and welcome," he said. "It was with

The actual cabin in which Jack lived while working his Henderson Creek claim.

The above signature was found on a log above the upper bunk on the back wall of the Henderson Creek cabin. "Jack London. Miner, author, Jan. 27, 1898."

some such purpose in mind that I brought it in." This was the first and last of Jack's whiskey, and he himself never had as much as a taste.

Good whiskey it was, Doc. Harvey said so, and he knew. One quarter of the bottle, or jug, went down his throat to steady his nerves, and the remainder of the whiskey saved the life of his patient.

For five months Jack London had had that jug of whiskey beneath his bunk, and to this day my temper gets the better of me when I see men shake their heads knowingly, and hear them call

him a drinking man. I know that here in our own sunny California, Jack that day gained five life-long champions—the wife and four children of my crippled partner, who, as soon as he could, informed them of his friend London's generosity and kindness.

For many weeks after he and his partners had separated, Jack camped with me and my mate in our tent in Dawson. If there had been trouble between them I did not know it, for he did not complain, and I did not ask. "Our food gave out," he said simply.

At the cabin site in 1969. From left to right: Eddie Albert, Russ Kingman, Sgt. Ralph Godfrey of the Oakland Police Department, and Jack Williamson, cinemaphotographer. Fred Reicker, Public Relations Director of the Port of Oakland, took the picture.

Memory still clings to the day he set out for the "outside." A small skiff and fifteen hundred miles of river before him, he sick with the scurvy, and sick with the failure consciousness that had gripped so many, and yet, as I bade him farewell, the well-known boyish, engaging smile took the sting out of our parting, though it haunts me still. "I shall be glad, Emil," he said, as his hand tightened around mine, "when some day next summer I shall open my door and find you waiting on the porch." And he was, for he never forgot.

At 4 P.M. on June 8, 1898, Jack London, John Thorson, and Charles M. Taylor left en route to St. Michael. The trip was uneventful and restful. Jack put his recollections on paper—the first notes he had made in the Klondike. It was probably the first time that he realized he could pan more gold from his pen than from Claim No. 54.

Saturday, June 18, they arrived in Anvik at 10 P.M. They were invited by the Episcopal missionary to stay over until Sunday. With great elation Jack recorded in his notes: "Given fresh potatoes & can of tomatoes for my scurvy, which has now almost crippled me from my waist down. Right leg drawing up, can no longer straighten it, even in walking must put my whole weight on toes. These few raw potatoes and tomatoes are worth more to me at the present stage of the game than an El Dorado claim. 'What mote it though a man gain illimitable wealth and lose his own life.' "

On June 28 they arrived in St. Michael. On July 2 or 3 they booked on the schooner *Bartlett* for Port Townsend. The fare was fifty-five dollars. W. C. "Cas" Prewitt had planned to go out with his friends Taylor and Peacock, but seeing Jack in such

a pitiful condition with his scurvy, he let him go in his place and gave him his ticket for the *Bartlett*.

It is commonly believed that John Thorson was on the boat from Dawson to St. Michael with Jack and Taylor, but it may have been W. T. Peacock instead. A letter from C. M. Taylor to Cas Prewitt dated at St. Michael on July 1, 1898, stated that the three men—London, Peacock, and Taylor—had gone down the Yukon together and had all left on the *Bartlett*. However, Jack always said it was John Thorson and that he stoked coal on a steamer from St. Michael to San Francisco in exchange for his passage. At least, they all got home.

BACK IN OAKLAND, 1898

In the Klondike Jack had found himself, learned patience, and become more steady. This was good, because on his return he discovered his father had died the previous October 15. His mother had begun raising little Johnny Miller, Jack's stepsister Ida's boy, and she had moved from 1645 Twenty-fifth Avenue to a small cottage at 1914 Foothill Boulevard. Times were hard. Work of any sort was difficult to get. Jack had to find food for three, since he was now head of the family. The rent was due and he needed a winter suit. It was no time to speculate on the future—it was time to locate a job, any job.

Unskilled labor is the first to feel hard times, and Jack had no trades save those of sailor and laundryman. With his new responsibilities he couldn't go to sea, as much as he wanted to, and the laundries weren't hiring. He failed to find a job at anything. He made applications at five employment bureaus and advertised in three newspapers. He looked up the few friends he knew who might help him find work, but they were either uninterested or unable to find anything for him.

The situation was desperate. He pawned his watch, his bicycle, and a mackintosh his father had left him. The coat was his sole legacy. It had cost fifteen dollars, and the pawnbroker let him have two dollars on it. A waterfront comrade of earlier years came by one day with a dress suit wrapped in newspapers. He gave no adequate explanation of

how he had come to have it, nor did Jack ask for one. He wanted the suit too badly. He traded his friend a lot of rubbish that, being unpawnable, was useless to Jack. His friend peddled the rubbish for several dollars, while Jack pledged the dress suit with his pawnbroker for five dollars.

Jack couldn't understand why he could find no work, he knew that he was a bargain in the labor market. He was twenty-two years old, weighed one hundred and sixty-five pounds, his scurvy was gone. Every possible opening for employment was tackled. He tried to become a studio model, he answered the advertisements of elderly invalids in need of companions, and he almost became a sewing machine agent. Along with these frivolous occupations, he was trying to get work as a laborer or stevedore, or anything. His vow to use brains and no brawn would have to be put aside for awhile. Now he couldn't even find muscle work. Winter was coming on, and the surplus labor army was pouring into the cities.

Early in August, in sheer desperation, he threw some of his mining equipment together, went to Traeger's Loan Office and pawned his remaining Klondike gold dust for $4.50, and headed for the Nevada gold sites. Little is known of this venture, but evidently the Klondike wasn't the only place short of gold, because in a matter of a few weeks Jack was back in Oakland hunting for work again and writing like mad. For years his muscles had been exploited, now he couldn't sell them. He would gladly have gone back to the power plant at this point—at least he would be able to pay the rent and buy food.

He worked days, and halfdays, at anything he could get. He mowed lawns and cleaned carpets. Between these odd jobs, he tried to earn ten dollars by writing a newspaper account of his voyage down the Yukon River in an open boat. He didn't know the first thing about the newspaper game, but was confident he'd get ten dollars for the article. He called this first attempt to pan literary gold "From Dawson to the Sea." He sent it to the editor of the *San Francisco Bulletin* with this letter:

Sept. 17, 1898
962 E. 16th St.
[Now 1914 Foothill Blvd.]
Oakland, Calif.

Editor of the "Bulletin"
Dear Sir:

I have just returned from a year's residence in the Klondike entering the country by the way of Dyea and Chilcoot Pass. I left by the way of St. Michael, thus making altogether a journey of 2,500 miles on the Yukon in a small boat. I have sailed and traveled quite extensively in other parts of the world and I have learned to seize upon that which is interesting, to grasp the true romance of things, and to understand the people I may be thrown amongst.

I have just completed an article of 4,000 words describing the trip from Dawson to St. Michael in a row boat. Kindly let me know if there would be any demand in your columns for it—of course thoroughly understanding that the acceptance of the manuscript is to depend upon its literary and intrinsic value.

Yours very respectfully,
Jack London

The letter was returned and in pencil at the bottom:

Interest in Alaska has subsided in an amazing degree. Then again so much has been written that I do not think it would pay us to buy your story.

Editor

Finding no work to support his family, Jack decided he could at least earn ten cents an hour as a writer, the same pittance his brute work had earned him. He wrote a twenty-one-thousand-word serial for the *Youth's Companion,* which he finished in seven days. Jack said, "I fancy that was what was the matter with it, for it came back." It took some time for it to go and come, and in the meantime he tried his hand at short stories and an essay or two.

BIRTH PANGS OF A WRITER

Jack had many liabilities and no assets. He had no income, several mouths to feed, and a poor widow as a landlady whose needs demanded that he should pay his rent with some degree of regularity. This was his economic situation when he attempted to sell his work to the magazines.

He knew nothing about the writing game. He lived in California, and the great publishing centers were in the East. He had no idea what an editor looked like. Nor did he know a soul who had ever published anything; nor yet again, a soul who had ever tried to write anything, much less tried to publish it.

There was no one to teach him the writing game, no one's experience to profit by. So he sat down and wrote in order to get experience of his own. He wrote everything—short stories, articles, anecdotes, jokes, essays, sonnets, ballads, villanelles, triolets, songs, light plays in iambic tetrameter, and heavy tragedies in blank verse. All of these creations were put in envelopes, with return postage enclosed, and dropped into the mailbox. He was prolific. Day by day manuscripts piled up until the finding of stamps for them became as great a problem as that of supporting his dependents.

All of his manuscripts came back. They continued to come back. He would drop a manuscript into the mailbox. After the lapse of a certain length of time, the manuscript arrived back in his mailbox. Accompanying the manuscript was a stereotyped rejection slip. A machine, some clever arrangement of cogs and wheels at the other end, (it couldn't have been a living, breathing man with blood in his veins) had transferred the manuscript to another envelope, taken the stamps from inside and pasted them outside, and added the rejection slip.

This went on for months. He had no idea what was marketable. Would it be poetry or prose, jokes or sonnets, short stories or essays? He had a vague idea that a minimum rate of ten dollars a thousand words was paid; that if he only could get two or three things published the editors would clamor for his work.

Jack was perfectly content to receive the minimum rate. He reasoned that he would have to write no more than three thousand words a day, five days a week. Thus he would have plenty of time for recreation and he would still earn six hundred dollars a month without overstocking the market. Actually, he would have been overjoyed if some editor paid him the old work beast rate of ten cents an hour.

Mabel was no help. She had little faith in his ability to earn a living with a pen. She was beside herself with joy when he told her about a Post Office ad in the *Examiner*. She urged him to take the postman's job as soon as it was available and settle down.

Jack's idol was again showing her feet of clay. He had fallen out of love with her a long time ago and was now more interested in a game of chess with Ted when he visited the Applegarths than in going biking with her. Mabel missed those days when Jack sat at her feet in awe. She prayed that a miracle would restore them. One day she was piqued because Jack and Ted were completely engrossed in their game, and she wanted to go for a ride on their bicycles. Walking over to the board, she swept the pieces across the room.

Jack was astounded, hurt, and thoroughly disillusioned. Not a word was said, but when, after what seemed a century to her, his eyes met hers she knew her prayers would never be answered. From that moment, any love that may have lingered became mere friendship. Jack realized that he had been in love with his idealization of her, not with Mabel herself. He felt sorry for her and feigned a romantic infatuation for many months rather than hurt her feelings. The truth was that they both realized what had happened to their love before Jack left for the Klondike gold fields. Now they could be close friends without pretense and they were just that through the years ahead.

Jack's desire to make a fortune in the Yukon was undiminished when scurvy forced him to come out. As soon as he was able he hoped to return and work his claim. In a letter to Ted Applegarth he said, "My partners are still on the inside and it all depends as to what they write me whether I go back in February or not. As to what I make out of our claims I don't know—maybe nothing, maybe several thousand . . . Quien Sabe?" A favorable report from his mining partners would let him escape the necessity for manual labor, and he could earn enough to go back to school. He could then build his writing career on a proper foundation. Realizing such a plan would probably never materialize, he took the examination for mail carrier at the Oakland Post Office on October 1.

About two weeks earlier he wrote Ted that Fred Jacobs and Herbert Shepard had enlisted in the Spanish-American War, or as Jack said, "The 'Yanko-Spanko War.'" "I assure you I don't envy them . . . not the danger or the hardship, for they are incomparable with an Alaskan trip, but what they must put up with from their superiors. A soldier's life is a dog's life at the best."

The Post Office showed no signs of an opening. Jack grew grim and depressed. In an unpublished manuscript, Frank Atherton, who visited him at the time, reveals the depth of his despair:

A few weeks later when I visited him, he made a strange confession. In a mood of utter despondency, he had contemplated suicide, having gone so far as to write farewell letters to his most intimate friends, intending to mail them just before ending his life.

"I could see nothing to live for," he explained in relating the incident. "All I could see was failure, complete failure. If I failed to succeed in writing," he continued, "there would be nothing else for me to do. I recalled all the various jobs I had worked at in the past, way back to my paper route. And the only bright spot in all my past experience was the open sea. But how could I go to sea again when my mother and Johnny Miller were depending on me?"

His argument seemed reasonable. "How could you be of any assistance to them if you were dead?" I interrupted him.

"Oh, I know I was crazy," he admitted, "but that was the way I felt about it. I had it all planned, the farewell letters all ready to mail. And then who should come to see me but ... well, there's no need to mention her name; but I've known her for some time. She came to say goodbye for the last time. The world had been cruel to her, and she decided to end it all.

"She saved my life," he continued reminiscently. "You see I began to reason with her, telling her how utterly foolish it is to entertain such a rash act, and in my argument I began to realize my own folly."

He smiled triumphantly, and I waited for him to proceed.

"I'm going to stick to my writing, and the publishers are going to accept it whether they like it or not. And some of these days they'll be glad to take the stuff they've rejected and pay me a good price for it; you just wait and see."

Thus aroused from his morbidity, Jack began one of the greatest battles of his life, to conquer the unconquerable, to achieve the impossible, and gain recognition from the literary world.

Jack was supposed to have gone to visit the Applegarths for Thanksgiving, but was unable to leave for San Jose because Frank was still visiting. On November 27 Jack wrote to Mabel:

Everything seems to have gone wrong—why, I haven't received my twenty dollars for those essays yet [two ten-dollar prizes for essays he had submitted to a Republican Club contest]. Not a word as to how I stood in my Civil Exs [later he discovered that he passed first with a grade of 85.38]. Not a word from the *Youth's Companion* [regarding "Where Boys Are Men"] and it means to me what no one can possibly realize.

Though it took me a long while, I have learned my lesson, and thanks to no one. I made ambitious efforts once. It makes me laugh to look back on them, though sometimes I am nearer to weeping. I was the greenest of tyros, dipping my brush into white-wash and coal-tar, and without the slightest knowledge of perspective, proportion or color, attempted masterpieces—without a soul to say "You are all wrong; herein you err; there is your mistake."

I shall not be ready for any flights till my flying machine is perfected, and to that perfection I am now applying myself. Until then to deuce with them. I shall subordinate thought to technique till the latter is mastered; then I shall do vice a versa.

I may be digging sewers or shoveling coal next week.

Convinced that Jack was far enough out of his despondency, Frank went home in early December. Jack was still low in spirit, however. Finally he received his first encouragement. The old manuscript rejection machine had been working without a flaw and his manuscripts were still making their regular round trips, until one morning the postman delivered a thin letter from the *Overland Monthly Magazine* regarding his short story "To The Man on Trail." As he tore open the envelope, he modestly expected to find a check for no more than forty dollars—four thousand words at the minimum ten dollars per thousand. Instead he read, "We have read your Ms. and are so greatly pleased with it, that, though we have an enormous quantity of accepted and paid for material on hand, we will at once publish it in the January number if you can content yourself with five dollars."

Five dollars! A dollar and a quarter per thousand words! He felt terrible. An article in the Sunday supplement of a local newspaper had convinced him that the minimum pay for writing was ten dollars per thousand words. The article had lied. He was finished, finished as only a very young, very sick, and very hungry young man could be. He was too miserable to think about anything except that he would never write again. But the postman brought another thin envelope. This one was from H. D. Umbstaetter of *The Black Cat* telling him that the four-thousand-word story he had submitted was more "lengthy than strengthy," but if he would give permission to have it cut in half, he would immediately be sent a check for forty dollars. The offer was equivalent to twenty dollars per thousand, or double the minimum rate. He told Umbstaetter that he could cut the story in "two halves" if he would only send the money along.

It was several months before Jack was able to collect his five dollars from the *Overland Monthly Magazine,* but in February, *The Black Cat* magazine paid him forty dollars for his story "A Thousand Deaths." In his introduction to *The Red Hot Dollar* in 1911, Jack said, "And that is just precisely how and why I stayed by the writing game. Literally and literarily, I was saved by the *Black Cat* short story."

Christmas had been bleak. It had been a bad year—full of hunger and failure, but at least his career was progressing. His letter written that day to Mabel reveals a young man who could face 1899 better armed for the conflict:

Xmas Morning [1898]
Oakland, Calif.

Dear Mabel:

About the lonliest Christmas I ever faced—guess I'll write to you. Nothing to speak of, though—everything quiet. How I wish I were down at College Park, if for no more than a couple of hours. Nobody to talk to, no friend to visit—nay, if there were, and if I so desired, I would not be in a position to. Hereafter and for some time to come, you'll have to content yourself with my beastly scrawl, for this is, most probably, the last machine made letter I shall send you.

Well, the FIRST BATTLE has been fought. While I have not conquered, I'll not confess defeat. Instead, I have learned the enemy's strongholds and weak places, and by the same I shall profit when the SECOND BATTLE comes off; and by what I learn through that, I will be better for the Third Battle—and so on, ad infinitum.

The typewriter goes back on the thirty-first of December. Till then I expect to be busy cleaning up my desk, writing business letters of various nature, and finishing the articles I am at present on. Then the New Year, and an entire change of front.

I have profited greatly, have learned much during the last three months. How much I cannot even approximate—I feel its worth and greatness, but it is too impalpable to put down in black and white. I have studied, read, and thought a great deal, and believe I am at last beginning to grasp the situation—the general situation, my situation, and the correlative situation between the two. But I am modest, as I say, I am only beginning to grasp—I realize, with all I have learned, I know less about it than I thought I did a couple of years ago.

Are you aware of the parodox entailed by progress? It makes me both jubilant and sad. You cannot help feeling sad when looking over back work and realizing its weak places, its errors, its inanities, and again, you cannot but rejoice at having so improved that you are aware of it, and feel capable of better things. I have learned more in the past three months than in all my High School and College; yet, of course, they were necessary from a preparatory standpoint.

And to-day is Christmas—it is at such periods

The story that saved Jack London's literary life

that the vagabondage of my nature succumbs to a latent taste for domesticity. Away with the many corners of this round world! I am deaf to the call of the East and West, the North and South—a picture such as Fred used to draw is before me. A comfortable little cottage, a couple of servants, a select coterie of friends, and above all, a neat little wife and a couple of diminutive models of us twain—a hanging of stockings last evening, a merry surprise this morning, the genial interchange of Christmas greeting; a cozy grate fire, the sleepy children cuddling on the floor ready for bed, a sort of dreamy communion between the fire, my wife, and myself; an assured, though quiet and monotonous, future in prospect; a satisfied knowledge of the many little amenities of civilized life which are mine and shall be mine; a genial, optomistic contemplation.

Ever feel that way? Fred dreamed of it, but never tasted; I suppose I am destined likewise. So be it. The ways of the gods are inscrutable—and do they make and break us just for fun? What a great old world! What a jolly old world! It contains so much which is worth striving for, and nevertheless, so much to avoid. But it's like a great Chinese puzzle—in every community are to be found the Islands of the Blest, and yet we know not where to look for them. And if we do, our ticket in Life's Lottery bears the wrong number. An auspicious mingling of all the elements which go to make up the totality of human happiness—the capital prize—there are various ways of winning it, and still more various ways of losing it. You may be born into it, you may tumble into it, you may be dragged into it; but verily, you may not knowingly walk into it. The whole thing is a gamble, and those least fitted to understand the game win the most. The most unfortunate gamblers are those who have, or think they have systems to beat the game—they always go broke. The same with life. There are numerous paths to earthly happiness; but to find them, skill in geography or typography is worse than useless.

I shall forsake my old dogmas, and henceforth, worship the true god. "There is no God but Chance, and Luck shall be his prophet!" He who stops to think or beget a system is lost. As in other creeds, faith alone atones. Numerous hecatombs, and many a fat firstling shall I sacrifice— you just watch my smoke (I beg pardon, I mean incense).

I started to write a letter; I became nonsensical; forgive me. I go to dine at my sisters. Happy New Year to all!

Jack

There is no record of Jack London receiving one penny for his writing efforts in 1898.

Jack kept all his work in circulation. He was his own literary agent. His manuscripts seldom sat idly at home and his record keeping was highly professional. Each item was recorded and as soon as a manuscript was returned it was sent to another publisher until it was sold. Those that didn't sell after repeated attempts were marked "retired" and filed away for possible future changes.

The year 1898 was not as bad a year as his financial records showed. He didn't return from the Klondike until July, and at least one month was spent in the Nevada gold hills. By December he had sold two short stories, and he was learning the writing game. He was also learning what it meant to collect rejection slips. In that short span he managed to obtain 44. Next year he would have a full year in which to keep his manuscripts moving from publisher to publisher, and would receive the most rejection slips of his career—a whopping 266!

1899—THE BUSIEST YEAR

Few authors ever wrote more steadily than did Jack London in 1899. In addition to his previously unsold items, he added sixty-one new stories, jokes, poems, essays, triolets, etc. These were mailed to seventy-four different magazines and twenty-one newspapers. According to his records, he went to the post office at least once on each of 140 days during the year to send one or more manuscripts on their way. A total of 287 mailings were made in 1899. A few manuscripts were sold quickly, but most of them saw a lot of travel as they brought the 266 rejection slips home to him.

Jack was gaining ground despite the rejections. Previously he had known mostly failure, but now he was selling and being published. Friends who formerly looked askance at him were now looking with appreciation and a little awe. He was being encouraged more, and the newspapers were printing favorable articles about Oakland's young author.

Early in 1899 Jack wrote to the corresponding editor of the *Youth's Companion*, who had advised that he make his living in some other way than writing:

I understand and appreciate your urging me to not make writing my means of livlihood. Enclosed ad is the one I am at present running in the local papers. Have been trying for work constantly. In the midst of Youth's Companion MS., broke off to take Civil Service Examinations for the Post Office. They are very slow at Washington, however, for I have yet to receive my standing in the same. I think I did very well.

Yet to me all work will be but a means to an end. I may labor till I am old and decrepit; but periods of idleness and sickness eating into the savings of labor and frugality, will have placed me in the proper position for the poor house. No, No, I have seen too much labor and too many laborers, not to understand the game. Some day I shall hit upon my *magnum opus*. And then, if my struggling expression at last finds tongue, I will not have to go to the poor house because my muscles can no longer work. And if not—well, so be it.

A few days later, on January 16, the Post Office notified him that because of his high score of 85.38 on the examination, his name was first on the list for mail carrier. A friend in the local post office advised that he could expect a call in April as an extra man at forty-five dollars a month. Six months later the salary would go to sixty-five dollars when he became a regular. This was a princely sum since the average wage earner was earning less than five hundred dollars per year.

"To the Man on Trail" had been published in January by the venerable *Overland Monthly Magazine*. Jack always believed that this was his first short story to be published. Actually the *Owl Magazine* published his "Two Gold Bricks" in September of 1897 while he was struggling over the Chilcoot Pass. Jack never saw the magazine or ever knew that this story was published.

The *Overland Monthly* was founded by Anton Roman in 1868. Roman astutely arranged for contributions from Charles Warren Stoddard, Bret Harte, and Ina Coolbrith, the "Golden Gate Trinity." Its main purpose was to promote Western literature and help young Western authors launch their careers. Jack London became one of their star contributors, but they paid so little that the early months of 1899 were trying times for Jack and his mother. From the notification of his placement on the mail carrier list until his call to go to work, they had to do some hard thinking. Jack was willing to face privations, for he had confidence in his ability to achieve literary success. But could he ask his mother and little Johnny Miller to hunger with him? At this time they were living from hand to mouth in the poorest of circumstances. They were actually subsisting on Flora's income from a small pension and her occasional piano pupils. Should he

SEPTEMBER.   5 CENTS.

The Owl *Magazine. Jack London's first story to appear in a magazine appeared in this magazine in the September issue of 1897.*

accept the security of Uncle Sam's payroll and provide his family with a decent life? Flora made the decision. She had not forgotten the prize he had won back in 1893. Now that the *Overland Monthly* had printed "To the Man on Trail," her circle of friends had expanded. She was willing to keep on and suggested that he pass up the mail carrier job and stick to his writing. As far as we know, this was the one great thing she did for Jack. Probably she reasoned that her "badge of shame" could now become her "entreé into high society," which, she felt, should have been her place all along. Besides, Flora was always willing to play her hunches—whether on a Chinese laundry ticket or on the hope of her son's future fame.

During this period Jack had little time for social life. He only saw the Applegarths on rare trips when he could spare the time to bike the long miles to San Jose. Success as a writer required not only the hard work of writing, but also the necessity of a thorough education, which meant long hours with the books—a rigid discipline he was willing to follow. The light in his little bedroom continued to burn into the early hours of the morning.

As Irving Stone explains in *Sailor on Horseback:*

He knew that if he thought clearly he would write clearly, for if he were badly educated, if his thoughts were confused and jumbled, how could he expect a lucid utterance? And if his thoughts were worthy so could his writing be worthy. He knew that he must have his hand on the inner pulse of life, that the sum of his working knowledge would be the *working philosophy* by which he would measure, weigh, balance, and interpret the world. He felt that he had to educate himself in history, biology, evolution, economics, and a hundred other important branches of learning because they would broaden his thought, lengthen his vistas, drive back the bounds of the field in which he was to work. They would give him a working philosophy which would be like unto no other man's and force him to original thinking, provide him with something new and vital for the jaded ear of the world. He had no intention of writing trivia, of administering chocolate-coated pills to constipated minds.

And so he went directly to the books and laid siege to the citadel of their wisdom. He was no college boy cramming sufficient facts to pass an examination, no casual passerby warming his hands at the great fires of knowledge. He was a passionate wooer and to him every new fact learned, every new theory absorbed, every old concept challenged and new concept gained was a personal victory, a cause for rejoicing. He questioned, selected, rejected, submitting everything he read to a searching analysis. He was not blinded or awed by reputations. Great minds made no impression upon him unless they could present him with great ideas. Conventional thinking meant little to this man who had broken every convention he had met; an image-maker himself, iconoclastic thinking on the part of others did not frighten or repulse him. He was honest, he was courageous, he could think straight, and he had a profound love for truth, four indispensables for the scholar.

Jack London never became a recognized authority in philosophy, biology, psychology, or in any other field of learning, but his grasp of these subjects was far superior to that of most laymen, and he could hold his own with many professors in their chosen fields. Late in 1916 Jack said in a transcript of evidence in a court trial, "I have acquired practically every bit of my knowledge from the books. I never was a graduate of a university; I never finished the first half of my freshman year at a university; yet I have thought it nothing to face a group of thirty or forty professors hammer-and-tongs on philosophy, sociology, and all the other 'ologies—the group including David Starr Jordan and others of the same high intellectual calibre. I was able to do that and hold a table of debate—I who had never been through a university—because I had gotten my knowledge from the same books they had got their knowledge from."

His views were not always conventional, and his many contradictions and inconsistencies are obvious, but Jack knew about them as well as anybody, and effected compromises with which he could live. His knowledge was wide ranging and sometimes deep, but not comprehensive. However, his popularity was not due to his depth of knowledge, except as it was reflected in his writing. It was due to his great ability as a creative writer and to his legendary personal life.

Searching for his own philosophy of life and his own style, Jack fished in the rich streams of Spencer, Darwin, Marx, Nietzsche, Kant, Mill, Smith, Malthus, Hobbs, Hume, Locke, Hegel, Berkeley, Leibnitz, Huxley, Wallace, James, Bacon, and many other authors. He took from them what he could accept and discarded the rest. Seeking polish and better style, he immersed himself in Shakespeare and the Bible. He reasoned that every book contained the best thought of the writer, and he wanted to know what they knew. Gradually he synthesized all the learning of the ages that he could and formulated his own philosophy based on scientific reasoning, and the facts he had discovered. He detested metaphysical reasoning or any other thinking that was not based on a positive and defensible platform.

When the January issue of the *Overland Monthly* was published, Jack was elated and depressed. No matter how much the story was praised, he could only think of the five-dollar payment, and he didn't even have that yet. He also knew that it wasn't a great story. It was eminently readable, but it had some bad flaws and didn't reflect the kind of story of which he knew himself capable. He never in his life made any pretense that he was writing for anything but money, but this is not to say that he neglected his constant pursuit of a better literary style. He knew that success as a writer depended upon a thorough study and knowledge of literature as it was commercially produced in his day and he attempted to write the highest-quality work possible that would still be acceptable to his market.

Early in his career, Jack's study of that market made him prophesy the decline of the novel. He therefore decided to specialize in the short story. A look into this genre showed that American readers were asking for tales of action and adventure. His own life's adventures seemed perfect material, so he sat down, pen in hand, and gave the public what it wanted.

This period was also marked by the glorification of rugged individualism, brute strength, and the racial superiority of the white man. It was a time of Kipling mania, and London was caught up in the trend. He has been accused of being a racist, and it is true, but only in the sense that was true of most people of the time. There was much race prejudice focused on the Chinese and Japanese, whose lower standard of living was interpreted as a strong threat to the white workingman's hope of employment. The "Yellow Peril" was a common slogan in early California, and seeped into much of its fiction. To call Jack London a racist in the context of our own times would be ridiculous.

Jack never stopped sharpening his literary skills. Without formal training of any kind it proved to be a difficult job, and one with which he was still struggling at the time of his death. From his early "formula" stories he moved on in a quest for better methods. He read that short story theoreticians were teaching their students that a short story should not be a condensed novel. Jack agreed, and began to think of the short story in a new way. He told a friend, "Remember this—confine a short story within the shortest possible time-limit—a day, an hour, if possible—or, if, as sometimes with the best of short stories, a long period of time must be covered—months—merely hint or sketch (incidentally) the passage of time, and tell the story only in its crucial moments ... the short story is a rounded fragment from life, a single mood, situation, or action."

From a loose first-person point of view that marred several earlier stories, Jack moved on to use better narrative control in his Northland stories.

He was beginning to use the third-person narrative method, but when the critics complained about the use of authorial intrusion, he used less. However, many admirers of London's style wish he had continued his excellent use of the author's "intrusion," which enabled him to create a philosophical depth that would have been out of place in the mouths of his characters.

His early essay-exemplum type of construction gave way to the frame story. No longer did he have to speak in his own authoritative voice. Now, by using a teller who was clearly not himself, he was free to delve into more complex social and moral issues.

By the end of 1902, Jack had acquired a highly professional understanding of short story craftsmanship, which, coupled with his innate ability to spin a yarn, soon made him one of the best and most popular short story writers in America.

In 1913 Jack referred to these early years:

I started writing when I was too poor to buy magazines to find out what a story was. In those days I went to the library and crammed myself full of the stories that were selling. Then I sailed in.

There are tricks and devices I use—tools in the art. I build a motive—a thesis, and my story has a dual nature. On the surface is the simple story any child can read—full of action, movement, color. Under that is the real story, philosophical, complex, full of meaning. One reader gets the interesting story, the other sees my philosophy of life.

If you are filled with enthusiasm for one thing, if you have one preachment, if you see with a wide vision and hold fast to that one thing, you'll succeed.

Since Jack London made more money as a writer than any other author of his time, young writers should have considered his advice:

Don't quit your job in order to write unless there is no one dependent upon you. Fiction pays best of all, and when it is of fair quality is more easily sold. A good joke will sell quicker than a good poem, and, measured in sweat and blood, will bring better remuneration. Avoid the unhappy ending, the harsh, the brutal, the tragic, the horrible—if you care to see in print the things you write. (In this connection don't do as I do, but do as I say.)

Humor is the hardest to write, easiest to sell,

and best rewarded. There are only a few who are able to do it. If you are able, do it by all means. You will find it a Klondike and a Rand rolled into one. Look at Mark Twain.

Don't dash off a six-thousand word story before breakfast. Don't write too much. Concentrate your sweat on one story, rather than dissipate it over a dozen. Don't loaf and invite inspiration; light out after it with a club, and if you don't get it you will nonetheless get something that looks remarkably like it. Set yourself a "stint," and see that you do that "stint" each day; you will have more words to your credit at the end of the year.

Study the tricks of the writers who have arrived. They have mastered the tools with which you are cutting your teeth. They are doing things, and their work bears the internal evidence of how it is done. Don't wait for some good Samaritan to tell you, but dig it out for yourself.

See that your pores are open and your digestion is good. That is, I am confident, the most important rule of all. And don't fling Carlyle in my teeth, please.

Keep a notebook. Travel with it, sleep with it. Slap into it every stray thought that flutters up into your brain. Cheap paper is less perishable than gray matter, and lead pencil marking endures longer than memory.

And work. Spell it in capital letters, WORK. WORK all the time. Find out about this earth, this universe, this force and matter, and the spirit that glimmers up through force and matter from the maggot to the Godhead. And by all this I mean WORK for a philosophy of life. It does not hurt how wrong your philosophy of life may be, so long as you have one and have it well.

The three great things are: GOOD HEALTH, WORK and a PHILOSOPHY OF LIFE. I may add, nay, must add, a fourth—SINCERITY. Without this, the other three are without avail. With it you may cleave to greatness and sit among the giants.

Jack London followed his own advice to the letter, and in less than four years from the publication of "To the Man on Trail" his name was rapidly becoming a household word in America, and he was gaining fame throughout the world. In just a few more years he was one of the most popular authors in the world, a position he still holds. He preferred cash to fame, and though he never had more than twenty-eight thousand dollars in the bank at one

Cloudesley Johns

time, he ran about one million dollars through his account in sixteen years.

But in 1899 he gained only local fame and very little money. He once said that he should at least be able to make ten cents an hour from his writing. He didn't quite make it that year. He seldom made less than thirty dollars per month during his work beast period. His last full-time job was in the Belmont Academy for thirty dollars per month plus room and board. From his writing in 1899 he earned an average of $29.73 per month, but he was steadily learning his trade.

His local fame caused some problems. Old shipmates, ex-cronies, and fellow Klondikers found his home with no trouble. It seemed they all had the same story: "Just returned from a long voyage. What a wonderful fellow Jack London is; never liked anybody in all the world so much; expect to get paid tomorrow ... say, Jack old boy, can you lend me a couple of dollars 'til payday?" Jack, whenever possible, scaled them down to about half of what they asked for, gave them the money, and let them go. Some of these he never heard from again; others came back over and over again.

A note in a letter to Cloudesley Johns explains another reason why Jack accumulated so many friends during his life. "My one great weakness is the study of human nature. Knowing no God, I have made of man my worship; and surely I have learned how vile he can be. But this only strengthens my regard, because it enhances the mighty heights he can bring himself to tread. How small he is, and how great he is, but this weakness, this desire to come in touch with every strange soul I meet, has caused me many a scrape."

Jack was always genuinely interested in people. He wanted to know what made them tick, like a kid with an old alarm clock. He trusted people even when he knew better. Yet Jack had very few close friends and less than a handful who were not simply basking in his fame. Cloudesley Johns and Jim Whitaker were true friends; they gave as much as they took and asked for nothing.

Early in February, Cloudesley sent Jack a letter congratulating him on the publication of "To the Man on Trail" in the *Overland Monthly*. It was the first word of cheer Jack had received and, poor as he was, it meant more at that time than a publisher's check. It precipitated the most active correspondence Jack ever had in his lifetime with any one person. Johns was a young writer and postmaster of a small desert post office in Harold, California. Their friendly literary correspondence through the years was of tremendous benefit to both writers. They candidly criticized each other's work, a practice that was good for both. They shared their philosophies of life, their aspirations, and their failures. Jack adored Cloudesley's grandmother, Mrs. Rebecca Spring. She talked with him about her literary friends—Emerson, Holmes, and Longfellow. He sat at her feet and drank in every word.

Besides Cloudesley Johns, Jack's more intimate friends included Anna Strunsky, Charles Warren Stoddard, George Sterling, Jim Whitaker, Xavier Martinez, Ted and Mabel Applegarth, Blanche Partington, Armine von Tempski, his brother-in-law Ernest Matthews, Senator James Duval Phelan, Frank Atherton, Finn Frolich, and Frederick Irons Bamford. In later years he and Charmian were on very friendly terms with Ed and Ida Winship in Napa.

Herman "Jim" Whitaker had an important influence on London. Born in Huddersfield in Yorkshire, England, in 1867, the son of a mill owner, Whitaker left home at sixteen to join the army and soon became an instructor in gymnastics and fencing at the Curragh Camp in Ireland. In 1884 he purchased his discharge and emigrated to Canada, where he pioneered north of Winnipeg and where he enjoyed many fabulous adventures. Moving to California in 1895, he settled in Oakland with his wife and six children.

Sidney Grundy, popular Victorian playwright, was Whitaker's great-uncle. When Grundy brought home a copy of Bret Harte, Jim read it and decided he would go to California and become a writer.

At the time Whitaker arrived in Oakland, Jack London was struggling through high school. For two months Jim's family lived on only eight dollars. During this period he was active among the local socialists who started a cooperative grocery store. Whitaker was hired to manage it on a thirty-dollar per month salary. About this time he met Jack at a street meeting and encouraged him to join the party. They immediately became close friends. After the store closed at night, they pulled

Herman Whitaker. This picture was taken during World War I when he was one of the leading war correspondents.

Jack fences with his friend Spiro Orfans.

the shades and Jim taught Jack the fine points of boxing and fencing.

Late in 1900 Whitaker asked, "Would you advise me, Jack, to throw up my job and have a 'go' at fiction?" Whitaker had only written one short story for the *Overland Monthly*.

"No," Jack answered, "I certainly wouldn't."

"Well, I am going to anyway."

"And so would I," Jack responded with a grin.

The two pals worked together for months. Jim's fine English education was shared with Jack and, in turn, Jack's enthusiasm, perseverance, and self-assurance were captured by Whitaker.

In less than three months Jim had been published in a national magazine; Jack was both pleased and astounded. By 1912 Whitaker had nearly as much space in the *International Who's Who* as Jack. Jim wrote seven novels—three of which were made into movies—many essays on socialism, and had short stories published in most of the popular magazines of his day.

London and Whitaker were both active in the Ruskin Club of Oakland. The Club was started by Frederick Irons Bamford, A. A. Denison, and Austin Lewis on December 9, 1898, at Maison de L'Opera. Nine charter members were present, including Jack London, Jim Whitaker, and George Sterling. It was a highly intellectual socialist group. A look at the programs of their meetings reveals

that Jack and Jim lectured often on socialism and economics. Whitaker once successfully debated David Starr Jordan, President of Stanford University.

Later, in 1913, Whitaker traveled for six months with Pancho Villa and in 1914 was a correspondent in Mexico for the *Oakland Tribune*. He was also a noted war correspondent during World War I, representing a number of magazines and newspapers.

Herman "Jim" Whitaker was known as one of the "West Coast Giants of Literature," but, tragically, he died of cancer before he could return home from the war and was soon forgotten. His writing was superior to many of the popular authors of the day, but never reached the quality or popularity of Jack's. He did not have his friend's charisma and his choice of material was dated and made no lasting impressions. However, *The Planter* and other books are an excellent source of historical information on Mexico; *The Settler* and *The Probationer* do the same for a study of the early settlers in Manitoba, Canada.

In a letter to Houghton Mifflin dated January 31, 1900, Jack described his own early work: "Hackwork all, or nearly so, from a comic joke or triolet to pseudoscientific nothing. Hackwork for dollars, that's all, setting aside practically all ambitious efforts to some future period of less financial stringence, thus my literary life is just thirteen months old." He talked of the period from 1895 through 1898 as his years of apprenticeship. He dated January, 1899, when "To the Man on Trail" was published, as the birth of his career.

Actually, some of his finest work was written in 1898. "The White Silence" is one example. It was first sent to *Godey's Magazine* as "Northland Episode." It was finally sold to the *Overland Monthly* on January 3, 1899, after also being turned down by *Lippincott's* in 1898. Of this story George Hamlin Fitch, a literary critic of the *San Francisco Chronicle*, said, "I would rather have written 'The White Silence' than anything that has appeared in fiction in the last ten years." Fitch's desire was widely shared. Many are the writers who wish they could create prose as timelessly evocative as Jack did in this short story, where he raised his words to the level of poetry:

> The afternoon wore on, and with the aura, born of the White Silence, the voiceless travellers bent to their work. Nature has many tricks wherewith she convinces man of his finity—the ceaseless flow of the tides, the fury of the storm, the shock of the earthquake, the long roll of heaven's artillery,—but the most tremendous, the most stupefying of all, is the passive phase of the White Silence. All movement ceases, the sky clears, the heavens are as brass; the slightest whisper seems sacrilege, and man becomes timid, afrighted at the sound of his own voice. Sole speck of life journeying across the ghostly wastes of a dead world, he trembles at his audacity, realizes that his is a maggot's life, nothing more. Strange thoughts arise unsummoned, and the mystery of all things strives for utterance. And the fear of death, of God, of the universe, comes over him—the hope of the Resurrection and the Life, the yearning for immortality, the vain striving of the imprisoned essence, it is then, if ever, man walks alone with God.

Jack's "In a Far Country," published in the June, 1899, issue of the *Overland Monthly* deals with the abilities of man to cope with an indifferent Nature. Two men are holed up in a Klondike cabin to hibernate through the winter months. They believe that they have made adequate preparation to survive. As Earle Labor points out, Jack uses the "Seven Deadly Sins" to show how ill prepared they actually are and to reveal the deadly workings of the law of the survival of the fittest, or better, the

nonsurvival of the incapables. Cuthfert and Weatherbee move through pride, lust, laziness, gluttony, covetousness, envy, and anger as they fail to adapt to the inescapable "Code of the North." Their failure to do so destroys the men as winter embraces them in its heartless cold and barrenness. Their shallowness of soul is beautifully portrayed. Those who see the surface motif of the story tend to empathize with the men in their struggle to live, but those who perceive the main motif see the symbolism of man's inhumanity to man, and the failure to recognize that man must adapt to his world.

All through his literary life Jack London hammered away at institutions designed and perpetuated to make the rich richer and the poor poorer. The wasteful use of natural resources and the failure to meet the needs of the people; the hypocrisy of political leaders who lead for personal gain rather than for the good of the country as a whole—these ate at London's very soul and influenced much of what he wrote. Public servants wanted to be served. The government had become a new aristocracy. The weak were the ones that suffered. It is the law, the immutable law of the universe, that the weak shall perish, but Jack devoted his life and work to fight it with all that was in him. He knew it was impossible, but he tried anyway. As least he might help a little.

Jack knew that he needed a better education to be a writer, but he resigned himself to the impossibility of resuming his studies at the university. He often wished that his years could have been condensed in such a way that he could have lived, at least temporarily, the scholar's life. Once more he turned to the books. Having little money, he happily discovered that Bull Durham tobacco was an answer—it was cheap and the tobacco tags that came with it could be swapped for books.

On his return from the Klondike Jack learned that his friend Fred Jacobs had died en route to the Spanish-American War on the troopship *Scandia*. Most of Jack's spare time was spent consoling Fred's fiancée, Bessie Maddern. Their friendship grew steadily until he found himself spending much more time on picnics with Bessie than in riding to San Jose to see the Applegarths.

By June Jack was studying harder than ever. He was particularly worried over his clumsiness of style and his inability to polish his work. Plots were especially difficult for him. He said, "Well, I can't construct plots worth a damn, but I can everlastingly elaborate." His favorite method of composition was to write fifty to three hundred words, then type it in manuscript form for submission. He was groping for his own particular style.

On June 4 his "From Dawson to the Sea" was published in *The Illustrated Buffalo Express*. "An Old Soldier's Story" had already been published in the *Orange Judd Farmer*, the *American Agriculturist*, and *The New England Homestead*, so his work was now being read from coast to coast. Literarily he was doing fine, but financially he was still nearly a pauper. On August 5 he went to Traeger's Loan Office, and pawned his Rambler bicycle for five dollars.

In September, having redeemed it, he took a bicycle vacation and toured the Peninsula area with a side trip to see the universe through the big telescope at Mount Hamilton Observatory. In addition, he audited several classes at Stanford University before returning home.

The last Sunday in September Jack and Bessie rode their bikes to Mill Valley, via the ferry be-

Jack London

Jack pawns his bicycle.

tween San Francisco and Sausalito, where they pedaled to the base of Mount Tamalpais (now Muir Woods). That evening they worked together developing the photos taken on the trip. This was not a courtship, but they were seeing a lot of each other.

The first big break in London's career was when he received his first large check for a story. It came from the *Atlantic Monthly* on October 30 for "An Odyssey of the North." Up to this time Jack's work had been published in fairly obscure magazines, and the prestige of being published in one of the very top national magazines was tantamount to success. After staring rapturously at the one-hundred-twenty-dollar check for some time, he celebrated this momentous event by purchasing a new typewriter, paying off his long-suffering butcher and grocer, and making life liveable again for his landlady by paying his long overdue rent.

On November 11 he told Cloudesley Johns that he was preparing a lecture to be given before the Oakland section of the Socialist Labor Party on the 25th. This was his first formal lecture, quite a step up from his street haranguing of 1896. He was evidently successful, for he was soon in great demand as a lecturer. It is also evident that he lectured for free, because on the 28th he went back to Traeger's Loan Office and left his black dress coat and vest, a gold bangle, and his gold watch. He was given four dollars.

In December he had the pleasure of seeing the University of California win the "Big Game" with Stanford 30–0. Curiously, Jack seldom attended organized sporting events other than boxing matches. A couple of times he went to the U.C.–Stanford football games, and he was seen at a bullfight in Ecuador. Even more curious was his attendance at three bullfights in Mexico in 1914, after he had publicly stated his hatred of them because, in his opinion, they were the most unsportsmanlike of all sporting events. He expressed his feelings in his short story "The Madness of John Harned." However, he loved to participate in several sports. His strong competitive spirit and desire to achieve led him to become an expert boxer, cyclist, swimmer, fencer, surfer, and one of the best small-boat sailors of his day.

The year 1899 had served its purpose. He had learned much, and had unlearned nearly as much. His finances were in terrible shape, but with his story coming out in the *Atlantic Monthly* in January he was anxiously looking forward to a new year and a new century.

THE TWENTIETH CENTURY ARRIVES

Jack London entered the literary scene at a most critical time in American life. The closing of the last frontier, the emergence of an industrial society, the growth of the cities, and the impact of new scientific concepts had challenged the thinking of the new generation. For too long the literary world failed to keep up with the changing scene.

The Mauve Decade was about to pass and so were the old traditions. The workingman was no longer content to be passive while exploited. He wanted more than the meager reward he had been receiving. He was demanding a place in the sun, and to get it he was willing to educate himself. The masses wanted reading material, but were too practical minded to accept the sugar-coated literature of the nineteenth century.

Magazine and book sales set new records and some of the newer magazines sensed the new trends and designed their output to meet the demands of a wider, more democratic reading public. S. S. McClure of the McClure Publishing Company, John Brisben Walker of *Cosmopolitan,* and Frank A. Munsey of *Munsey's Magazine* were to become three of the giants. They put out cheaper magazines loaded with lively fiction and controversial articles that appealed to this new readership. Even some of the conservatives like *Harper's, Century, Scribner's,* and the staid old *Atlantic Monthly* pepped up their offerings with new robust action stories.

In fact, the first issue of *Atlantic Monthly* printed in the new century hit the stands with Jack's "An Odyssey of the North." As the church bells were ringing in the year 1900, Jack London exploded upon the national literary scene and gave the world its first popular naturalistic fiction.

A few men before London had paved the way for this change by not being afraid to discuss poverty, exploitation, and the problems of society. Some of these even dared to attack religious institutions. Hamlin Garland, Stephen Crane, and Frank Norris had opened the wedge into which young Jack London drove with the full intenstiy of his passionate personality.

London's description of his hero Martin Eden's brand of realism also describes the type of writing Jack himself was turning out at this time:

His work was realism, though he endeavored to fuse it with the fancies and beauties of imagination. What he sought was an impassioned realism, shot through with human aspiration and faith. What he wanted was life as it was, with all its spirit-groping and soul-reaching left in.

London's work was shocking to Victorian prudery, but Jack agreed with Crane—to hell with Tradition. He would rather write for men than nice old ladies. His work was often sordid and brutal, but only when these qualities had significance to the story. Although he dealt graphically with brutal events and painted a most sanguinary picture of nature in the raw, replete with a Darwinian struggle for existence, he was essentially an artist. Because he blended romantic truths with the facts of realism, his work was as historical as it was fictional—he was a true interpreter of his times.

A GOOD YEAR

Nineteen hundred was a good year for Jack. When he compared his earnings of $2,534.13 for the year against the $780.00 he would have earned as a full-time mail carrier, he knew he had made a wise decision. In one year he had earned as much as he would have earned in three and a quarter years in the post office.

It was also a year of hard work. His records reveal that he submitted thirty new items as well as rewriting and resubmitting much of his past work. He was at the post office almost as much as if he worked there, mailing one or more manuscripts on each of 127 days to fifty-one different magazines, four newspapers, and three syndicates. Twenty-seven manuscripts were published, including sixteen short stories. There were only 108 rejections compared to the 266 he received in 1899.

THE FIRST MARRIAGE

During these early years after the Klondike, Jack had few possessions, and they were usually on the move—in and out of Traeger's Loan Office. The mackintosh, a fairly good suit of clothes, and a bicycle all went in and out in that order. When things became really tight, the rented typewriter went back to the shop until odd jobs brought in a few dollars or a publisher's check arrived.

The hours were long, and he had relatively few close friends. Flora was still lavishing all her love on little Johnny Miller and none on Jack, as usual, but at least she was fighting the battle with few complaints. She wanted Jack to succeed as much as he did, but for different reasons. Hers was a matter of pride and prestige in the community. The members of the Socialist Labor Party were all older than Jack and, although their goals were the same, there was little companionship. His only companion on the literary trail was Jim Whitaker, and his boyhood friend Frank Atherton was always around when needed.

He found himself spending more and more time with Bessie Maddern. She had followed his progress and knew how far he had come. She shared his high moments and went through his trials with him, quietly reassuring him when he became discouraged. After going over his manuscripts together, they would jump on their bikes for a picnic in the hills or maybe just disappear on a forty-or fifty-mile biking trip. They were comfortable together.

Bessie was a few months younger than Jack. She was very attractive, slender and athletic, with blue-black hair and hazel eyes. Jack admired her independence and self-sufficiency. At business school and later on her own, she had mastered mathematics and made her living tutoring students who hadn't. Being an excellent typist, and good organizer, she was constantly helping him with his work.

There was little money in the old Klondike poke he carried, but success was now just a matter of

Jack and Bessie begin their honeymoon by bicycle.

1130 East Fifteenth Street, East Oakland.
Jack and Bessie's first home. Joan, their first daughter,
was born here on January 15, 1901.

time. Because the little bungalow was much too small for his family, he rented a large, spacious seven-room home a few blocks away at 1130 East Fifteenth Street. One night as Bessie was helping Eliza and Flora put up curtains, Jack decided he might as well add the joys of a wife to his family and impulsively asked Bessie to marry him. The following Saturday morning they were married at her home. Flora was crestfallen—her dream of being the hostess of Jack's home evaporated with the marriage and lowered her to the status of an unappreciated guest.

Jack had made it clear to Bessie that he did not love her, but that he liked her enough to make a successful marriage. She was still trying to recover from the death of her fiancé, Fred Jacobs, whose body had been returned for burial just a month before. Bessie was sure that in a short time they would be in love with one another. She was half correct. She fell deeply in love with him, but he never was able to reciprocate.

Charmian in 1900

Charmian Kittredge about 1900

The marriage was doomed from the beginning. Jack was gregarious to a fault; Bessie abhorred company. Jack loved humor and practical jokes, while Bessie had no humor at all. She was an excellent housekeeper and secretary, but an exceptionally poor cook. Her Victorian prudery ruined their love life. It was inevitable that Jack would seek more congenial company elsewhere, which inflamed her jealousy and destroyed their companionship.

A lot of heartache would have been avoided had Jack only realized that Charmian was the ideal woman for him. When Ninetta Eames interviewed him for the *Overland Monthly* in January she brought along her foster-daughter, Charmian Kittredge. Neither Jack nor Charmian was much impressed with the other, but they did have a luncheon date for April 7—a date Jack had to break, explaining that he had had a change of plans and was getting married that day. Although Charmian was destined to play an extremely strong role in the life of Jack London, neither would have believed it at their first meeting.

April 7, the day of his marriage, saw the publication of his first book, *The Son of the Wolf.* It was so well received that in a short time Jack was hailed as the "Kipling of the North"—a tribute he loved, since Kipling had always been his hero. This tribute thrilled him as much as the one George Bernard Shaw paid him in an interview for the *Dallas Times-Herald* in 1905, when Shaw told the reporter, "If you wish to compliment me, call me the Jack London of the British Isles."

In *John Barleycorn* Jack wrote:

Critics have complained about the swift education one of my characters, Martin Eden, achieved. In three years, from a sailor with a common school education, I made a successful writer of him. The critics say this is impossible. Yet I was Martin Eden. At the end of three working years, two of which were spent in high school and the university and one spent at writing, and all three in studying immensely and intensely, I was publishing stories in magazines such as the *Atlantic Monthly,* was correcting proofs of my first book (issued by Houghton, Mifflin Co.), was selling sociological articles to *Cosmopolitan* and *McClures,* had declined an associate editorship proferred me by telegraph from New York City [by John Brisben Walker of *Cosmopolitan*] and was getting ready to marry.

Jack's arithmetic was a little off. His was not quite the record he gave to Martin Eden. He entered high school in 1895 and was getting ready to marry in April of 1900—closer to five and a third years—but it was still a fantastic success story matched by few.

The Son of the Wolf and his early work were indicative of what was to follow. Because Jack had been forced by his home environment and study to question the religious structures of his day, his stories were shot through with valid criticisms of the organized churches and with underlying propaganda for the socialist cause. There would always be a few contradictions and inconsistencies to the reader who was unfamiliar with London's own unorthodox beliefs. Sometimes he was more mystical than materialist, and his dualism and individualism sometimes warred against his monism and socialism. It is these inconsistencies that have confused his critics, but not Jack, for consistency was never a worry for him.

Nineteen hundred was a year of work and study. He was always studying. Every night he spent the last several hours in bed with his books. He was interested in all knowledge. His principle studies at this time were scientific, sociological, and ethical, but he gave equal time to his study of literature.

Late in February *McClure's* paid three hundred dollars for "The Man with the Gash," "The God of His Fathers," and "The Question of the Maximum." It was the best pay he had ever received—twenty dollars per thousand words. The three hundred dollars went to pay past bills, leaving him wondering where he could find enough money to pay his moving expenses.

The new home on Fifteenth Street was bedlam until Jack realized that there was no way his mother could live amicably with another woman in the house. Accordingly, he moved Flora into a little house a block behind them. The ensuing peace was well worth the added expense. Bessie, with her major burden lifted, was like a new person until Jack began his famous "Wednesday Nights," when he set aside the afternoon and evening for any of his friends to come by and share his board. The afternoons were given to games and frolic, evenings to whim. At times Jack would read his newest material to the guests. Other nights would be devoted to card playing or to a "rap" session. It was good clean fun, and none of the participants ever forgot their Wednesday evenings at Jack's house.

These Wednesday Nights added to an already strained budget. In an attempt to get it back in balance, Jack proposed a novel to S. S. McClure, *A Daughter of the Snows.* McClure accepted and advanced him $125 per month until the book was finished. Now, with his worst financial problems solved, he could write at a more leisurely pace. Each morning was devoted to his one-thousand-word stint, leaving the rest of the day for study.

However, even with the steady $125 each month Jack still had to write a few potboilers to keep pace with ever mounting bills. With two households to support and an occasional helping hand to old friends, he was careful to maintain good relations with Traeger's Loan Office.

Jack and Bessie still loved their biking trips. In a letter to Ida Meacham Strobridge in June he said:

Ever bike? Now that's something that makes life worth living! I take exercise every afternoon that way. O, to just grip your handle bars, and lay down to it (lie doesn't hit it at all), and go ripping and tearing through streets and road, over railroad tracks and bridges, threading crowds, avoiding collisions, at twenty miles or more an hour, and wondering all the time when you're going to smash up. Well, now, that's something. And then home again after three hours of it, into the tub, rub down well, then into a soft shirt, and down to the dinner table, with the evening paper and a cigarette in prospect— and then to think that tomorrow I can do it all over again!

By fall Jack and Bessie were quite happy together. She had announced the coming arrival of a baby around the beginning of the new year. Jack's dream of fatherhood was to become reality, and all was well with his world. The novel was progressing and there was no reason to be unhappy. To add to his sense of well-being, now that they were under separate roofs Flora and Bessie were becoming good friends, especially with a grandchild in the offing.

Bessie London

Jack in a relaxing mood

From their first meeting at a socialist lecture given by Austin Lewis at the old Turk Street Temple in San Francisco early in December of 1899, Jack and Anna Strunsky carried on a correspondence about love, world economics, and socialism.

Anna was two years younger than Jack and a student at Stanford University. In 1897 Jack was known as the "boy socialist" of Oakland, and Anna was called the "girl socialist" of San Francisco, so it is probable that they knew of each other or might even have met before the Austin Lewis lecture.

Anna was born in Babinotz, Russia, on March 21, 1878. With her parents, radicals in old Russia, she came to San Francisco, where she was educated. She was vitally interested in social problems, literature, and the labor movement.

She had the high cheekbones of her Tartar ancestors; her skin was dark and her lustrous black hair and eyes were distinctly Oriental. Jack thought she was a beautiful genius.

Anna and her family lived in the home of her brother, Dr. Max Strunsky. She and her sister Rose were members of a radical group of young California writers and artists that included Jack London, Jim Whitaker, George Sterling, and others. The Strunsky sisters were leaders of the intelligentsia that flourished in San Francisco at the turn of the century.

Jack and Anna were regular participants in the activities of the Bay Area socialists. They were very good friends, and at first did not think of each other romantically. Theirs was an affair of two highly intellectual minds with similar ideas and dreams. Anna Strunsky was a powerful influence in the life of Jack London. Except for a short period in 1902 when Jack fell in love with her, they were only very close friends. Anna was never in love with Jack, but always had the deepest respect for him.

By late 1900 their letters about the nature of love evolved into their collaboration on *The Kempton-Wace Letters*. Jack, as Herbert Wace, would discuss love from the biological point of view; and Anna, as Dane Kempton, would take the idealistic and emotional viewpoint. *The Kempton-Wace Letters* were published in 1903, and they constitute one of the most interesting and curious books in the whole literature of love. The book was brilliant, superbly youthful and audacious for its time, and it still reads well today.

It is unlikely that anybody knew the real Jack London of that period better than Anna. A portion of her "Memories of Jack London" published in *The Bowery News* in 1960 gives us a glimpse of what she thought:

"Take me this way: a stray guest, a bird of passage splashing with salt-rimed wings through a brief moment of your life—a rude and blundering bird, used to large airs and great spaces, unaccustomed to the amenities of confined existence," so he wrote in a letter to me dated Oakland, California, December 21, 1899, in the twenty-fourth year of his life. A bird of passage, splashing with salt-rimed wings not only through my life but through life itself, and not for a brief moment but for eternity.

For who shall say when that of wonder and beauty which was Jack London will pass from the earth? Who that ever knew him can forget him, and how will life ever forget one who was so indissolubly a part of her? He was youth, adventure, romance. He was a poet and a thinker. He had a genius for friendship. He loved greatly and was greatly loved.

But how to fix in words that quality of personality that made him different from everyone else in the world? How to convey an idea of his magnetism and the poetic quality of his nature? He came out of the abyss in which millions of his generation and the generations preceding him throughout time have been hopelessly lost. He rose out of the abyss and he escaped from the abyss to become as large as the race and to be identified with the forces that shape the future of mankind.

His standard of life was high. He for one would have the happiness of power, of genius, of love and the vast comforts and ease of wealth. Napoleon and Nietzsche had a part in him, but his Nietzschean philosophy became transmuted into Socialism and it was by the force of his Napoleonic temperament that he conceived the idea of an incredible success, and had the will to obtain it.

Such colossal energy, and yet he could not trust himself! He lived by rule. Law, Order and Restraint was the creed of this vital, passionate youth. His stint was a thousand words a day

Anna Strunsky

Cause; to "show them" that Socialists were not derelicts and failures had certain propaganda value. So he succeeded—became a kind of Napoleon of the pen.

Late in 1900 Anna's Napoleon of the Pen was still struggling for his own literary style. He wrote to Elwyn Hoffman, "In my collection of tales there are about one hundred polysyllable words I would like to be able to strike out; though of course at the time they suited me immensely."

He was also wrestling with photography. "I have just recently invested in a camera, and I can't do any work at all with it, and I can't find the time to learn." However, he did find the time and his photographic know-how reached professional status by the time he needed the expertise to illustrate his book on the English slums in 1902. And his photographic record of the Russo-Japanese War was a credit to the finest in photojournalism. No other author before or since left a better photographic history of himself than did Jack in nearly one hundred photograph albums.

Early in his career he had laboriously rewritten much of Rudyard Kipling's work in longhand to capture some of his style. In a letter to Elwyn Hoffman on October 27, 1900, he acknowledged his indebtedness: "As for myself, there is no end of Kipling in my work. I have even quoted him. I would never have possibly written anywhere near the way I did had Kipling never been. True, true, every bit of it. And if several other men had never existed, Kipling would never have written as he did."

The year ended on a low note for Jack. His self-esteem and superb confidence were suffering because of *A Daughter of the Snows*. His first novel was a failure, but doggedly he finished it. For one thing, he needed the monthly advance, and, besides, it was already sold. Because he lacked experience with a novel, he attempted to compensate by squandering enough material on it for a dozen novels, which aggravated his problem. He was frustrated and sick at heart. Second thoughts about his scientific marriage, brought on by Bessie's cold nature, added to his mental discomfort. Anna's letters made marriage between "lovers" more appealing every time she wrote. He wondered if he were falling in love with her.

As the months rolled on, he spent more and more time with her as they worked on *The Kempton-Wace*

revised and typed. He allowed himself only four and one-half hours of sleep and began his work regularly at dawn for years.

The nights were devoted to extensive reading of science, history and sociology. He called it getting his scientific basis. One day a week he devoted to the work of a struggling friend [Jim Whitaker]. For recreation he boxed and fenced and swam—he was a great swimmer. He sailed too and spent much time flying kites, of which he had a large collection.

Sincerity was the greatest trait of his character. He never made pretensions and he built neither his works nor his life on sophism and evasions. If literature was marketable and had a price and he put the products of his brain for sale, then he could not stoop to pretend that he was following art for art's sake and was not writing for money.

To know him was immediately to receive an accelerated enthusiasm for everybody.

He was a Socialist, but he wanted to beat the Capitalist at his own game. To succeed in doing this, he thought, was in itself a service to the

Letters. Jack at first began his letters "Dear Miss Strunsky." Later he started them "Dear Anna" and then "Dear You" and finally "Dear dear you." Although he was married to a good wife, he found Bessie could never be a "mate-woman." Maybe Anna would be. But she was not so inclined. She considered Jack to be something extra special, but realized the impossibility of a marital relationship.

After the publication of *The Son of the Wolf,* the newspapers and magazines were calling Jack "A New Kipling," "Another Bret Harte," and so on. They were much less complimentary to *A Daughter of the Snows.*

McClure was thoroughly disappointed with the novel; so was Jack. One aspect of it that proved unpopular was its blatant Anglo-Saxon chauvinism. Another of its weaknesses was its improbable heroine. All through his career Jack would be accused of poor female character portrayal. The truth was that he was one of the few who portrayed the nontypical women of his time. Contemporary writers either put their women on a pedestal or in front of a hot kitchen stove. There was seldom any middle ground. Jack was ahead of his time in liberating women when he introduced Frona Welse in his first novel. She was too unconventional and free for that period. She was durable and different. The daughter of a Yukon trader, with a penchant for boxing and the outdoors, was unbelievable except to those who had met women like her in the Yukon. Jack put real people in his stories and the mood was their mood, the setting was their setting—they had to be real. Yet, because Frona was not the kind of woman the average professor knew, she was called "unreal." In a sense she was, but not to the extremes claimed by the critics. Jack added a few too many of his own beliefs to his heroine's character, so she was unacceptable to an age that was just emerging from Victorianism. Could she have actually chinned herself twenty times? Nobody could know the answer to that question unless they had met the real person upon whom the fictional Frona was based, as Jack had.

The fact that he expected a poor reception for his first novel didn't make him feel any better when it actually happened. His pessimism at this time is reflected in "The Law of Life," a short story that shows man trapped in a meaningless, mechanical existence with death his only destiny. This story is unlike most of his work, which stressed the will to live and man's enthusiastic victory over his environment, whether it be in the ghettoes of Oakland, the frozen wilds of the Klondike, or the depressing, debilitating heat of the South Seas.

Despite its pessimism, "The Law of Life" is an excellent story and exhibits solid craftsmanship based on Jack's use of the frame story. In one of the most thorough critiques of his own work, he told Cloudesley about it:

It is short, applies the particular to the universal, deals with a lonely death, of an old man, in which beasts consummate the tragedy. My man is an old Indian, abandoned in the snow by his tribe because he cannot keep up. He has a little fire, a few sticks of wood, the frost and silence about him. He is blind. How do I approach the event? What point of view do I take? Why, the old Indian's, of course. It opens up with him sitting by his little fire, listening to his tribesmen breaking camp, harnessing dogs, and departing. The reader listens with him to every familiar sound; hears the last draw away; feels the silence settle down. The old man wanders back into his past; the reader wanders with him—thus is the whole theme exploited through the soul of the Indian. Down to the consummation, when the wolves draw in upon him in a circle. Don't you see, nothing, even the moralizing and generalizing, is done, save through him, in expressions of his experience.

Jack had burned another bridge behind him when he turned down a lucrative editor's job with *Cosmopolitan* magazine, indicating that he was satisfied with the progress of his career. Fame was actually coming faster than he had hoped for, but he cared little for it except that it meant a better market for his stories. Fame demanded a better product, however, and he wasn't sure he was ready yet. He would have to develop better style, especially with novels, and he must also give himself a continually improved philosophy of life and both must be nurtured by a never ending study of as many branches of knowledge as possible. As 1900 drew to a close, Jack pulled himself together and vowed that 1901 would be even better.

Being three thousand dollars in debt, Jack started 1901 with a lot of determination but full of worries and disappointment. The birth of his daughter Joan on January 15 brought mixed emotions and added responsibility and expense. The fact that his firstborn was a girl didn't bother him too much. What did bother him was that a child tied him more tightly into a marriage he was not too happy about. Financial problems bothered him throughout the year. His entire income for the year from literary sources only amounted to $2,650.80 (including advances)—not an auspicious sum for a person supporting two households, and in debt by more than his yearly income.

Jack and his families continued to live on the $125-a-month income from McClure until October 1, when McClure terminated the agreement because he had lost faith in Jack's future as a writer. Everything he sent to McClure, including his only book published in 1901, *The God of His Fathers,* brought no income. Every nickel of royalty was retained by McClure to pay off advances already made.

The Son of the Wolf was still receiving excellent reviews in 1901. A typical review of this book was written in December of 1900 by the Boston *Beacon:*

"The impression gains ground that Jack London is a coming author, that it is merely a matter of a few years when he will be recognized as a writer as forceful as Kipling, as finished and discerning as Lafcadio Hearn"; and that "what Kipling has done for India, and Lafcadio Hearn for Japan, Jack London has done for the Arctic." So writes Howard V. Sutherland in Impressions of San Francisco, in taking up for the second time London's The Son of the Wolf. "It is only a matter of time," he concludes, "when he will take his place among the few writers of really international reputation."

Jack was also getting more and more involved in local socialist work. The party was beginning to exploit his fame as much as capitalists had exploited his brawn in earlier years, but this was different. It was a cause in which he was willing to be exploited. Realizing that his burgeoning literary reputation would draw a lot of publicity, the socialists asked him to run for Mayor of Oakland on their ticket. Since there wasn't a possible chance for election, Jack agreed to let his name be used. As predicted, the press gave a lot of space to Jack London—both good and bad. *The Evening Post* in San Francisco on January 26, 1901, printed:

Jack London (The Son of the Wolf) is announced as a candidate for Mayor of Oakland on the ticket of the Social Democrats. I don't know what a Social Democrat is, but if it is anything like some of Jack London's stories, it must be something awful. I understand that as soon as

Joan learns how to blow out her daddy's match.

Jack London is elected Mayor of Oakland by the Social Democrats the name of the place will be changed. The Social Democrats, however, have not yet decided whether they will call it London or Jacktown.

In the fall elections he received only 245 votes, but the party had achieved its purpose of getting its name before the voters. The election did nothing for Jack except close forever most of the opportunities he might have had in social circles other than those of his socialist friends. The Oakland social set wanted no part of socialists, and with all the publicity of the election everybody knew that Jack was still one of them.

Social life had been denied to him in his early years, and when he had been invited to the houses of prominent people, he went to broaden his experience and because he believed it a complement to his efforts as an author. He thought that social acceptance was one of the things he was fighting for when he sought fame and success. Surely in the upper-class homes he would find interesting people and scintillating conversation, since they had had all the advantages of education and culture. He was soon disillusioned by the discovery that he was merely being used as a curiosity piece for the amusement of guests or to satisfy the ego of his hostess. He didn't find these people interesting either, and their talk was usually shallow and dull. He decided that he had learned all that was necessary from such experiences and cut them completely out of the rest of his life.

Jack had studied Karl Marx in depth and had recommended his *Capital* for several years. The book had been constantly recommended to the readers of most socialist papers since its translation and publication into English by Otto Weydemeyer in 1877. A few years earlier Jack's socialist friends were amused and gave Jack a lot of good-natured kidding when a local newspaper made a glaring typographical error in printing a report that Jack recommended the reading of "Carl Marks' *Capital.*" A letter to Cloudesley John in February of 1901 reveals an astute understanding of Marx's theories that escaped most socialist thinkers:

I should like to have socialism; yet I know that socialism is not the very next step; I know that capitalism must live its life first, that the world must be exploited to the utmost first; that first must intervene a struggle for life among the na-

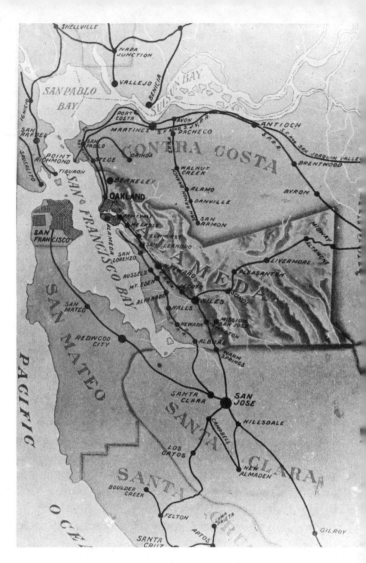

The area around San Francisco Bay about 1900. From 1903 until his death, Jack often sailed in the Suisun Bay area.

tions, severer, intenser, more widespread than ever before. I should much more prefer to wake tomorrow in a smoothly-running socialist state; but I know I shall not; I know it cannot come that way. I know that the child must go through the child's sicknesses ere it becomes a man. So, always remember that I speak of things that are; not of the things that should be.

Jack was still helping Whitaker, both financially and in getting his work sold, and Jim was still teaching Jack how to box and fence. They spent many happy hours together discussing socialism, philosophy, and literature. Both had lived unusual lives. Jack was spellbound as Jim told him of his experiences in the British Army and in the wilderness of Manitoba. Jack especially enjoyed the Indian tales but he never used them for plots, leaving them for his friend to exploit. Jack couln't get over the nerve of his friend when with seven children to support, Jim threw caution to the winds and embarked on a totally new career. It hadn't been easy for Whitaker over the past months. He had jumped into print in a very short time, but was still struggling to get enough stories sold to pay his bills. But, Jack noted with satisfaction and admiration, Jim had the courage and determination to see it through.

VILLA LA CAPRICCIOSO

Early spring rains turned the London home on Fifteenth Street into a lakeside villa—except that all the water was in the basement and in the yard. They had to move immediately. Fortunately Jack's sculptor friend, Felix Peano, had an ornate, pseudo-Italian villa about a block away from Lake Merritt. Peano was short on cash for groceries, so he offered to share his home, provided the Londons would supply the food and cooking.

Jack had enough romance in his soul to love the wild, flamboyant architecture of Villa La Capriccioso, but Bessie, having no romantic inclinations, hated it—all she saw were the tiny doorways, the odd arrangement of rooms, and the numerous narrow winding staircases. She felt as though she were living in a cemetery salesman's showroom—every place she turned she bumped into one of Peano's sculptural creations.

Bessie's hatred of Jack's Wednesday open houses grew stronger, and Jack's desire for them increased proportionately. It seemed to Bessie that all of Jack's friends and his friends' friends wanted to see the inside of that crazy house. She found it impossible to stretch the money enough for this entertainment, but somewhere or somehow Jack always managed to come up with the money, so on they went.

During this stay with Peano at 1062 First Avenue, *A Daughter of the Snows* was completed to the satisfaction of neither McClure nor Jack. Believing that Jack could deliver better material, McClure continued to send advances until October, at which time, by mutual consent, they severed relations.

Throughout 1901 Jack gave lectures on "War," "Women's Suffrage," "What the Community Loses by the Competitive System," "Competitive Waste," "The Tramp," "Land of Democracy," and "Wanted: A New Law of Development." The highlight of the lectures was his invitation to speak on "An Odyssey of the North" in the chapel at Stanford University.

From June 14 through July 6 Jack was the fea-

La Capriccioso. Jack, Bessie, and Joan lived here for several months in 1901 with Jack's sculptor friend, Felix Peano. It was located at 1602 First Avenue, almost on the shore of Lake Merritt.

Jack plays the part of the "Irresistible Villain" in the Camp Reverie play,
Manitoba Jim's Revenge

Jack during an outdoor lecture at Camp Reverie in June of 1901

Jack, Jim Whitaker, and others put on the play Manitoba Jim's Revenge *for the campers at Camp Reverie in June 1901.*

tured lecturer for the Camp Reverie Association in Forestville, Sonoma County. The camp, modeled after Brook Farm, was located in a grove of stately redwoods on the Russian River, about twelve miles northwest of Santa Rosa. While Jack was busy lecturing, his daughter Joan was fully occupied as camp mascot.

Shortly before his lecture/vacation at Camp Reverie, the *San Francisco Examiner* commissioned him to report on the Schutzenfest shooting competition in Oakland and to write several special articles for their Sunday supplement section. The Saturday morning *Examiner,* July 13, 1901, printed:

Jack London, the story writer, the young man who has made fame for himself and California in the world of letters, will write a description of the opening of the third great national Bundes shooting festival. He will watch the Sunday morning parade in this city and will then go to Shell Mound Park to witness the lining up at the butts of the men of steady nerves, iron hand, and keen sight. Then he will write in his own graphic style what he has seen.

The ten daily Schutzenfest articles netted him a total of two hundred dollars. The June 13 article "Victory Over War and Wave: Home the *Oregon* Comes Again" paid forty dollars. An article published June 16, "Washoe Indians Resolve to be White Men" brought twenty-five dollars, while his July 21 feature, "Girl Who Crossed Swords with a Burglar," earned him another twenty-five dollars. The total income from this summer series was only two hundred ninety dollars, but the publicity was worth far more. The Sunday supplements were full page and very well illustrated—excellent exposure for any young writer seeking a reputation.

Toward the end of the summer Jack and Anna, working steadily together, had *The Kempton-Wace Letters* over half-completed. He was also working on *Children of the Frost,* a book about the Indians of the Northland. There was no end of work, study, and worry about finance. Because the La Capriccioso arrangements failed, Jack was faced with a major decision in September. Financially speaking, he should have moved back to a low-rent district in East Oakland, but he decided that his career would

be enhanced by a more prosperous address. He settled his family in a fine home in the lower foothills above Oakland at 56 Bayo Vista, a fashionable new district. A check for one hundred dollars on September 15 from *Ainslees* for "Keesh, the Son of Keesh" helped pay the moving bills.

By this time Jack was hoping to get away from the Klondike as story material, but this seemed to be the only material that sold. However, he had already panned all the stories he could from the bed rock of his own memory, and began to write to Klondike friends for plot ideas. He also began surveying old newspaper articles about the gold rush, and read books about it, hoping to strike another Bonanza. It was as hard work as digging through the frozen ground at Henderson Creek. In November he wrote to Johns, "A man does one thing in a passable manner and the dear public insists on his continuing to do it to the end of his days." In December he wrote again, "Am hammering away in seclusion, trying to get out of Alaska. Guess I'll succeed in accomplishing it in a couple of years."

It was not a banner year, but his work was still selling and his name was becoming better known every month. In December George P. Brett, president of the Macmillan Publishing Company, wrote asking him for material that he could publish in America and England. The part of the letter that warmed Jack's heart and gave him new assurance was Brett's comment that his stories represented the very best work of the kind that had been done in America—high praise from one of the foremost publishers in the world.

In January, answering Brett's request, Jack wrote stating that he had no readable copies of the manuscript for *Children of the Frost,* but explained what he was doing and asked for an advance of a couple of hundred dollars. Brett quickly replied with a contract, the two hundred dollars, and a promise to publish *Children of the Frost* in October of 1902. Jack signed the contract on April 21, 1902, according to which he would get an advance of another three hundred dollars on publication and royalties of 15 percent for the first five thousand sold and 20 percent thereafter. By May 1, 1903 royalties earned for the 2,172 copies sold brought Jack $448.70, leaving him in debt to Macmillan for $11.30.

Jack had become friendly with George Sterling, later the unofficial poet laureate of San Francisco, who told him that the old Worcester place near him was for rent. After one look, Jack made the necessary arrangements and moved in. He liked the location of his new home, for he could escape from the city, enjoy the comforts of country life, and still be only thirty minutes from the Oakland Estuary. As he put it to Johns:

Am beautifully located in a new house. We have a big living room, every inch of it, floor and ceiling, finished in redwood. We could put the floor space of almost four cottages (the size of the one you can remember) into this one living room alone. The rest of the house is finished in redwood, too, very comfortable. We have also the cutest, snuggest little cottage on the same ground with us, in which live my mother and my nephew. Chicken houses and yards for 500 chickens. Barn for a dozen horses, big pigeon houses, laundry, creamery, etc., etc. A most famous porch, broad and long and cool, a big clump of magnificent pines, flowers and flowers and flowers galore, five acres of ground sold the last time at $2000 per acre, half of ground in bearing orchard and half sprinkled with California pop-pies; we are twenty-four minutes from the door to the heart of Oakland and an hour and five minutes to San Francisco; our nearest neighbor is a block away (and there isn't a vacant lot within a mile), our view commands all of San Francisco Bay for a sweep of thirty or forty miles, and all the opposing shores such as San Francisco, Marin County and Mount Tamalpais (to say nothing of the Golden Gate and the Pacific Ocean)—and all for $35.00 per month. I couldn't buy the place for $15,000. And some day I'll have to be fired out.

In the same letter he said, "Lord, what a stack of hack I'm turning out! Five mouths and ten feet, and sometimes more, so one hustles. I wonder if ever I'll get clear of debt." He never was, except for a short period in 1904, when he returned from the Russo-Japanese War with nearly four thousand dollars in the bank. This condition lasted just a few weeks, but he became a master of deficit spending, and being in debt became a way of life.

The years 1901-1902 were good years. The bungalow was ideal for his needs. It gave him plenty of room to entertain his friends, fly his kites, and do his work. The morning stint of one thousand words was rigidly adhered to, and afternoons were spent

George Sterling, who became Jack's closest and most trusted friend

The Bungalow on Blair Avenue in the Piedmont hills above Oakland

with "the crowd," in study, or in relaxation. The "Wednesdays with Jack" were better than ever. Even Bessie was happy now that Jack was able to provide servants to care for the house.

It was also a good literary year. Sixteen short stories, seven major articles, and three books were published. But financially it was a disaster. He received only a few dollars from his book sales. The rest went to reduce the debt from advances. Other than books, his literary efforts totalled only $1,103.75. Nevertheless, he was holding his own. The year began with an indebtedness of three thousand dollars and he still owed the same amount in August. In addition to books, he submitted fourteen new manuscripts and collected 130 rejection slips during the year.

MATERIALIST MONIST

Jack had been knocking around at his philosophy of life for a long time and finally discovered what he was. "I have at last discovered what I am. I am a materialist monist, and there's damn little satisfaction in it." The monist believes that all phenomena is due to a single underlying substance or causation. They do not believe that the spirit and nature coexist in man.

His home environment of spiritualism had kept him away from organized Christianity, even though one of his heroes was Jesus Christ. ". . . I was born among spiritualists and lived my childhood and boyhood among spiritualists. The result of this close contact was to make an unbeliever of me. I don't know whether Jesus Christ was a myth or not, but taking him just as I find him, just as I read him, I have two heroes—one is Jesus Christ, the other Abraham Lincoln."

During his early years Jack had sought a Christian experience, but lack of dedication and sincerity on the part of the ministers and Christians he met had kept him from it. Much of his work reveals a dislike for organized religion, but he never produced an indictment of Christianity itself. Never having been convinced of the church's claim that Christ was divine, he always called himself an atheist. Interestingly, though, he was an avid Bible scholar and did go to church on occasion. He once classified himself as an agnostic, but usually he held to his atheistic position.

A classic example of Jack's belief in the brotherhood doctrines of Christ is found in *The Iron Heel*, published in 1908. Bishop Morehouse is led out of his self-satisfied lip service to become an active follower of what Jack considered the real mission that Christ called him to—service to his fellow man and especially to the poor.

Jack's life and writings were strangely influenced by an inner war in his own nature—a war in which his materialism represented one force and his deeply spiritual instincts the other. He read the Bible in depth and everything else he could find on the subject, and synthesized every possible argument until he could declare himself the strictest, most inflexible of all materialists. He was a scientific thinker and firm follower of the positivist school, but in everything he did and in much of his writings there is strong evidence of his spiritual and idealistic nature.

An early Arnold Genthe portrait

An interesting episode occurs in *The Sea-Wolf*—a book that was written to discredit the superman concept. Note the unusual passage where Van Weyden watches Wolf Larsen mete out a merciless beating to one of the crew:

In his action I found a complete refutation of Wolf Larsen's materialism. The sailor Johnson was swayed by an idea, by principle, the truth, and sincerity. He was right, he knew he was right, and he was unafraid. He would die for the right if needs be, he would be true to himself, sincere in his own soul and in this was portrayed the victory of the spirit over flesh, the indomitability and moral grandeur of the soul that knows no restriction and rises above time and space and matter with a surety and invincibleness born of nothing less than eternity and immortality.

Why did Jack write passages like the above that refuted the things he claimed to believe? Were they the words of Van Weyden or Jack? The simple answer is that he constantly came to situations with which his materialism and atheism couldn't cope, and he therefore turned to his inner spiritual resources for adequate answers.

In a letter to Anna he stated that he had "an idealism which is an inner sanctuary and which must be resolutely throttled in dealing with my kind, but which remains within the holy of holies, like an oracle, to be cherished always but to be made manifest or be consulted not on every occasion I go to market."

Jack was a thorough student of the Bible and had theological insights deeper than many theologians of his day. We know this because he left for posterity one of the finest studies of the Crucifixion of Christ in the seventeenth chapter of *The Star Rover*. The setting is in the household of Pontius Pilate. Ragnar Lodbrog, in command of a Roman legion, is in love with Miriam, a friend of Pilate's wife. Miriam is a follower of the Christ and begs Ragnar to save Him from the Crucifixion:

"Pilate has weakened. He is going to crucify Him," Miriam said. "But there is time. Your own men are ready. Ride with them. Only a centurion and a handful of soldiers are with Him. They have not started. As soon as they do start, follow. They must not reach Golgotha. But wait until they are outside the city wall, then countermand the order. Take an extra horse for Him to ride. The rest is easy. Ride away into Syria with Him, or into Idumaea, or anywhere so long as He is saved."

After much more pleading by Miriam, Lodbrog replies:

"Then who am I to make liars of the prophets? To make of the Messiah a false Messiah? Is the prophecy of your people so feeble a thing that I, a stupid stranger, a yellow northling in the Roman harness, can give the lie to prophecy and compel to be unfulfilled the very thing willed by the gods and foretold by the wise men?"

Simple theology? Yes! But it has been the simple things that have been the major stumbling blocks to theologians down the centuries. Jack's stories are replete with biblical phrases, and Christian ideals are often expounded. He said he was a materialist monist and an atheist, but sometimes the things he said and did refuted what he wrote.

THE PEOPLE OF THE ABYSS

On July 21, 1902, Jack was still three thousand dollars in debt, when the American Press Association in New York asked him to go to South Africa. The Boer War had ended seven weeks before with the signing of articles of peace at Pretoria, and the APA wanted him to interview General DeWitt and Botha and other famed officers. Before his arrival in New York, the newspapers reported that most of the leaders had left for Capetown en route to Europe, so Jack's commission was cancelled. With his plans made for the trip and his ticket in his pocket, he came up with a new idea—he would go into the East End of London and write a book about the conditions there. On arrival in New York, he broached the subject to his publishers, and Brett gave him a green light for the project.

While in New York, Jack stayed at the Harvard Club and left for Liverpool July 30 on the R.M.S.

A workhouse in the East End of London

Majestic. The next day he wrote to Anna about his plans to view the Coronation on August 9 with the East Enders.

He arranged for a room, probably with Johnny Upright, a veteran of thirty years with the London detectives, on Dempsey Street near Commercial. On August 23 he was using the address, 89 Dempsey Street, Stepney. Then he swapped his clothes for a used outfit that would be in keeping with his new identity of a stranded American sailor and merged into the life of the East Enders. He lived with them, went from workhouse to workhouse with them, and shared their miserable, hungry, hopeless lives.

His East End report concentrated on the forgotten ones who could no longer meet the requirements of employers and were thrown into a human scrap heap. There were many merchants and workers in the East End who were able to eke out a precarious, but to them satisfactory, existence. The conditions he found here were about the same as in the slums of New York, and both were inexcusable in cities as prosperous as these. Once again he saw a picture of exploitation where a society refused to provide for those of its members who could no longer contribute—people who had never been able to save money for their old age on their meager

wages. He also found many other unfortunates who were willing to work but simply could find no jobs.

In late August Jack wrote, ". . . out all night with homeless ones, walking the streets in the bitter rain, drenched to the skin, wondering when dawn would come. Sunday I spent with the homeless ones in the fierce struggle for something to eat. I returned to my rooms Sunday evening, after thirty-six hours continuous work and short one night's sleep."

On several occasions he "Carried the Banner" with them. They were never allowed to sleep in the park, on benches along the Thames, or in the streets during the night. They just walked and walked until dawn, when they were allowed to sleep in areas where they wouldn't be seen. In this way the more prosperous residents of London wouldn't be bothered. All this was allowed to occur, according to Jack, in the year of our Lord 1902, in the heart of the greatest, wealthiest, and most powerful empire the world had ever seen.

A typical night: " 'Carried the Banner' all night. I did not sleep in Green Park—heard of a place on Surrey side of Thames where Salvation Army gave breakfast to unwashed (The Peg). A weary walk: Down St. James Street—along Pall Mall—past Trafalgar Square to the Strand—across the Waterloo Bridge to Surrey side—cut across to Blackfriar's

Waiting for food at the Salvation Army Workhouse in the East End of London

A postcard sent to Bessie and Joan while researching The People of the Abyss

Bert went to Kent with Jack to pick hops.

The other side of the postcard sent to Bessie and Joan from London

Dear Bess & Joan:

And how do you like Daddy now? Would you gi' me a bit o' juml if I battered your back door?

With all sorts of love —

Jack.

East London,
August 31, 1902

Road and came out near the Surrey Theatre—to Salvation [Army] barracks."

In his research Jack discovered that these people who lived in the slums did so not by choice and not through laziness, but because of old age, disease, or accidents that had reduced their labor value. Escape from the slums was next to impossible, for their tiny wages did not permit them to live elsewhere. They had no resources, no money, and no strength left. Slow starvation was the common end.

In eighty-six days he gathered an enormous amount of material, read hundreds of books and thousands of pamphlets, newspapers, and Parliamentary reports, composed his book, typed it all out, took two-thirds of the photographs with his own camera, took a short vacation in France, Germany, Italy, and other points in Europe, and landed in New York City with the complete manuscript of *The People of the Abyss* in his suitcase.

The book is one of the finest sociological works ever done in this country. London said he put more

Taken while in the East End of London, 1902

of his heart into this book than any other on his long shelf. He lived with the people and wrote the story as it was. No preaching! No suggestions for a cure! He simply wrote the facts as he saw them in such a descriptive way that no authority could ever say that he did not know the conditions of the "submerged tenth" in the East End of London.

Jack London has been criticized for failing to tell the true story of the London slums, but two years after Jack's visit to England the Archbishop of Canterbury, the highest personage in Great Britain next to the Royal Family, with a seat in the House of Lords, made a tour of the slums of New York with Booker T. Washington and Jacob A. Riis. The Archbishop stated to the press, "Amazing! I am astonished at it all. The slums of New York are not nearly so bad as the slums of London and the mean streets not so mean as the East End of our great English city."

When Jack read the above statement, he doubtlessly wondered why the Archbishop didn't use part of his seventy-five-thousand-dollar-a-year salary to alleviate some of the suffering in the East End. It is probable that Bishop Morehouse in *The Iron Heel* was inspired by this incident.

In George Wharton James's copy of *The People of the Abyss,* Jack wrote, "God's still in his heaven, but all's not well with the world. Read here some of the reasons of my socialism, and some of my socialism. Walk with me here, among the creatures damned by men and then wonder not that I sign myself, Yours for the Revolution."

Among some of Jack's notes in the Huntington Library is this one that reveals a compassion for the poor unfortunates who had been caught in a trap not of their own making and the society that let it happen: "Anyway, if I were God one hour, I'd blot out all London and its 6,000,000 people, as Sodom and Gomorrah were blotted out, and look upon my work and call it good." This is an extremely strong statement for one who always admired and identified with the British Empire.

Arriving in New York City on November 4, Jack rushed to borrow one hundred fifty dollars from Brett at Macmillan to get home. On the train heading West his thoughts were of home and his new daugther, Bess, born on October 20 while he was in Europe. During his time in London he had written his first love letter to Bessie and was determined to make a success of their marriage.

Jack returned to the Bungalow, where he and Bessie both worked diligently at making a home for their two daughters. The Wednesday nights were better than ever as he shared his recent experiences in England and Europe with the crowd.

A few days after his return he wrote to Brett explaining that he wanted to move out of the Northland and write several books. If Brett would advance him one hundred fifty dollars per month, he could complete *Tales of the Fish Patrol,* a new collection of Klondike stories *(The Faith of Men), The Kempton-Wace Letters, The Flight of the Duchess* (never written), and *The Mercy of the Sea* (title changed to *The Sea-Wolf).*

A telegram of acceptance early in December enabled him to forget his major financial worries. This, coupled with his recent adventures abroad, let him settle down and relax. Before starting on his "big work," Jack decided to get something out of his system. Being an animal lover, he had felt guilty over his story "Diable—A Dog" (later changed to "Bâtard" when collected in *Faith of Men)* in which he had portrayed a dog as a vicious beast, and decided to write one that would make the dog a worthy creature. He planned about four thousand words, but it got away from him and ran to over thirty-two thousand words.

On January 26, 1903, he submitted the completed manuscript of *The Call of the Wild* to the *Saturday Evening Post.* On February 12 the editor agreed to purchase the story if he would cut it by five thousand words, and they asked him to set his price. Jack agreed to shorten it and set the price at three cents a word. On March 3 he received a check for seven hundred and fifty dollars. Twenty-two days later Macmillan bought the book rights for two thousand dollars with a promise to give it extensive advertising. At the time it seemed a very sensible thing to do. His previous books had not hit the best seller lists, and neither he nor Brett had any idea that *The Call of the Wild* would do much better. If Jack had known at the time that this book would become a classic in American literature, and that royalties from it would have made him wealthy, he would have bargained differently. Yet, without the extensive promotional program, it could have easily become just another dog book.

The answer will never be known, but Jack never regretted his decision, feeling that the extra promotion by Macmillan had been a major factor in its success.

The book was a passport to instant world acclaim. It not only became a classic, but it also opened a new era of literature. Mush was out, and courageous, raw, red-blooded life was in. *The Call of the Wild* proved that realism was what the new generation wanted. The reviewers and critics had mixed emotions—some called it "just another dog story," while others acclaimed it as "the best dog story ever written."

The book has never been out of print during the last seventy-five years, and critics still rave about it. A few years ago Carl Sandburg said, *"The Call of the Wild* is the greatest dog story ever written and is at the same time a study of one of the most curious and profound motives that play hide-and-seek in the human soul."

The book is a significant philosophical novel, and is a human allegory concealed within the dog's life and death struggle to adapt to a hostile environment. The allegory was purely unintentional but not accidental. London's experience with the people in the slums of England set him thinking of the contrast between them and the clean, beautiful, but primitive world of the North. These thoughts, coupled with the memories of his own background and his superb philosophical knowledge, made the allegory inevitable. It was a book that wrote itself. Jack's unusual power of observation and his unsurpassed ability to describe what he saw made him one of America's leading storytellers. When all of these things are added to his belief in adaptation as the only means of survival, it is easier to understand the phenomenal success of *The Call of the Wild.*

Andrew Flink, in his *"The Call of the Wild*—Jack London's Catharsis," has provided some interesting insights into the book. He feels that "In Jack London's life his sensitivity was assailed by two major events, the rejection of fatherhood by Chaney and the experience of the Erie County Penitentiary, both of which seemed to be highly traumatic for him. The Erie County experience, shock that it was, became the turning point of his life . . . steering his

Marshall and Louis Bond's cabin in Dawson City. Jack's tent was pitched next to this cabin during his short stay there. The Bonds' dog Jack (Buck in The Call of the Wild) *is at the left.*

course to education and ultimately to writing." Flink's article goes on to point out the many similarities in *The Call of the Wild* and the life of London. One example he used was a quote from *The Road:*

I was forced to toil hard on a diet of bread and water, and to march the shameful lock-step with armed guards over me and all for what? What had I done? What crime had I committed against the good citizens of Niagara Falls that all this vengeance should be wreaked upon me? I had not even violated their "sleeping-out" ordinance. I had slept outside their jurisdiction in the country that night. I had not even begged for a meal, or bartered for a "light piece" on their streets. All I had done was to walk along their sidewalk and gaze at their picayune waterfall and what crime was there in that?

...I wanted to send for a lawyer. The guard laughed at me. So did the other guards. I really was incommunicado.

Buck was equally confused in *The Call of the Wild:*

There he lay for the remainder of the weary night, nursing his wrath and wounded pride. He did not understand what it all meant. What did they want of him, these strange men? Why were they keeping him pent up in this narrow crate? He did not know why, but he felt oppressed by a vague sense of impending calamity. Several times during the night he sprang to his feet when the shed door opened expecting to see the Judge,

or the boys at least. But each time it was the bulging face of the saloon keeper that peered in at him by the sickly light of the tallow candle.

Flink continues: "What does this all mean? Maybe nothing! Then again, it might mean that *The Call of the Wild* became the success it did because of the trauma of the Erie County Penitentiary, his nebulous parentage, and the fact that *The Call of the Wild* was an autobiographical purging of the strongest elements of his life up to the point of writing his haunting novella, London's catharsis, as it were. This, too, could be one reason why the story just about wrote itself."

The plot of the story is quite simple, in that Jack sets out to show that Buck's domesticity is merely the result of environment and training. Remove these conditions, and he reverts to the primitive type of his wild ancestors.

The hero of the story is based on Jack, a dog who belonged to the sons of Judge Bond on whose ranch in Santa Clara he had been raised. Marshall and Louis Bond were Jack London's neighbors during his winter visit to Dawson City in the Klondike days. London and Jack became very good friends. For obvious reasons, Jack became Buck in the story.

Buck had never known anything but kindness and affection until he was sold by an unscrupulous servant and transplanted from the gentle California climate to the icy wilderness of the Klondike to join the canine work force of the gold rush. One by one Buck drops the ways he had known and slowly adapts to the law of the wild—the law that says that only the fit can survive. His dormant instincts come to the surface until finally, with the death of John Thornton, his last human friend and master, the one he loves above all humans, he breaks all ties with civilization and joins a pack of wolves. He roams and hunts with the pack until he becomes the leader.

The ending of the book is powerful: "But he is not always alone. When the long winter nights come on and the wolves follow their meat into the lower valleys, he may be seen running at the head of the pack through the pale moonlight or glimmering borealis, leaping gigantic above his fellows, his great throat a-bellow as he sings a song of the younger world, which is the song of the pack."

PLAGIARISM AND SPURIOUS WORKS

Jack was often accused of plagiarism because he had taken a plot from someone's story or had built his story on the same newspaper account someone else had used.

The Call of the Wild brought loud cries of plagiarism from Egerton R. Young, who claimed that too much of Jack's book was taken from his *My Dogs in the Northland.* Jack did not deny the charges that he had used Young's book as one of his sources and claimed to have written his thanks for the material used.

His short story "Love of Life" brought charges of "identity of time and situation" with "Lost in the Land of the Midnight Sun" by Augustus Biddle and J. K. MacDonald. The *New York Sunday World* printed eighteen excerpts side by side with London's work in "deadly parallel" columns.

Stanley Waterloo, author of *The Story of Ab,* claimed London plagiarized his book when he wrote *Before Adam.* Once again "deadly parallels" were published, this time by *The Argonaut.*

In 1901 Frank Harris published "The Bishop of London and Public Morality" in *Candid Friend,* a British magazine. London lifted the article, almost *in toto,* and used it in *The Iron Heel,* where it became "The Bishop's Vision." Jack defended himself against Harris's charges by claiming that he had read the article in question in an American newspaper and believed it to be an authentic speech delivered by the Bishop of London at a public meeting.

Franklin Walker has pointed out that "Moon-Face" is particularly interesting because it uses the same situation employed by Frank Norris in "The Passing of Cock-Eye Blacklock," which appeared in *Century* the same month that London's story appeared in *The Argonaut.* When charges of plagiarism appeared thick and fast, it turned out that both Norris and London had borrowed the idea of having a dog accidentally retrieve a stick of dynamite from a story published in *The Black Cat* a year earlier, and that the author of *that* story had taken it from an even earlier yarn.

Jack never tried to hide anything. He was as candid about his sources as he was about everything else he did. "Identity of time and situation" was bound to crop up. He used articles from newspapers and magazines, yarns told by friends, ideas in books by other authors, and other sources he ran into. He often admitted his difficulty in creating, but considered himself "one hell of an elaborator." "I, in the course of making my living by turning journalism into literature, used material from various sources, which had been collected and narrated by men who made their living by turning the facts of life into journalism. Along comes the space-writer of the *World* who makes his living by turning the doings of other men into sensation. . . .Well, all three of us made our living, and who's got any kick coming."

Jack also bought story plots from Sinclair Lewis, George Sterling, and probably others we know nothing about. His friend Cloudesley Johns also furnished plots and ideas and, no doubt, so did Charmian, Bessie, Finn Frolich, Jim Whitaker, and others of "the crowd." He never tried to hide these sources, believing that his job was to "elaborate" them into saleable fiction.

Jack London's name appears as author or co-author of books, plays, articles, poems, and stories that he did not write. One or two were altered slightly by him in order to make the use of his name somewhat legal. In some cases, like "The First Poet," "Daughters of the Rich," *Gold,* and *The Great Interrogation* (play), he authorized the writers to list him as author or co-author to make their work sell better. On other occasions, due to a shortage of time, he allowed someone else to write the preface, endorsement, or introduction and use his name. Typical is the following case.

In a letter to Sanger & Jordan, April 4, 1914: "I am sending you today, under separate cover, a play entitled *Gold,* written by Herbert Heron, and based upon a short story of mine entitled "A Day's Lodging." ... If you cannot do anything with this play as it stands, how about putting my name to it as joint collaborator with Herbert Heron? Or, how about my putting my name to it as sole author of said play? Still further, supposing such play is too rotten for anything ... how about having somebody make a new play, using my name, or not, as collaborator, and using Herbert Heron's name, or eliminating Herbert Heron's name."

And again, to Osias L. Schwartz regarding a preface for *General Types of Superior Men*—"I positively cannot find time to re-read your manuscript and, therefore, I suggest to you that you write a general, strong introduction, embodying what little I said in my letter, what Nordau said (in different language), send same to me, and I will sign same so that it may be published as an introduction over my name."

To Lee Bascom—"In the matter of the dramatization of my story "The Great Interrogation," it is understood that my name shall appear as collaborator."

To Michael Williams—"Now as regards that Art Museum proposition. If you will write up something that I know you are able to do, that will sound like me, and submit to me, I shall gladly sign my name to it."

To V. R. Sinclair—"If you can yourself, or if you can find somebody else, who will do it, will you please have a few lines, or a short article, written that you may esteem characteristic of me, and publish same over my name. I hereby authenticate this procedure."

To Mr. Esenmein—"Won't you just write out an endorsement for me of the *Writer's Monthly,* then submit the endorsement to me and I shall sign it and return it to you."

To William W. Hodkinson—"Suppose you yourself, or somebody in your office, write such an autograph-letter for me. Send it to me, and I shall immediately affix my autograph to same and return to you."

To J. A. Waldron by Charmian—"Jack suggests ... that you yourself write up the short semi-humorous article, and publish it over his name ... first, of course, letting him go over it in order to lend it his touch."

In like manner Francis A. Cox was authorized to write a foreword to his *What Do You Know About a Horse?* using Jack's name as author. Others just used his name without approval. "The Good Soldier," published under Jack's name by an anonymous author, caused him all kinds of trouble with the military, since it was a vitriolic denunciation of a soldier's life. He wrote denial after denial, but even today it crops up as his. Whoever wrote it used his style and signed Jack's name. Shortly after Jack's death, ex-President Theodore Roosevelt wrote Charmian and stated that he was convinced that Jack had never written "The Good Soldier."

IMPOSTERS AND FALSE ARTICLES

Imposters were a constant source of irritation and became part of the myth-making process that still lingers today. Jack received a letter from a bank in Billings, Montana, informing him that two checks bearing his signature had been returned from Chicago marked "No Funds." Jack sent a copy of his signature and informed the bank that he had never been in Billings, except to pass through on the train, and had no account in Chicago. The bank was finally convinced.

Newspapers all over the country and in the Bay Area carried stories of his exploits as a revolutionary in Mexico long before he went there for the first time. Jack just laughed and worked away at the ranch in Glen Ellen. Another imposter was wined and dined at the famous 101 Ranch and other points in Oklahoma. Others relieved many young girls of their virtue in the name of Jack London, stole books from libraries, or passed bad checks. Jack London was a very common name, and many who shared his name took advantage of it and were as bad as the outright imposters.

In addition to problems with imposters, newspapers everywhere printed anything given to them and seldom bothered to check whether it was the real Jack London or, for that matter, whether it was even true.

During their one-week stay in Eureka in 1911 Jack and Charmian were given the use of a lovely houseboat belonging to H. L. Ricks. In a letter to Ricks August 17, 1911, Jack said, "I read in today's paper that your son-in-law has given me a black eye, and that my wife has deserted me! In yesterday's paper I read that I had been fishing in a Washington lake for Beardslee trout with a diamond stud attached to my troll for a lure. One reads very many things." At the time these incidents were supposed to have happened, Jack and Charmian were camped many miles away. Thus it is possible for a biographer of Jack London to research well and still produce a book full of errors and misunderstandings.

As an example—for many years Jack London, the author, was given credit for the lyrics of "On the Face of the Earth, You Are the One" until Jack Neiburg identified the writer as Jack London, a Boston songwriter.

And these are just a few of the impersonations, misunderstandings, misinterpretations, exaggerations, deliberate lies, and misquotes that still plague his memory and his works. Sadly, when one biographer makes a mistake many others compound his mistake in their biographies or in articles for newspapers and magazines. Some of these are so ludicrous that a Jack London scholar would hardly recognize the man they are describing. Myths that have been based on erroneous interpretations, suppositions, speculation, unsubstantiated information, and inadequate research have given the public the inaccurate picture of Jack London as a

A caricature of Jack London the sailor

suicide, a drug addict, a homosexual, a woman-chaser, and many other unsavory characteristics. None of these are true but an avalanche of truth will never be able to undo the harm that has been done.

This phenomenon works the other way, too. Those with a bias in Jack London's favor tend to minimize his faults or just ignore them entirely. An example of this can be found in Volume One of Charmian London's *Book of Jack London.* For several pages she cites Jack's English ancestry. But even a shallow London student knows that John London married Flora when Jack was already eight months old. Actually John London didn't even know Flora at the time of Jack's conception. However, Charmian did not invent this myth. She merely perpetuated one that Jack established himself when Ninetta Eames interviewed him for an article she was writing for the *Overland Monthly* in 1900. From that date he adopted his stepfather's genealogy. Maybe he reasoned that the public would be reluctant to accept him because of his having been born to unmarried parents, or perhaps it was a way of settling his own inner conflicts. Since he had been unable to determine who his real father was, he may have decided to solve the dilemma by simply accepting his stepfather as his real father. Whatever the reason, he chose that course of action for the rest of his life. Charmian honored his decision in her book. A careful reading of her two-volume work and a thorough study of their marital relationship reveals that she depicts the real Jack London as only a loving wife and one dedicated to the memory of her husband could do.

SEPARATION AND *THE SEA-WOLF*

Jack decided to buy a small sailboat with part of his earnings from *The Call of the Wild*. His brother-in-law, Ernest Matthews, had found the *Spray* for him, and he bought it. On its maiden voyage to Petaluma, Jack signed the flag and gave it to Ernest as a souvenir. He told Ernest he was buying the boat to recapture the feel of the water for his next book—*The Sea-Wolf*.

Ninetta Eames had a nice home in Glen Ellen. Since there were several rental cottages on the property, and it was surrounded by the beautiful Wake-Robins, she called it Wake Robin Lodge. In May of 1903 Jack brought his wife and two daughters to Wake Robin and rented a cabin for the summer. He returned later to the bungalow in Piedmont so he could sail on the *Spray* and work on *The Sea-Wolf*.

The breakup of his marriage was imminent. He simply couldn't endure it any longer. Bessie was a fine woman, but they were extremely incompatible. Jack was struggling with his strong sense of family responsibility and an equally strong realization that to continue living with Bessie was impossible. Other than the days when "the crowd" gathered for an afternoon or evening of good clean fun, he was living a shallow, frustrating life. There was no love left. Even companionship and respect had gone out of his marriage. Bessie was the mother of his girls, and they occupied all of her time and interest. Their bicycle excursions were dead and so was just about everything else in their marriage. Yet Jack was still so kind and gentle with Bessie that when Cloudesley Johns was a house guest in February of 1903 he didn't suspect a breakup of their marriage. Johns must have noticed how egocentric Bessie had become, but he failed to see her other faults and had no reason to know that she was a compulsive neighborhood gossip with no

Ninetta Eames with her second husband, Edward Biron Payne, and friends in front of one of the cabins at Wake Robin Lodge.

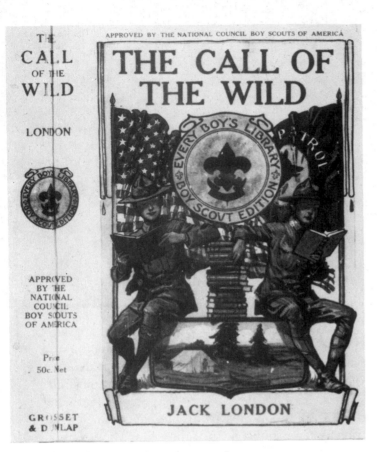

The Call of the Wild *has been published in at least four hundred different editions. The Boy Scouts of America endorsed* The Call of the Wild, The Sea-Wolf, *and* White Fang *for scouting.*

qualms about adding untruths to what she had to say. It was a miracle that Jack lingered as long as he did.

Jack finally threw restraint overboard and decided to take a mistress for a sail on the *Spray*. He mulled over the girls of "the crowd" and selected a few who would be good candidates—Mab Lachmund, Blanche Partington, and Charmian Kittredge came to mind. Maybe he could entice one of them. Come Monday he would try, but first he was to spend the weekend at the Sterlings' camp in the hills. Monday morning on the way back to Oakland a wheel broke on the buggy. In the accident Jack acquired many bruises and a badly injured knee. It seemed that the philandering and the *Spray* would have to wait.

But Bessie had asked Charmian to pick up some things for her and give them to Jack, who would take them to Glen Ellen. Charmian called Jack to tell him the things were ready. On discovering his plight, she took them to him. When Charmian left he impulsively kissed her. At the time Charmian

was in love with another man, and Jack was only thinking of the possibility of a few days on the *Spray* with her when his knee was well.

Coincidentally, both went to Glen Ellen, Jack to be with his family and Charmian to be with her foster-mother, Ninetta Eames. During this short period in June and July they fell in love, but their deportment was such that Bessie had no idea that Charmian was the other woman. Late in July, Jack told Bessie that he was leaving her and returned to the Piedmont Bungalow on July 24 with his affairs in total confusion.

Early in the year Frank Atherton, his wife, and baby had visited Jack and Bessie at the Bungalow. Jack was out flying kites. He had six in the air at the moment. As Frank was about to leave, Jack said, "Say, Frank, why can't you and your wife and kid come up here and take that vacant place. There's plenty of room for three, and it won't cost you a cent of rent. It's better than living in town."

Frank and his family moved in bag and baggage. Jack refused his attempts to pay rent, but let him do maintenance work on the place and always had him over to the many parties. Frank remembered meeting Stewart Edward White, George Sterling, Jim Whitaker, Cloudesley Johns, and many other writers and dignitaries. Occasionally Joaquin Miller rode over to discuss literature. Frank said, "The afternoons and evenings at the Bungalow were al-

Joan, Bess, and Bessie about the time of the divorce

Piedmont Baths in Oakland. This was one of Jack's favorite recreation spots.

ways enjoyable. Debates, recitations, discussions on various topics, music, and general sociability."

When Jack came back from Glen Ellen and told him about his plans to separate, Frank was astonished. He had never suspected any trouble between them. Jack asked Frank to find a suitable house for him—a place where he could write in privacy and entertain company. It didn't have to be too spacious since he would be spending most of his time on the *Spray*—just a place to keep his gear and where he could have a few friends in now and then. Frank found a six-room flat at 1216 Telegraph Avenue (later 2820).

Jack proposed that the Athertons share the apartment with him. He would pay the rent and board with them. For several months Jack was

their star boarder. He also rented a house at 919 Jefferson Street for Flora and John London's grandson, Johnny Miller.

To celebrate the finding of his new apartment, Jack took Frank on a whirlwind tour of his favorite Oakland saloons, buying drinks for everybody and playing the slot machines with abandon. Frank admonished him to economize and Jack promised to do so, but only after this celebration.

Frank reminisced about this period when he and Jack shared the apartment:

Still, after that day, I could see no difference. He would plunge wildly into whatever suited his fancy, going to the extreme in pursuit of recreation. Whatever others did, he would go them one better. If someone took one drink, he would take

123

1216 (later changed to 2820) Telegraph Avenue. Jack and the Athertons lived in the upper left apartment.

two. But this I can truthfully say; in all the years of our intimate association I never saw him drunk. By the word drunk, I mean staggering or swaggering, foolish or unmindful of what he was doing.

Sometimes Jack would go out for an afternoon with George Sterling. I well remember one night when they had been together. It was quite late when Jack came home. His eyes looked glassy, and apparently he had been drinking too much. Still he was very quiet, retiring immediately. We didn't see him again until the next morning when he related his experience of the previous night. He and George had tentatively indulged in hashish.

"To one who has never entered the land of hashish," he said, "an explanation would mean nothing. But to me, last night was like a thousand years. I was obsessed with indescribable sensations; alternating visions of excessive happiness and oppressive moods of extreme sorrow. I wandered for aeons through countless worlds, mingling with all types of humanity, from the most saintly persons down to the lowest type of abysmal brute."

"But why in the devil did you want to take the damned stuff?" I asked him. "It's a wonder you and George didn't go crazy."

Jack smiled evasively. "Say, Frank, you've read some of Marie Corelli's books, haven't you? No doubt you've read *Wormwood.*"

"Yes, I have, but what has that to do with hashish?"

"Everything," Jack replied. "Marie Corelli couldn't have written *Wormwood* if she hadn't drunk enough absinthe to experience all those

strange dreams and fancies described in *Wormwood.* And I've read that she even became an inmate of brothels to get the material for other books. So you see in order to write intelligently one must have certain experiences that coincide with the subject."

On August 14, Jack wrote to Fannie K. Hamilton, saying in part, "As you will notice by my above address, the Bungalow is no more. I never loved a habitation so greatly in my life. And alas! it is no more. Ere this you may have heard things concerning me in the Eastern papers. At least believe this of me: that whatever I have done I have done with the sanction of my conscience, that I have performed what I consider the very highest of right acts."

Cloudesley Johns came up from Southern California on vacation, and he and Jack sailed out from the Oakland Estuary on the morning tide October 22 for a two-month working vacation about the waters of the Bay and up the Sacramento, San Joaquin, and Napa rivers. Cloudesley was working on several literary projects and Jack was putting the finishing touches to *The Sea-Wolf.*

A few days prior to sailing Jack and Charmian managed to have a weekend of intimacy—probably aboard the *Spray.* A new appreciation of the ideals of love in all its passionate ways enveloped him. Charmian was feminine, delicate, sexy, and available now that she and her lover had broken off. She was not beautiful by any means, but she had a fabulous figure and knew how to dress to emphasize it. She was coquettish and had no prudish inhibitions, since her foster-mother had taught her the ways of the infamous Victoria Woodhull and the doctrine of free love.

They were an ideal match. It had to happen. Charmian was the comrade for whom Jack had sought. She was fearless and game for any adventure he might dream up and yet always ultra-feminine. She filled his every need and more during their years of marriage.

The Kempton-Wace Letters had been published and the book received mixed but generally favorable reviews. The Buffalo *Commercial* said, "We say again as we have said frequently before, that *The Kempton-Wace Letters,* which The Macmillan Company published, consists in a correspondence about the function and meaning and purpose of love and the place which it should have in our lives. To

Jack working on The Sea-Wolf *near Wake Robin Lodge on the bank of Graham Creek*

presses one so much, though the writers often know their subjects. . . . These stories are simply admirable."

In September, as Jack was completing what was to become another American classic, he was still reading laudatory reviews of *The Call of the Wild.* The *Criterion* in New York City said about it, "The most virile, freshly conceived, dramatically told, and firmly sustained book of the season is unquestionably Jack London's *Call of the Wild.* Such books as these clarify the literary atmosphere and give a new, clean vibrant breath in a depression of romances and problems; they act like an invigorating wind from the open sea upon the dullness of a sultry day."

The Sea-Wolf was started on a mossy shelf down the slope from Wake Robin Lodge on the bank of Graham Creek during the time of Jack's breakup with Bessie. The last half was written during his torrid romance with Charmian Kittredge.

According to Jack, most of the events in the book were drawn from his own experiences aboard the *Sophia Sutherland,* but actually they were more from the "sea yarns" related either by some of the old seafarers who were his shipmates or by the newspaper accounts of Captain Alexander McLean, who was the prototype for Wolf Larsen.

The Sea-Wolf was a protest against the philosophy of Nietzsche, insofar as that philosophy expounded strength and individualism against cooperation, democracy, and socialism. Jack said, "I attacked Nietzsche and his super-man idea. This was in *The Sea-Wolf.* Lots of people read *The Sea-Wolf,* no one discovered that it was an attack on the super-man philosophy." The idea was to present a plain tale with underlying psychological substance—an attempt to prove that the superman cannot be a success in modern life because his antisocial concepts are bound to bring defeat in a complex society.

One wonders what kind of reception *The Sea-Wolf* would have had if Jack could have written it today in a more permissive society. Most critics acknowledge that it is one of the finest classics of the sea up to the time that Maud Brewster is rescued and brought aboard the *Ghost.* Ambrose Bierce, by no means a Jack London fan, said to George Sterling, "But the great thing—and it is among the greatest of things—is that tremendous creation, Wolf Larsen . . . the hewing out and set-

Dane Kempton, the foster-father of Herbert and Barbara Wace, love is nearly the whole of life; at least, life has passed by him who had not loved. And through these letters the woman's side of the problem appears and reappears. Aside from the thought and the ideas and the philosophy in this book, it is especially attractive on account of the sheer charm of its prose. The book 'caught on' at once, and holds firmly its place in the front rank of the best of the season's publications."

The Cruise of the Dazzler brought excellent reviews and placed Jack in the top rank of children's authors. *Children of the Frost* brought rave reviews in America and England. The *Queen,* a British publication, said of it, "The *Children of the Frost* by Jack London is an excellent book. Nothing but praise need be given to it. The first story, "In the Forests of the North," is admirable. It has a strength in treating Canadian subjects worthy of Mr. Kipling. Very few books about the noble Red Man im-

ting up of such a figure is enough for a man to do in one lifetime." Bierce also said, "The love element, with its absurd suppressions and impossible proprieties, is awful. I confess to an overwhelming contempt for both the sexless lovers." He was correct in both assertions, but failed to realize that had Jack written the true love story, based on his love affair with Miss Kittredge, the publishers would never have printed the book.

Both R. W. Gilder, editor of *Century,* who published the magazine serial, and George Brett of Macmillan were deeply concerned about how Jack would handle the adventures of the couple all alone on a desert island. Jack assured Brett, "I am absolutely confident myself that the American prudes will not be shocked by the last half of the book."

The decision to save the blush from young maidens' cheeks kept *The Sea-Wolf* from being one of the greatest of American classics, but did make it a best seller. *The Sea-Wolf* and *The Call of the Wild* were the only two books of Jack London to make number one on the best seller list. The first edition of *The Sea-Wolf* sold all forty thousand copies before publication and the second edition sold over fifteen thousand copies before it was published. The *Ladies' Home Journal* bought several thousand copies for premiums, and Jack chuckled, since the reviewers insisted that it was a man's book and women would not care for it.

The Albany *Argus* on November 25, 1904, said: "Mr. Jack London has produced in *The Sea-Wolf,* his first [sic] novel, one of the strongest pieces of literature sent forth by any writer of to-day. It has been running its course as a serial in the *Century* and there is scarcely a question but that it is the novel of the year in America. It is a remarkable book from several standpoints, but chiefly it is a daring study in the moralities." The Boston *Herald*'s review reported, "Jack London's standing as one of the foremost of our young authors is advanced by his latest novel, *The Sea-Wolf,* just completed in serial form. It is an uncommonly vigorous piece of work, admirably developed—one of the best sea tales in recent literature." The majority of reviews were extremely favorable but, as usual, there were a few who saw the book as no better than the average "dime novel."

Probably the compliment most appreciated by Jack was in a letter from Thomas T. Horton on the U.S.S. *Wyoming,* who wrote to him after reading *The Sea-Wolf:* "If the ocean needed a 'Boswell' you would land the job." He would also appreciate Carl Sandburg's statement, *"The Sea-Wolf* bore down on me for all my brain-traffic would bear."

The year 1903 had been a year of happiness and also one full of trauma. The early months of the year constituted one of the best periods in Jack's life and are best revealed by Fannie K. Hamilton in an interview for *The Reader* at the Bungalow:

Mr. London's California home, high up in the Piedmont hills, is at the end of a trail winding through a most romantic and beautiful country. The bungalow, deep verandaed and vine-shaded, looks upon a superb panorama, across great sweeps of plain and mountain and wooded steeps, to Oakland, flattened and remote, a mere fringe of green-shored city at the base of the foothills, and afar across San Francisco Bay to the Golden Gate and the Pacific Ocean.

Here in this open-air sitting room, around which sings and sighs the drowsy music of the woods, one may find Mr. London at leisure on Wednesday afternoons. He is one of the most approachable of men, unconventional, responsive and genuine, with a warmth of hospitality which places the visitor on the immediate footing of a friend. In fact, Jack London, boyish, noble and lovable, is made up of qualities that reach straight for the heart.

Ominous war clouds hovered over Japan and Russia as the new year began. Five major syndicates asked Jack to go to the Orient and cover the threatening hostilities. He liked the offer from Hearst best and accepted his first assignment as a war correspondent. He rushed *The Sea-Wolf* to completion in book form, requested Macmillan to send monthly checks to Bessie and the girls, told Eliza to give Miss Kittredge anything she wanted, and arranged for George Sterling and Charmian to edit and proofread *The Sea-Wolf* for him. On January 7, 1904, he sailed through the Golden Gate on the S.S. *Siberia* headed for Yokohama and Korea.

Before arriving in Honolulu, Jack came down with "La Grippe," but attended a concert the night of January 13, aching bones and all. One day out of Honolulu, still suffering from "La Grippe," he jumped from a height of about three and a half feet and landed on a round stick the size of a broom handle, straining one side of his left ankle and spraining the other side. For sixty-five hours he lay flat on his back and then each day Phillips, the English correspondent, carried him on deck for a couple hours of sun.

Undoubtedly he came in for a lot of good-hearted joshing from the other correspondents. He had to admit that a pair of crutches did tone down his swashbuckling image a bit.

On the voyage he met Jimmy Hare and R. L. Dunn of *Collier's* and they became immediate and permanent friends. He also met Ed and Ida Winship from Napa, California, and in the later ranch years this chance acquaintance grew into a close

friendship. In fact, the Winships were probably the closest friends Jack and Charmian had during his last years.

The world's leading war correspondents were detained in Japan. Every pretext possible was used to keep them there. Permits of every kind were required, and each was preceded by miles of Japanese red tape. R. L. Dunn had gone to Korea, correctly guessing that the Japanese Army would make a surprise landing there. Jack noted that Dunn had slipped away and guessed what he had guessed, so three days after landing in Yokohama, on January 25, he set out on an all-day journey to Kobe.

The following morning he plunged out of Kobe in three rickshaws, with push-boys and pull-boys, racing to catch the express for Nagasaki. Then he traveled from Nagasaki to Moji searching for a steamer to Chemulpo. On arrival at Moji he bought a ticket to sail on Monday. Two days later

War correspondents aboard the S.S. Siberia *en route to Yokohama and the Russo-Japanese War. From left to right: James H. Hare, Robert L. Dunn, David Fraser, Sheldon Williams, Jack London, Percival Phillips, Frederick Palmer, Lionel James, and O. K. Davis.*

Jack snaps picture of fellow travelers before going aboard the train to Nagasaki.

Jack charters a junk to get from Makpo to Chemulpo.

he was still waiting and, as Jack put it, "Thereby hangs a tale of war and disaster, which runs the gamut of the emotions from surprise and anger to sorrow and brotherly love, and which culminates in arrest, felonious guilt and confiscation of property, to say nothing of monetary fines or alternative imprisonment.

"For know that Moji is a fortified place, one is not permitted to photograph land or water scenery. I did not know it, and I photographed neither land nor water scenery; but I know it now just the same.

"Having bought my ticket at the Osaka Shosen Kaisha office, I tucked it into my pocket and stepped out the door. Came four coolies carrying a bale of cotton. Snap went my camera. Five little boys at play—snap again. A line of coolies carrying coal—and again snap, and last snap."

He was arrested by the police on February 1 and taken to jail in Kokura. The next day he appeared before the Public Procurator of the Kokura District Court and was fined five yen and had his camera confiscated. Had it not been for the intervention of United States Minister Griscom from the military prison at Shimonaseki he would have spent much more time in jail.

He was scheduled to sail on the *Keigo Maru* on the 8th, but discovered that the ship had been taken over by the government. Then he made a wild dash to catch a small steamer as it was getting underway for Fusan. He arrived aboard soaking

128

The steersman on the sampan trip across the Yellow Sea during February 1904 in subzero weather

wet from having to retrieve one of his trunks that fell overboard in the confusion. At Fusan he caught a little one-hundred-twenty-ton steamer loaded with Koreans and Japanese. The deck was piled so high it arrived at Mokpo with a thirty-degree starboard list. At Mokpo the ship was taken over by the Japanese Government, and the passengers were taken ashore.

Now Jack was mad and determined to get to Chemulpo. Chartering a junk, he sailed out into the Yellow Sea and along the coast of Korea. His Korean crew of three spoke no English, but somehow they all managed to keep going. It was a cold, miserable, stormy voyage. By nightfall they arrived in Kun San minus a mast and with a smashed rudder. Five Japanese had been given passage on the trip to Kun San. At the height of the storm, Jack had one man at the tiller, a Korean at each sheet, four scared Japanese, and a fifth too seasick to be scared.

That night Jack was a guest in the village. Five native maidens helped him undress, take a bath, and get into bed. There was a repeat performance the next morning. The Mayor of Kun San, the Captain of Police, and most of the leading citizens crowded into the bedroom while he was shaved, washed, and dressed. All screamed "Sayonara" as the junk put out to sea.

Because the old junk was too badly damaged to

be of use, he had to charter a new one. This time he had five Japanese crew members who knew no English. In Kun San there were rumors of fighting, but nobody knew whether war had been declared. It was so cold that the salt water froze as the breakers splashed over the side. There were no stoves—only charcoal boxes with a half dozen embers. Jack had bought one at a tiny Korean village for twelve and a half cents when they had landed for water.

Perhaps the liveliest eight days of Jack London's life were spent in this small boat on the West Coast of Korea. The voyage turned out to be more adventuresome than even he wanted. He was voyaging up the Yellow Sea during February in below-zero

Five passengers on Jack's junk en route to Kun-San

Jack's crew on the sampan trip

weather. All he had to keep warm, other than the pitiful little charcoal box, was the thought of the rest of the correspondents bottled up in Japan—he was on the way to the front.

He was in an open boat, a sampan, on a rocky coast where there were no lighthouses, and where the tides ran from thirty to sixty feet. His crew members were Japanese fishermen. They couldn't understand him, and he couldn't understand them. However, there was nothing monotonous about the trip. Jack never forgot one particular cold, bitter dawn, when, in the thick of driving snow, they took in the sail and dropped their small anchor. The wind was howling out of the northwest and they were on a lee shore. Ahead and astern all escape was cut off by rocky headlands, against whose bases burst the unbroken seas. To windward a short distance, seen only between snow squalls, was a low, rocky reef. It was this reef that inadequately protected them from the whole Yellow Sea that thundered in upon them.

The Japanese crawled under a rice mat and went to sleep. Jack joined them, and for several hours they dozed fitfully. Then a sea deluged them with icy water, and they found several inches of snow and ice on top of the mat. The reef to windward was disappearing under the rising tide, and moment by moment the seas crashed stronger and stronger over the rocks. The fishermen studied the shores anxiously. So did Jack, and with a trained sailor's eye, though he could see little chance for a swimmer to gain that surf-hammered line of rocks. He made signs toward the headlands on their flank. The Japanese shook their heads. He indicated that dreadful lee shore. Still they shook their heads and did nothing. He concluded that they were paralyzed by the hopelessness of the situation. Yet their danger increased every minute, for the rising tide was robbing them of the reef that had been serving as a buffer. The sea was splashing aboard in growing volume, and they bailed constantly. And still the fishermen eyed the surf-battered shore and did nothing.

At last, after many narrow escapes from complete swamping, the fishermen got into action. All hands toiled on the anchor and hove it up. Forward, as the boat's head paid off, they set a patch of sail about the size of a flour sack, and they headed straight for shore. Jack unlaced his shoes, unbuttoned his great coat, and made ready for a quick partial strip a minute or so before they struck. But they didn't strike, and, as they rushed in, he saw the beauty of what was happening. Before them opened a narrow channel, filled at its mouth with breaking sea. Jack had forgotten the rising tide, and it was for that tide that the Japanese had so precariously waited. They ran through the breakers, sailed into a tiny sheltered bay, and landed on a beach where the salt sea of the last tide lay frozen in long, curving lines.

Sunday, February 14, they put into a Korean fishing village and spent the day and night. As Jack, exaggerating a little for emphasis, put it, "Five sailors, myself, and about twenty men, women, and children slept in a hut whose floor space equalled the size of a standard double bed." Jack was the first white man ever seen in the village and was the center of attention for all. At midnight he made the mistake of showing his false upper teeth to an old man, who immediately aroused the house to see this miracle. At three o'clock everybody woke up for another series of demonstrations.

Monday the 15th they were on the last leg of the trip up the wild coast in the bitter cold. Jack wondered several times during the long day if he could stay alive long enough to make it. He nearly didn't. R. L. Dunn was there when Jack landed and tells us about it:

I want to say that Jack London is one of the grittiest men that it has been my good fortune to meet. He is just as heroic as any of the characters in his novels. He is a man that will stay with you through thick and thin. He doesn't know the meaning of fear and is willing to risk his life in the performance of his duty.

I got to Korea one month before London. Immediately after my arrival at Chemulpo the port was closed. London knew that. So did the other correspondents who were at that time in Japan. London had another idea. He came over to Korea in a junk. From Fusan where he landed, he came to Chemulpo in a sampan. A sampan is an open boat, big enough to carry several men. It took him seven days to make the trip from Fusan to Chemulpo. In crossing the Straits to Korea in mid-winter Jack had again shown the stuff of which he was made, but he explained to me that he was most proud of the fact that with an "excuse please, so sorry!" he had also been able to leave all the noted writers in Japan.

The weather during this trip was at the zero mark. When London arrived in Chemulpo I did not recognize him. He was a physical wreck. His ears were frozen; his fingers were frozen; his feet were frozen. He said that he didn't mind his condition so long as he got to the front. He said his physical collapse counted for nothing. He had been sent to the front to do newspaper work, and he wanted to do it.

As soon as he was able to move about he and I started for the front. The Japanese monopolized the regular roads. We had to make our way through the ice-crusted rice fields.

Korea is a very mountainous country and traveling under the best conditions in winter can be a tragedy. We had to beat the soldiers to a village in order to get a place to sleep. A village containing six houses would be utilized by a regiment of infantry.

If we got to a village first we had a room against the soldiers. If they got there first we had no place to sleep.

Our entire stay in Korea was a succession of hardships that is almost impossible for anybody who has not visited the country during the winter to realize. We were held at Ping Yang by the Japanese Consul for a week. Our forced stay at Ping Yang was the result of a complaint lodged with the Japanese Government by the correspondents of Tokyo who did not have the grit or the enterprise to get anywhere near the field of action. Finally we reached Sunan, one of the most northern towns of Korea. There we were put in a military prison for four days. Then they sent us back to Seoul.

Dunn and Jack headed north over frozen mountains and through ice-covered valleys. When night came, they huddled up on the frozen ground and hoped that they would live long enough to get back home. At times it seemed an impossible dream. By February 24 they had arrived at Seoul and were staying at the Grand Hotel. Jack's entourage consisted of three pack horses, two riding horses, one Japanese interpreter (Mr. Yamada), one cook (Manyoungi), and two Mapus (Korean grooms).

By March 4 they had reached Ping Yang. Jack traveled one hundred eighty miles on horseback on Belle, the horse formerly owned by the Russian minister in Seoul. Their plan was to head north for Anju and maybe the Yalu River. C. Shinjo,

Japan, Korea, and Manchuria

Taking refuge on a beach. Note the line of frozen salt water.

Jack and R. L. Dunn in a mild protest at the Grand Hotel's increase in prices

Manyoungi checks out the food supply

132

Ever north

Jack stops along the way for a short visit and, hopefully, for information.

Jack and Belle at Jack's camp

Japanese acting consul forbade them to go any farther north, but late in the afternoon of March 8 they arrived at Poval Colli, a forlorn little village full of scared, cold people. It was snowing and everybody, including Dunn and London, was generally miserable.

The following day they were captured by Japanese soldiers and given strict orders to venture no farther north than one hundred yards. Dunn, the photographer/correspondent, and London, the correspondent/photographer, were disgusted and exasperated. The front was still forty miles away. The fact that they had penetrated farther north than any other correspondents in the war gave little solace. Dunn rode back to Seoul to beg permission for them to go on to the front. Jack remained in Sunan taking pictures. On March 13 the Japanese insisted that he return to Seoul.

No war ever saw as many correspondents ready to wield pen and camera who had so little opportunity to do so. While the battles raged, the world's leading war correspondents were bottled up in Seoul and Tokyo. Finally the Japanese headquarters decided to let a few correspondents go with Kuroki's First Army. Writing to Brett, Jack said, "Am now waiting in Seoul (under instructions) for the correspondents in Tokio to get permission to start and to overtake me. Then I may go on. Believe me, it has all the appearance now (so far as we are concerned) of a personally conducted Cook's tourist proposition."

At last, on April 16, he was able to leave Seoul and five days later arrived in Wiju. There he watched the army move up and wrote an article, "Japanese Supplies Rushed to Front by Man and Beast." On May 1 he rode across the Yalu River to Kuel-ina-Ching and on to the Chinese city of Antung, where he wrote "Give Battle to Retard Enemy."

With Jack at First Army Headquarters were John Bass, Robert M. Collins, Walter Kirton, Oscar K. Davis, William Dinwiddie, James B. Hare, and Frederick Palmer. They were confined in a grove of pines on a hill slope near a temple located five miles from the Yalu and well out of sight of the river. Any hope of seeing a battle was futile since they were limited to riding or walking within a circle of two miles. The nearest contact with the front occurred when the Japanese general allowed them to watch the battle of Yalu—probably because he was fairly confident of victory with his

Jack's trip north was constantly interrupted by military checkpoints

fifty thousand men pitted against Russia's five thousand. The Japanese even set up a fine place from which to view the fighting, several miles from the front on a high bluff. At least the correspondents could let the world know that whenever battles were fought there was smoke. However, they were so far away that they weren't certain any noise was involved.

By the time the army headquarters and the correspondents had moved up to Feng-hwang-Cheng, Jack had sent nineteen articles and hundreds of pictures to Hearst, but had no idea whether any had reached San Francisco.

It became difficult for him to wheedle any particular favors, due to an altercation just prior to leaving for Seoul. Robert Dunn said, "When London finally left for the First Army front, near Yalu, he did paste a Japanese servant he caught stealing.

Jack seeks information after his credentials are approved.

Sentry checks Jack's credentials.

War correspondents cooled their heels in this camp in a grove of trees near the First Japanese Army Headquarters near Wiju.

Correspondents with the First Japanese Army watching the Battle of the Yalu on May 1, 1904

"So that Americans might see London at work in a land thousands of miles from home I made the picture herewith. It shows Jack crouched in a filthy hut, half frozen, yet giving his best thoughts of a war torn country, a country though neutral, being stripped of every vestige of things worth while." R. L. Dunn

Headquarters dressed Jack down, and kept him under arrest without a hearing in a military-racial ruckus." Palmer fills in the details, "It was solved by explaining that London was a most gifted writer, with a strong sense of the pioneer American *bushido,* which responded with a blow of a fist to an insult."

By June 4 Jack was thoroughly disgusted and gave up all hope of being able to accomplish anything that he was sent out to do. He decided to return home. Palmer reported that Jack was particularly irked at the restraints. When Palmer told him that he had to understand the Japanese way of doing things and suggested that, at least, the Japanese were very brave soldiers, Jack responded, "They may be brave, but so are the South American peccary pigs in their herd charges."

The only redeeming feature of the whole Russo-Japanese War was the camaraderie he had enjoyed with Bobby Dunn. He told Dunn, "I've wasted five months of my life in this war." A little humor had brought Dunn and London through many distressful situations, enabling them to do about the only reporting of any consequence that came out of the war. Jack's humor was still intact as he said goodbye to his friend, "If we ever meet again, Bob, my memory will be your laughing at me and my laughing at you, and your knowing, and my knowing you know I am."

Jack's camp

One of a series of articles written for the San Francisco Examiner *by Jack London*

FRESH BATTLE RAGING AT PORT ARTHUR

VICEROY ALEXIEFF'S WAR REIGN IS ENDED

ST. PETERSBURG, April 19.---Viceroy Alexieff has applied by telegraph to the Emperor to be relieved of his position of Viceroy in the Far East. It is expected that the request will be immediately granted. While no official announcement has yet been made there is reason to believe that the above statement is correct.

EXCLUSIVE WAR PHOTOGRAPH MADE FOR THE 'EXAMINER' BY JACK LONDON

JAPANESE DIGGING TRENCHES JUST BEYOND THE KOREAN VILLAGE OF SUNAN

Expenses 2 paid

books	$ 45.00
special delivery	5.00
underclothes	18.00
socks	3.00
case for glass	2.50
Camera	67.50
steamer tips	12.00
onion-skin paper	2.50
carbon	1.50
stylographic	1.00
	$158.00

Yokohama

dress suit, Tuxedo	$45.00
shirts, etc.	15.00
brush, slippers	3.50
pajamas	4.50
shirts	8.75
Incidentals	6.00
cigarettes	1.50
	$84.25

I brought ashore with me 18.20
$66.05

$158.00
66.05
$91.95 — bal due me Jan 29/04

Moji
Incidentals — $3.50
cigarettes .75
$4.25

$91.95
4.25
$87.70 — bal due me Feb 3/04

Jack kept excellent records of his expenses.

DIVORCE

Suit for divorce was filed by Bessie on June 28, 1904, on the grounds of desertion. Besides bringing the suit for divorce, she had also filed a petition for an order restraining the Central Bank of Oakland and Jack's publishers from paying to her husband any money on deposit or due him pending the settlement of the divorce proceedings. Jack was served divorce papers on board the S.S. *Siberia* before landing in San Francisco. Newspaper headlines gave equal space to his brilliant work for Hearst in the Russo-Japanese War and to his divorce.

Anna Strunsky was not accused of any wrongdoing, but was named as the cause of the separation. Bessie did claim that Jack had declared his love for Anna on several occasions, and hinted that she had seen several letters that proved their relationship to be far from platonic. This was really just another of Bessie's embellishments, and many writers since have used her accusation to prove that Anna reciprocated Jack's love for her. Actually, if anybody really wants to know the truth of their relationship, he need only look at the letters they left behind them.

Anna stated for the press at the time:

Absurd is hardly a word strong enough to be used in regard to the silly stories about the love-making that went on before Mrs. London's eyes. Mr. London and I were very good friends, and we treated one another as such—no more. Besides, Jack London is hardly the man to make love to another woman in his own house, invited there on another errand altogether. His behaviour was most circumspect toward me, and always has been.

The ridiculous part of the whole thing is the fact that my visit to the Londons' house occurred exactly two and a half years ago. At that time there was not a breath of rumor to the effect that their married life was not happy. My observations at the time served to convince me that he was blindly in love with his wife—and whatever other affection he had to give was lavished on his two children.

Since 1901, I have seen Mr. London but three or four times. Immediately after my visit to his home, I went to New York, from there to London, and I have spent the greater part of my time since then in Italy; returning from Naples only four months ago.

Flora London was quoted by the *San Francisco Chronicle* on June 30, 1904:

I can hardly believe that Bessie has made such charges. "Cruelty and desertion" indeed! During my whole life with them I do not recall where Jack once said an unkind word to her or did anything that could in any way hurt her feelings. He was loving, affectionate and generous to a fault during the first two years of that marriage. Then there began to grow a gradual coolness between them, due to her not understanding the needs of his literary work, and partly caused by the "hero worship" of a lot of silly girls who wrote him letters and veritably dogged his footsteps whenever he left the house. Jack looked upon the latter as a joke, and would often laugh about it. Perhaps he took it all too lightly, for things went from bad to worse between husband and wife, and a year ago, they decided to separate . . . Jack has made her a liberal allowance, and has done all in his power to promote her comfort and that of the little girls.

So far as Anna Strunsky is concerned, she was at our house several years ago, when she and Jack were finishing their book together. Her behaviour was always that of a good friend to all of the family. I think there is no reason for the connection of her name with Jack's.

Judge Greene, with Bessie's consent, set aside the restraining orders on Jack's bank and his publishers on July 12, when Jack agreed to Bessie's financial demands and promised to build her a house. In August Bessie dismissed her earlier actions and instituted a second, alleging simple desertion as the ground for her complaint.

On August 30 a deed was placed on record conveying a lot at 519 Thirty-first Street in Oakland from Jack to Bessie. She could retain the property as long as she remained single. A contract was signed with C. M. McGregor to construct a house on the lot for $2,175.

On his return from Korea Jack had nearly four thousand dollars in the bank—the first and only

"Jack's House" in Glen Ellen, California

time in his adult life when he wasn't actually in debt—but that condition lasted only until he wrote McGregor's check and paid the sixteen hundred dollars for the lot. Now he was back in debt and remained that way until he died. However, he managed to live a full life as a wizard of deficit financing.

Judge Ellsworth granted Bessie an interlocutory decree of divorce on November 11, 1904, making it possible for Jack and Charmian to marry after a one-year waiting period.

In the meantime Charmian had fled to Newton, Iowa, to escape scandal. Jack went to Glen Ellen in July and rented a small house next door to Wake Robin Lodge, sent transportation money to Charmian, and waited impatiently for her return home. Charmian returned to Oakland in November. At the time Jack was living at 1216 Telegraph Avenue with his mother, nephew, and his Korean houseboy, Manyoungi, whom he had brought to America from Korea.

Brett mailed Jack a three-thousand-dollar royalty check so he could clear up some of his debts. *The Sea-Wolf* had been published a month before and was selling extremely well. It was drawing the same favorable critical reviews that the serial publication had enjoyed. At Brett's suggestion he cut the "Salt of the Earth" from his *Salt of the Earth* anthology and submitted it for publication under the title of *The War of the Classes*. Earlier in December he wrote to Macmillan about his plans for *White Fang,* to be a companion book to *The Call of*

At the Bohemian Club's Annual High Jinks in 1904

In late 1904 The Son of the Wolf *was still selling well. Houghton, Mifflin and Company capitalized on the popularity of* The Call of the Wild.

the Wild: "I'm going to reverse the process. Instead of the devolution or decivilization of a dog, I'm going to give the evolution, the civilization of a dog—development of domesticity, faithfulness, love, morality, and all the amenities and virtues."

Jack London's literary output in 1904, other than his extraordinary work in the Russo-Japanese War, was meager. *The Game,* "A Nose for the King," "Explanation of Socialist Vote in U.S.," and "Korean Money" were the only items that were submitted for the first time. Only six items in all were submitted by him, and his collection of rejection slips was only increased by four.

Financially, other than his excellent pay from Hearst for his war work, 1904 was a mediocre year. According to his records, he received $27.50 from *Holiday* magazine for "The Story of Keesh," fifty dollars from the *San Francisco Examiner* for "Explanation of Socialist Vote in U.S.," and a three thousand-dollar advance from the Macmillan Company—a total of $3,077.50.

In *Jack London, 1905,* Lois Rather pictures Jack as he faced the New Year: "Jack London in 1905 was a complex of contrasts. Handsome, much admired by friends of both sexes, a popular writer who had won a smashing success with an early book, *The Call of the Wild* (July, 1903), followed by another with *The Sea-Wolf* (October, 1904), living a self-indulgent life attended by an obsequious Korean valet, he was beset by problems. He had fallen in love with a woman somewhat older than himself, had separated from his wife and two small daughters, was constantly worried by financial demands of three households, his own, his mother's, and that of his first wife. On top of all this, he was a zealot thoroughly convinced of the over-riding rights of the common man, an active socialist and an ardent revolutionist."

The first week of the year was spent with his friend Cloudesley Johns at 500 North Soto Street in Los Angeles. While there, he lectured for the socialist local. Julian Hawthorne, son of Nathaniel Hawthorne, wrote for the *Los Angeles Examiner:* "It is pleasant to look upon Mr. London. He is as simple and straightforward as a grizzley bear. Upon his big, hearty, healthy nature is based a brain of unusual clearness and insight. His heart is warm, his sympathies wide, his opinions are his own—independent, courageously expounded; with no trace of pose in him." Unfortunately, many newspapers were not as kind in reporting his many lectures during the year. His fame as a writer was gradually overshadowed by his notoriety as a socialist agitator. Headlines like the following in the *New York American* for January 29, 1905, were typical: "Jack London Out in Condemnation of Capitalists." It was occasioned by Jack's lecture at the University of California in Berkeley. President Benjamin Ide Wheeler invited him to lecture on any subject of his choice. Jack chose "Revolution," denouncing the capitalistic mismanagement of the country. More abrasive than persuasive, he alienated his audience and caused them to fear socialism rather than accept it. His only converts were among the disaffected youth, rebels looking for a cause. He seldom pleaded. Instead, he hammered away dogmatically. His approach was wonderfully effective in his lectures to socialists and dissidents, but equally ineffective in converting capitalists to his cause. After the lecture he accused the University of using antiquated texts in its literary courses. When Dr. Gayley happily informed him that *The Call of the Wild* was being used, Jack joined in the hearty laughter.

The faculty and most members of the audience were furious at the audacious attack on the status quo, but one group of young listeners formed a Socialist Club. This was the forerunner of "The collegiate Socialist Society" founded September, 1905, at Peck's Restaurant on Fulton Street in New York City with Jack London as its first president, and Upton Sinclair as its first vice president.

When the newspapers weren't busy reporting Jack's left-wing activities, they were publishing accounts of his amours. A headline in the *Los Angeles Examiner* for January 27, 1905, said: "Reported Blanche Bates Will Wed Jack London."

Blanche Bates was playing the title role in *The Darling of the Gods* in Oakland. Thinking she might be the one to play Freda in his play *Scorn of Women,* based on his short story by the same name, Jack

Bess (Becky) London was an early reader and, like her father, has been a voracious reader all her life.

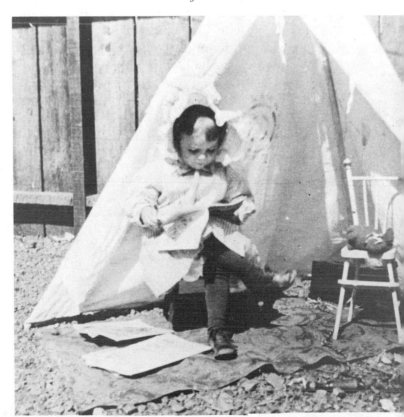

bought a front-row seat at the Macdonough Theatre and watched her every move. A reporter covering the play noted his presence, but thought little of it since Jack was a regular patron of the theatre. But when he saw him there in the same seat for the next two nights, he sensed a story. Jack appeared to be more interested in Miss Bates than in her performance. When he saw Jack enter her room at the Metropole Hotel and was told that he was there again the next night after the show, his hunch appeared to have been correct. Then when Jack gave a dinner in her honor he was certain, and wrote a story that caused newspapers all over the United States to publish in bold headlines that the famous author and Miss Bates would soon wed. A simple business venture had been turned into a love affair by a careless reporter.

At the time, Charmian was in Glen Ellen practicing piano and brushing up on shorthand and typing for her new responsibility as an author's wife. She had no illusions about this role and knew that it would include marriage to his writing career. But this posed no problem, since she was in love with both. Jack lost no time in assuring her there was no basis to the rumors of his romance with Miss Bates.

This publicity brought Jack's name to the attention of Ethel Barrymore, who promptly asked him to write a play for her. On February 12 the *Springfield Union* ran this story: "Miss Ethel Barrymore is an enthusiastic admirer of Jack London, who, she thinks, shares with Conrad the credit and distinction of writing about the only 'big stuff' that is being done today. She met Mr. London in California recently and found him a most interesting personality. 'He's the sailor, all over,' Miss Barrymore told a reporter, 'with all the charm of a free life about him. We talked about the play that he is

LONDON'S LITERARY MAJORING ON WATERFRONT
. . . famed cartoon by James Swinnerton,
onetime Examiner artist

Jack London was one of Swinnerton's favorite subjects.

going to write for me. It will be a Klondyke play, and there are all sorts of backgrounds and characters and romance available. I keep thinking about it all the time, for it has a strong hold upon the imagination."

The play she mentioned was *Scorn of Women*, which Miss Bates had decided against appearing in. The setting was Dawson City; the principal character was Freda Maloof, a dancer. As she read the play, Miss Barrymore saw that she could never realize the subtleties of the unconventional and intensely human Freda, and decided not to attempt the play.

JACK LONDON FOR MAYOR

During the first week in February of 1905 Jack and Cloudesley Johns boarded Jack's *Spray* and headed up the Sacramento River for the many sloughs in the Delta. Just before leaving the Oakland City Wharf, Jack accepted the Socialist nomination for Mayor of Oakland.

Already he was leaning heavily on Charmian.

On February 4 he sent a note to her in Glen Ellen, ". . . for 'The Class Struggle,' full proofsheets of same which I must correct in next 48 hours. May I then send proofsheets to you, on your own responsibility to change grammar, bad construction, etc., and forward immediately to the publisher."

Late in February Jack cruised into Stockton and

The Hotel Metropole

When The Youth's Companion *started publishing the stories that were collected later in* Tales of the Fish Patrol, *they were an instant success. Each story is based either on Jack's own experiences or those of his fellow patrolmen.*

on the 26th lectured to a group of businessmen in the home of his friend Johannes Reimers. Up until now society had lionized him. It thought his socialism a pose, but in the Stockton lecture and subsequent lectures during the Mayoral campaign, Jack made some reckless and foolish statements that created a barrier between him and Bay Area society for the rest of his life. The social set's decision to ignore him was actually a relief to Jack, because he had already found that their manner of living was not for him. The *Los Angeles Examiner* headlines read, "Socialism Ends Jack London's Pink Teas—Society closes gates on young author after lectures at Berkeley and Stockton and does not like his ideas. The 'Drones and Parasites' like fiction and thought socialist theories only a fad, but now see mistake."

There was no longer a question about Jack's intentions or his beliefs. Capitalists and their families preferred Paris frocks and flashy automobiles to sharing their prosperity with the poor. Jack London was now a threat and could no longer be tolerated. His words had been quite clear, "You are drones that cluster around the capitalistic honeyvats. You are ignoramuses. Your fatuous self-sufficiency blinds you to the revolution that is surely, surely coming, and which will as surely wipe you

and your silk-lined, puffed up leisure off the face of the map. You are parasites on the back of labor."

Readers were aghast when newspaper headlines blazoned another of his statements: "I think and speak of the assassins in Russia as my comrades, as do all comrades in America." They had forgotten that he also had said, "If the law of the land permits, they fight for this end peaceably at the ballot box. If the law of the land does not permit and if force is meted out to them, they resort to force themselves." Jack was sincere in his belief that the American Constitution gave every citizen the right to persuade 51 percent of the voters to form a better government as long as it was done legally and within the framework of that Constitution. His mistake was in his dogmatic presentation and thoughtless choice of words, which produced fear of, instead of sympathy for, the working class he represented.

His greatest notoriety came when he gave another lecture, in which he quoted General Sherman Bell as saying, "To hell with the Constitution!" when he condemned slavery in a speech in 1856. Jack used the quote because Bell had used the same term in later years when he was dealing with strikers. What Jack said to his listeners was that "if acts of tyranny are justified by the Constitution and their doers protected by it, then 'to hell with the Constitution' would be a proper statement." Jack believed his sentiment was profoundly American, but most newspapers distorted his view with their headlines—"Jack London Says to Hell With the Constitution."

The *San Francisco Newsletter* of March 25, 1905, reported, "London is no Socialist. He is a firebrand and red-flag anarchist, by his own confession, made in Oakland and in Stockton, and he should be arrested and prosecuted for Treason." A terrible distortion this, but, as usual, the gullible readers believed. And to this day a large percentage of California people believe these blatant untruths about a man who loved his country so thoroughly that he did everything in his power to make it a land of equal opportunity, a place where an equitable distribution of its wealth would obtain.

Jack's campaign for Mayor damaged his reputation as a writer and adversely affected the sales of his books. The capitalists controlled the presses and everything else in America, and it was a miracle that his books and stories continued to be pub-lished at all. Only the fact that he made money for his publishers kept him in print. His ability and sincerity made it possible for him to become one of America's most popular writers in his own lifetime, despite the notoriety of his socialist beliefs.

When the citizens of Oakland marched to the polls, they cast only 981 votes for Jack London. Though this was only one-twelfth of the total vote cast, it was four times the 245 votes he received in 1901. It was no surprise to Jack or the Socialist Party. Oakland was a Republican stronghold and a bourgeois town. Besides, the Socialists didn't run to win—they only used the opportunity for publicity. If Jack had even the remotest idea that he might become Mayor, he would have never allowed his name to be put on the ballot.

In the middle of all the adverse publicity, the *San Francisco Bulletin* stated, "The hot sincerity and hatred of wrong that burns in the revolutionary heart of young Jack London is the same spirit that characterized the tea-overboard party in Boston Harbor. It is the spirit that will ultimately reserve for the Republic all that is best, for it is the opposite of the dull spirit of slavish respect for the Established, which slavishness is composed of abasement of mind, and selfishness of character." This was a real surprise to Jack, since the *Bulletin* was neither a radical nor a socialist paper.

The Raven also picked up Jack's spirit when it wrote, just after the election, "Mr. London's first, last and only campaign speech was made on the Sunday evening previous to the election. The several hundred Socialists and admirers of the man willingly paid the admission fee, ranging from ten cents to fifty cents. This class of politicians believe in paying for what they receive, and in this instance, they got full value for the money received. To hear a great man speak is always a pleasure; to hear Mr. London is an education. His ideas are so unique, so free from convention, so overpowering."

At the height of the headline spree, the *War of the Classes* was published. It was astoundingly successful for a collection of revolutionary articles. It caused people to think and gave them a chance to read some of Jack's ideas without the usual reportorial distortion. The book made it clear that there was and had been a class war going on in the United States and that everyone was participating in it. Jack never had anything to say about policy in the Socialist Party and stayed rigidly within its guidelines; but by 1905 he had become America's leading propagandist for the Party, a role he continued to play for many years.

In mid-March Jack and Cloudesley completed their month-and-a-half sailing cruise and returned to Oakland. An old injury had been causing Jack a lot of pain and worry. Dr. Nicholson diagnosed it as a tumor and operated at the Shingle Sanitarium in Oakland on March 25. The tumor proved to be nonmalignant, and after a few days' recovering at 1216 Telegraph Jack put the *Spray* back in her moorings and went to Glen Ellen for the summer. Here there were no telephones, no people, no engagements, nothing but work, sunshine, and health—and hopefully no more headlines.

While Jack was in the Sanitarium, Charmian bought Washoe Ban—a beautiful thoroughbred horse—from Dr. Miner for two hundred fifty dollars, using part of the three hundred fifty dollars Jack had received for winning *The Black Cat* magazine contest with his story "A Nose for the King." On April 13 Charmian rode the horse to Oakland, took the ferry to San Francisco, and then boarded the river steamer *Sonoma* to Petaluma. She spent the night there at the American Hotel, and on the following day astride Ban rode the twenty-two miles over Sonoma Mountain to Glen Ellen.

The Southern Pacific depot in Glen Ellen. The town was also serviced by the Northwestern Pacific.

Main Street in Glen Ellen in Jack's time

Jack on Washoe Ban

Jack and Manyoungi moved into "Jack's House" next to Wake Robin Lodge, where Charmian lived with her Aunt Netta and Uncle Roscoe Eames. The first morning that Jack felt strong enough to go outside he went out to see Ban. He ran his hand across his coat of purest chestnut-gold and quickly decided that Charmian knew what she was doing when she bought horses.

Jack and Charmian had an excellent opportunity to get to know each other thoroughly before their wedding in November. Mornings were spent in Jack's little two-room cottage, Jack writing his one thousand words and answering his ever increasing volume of mail, while Charmian banged away at her new Remington No. 7 in a valiant and usually successful effort to keep up with the typing of Jack's manuscripts and letters. Knowledge of her Uncle Roscoe's unorthodox method of shorthand was an excellent asset to their work together through the years.

In the afternoons Jack and Charmian mounted Ban and Belle and rode together through the beautiful Valley of the Moon, exploring every little byway and secluded glen. They rode through the vineyards, up to the "secret meadow" and the falls, and wandered among growths of redwoods on Sonoma Mountain. One of their most pleasurable outings was when they rode through the ethereal magnificence of Nun's Canyon.

They visited the hot springs in Agua Caliente and Boyes. At Boyes Hot Springs they chatted with Captain and Mrs. H. E. Boyes in their quaint English cottage. Captain Boyes showed Jack a letter from Rudyard Kipling in which the English author asked the Captain if he had run across Jack London around Sonoma. Kipling enclosed a copy of "Mainly About People," containing a flattering criticism of Jack's work. Being called a genius by a man he admired greatly brought a lump to Jack's throat.

Jack and Charmian boxed, swam, and did everything except walk. Jack never walked unless it was impossible to get from one place to another in any other way. He had walked enough with Kelly's Army during his tramp days.

As the days grew warmer, the summer campers began to swarm into the little town of Glen Ellen. Its eight hotels and an equal number of bars were kept full by the two railroads, the Northwestern Pacific and the Southern Pacific, bringing visitors and campers from San Francisco and Oakland.

Wake Robin's cabins were soon full, and the swimming pool in Sonoma Creek was a place of wild fun daily. Jack loved to teach the youngsters how to swim and dive. Then after a frolic in the water they got lessons in boxing and wrestling, or just relaxed while he read to them. Evenings were quiet times in the country—usually spent playing cards, talking, or listening to Charmian play the piano. One evening Jack and Charmian's Uncle Roscoe were discussing Joshua Slocum's voyage aboard the *Spray*.

"If Slocum could do it alone in a thirty-five-foot sloop, with an old tin clock for a chronometer, why couldn't we do it in a ten-foot-longer boat with better equipment and more company?"

After discussing the proposition Jack turned to Charmian. "What do you say, Charmian?—suppose five years from now, after we're married and have built our house somewhere, we start on a voyage around the world in a forty-five-foot yacht."

Eager to be on the adventure trail with Jack, Charmian responded quickly, "I'm with you, every foot of the way, but why wait five years? Why not begin construction in the spring and let the house wait? No use putting up a home and running right away and leaving it! I love a boat, you love a boat; let's call the boat our house until we get ready to stay a little while in one place."

Thus the cruise of the *Snark* was born. Much of the rest of the summer was spent by the two lovers in planning their "round-the-world" trip. They would build their boat after completion of the Eastern lecture tour early in 1906 and leave as soon as it was ready.

In August Jack and Charmian went to see *The Great Interrogation*—a play based on Jack's story of the same name. The play was written by Ada Lee Bascom (Mrs. George Hamilton Marsden) and since it was based on his story, it carried Jack's name as collaborator.

The play was a huge success. The audience clamored and waited for Jack to appear. Ashton Stevens in the *San Francisco Examiner* reported, "Success was

POST OFFICE GLEN ELLEN CAL.

The Chawet Hotel on the left, post office and general store on the right, in Glen Ellen

Edward Biron Payne and Ninetta Eames in front of Wake Robin Lodge

WAKE ROBIN LODGE

Evidently Charmian goofed.

Jack and Charmian and the old No. 7 Remington

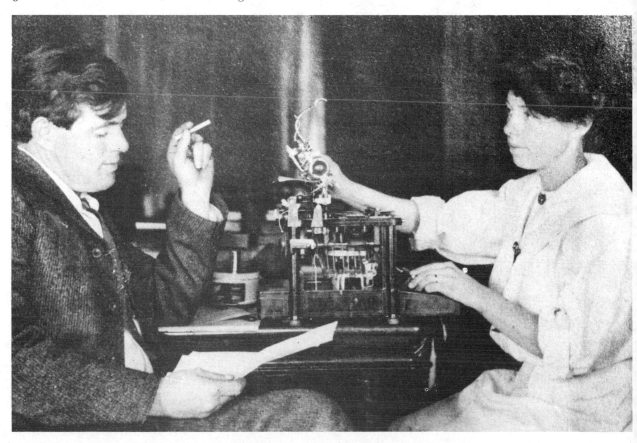

149

The Northwestern Pacific Railroad station in Glen Ellen

Jack and Charmian had fun in everything they did.

Hotel Riverside in Glen Ellen

a riot. The calls for the author were bringing in the police when finally somebody discovered Jack London sitting in a twenty-five-cent seat in the gallery. He was hustled to the stage, and with him went Lee Bascom, who collaborated." Jack attributed to Miss Bascom whatever excellence the drama possessed. Of Jack's disclaimer of credit Stevens commented: "It was a pretty nervous, shaky explanation. The man that can talk the ears off a thousand

The newspapers couldn't believe that Jack London had written a very successful play—
The Great Interrogation

HOTEL RIVERSIDE

socialists, who is at home on any rostrum from the cart to the curb, was obviously rattled." He had good reason to be rattled. He had had nothing to do with the dramatization and had sat in the gallery, hopefully unseen, so Lee Bascom would get the credit she deserved.

By now Jack was certain that, after the cruise, he would tie himself to the Valley of the Moon for life. Back in June he and Charmian had looked over the old "Greenlaw place" now owned by Robert P. Hill and fell in love with its romantic knolls. Its irregular diamond shape was bounded by the magnificently wooded gorge of old Asbury Creek to the southeast. The whole place was a wilderness of every type of California timber and shrubbery, save some forty acres of cleared land that had once yielded an abundance of wine grapes. Jack had to have it. This was the anchor he so desperately

Ashton Stevens did a full-page interview with Jack when The Great Interrogation *was playing at the Alcazar Theatre.*

wanted. It would be an escape from the social life of the city, which had snubbed him and for which he cared little.

On June 4 Jack, Charmian, and Manyoungi went to the Hill Ranch for a picnic and a long talk with the Allens—tenants on the place. The following day they drove to Eldridge to talk with the Hills. Two days later Jack put a five-hundred-dollar binder on the property and wired Brett for an advance of sixty-five hundred to complete the transaction. A few days later the check arrived and Jack became a farmer. For another six hundred dollars he bought the Allens' livestock and farm equipment and hired Mr. Werner Wiget as foreman. The Jack London Ranch became a reality.

Jack was creating few new headlines, but his books and stories kept his name before the public. *The Sea-Wolf* reached the top of the best-seller list, while *War of the Classes* went through several printings and kept the socialist *v.* capitalist controversy

active, and his new boxing story, *The Game*, was running serially in the *Metropolitan Magazine*.

The Game created headlines when critics claimed the story was unreal—that no fighter could be killed by hitting his head on the canvas. Jack replied that he had seen this actually happen in the West Oakland Athletic Club. The furor died down considerably when Jimmy Britt, lightweight champion of the world, reviewed *The Game* for the *San Francisco Examiner* and said, with a reproduction of a letter from Jack, "With nothing more than the above letter to assure me that Jack London is strictly on the 'level' and nothing more to guarantee me that he knows 'The Game' than his description of his fictional prize-fight, I would, if he were a part of our world, propose or accept him as referee of my impending battle with Nelson. *The Game* is certainly an epic on pugilism." Jack didn't referee the fight, but on September 9 he went to Colma and reported it for the *Examiner*.

On July 2 he started *White Fang*, his companion novel to *The Call of the Wild*—a marvelous story of the controlling and modifying influences and the civilizing and uplifting powers of love and tenderness, of the real spirit of humanity.

Jack said, "People find fault with me for my 'disgusting realism.' Life is full of disgusting realism. I know men and women as they are—millions of them yet in the slime stage. But I am an evolutionist, therefore a broad optimist, hence my love for the human (in the slime though he be) comes from my knowing him as he is and seeing the divine possibilities ahead of him. That's the whole motive of my *White Fang*. Every atom of organic life is plastic. The finest specimens now in existence were once all pulpy infants capable of being molded this way or that. Let the pressure be one way and we have atavism—the reversion to the wild; the other domestication, civilization. I have always been impressed with the awful plasticity of life and I feel that I can never lay enough stress upon the marvelous power and influence of environment."

The summer of 1905 was relaxing, but not monotonous. George Sterling had visited before leaving for Carmel, Flora and little Johnny had been up to see his new ranch, he had started the building of a beautiful new barn on his property, and had spent much time reading Nietzsche, Maeterlinck, Schopenhauer, and other authors by the dozen. In

Jack and George Wharton James discuss a passage in one of Jack's books.

George Sterling

From left to right: Xavier Martinez, Jim Whitaker, and Jack London. Blowing bubbles was a favorite pastime at Wake Robin Lodge.

addition he had been preparing for his fall lecture trip. He also completed "The Unexpected," a review of *The Walking Delegate*, "All Gold Canyon," "Planchette," a review of *The Long Day*, the "Holy Jumpers" article, and most of *White Fang*.

On October 4 he was heavily in debt, with only $207.83 in his checking account. His biggest worry was financing his trip East for the Slayton Lecture Bureau. Jack had to pay his expenses and those of his valet, Manyoungi, and Charmian, who was to follow him the following day to Newton, Iowa, where she was to wait for his call from Chicago the minute he was notified that his divorce was final. However, the future wasn't as bleak as it looked. In November he would receive thirty-seven hundred dollars from *Outing* as the first half payment for magazine rights to *White Fang*. He had also signed a one-year contract with Brett at Macmillan, which, starting December 1, would bring him three hundred dollars per month on general royalties; and the Slayton Lecture Bureau would be paying him six hundred dollars a week plus expenses for two when he started the lecture tour.

LECTURE TOUR—1905–1906

On October 18 Jack was on the train en route to his first lecture, in Kansas City. From there, he traveled to the following cities, lecturing every night: Matoon, Kansas; Mt. Vernon, Iowa; Chicago, Illinois; Lincoln, Nebraska; Ames, Iowa; Indianapolis, Indiana; Evanston, Illinois; Toledo, Ohio; Madison, Wisconsin; Oberlin, Ohio; Mercersburg, Pennsylvania; Orange, New Jersey; Brooklyn Height, New Jersey; New York, New York; Oneonta, New York; York, Pennsylvania; Oxford, Ohio; Sandusky, Ohio; New Kensington, Pennsylvania; and Elyria, Ohio.

Finally the news reached him at Elyria on November 18 that Judge Ellsworth of Oakland had signed the final decree of divorce. Jack wired Charmian to come as fast as possible to Chicago. She grabbed the early train on the 19th and Jack and Manyoungi met her at the station. They rushed by cab to the *Chicago American* office for the license and took the elevated to the Westside where

they were married by Notary Public J. J. Grant. Mr. Harstone of the *American* and Manyoungi were the witnesses. Their wedding night at the Victoria Hotel was worse than a Vermont "shivaree" with a squad of reporters pounding on their door and clamoring for a story.

The following day newspapers carried banner headlines. The nation was shocked because the couple had been married the day after the divorce. The reporters had neglected to mention that it had been well over two years since their decision to marry. To make things worse, the local papers carried the news that the marriage was invalid because divorced people had to wait a year before remarriage in Illinois.

Jack exclaimed, "Great Scott! Is that so? Well, we will get married tomorrow in Wisconsin and every other state in the union, if necessary . . ." They didn't have to, because the authorities finally decided it was legal after all. But Victorian Amer-

A caricature of Jack as socialist lecturer

ica didn't forgive that easily. Some lectures were cancelled, people refused to read Jack's books, and a few libraries would no longer put a Jack London book on their shelves. The two lovers couldn't have cared less. At last they were married, and this time there was no doubt about it. No two people were ever more compatible, and it would have been impossible for Jack to have found a more perfect mate.

Two days after their marriage they were on the grueling lecture trail again. From Chicago to Elwood, Indiana; Champaign, Illinois; to Grinnell College in Iowa. After the lecture at Grinnell, they had a short rest with friends in Newton, Iowa. Six days later Jack lectured in Des Moines, Iowa, and then the newlyweds headed straight for Boston to depart for Jamaica on December 27 on their long awaited honeymoon. Meanwhile, while waiting for the departure date, Jack lectured at Bowdoin College in New Brunswick, Maine. The week following this lecture was spent with Charmian's relatives in that state. Returning to Boston, they were entertained by friends, and Jack lectured at the Fremont Temple, at Faneuil Hall, and at Harvard.

Sailing date finally arrived, and Jack, Charmian, and Manyoungi boarded the United Fruit Company's steamship *Farragut* bound for Jamaica. The two lovers were perhaps the happiest people on the ship. Charmian had waited many years for the right man. She had wanted a successful man with fire, one who could sail, ride horseback with her—a fun person with brains and drive. Jack was handsome, famous, loaded with charisma, and sought after by the fairer sex wherever he went. He could have chosen from thousands, but was thoroughly satisfied that he had chosen the right mate. It was a happy couple who ended the year of 1905 aboard the *Farragut* in sight of Port Antonio, Jamaica.

HONEYMOON IN JAMAICA

Happily threading their way through the ever present reporters and admirers, Jack and Charmian registered at the Titchfield Hotel. In the evening they were welcomed by a host of new friends. Among them was Ella Wheeler Wilcox, who at the time was one of America's most famous poets.

Honeymoon notwithstanding, mornings were spent getting out those thousand words. It was no mania that dictated this routine, but a thoroughly developed work habit—a writing schedule that worked for him and was followed inflexibly throughout his writing career. Brett and many others tried to convince him that such a routine was not conducive to the best work a man could do. Jack wasn't interested in the best work he could do. A thousand words a day at ten cents a word was

better than five hundred fine words at the same ten cents a word. Moreover, he knew what the editors would buy and he was writing for a living, not to achieve a chair at Harvard.

After an interview for *Western Comrade*, Emanuel Julius quoted Jack as saying, "I am nothing more than a fairly good artisan. The only reason I write is because I am well paid for my labor—that's what I call it—labor. I get lots of money for my books and stories. I always write what the editors want, not what I'd like to write. I grind out what the capitalist editors want, and the editors buy only what the business and editorial departments permit. The editors are not interested in the truth; they don't want to tell the truth. A writer can't sell a story when it tells the truth, so why should he batter his head against a stone wall? He gives the editors what they want, for he knows that the stuff he believes in and loves to write will never be published."

The afternoon after their arrival was spent in the saddle sightseeing in Port Antonio and visiting a pineapple plantation; then to Moortown where many descendants of Spanish slaves made their home. The next day found them on a train heading for Buff Bay, where they picked up a couple of horses and rode to Chester Vale and then over the Blue Ridge Range, through Hardware Gap, Silver Hill Gap, Greenwich, Newcastle Barracks, Gordontown, and Kingston. On January 5 they said goodbye to their riding companion, Harry Schauffler, a friend they had met in Port Antonio, and traveled to Santiago Harbor, Cuba, on a dirty little Spanish steamer, the *Oteri*. Here they visited San Juan Hill and other tourist attractions.

The Londons sailed from Cuba on the steamer *Halifax* to Key West, and then transferred to the *Shinnecock* bound for Miami. Boating, angling, driving in the Everglades, a visit to an alligator and crocodile farm, and a shopping trip for curios and snakeskins filled their leisure time in this city. From there they traveled on to Daytona Beach. Finally time ran out, and on January 17, they went to Jacksonville and on to New York City. Jack was so sick on arrival that he should have gone to bed. Instead, he gathered together enough strength to give a scheduled lecture at Grand Central Palace.

It had been a good honeymoon. Everywhere they went the red carpet was rolled out in greeting, and the usual crowd of reporters and hero worshippers were always at hand. Now and then they were able to wander around without recognition—a welcome change. But, as with most vacationers, they returned to face Jack's demanding lecture schedule worn out from travel and sightseeing. If there was something to see or do he did it with his customary gusto. Charmian was just as bad. They could always relax tomorrow or at least some tomorrow.

BACK ON THE LECTURE TOUR

The Jack London lectures were causing talk from coast to coast and the reactions were mixed. The spectacle of the president of the Intercollegiate Socialist Society, whom the International Socialist Review had described as a "genuine, old-fashioned, proletarian, class-struggle socialist," traveling by train from lecture to lecture in a drawing room with a Korean valet was quite startling to a lot of people and especially to his fellow socialists, who were far more critical than others. Nobody realized that Jack had to have a place where he could write mornings and where Charmian, due to her insomnia, could get the most sleep possible. Traveling in privacy was a necessity—not a luxury.

Very few people recognized London's devout belief in the socialist cause and his willingness to give up all he had to see socialism adopted in the United States. But until it became law, Jack knew that he had to make his way among the capitalists. His hatred for capitalism and his faith in socialism were the driving forces of his character. Reconciling his way of earning a living with his preference for socialism was a disturbing problem. In his article "The House Beautiful," he wrote, "I often regret that I was born in this particular period of the world. In the matter of servants, how I wish I were living in the golden future of the world, where there will be no servants—naught but service of love. But in the meantime, living here and now, being practical, understanding the rationality and necessity of the division of labor, I accept servants. But such acceptance does not justify me in lack of consideration for them. In my house beautiful, their rooms shall not be dens and holes. And on this score I foresee a fight with the architect. They shall have bath-rooms, toilet conveniences, and comforts for their leisure time and human life—if I have to work Sundays to pay for it. Even under the division of labor I recognize that no man has a right to servants who will not treat them as humans compounded of the same clay as himself, with similar bundles of nerves and desires, contradictions, irritabilities, and lovablenesses. Heaven in the drawing-room and hell in the kitchen is not an atmosphere for a growing child to breathe—nor an adult either . . . I'd prefer that the servants had three hours to go swimming (or hammocking) than be compelled to spend those three hours in keeping the house spick and span. Therefore, it devolves upon me to build a house that can be kept clean and orderly without the need of those three hours."

Jack did not hate capitalists, but he did hate their economic system and their control of the system of government. Had there been equality for everybody under its system, if its leadership had written laws guaranteeing a fair distribution of profits between capital and labor, and if adequate provision had been made for those who found it impossible to compete, London would probably have accepted the system and written material like Rex Beach, Richard Harding Davis, or Harry Leon Wilson.

In June of 1906 he wrote "The Somnambulists," a strong indictment of the system he lived under. He describes the types he despised:

He bribes legislatures, buys judges, "controls" primaries, and then goes and hires other men to tell him that it is all glorious and right.

He is fastidiously nauseated at the thought of two prize-fighters bruising each other with their fists; but at the same time, because it will cost him some money, he will refuse to protect the machines in his factory, though he is aware that the lack of protection every year mangles, batters, and destroys out of all humanness thousands of working men, women, and children. He will chatter about things refined and spiritual and godlike like himself, and he and the men who herd with him will calmly adulterate the commodities they put upon the market and which annually kill tens of thousands of babies and young children.

He will recoil at the suggestion of the horrid spectacle of two men confronting each other with gloved hands in the roped arena, and at the same time he will clamor for larger armies and larger navies, for more destructive war machines, which, with a single discharge, will disrupt and rip to pieces more human beings than have died in the whole history of prize-fighting. He will bribe a city council for a franchise or a state legislature for a commercial privilege; but he has never been known, in all his sleep-walking history, to bribe any legislative body in order to achieve any moral end, such as, for instance, abolition of prize-fighting, child labor laws, pure food bills, or old age pensions.

Our statesmen sell themselves and their country for gold. Our municipal servants and state legislators commit countless treasons. The world of graft! The world of betrayal!

These were but a few of the things that aroused Jack London's ire. In the lecture he gave so many times during his lecture tour, "Revolution" (sometimes camouflaged under another name), he gave example after example of those who were suffering under the inequalities of the system:

In the United States there are 10,000,000 people living in poverty. By poverty is meant that condition of life in which, through lack of food and adequate shelter, the mere standard of working efficiency cannot be maintained.

In Chicago there is a woman who toiled sixty hours per week. She was a garment worker. She sewed buttons on clothes. Among the Italian garment workers of Chicago, the average weekly wage of the dressmakers is 90 cents, but they work every week of the year. The average weekly wage of the pants finishers is $1.31, and the average number of weeks employed in the year is 27.85. The average yearly earnings of the dressmakers is $37.00; of the pants finishers $42.41. Such wages mean no childhood for the children, beastliness of living, and starvation for all.

On a pile of rags in a room bare of furniture and freezing cold, Mrs. Mary Gallin, dead from starvation, with an emaciated baby four months old crying at her breast, was found at 513 Myrtle Avenue, Brooklyn, by Policeman McCommon of the Flushing Avenue Station. Huddled together for warmth in another part of the room were the father, James Gallin, and three children ranging from two to eight years of age. The children looked at the policeman much as ravenous animals might have done. They were famished, and there was not a vestige of food in their comfortless home.

In lecture after lecture Jack told his audience that the capitalist class had an opportunity such as was vouchsafed no previous ruling class in the history of the world, but it had failed deplorably, ignobly, and horribly. He not only told them that the capitalists had failed, but went on to prove his assertion with proof after proof, until the capitalists cringed in their seats and the socialists yelled in approval.

But not all socialists were yelling approval. Some accused him of retarding socialist work in America by twenty years by his overzealous approach and style of life. Smiling at the bitter accusation, Jack said, "On the contrary, I believe I still have accelerated the revolution by at least five minutes." The fashionable Averill Women's Club passed a resolution denouncing college football and Jack London. However, both have survived.

Dr. Alexander Irvine, handsome minister of Pilgrim's Church in New Haven and head of the socialist local there, went to New York to plead with Jack to lecture at Yale University. Jack was more than willing, so Irvine raced back to New Haven to make arrangements. President Hadley agreed with one of his professors who stated, "Yale is a University and not a monastery. Besides, Jack London is one of the most distinguished men in America." The New Haven committee did a fabulous job of promotion. Comrade Max Dellfant painted a striking poster of Jack for the occasion.

On the morning of January 26, 1906, students and faculty were startled to see the posters on nearly every tree and billboard. This advance publicity nearly precipitated war on the campus, but Professors Kent and Phelps did a masterful job of calming things down with their request for fair play. When the tumult had settled, Charles M. Field said, "Yale Union and Yale Faculty are sweating under the collar for fear that London might say something Socialistic."

The *New Haven Leader* sent a reporter to cover the lecture. Here is his report:

It was the newest thing under the sun! Woolsey Hall—that white dream of an auditorium filled to the doors with society folk, students, professors and hundreds of workingmen, socialists. It was interesting to notice President Hadley there and Prof. Sumner and Col. Osborn. The crowd was representative of all classes in the community.

It was dignified. At Harvard the students were vociferous, there was some horse play, but the great body of Yale students sat there for over two hours and listened to the gospel of socialism. It was probably the straightest thing they had ever heard. London spoke extemporaneously in his introduction, but his paper was carefully prepared. "It was prepared," said Jack, "to hit the students between the eyes." It was truth by the chunk.

This was verily bearding the lions. In the school filled with the sons of the high priests of capitalism this young man of 30 who had played

Jack and Dr. Alexander Irvine

the game of life in many climes hit out straight from the shoulder.

Some of the boys under whose auspices he spoke nearly had St. Vitus's dance when it was mooted that he had "socialistic tendencies." They were awfully worried and kept buzzing around until the last minute, then they faced the inevitable and introduced him. The applause was hearty. They applauded twice—at the beginning and at the close. Jack is no orator, but he delivered the goods with the precision of a social marksman (Marxman).

After the lecture the students lured him to a big dormitory and there they piled in until not another man could find room. He is very gentle. He speaks softly in conversation, but the boys were conscious that behind the gentle voice was the heart and nature of a lion.

Max Dellfant's poster for Jack London's lecture at Yale, January 26, 1906

When he arrived home at midnight there was a reception awaiting him again.

An intercollegiate socialist society was formed after the lecture.

"A professor of Yale," Dr. Irvine said, "told me a few days after the lecture that it was the greatest intellectual stimulus Yale had had in many years, and he sincerely hoped that London would return and expound the socialist program in the same hall."

The Yale lecture was typical. It was well attended and stimulated a great deal of thinking. One of the newspapers reporting it gives us a glimpse of Jack's technique: ". . . he walked to the edge of the stage and began to speak in a clear voice, which reached easily to the fartherest corner of the hall. He used scarcely any gestures, and rarely raised his voice even to emphasize a point. His emphasis he got by reiteration."

The New Haven press was unusual in that it gave an unbiased report. The press in most instances twisted the words to sell extra copies or to satisfy their owners and subscribers. Jack's notoriety was in full swing. Many papers who had been extolling "the brilliant young author" now said, "pathologically he is neurasthenic," or simply disposed of him as "that socialist sensation-monger who calls himself Jack London." The "To hell with the Constitution" quote was still being printed as though Jack had coined it. But interestingly, the editor of *The Morning Gleaner* in Flora London's hometown, Massillon, Ohio, quipped, "Must a novelist necessarily admire the Constitution?"

Following Yale, the lecture trail led Jack and Charmian to Chicago, where he appeared in the hallowed Model Hall of the University of Chicago and the Cook County Normal Training School; to the Central Presbyterian Church in St. Paul, Minnesota; and, at last, to the final lectures of the trip in Grand Forks, North Dakota, where he lectured at the State University in the morning and at the Opera House that night.

While on the tour, Jack met old friends and made many new ones. Upton Sinclair lunched with him in New York, and they became friends for life—a friendship by mail, however, since teetotaller Sinclair couldn't stand being with anyone who drank, and "Jack," Sinclair recalled, "was owlishly determined to have his fun with me." Jack drank more than usual on this occasion and Sinclair continued, "He told tales of incredible debauches; tales of opium and hashish, and I know not what other strange ingredients; tales of whiskey bouts lasting for weeks." Jack had a lot of fun with Upton in this manner, but Sinclair had the last laugh when he wrote *The Cup of Fury* by further exaggerating the exaggerations that Jack had made of his own drinking.

At Yale, London met Sinclair Lewis, and another lifelong friendship was formed. In 1910 and 1911 Lewis sold a number of story plots to Jack. It was a perfect solution to the problems of both. One needed money and the other needed ideas.

Earlier Jack had confessed to a friend. "No, I'm darned if any stories just came to me. I had to work like the devil for the themes. Then, of course, it was easy to just write them down. Expression, you see—with me—is far easier than invention. It is with the latter I have the greatest trouble, and work the hardest. To find some thought worthy of being clothed with enough verbiage to make a story, there's the rub."

On September 28, 1910, Lewis wrote to Jack, "I was very glad to receive your note suggesting that you are willing to look at some short story plots, etc. I am enclosing a big bunch, at the completion of which I have been working day and night since hearing from you. . . . I hope to gawd that you will feel like taking a considerable part of them, because, if you do, it will probably finally give me the chance to get back to free lancing—nothing but writing—which I haven't done for over a year; can the job and really get at decent work."

Jack had just returned from the cruise of the *Snark,* and needing plots, he was more than willing to buy fifteen of them for seventy dollars. Besides, he was always ready to reach for his billfold to help a young writer in need. Some of these ideas were used for London's "When the World Was Young," "Winged Blackmail," and *The Assassination Bureau, Ltd.* A plot bought later was used for the *The Abysmal Brute.*

According to Dr. Franklin Walker, Jack bought twenty-seven of the fifty-five plots submitted by

Upton Sinclair

Lewis for a total of $137.50. For Lewis this was welcome money, and the added thrill of having worked with the famous Jack London was nice, too. Maule and Cane in *The Man from Main Street* said, "The great man was extremely friendly to the skinny, the red-headed, the practically anonymous secretary." In a letter to Harvey Taylor, literary agent of the Jack London Estate in the early '30s, Lewis said further, "Now that I am older than he was at the time I understand what he told me—that a fresh scheme gave him a new urge to his own vast experience. It was to me a very exciting and helpful thing to be permitted to suggest fresh slants on his own wisdom."

With the lecture tour now at an end due to cancellations caused by the newspaper notoriety and his own anxiety to return home, he and Charmian boarded a train for Oakland. Those who had listened to Jack's fervent pleas fully expected to wake up in the morning to the sound of bugles announcing the arrival of the Revolution, but at the moment Jack London was more concerned with getting started on the building of his boat and his trip around the world. The Revolution could go on without him.

Joan (left) and Becky around 1906. They are standing in front of their home at 519 Thirty-first Street.

THE YEAR OF THE *SNARK*

There is no indication that any correspondence or any plans were made regarding the building of the *Snark* during the lecture tour. However, Jack must have made some arrangements with the Anderson Ways, a San Francisco shipyard, prior to the tour, for only ten days after his arrival in Oakland he wrote to Bailey Millard of *Cosmopolitan* stating, "the keel is laid." This may have been a metaphor for "the decision has been made," since there is no mention of any construction of the *Snark* in Charmian's diary until after the earthquake, when mention was made that the iron keel for the *Snark* was to have been laid on the day of the earthquake. She had noted, on March 18, 1906, that the first thousand dollars was paid to the shipbuilder, probably to bind the contract.

The name *Snark* was taken from Lewis Carroll's *The Hunting of the Snark.* The boat was to be forty-five feet long but somehow during construction two feet disappeared and the final measurements were forty-three feet on the waterline and fifty-five feet over all, with a fifteen-foot beam and seven feet, eight inches draft. Headroom below decks was six feet. There were four watertight compartments that leaked profusely all the way to Honolulu, where the boat was put into seaworthy condition. Auxiliary power was furnished by a seventy-horse power Century engine built by the New York Yacht, Launch & Engine Co. of Morris Heights, New Jersey. There were three staterooms, an engine room, bathroom, and galley. Her speed was estimated at ten knots under sail and eight knots with motor power.

No ballast was necessary, since her iron keel weighed five tons. She was built at Anderson Ways near Hunter's Point in San Francisco and outfitted alongside the Twelfth Street bridge in Oakland. But it was a long, rough road between Jack's statement February 18, 1906, that "the keel was laid" and sailing date, April 23, 1907.

The most important business of the year would be the boat, but in order to pay for it, Jack had to write furiously and arrange for future articles with advances. He put his wife's Uncle Roscoe on salary of fifty dollars per month to keep an eye on the boatbuilding, and went to work.

Putting engine in Jack London's "Snark" — my Dad

Installing the engine on the Snark

Jack kept a close eye on the Snark's construction.

Since he had to move from the flat at 1216 Telegraph Avenue to the Wake Robin Lodge annex, a place had to be found for Flora and Johnny Miller. After a short hunt Jack bought a respectable home at 490 Twenty-seventh Street, turning it over to them while reserving an upstairs room for himself and Charmian to use as their Oakland "townhouse." He never shirked his responsibility to those who were dependent upon him. In a day when the average income in the United States was five hundred per year, he gave his mother sixty dollars per month, furnished her a home, and paid all her expenses. He was equally generous to Aunt Jennie and cared for her all his life; Charmian continued the same care after his death.

As soon as Jack and Charmian were settled in at Glen Ellen, Jack started his fund-raising activities. He carefully divided his future writing efforts for the *Snark* into four divisions—news, industrial, political, and the story of the trip itself. He then offered various magazines exclusive rights to his work in the category that would best fit their needs. To *Cosmopolitan* he offered the travelogue, asking for a three-thousand-dollar advance. Bailey Millard, editor, accepted the proposition, but scaled the advance down to two thousand dollars and included a check. Jack attempted to make similar arrangements to do illustrated articles on events of large news value for *Collier's,* and studies of home life

490 Twenty-seventh Street, Oakland

through the South Seas and around the world for *Woman's Home Companion.* The *Companion* agreed with his plans.

Now that funds for the trip were assured, Jack had to turn his attention to raising money for his ever increasing financial struggle at home, sometimes whimsically called "Jack's Monthly Miracle" by his sister Eliza. He was supporting Flora, Johnny, and Mammy Jennie at 490 Twenty-seventh Street; Bessie, Joan, and Bess at 519 Thirty-first Street; Charmian and himself at Wake Robin Lodge; paying Werner Wiget and the hired men on the ranch; and partially supporting Roscoe and Ninetta Eames at Wake Robin.

The old ink-pencil was now pushing more than a thousand words a day. In March "A Day's Lodg-

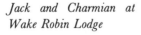

Jack and Charmian at Wake Robin Lodge

163

ing" was finished and "When God Laughs" was begun. "What Life Means to Me" was published in *Cosmopolitan.* It was an immediate hit and did much to improve Jack's reputation, which had been damaged in the lecture tour.

Cosmopolitan had asked many famous people to write an article entitled "What Life Means to Me," publishing one installment each month. While in New York, Jack had discussed the series with Edwin Markham, asking him how he was going to approach it. One of Markham's observations was that *Cosmopolitan* would blue-pencil ideas about socialism, but Jack's version appeared intact. In June an article in *Cosmopolitan* stated, "Jack London was the first to write on 'What Life Means to Me,' and his contribution has gone all over the country, and has been lauded as the best thing he ever wrote." The *New York Independent* reported, "We have had many ambitious studies of American life, from DeTocqueville to Münsterberg, but not one of them has penetrated so deeply into the heart of it as does this frank self-revelation of an American gifted with the divine fire, who has intensely lived it."

Editors of hundreds of papers swamped *Cosmopolitan* with requests for permission to reprint the article. The July *Cosmopolitan* said that Jack London's "What Life Means to Me" was the most discussed, sought after, and lauded magazine article of the year. Margaret Dunn's letter of April 19, 1906, was published. It stated, "Then that series of articles on 'What Life Means to Me'—well, I will just say that I skipped all the rest for a time to read that

first, for I had read Jack London's article in the March issue—which, by the way, was alone worth more than the price of the whole year's subscription." This was just one letter of thousands received by *Cosmopolitan* during the year. The Christmas issue in 1906 stated proudly, " 'What Life Means to Me' by Jack London has already been spoken of as the greatest magazine article of the year."

By the middle of the year the *Snark* had already consumed over ten thousand dollars and was only one-third completed. Jack had figured the total cost should be about seven thousand. However, his original figures had not taken into account the San Francisco earthquake and fire, which caused havoc with prices when the city attempted to climb out of its ashes. Materials and skilled labor were in great demand and got whatever prices were asked. Jack would have loved to cancel the whole thing, buy a boat, and take off for the South Seas, but he was caught in a trap of his own making. *Cosmopolitan* and the *Woman's Home Companion* had already signed contracts. The contract had also been signed with the shipyard, materials were either on the site or ordered, and the engine was en route from New Jersey. There was nothing he could do but go ahead with the plans as they were and hope for the best. The building of his own boat was part of the intrigue and interest in the project. Besides, he needed separate quarters for Charmian, himself, Roscoe Eames, and the crew, and it would have been nearly impossible to find a boat the size he wanted that would fit his particular needs.

THE SAN FRANCISCO EARTHQUAKE

On the morning of April 18, Charmian was fast asleep in an upstairs bedroom at Wake Robin. Jack was sleeping downstairs in the Annex. From early childhood Charmian had suffered from insomnia, apparently inherited from her mother, Dayelle Kittredge. Jack and Charmian always occupied separate sleeping quarters, due to her insomnia and Jack's bedtime habits of reading, writing, smoking, and coughing.

At 5:14 Charmian and everybody else in Northern California were rudely shaken awake by a gi-

gantic earthquake. Meeting Jack downstairs, they grabbed clothes and ran to the barn, where they threw saddles on Ban and Belle. By 6:00 A.M. they were atop Sonoma Mountain. Here they could see the clouds of smoke arising over San Francisco. In the other direction another column of smoke billowed above Santa Rosa.

A look at their ranch revealed extensive damage to the foundation of the new barn. Back in July of 1905 they had hired Martin Pasquini to do the stone and concrete work for the barn, but by the

San Francisco in ruins. Pictures taken by Jack London.

time the walls were completed the actual building had been postponed so that only the walls were destroyed when the quake hit.

There was no time for further inspection. With their characteristic love for adventure and concern for people, the Londons rushed to the scene of the disaster as fast as others fled from it. They hurried by train to Santa Rosa, where they saw a devastated city; then another train took them to San Francisco.

Less than twelve hours after the first shock Jack and Charmian were in the midst of the devastation. All Wednesday night they wandered up old Broadway and to other familiar haunts now in the path of the ravaging flames. The constant detona-

tions of dynamite were earsplitting, as General Funston and his men fought a heroic battle to save as much as possible. Fighting the fire was an impossible task without water, but they tried valiantly. After walking at least forty miles, according to Charmian, they curled up in a doorway on Nob Hill and slept till dawn. Then, making their way through the rubble of Mission Street to the docks, they grabbed a ferry for Oakland and tumbled into bed at 490 Twenty-seventh at noon and slept the clock around.

"No," Jack said, "I'll never write a word about it. What use trying? One could only string big words together, and curse the futility of them." But when *Collier's* offered him twenty-five cents a word for a

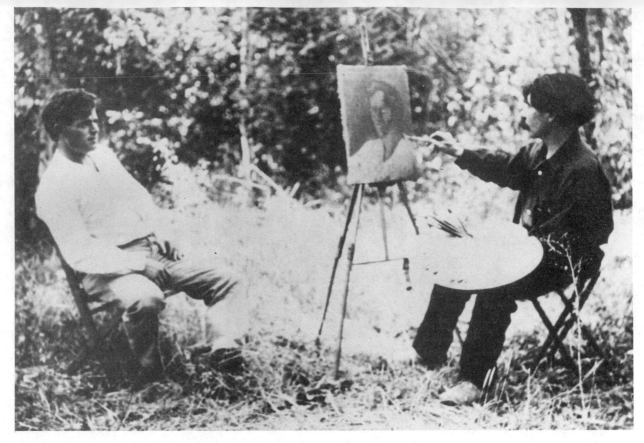

"Marty" paints Jack at Wake Robin Lodge. The painting burned in the fire following the San Francisco earthquake.

twenty-five-hundred-word article, he changed his mind and wrote "The Story of an Eyewitness."

Three weeks after the quake Jack and Charmian mounted Washoe Ban and Fleet and rode three hundred fifty miles throughout Northern California to see how the rest of the area had withstood the earthquake. Jack did no work on the trip—it was to be purely vacation and sightseeing. A few days after their return Ban got caught in a strand of barbed wire and sawed one of his hind legs nearly through. The only humane thing was a merciful bullet by the ranch foreman. Jack and Charmian sat stiffly together in a hammock at Wake Robin awaiting the sound of the gun. When it came they wept without restraint in each other's arms. They had lost a very dear friend.

SUMMER AND FALL OF 1906

By June 7 *Before Adam* was completed. On July 19 *Everybody's Magazine* accepted it by telegram and published it in serial form starting with the October issue. The story takes place before man's use of fire, before the wearing of clothes, before the use of weapons—at a time when man was in the process of becoming. It was a time when he spoke no language and used sounds instead of words. Three stages of man appear in the book—tree dwellers, cave dwellers, and fire makers. The stages were overlapped to increase the action and give the reader a better view of their evolutionary background.

The *New York Times* said, "Jack London has performed a wonderful feat in so describing the lives and passions of these rudimentary beings. He has builded a romance of the unknown ages, of the creatures that may have been, and endowed it all with poignant reality." Professor A. J. Keller of Yale University said, *"Before Adam* is in all essentials correct and scientific in its conception of early man," and promptly used it as a textbook for his anthropology classes. In 1962 Professor Loren Eiseley of the University of Pennsylvania said in his epilogue to the Bantam paper edition, "Fifty-five years have passed since *Before Adam* was written. Within that time many men have tried their hand at picturing the lives of our remote ancestors. Most have confined themselves to those later folk whom London called 'The Fire People.' In all this long

Brown Wolf snoozes while Jack catches up on some reading.

half-century, though our knowledge of human evolution has increased tremendously, it is my belief that no writer has since produced so moving and vivid a picture of man's primordial past as has Jack London."

It was a busy summer of writing. From April 24 through August 20 Jack submitted for publication "The Story of an Eyewitness," "Brown Wolf," a review of Upton Sinclair's *The Jungle,* an article on the Moyer-Haywood affair in Idaho, "A Day's Lodging," "When God Laughs," "The Apostate," "My Best Short Story," *Before Adam,* "The Somnambulists," "Created He Them," "A Wicked Woman," "The Wit of Porportuk," "Finis," and "Just Meat." All were well received, but probably the most powerful was "The Apostate."

The Londons had scarcely settled at Wake Robin when the editor of a large Eastern magazine tried to talk Jack into going into the Southern States to write a firsthand report on the child labor conditions in the cotton mills. He wanted to do it and was disappointed when he had to refuse. Not being able to do this vital work for the war against child labor, Jack decided to take time out of his busy schedule to write "The Apostate," which was the lead story in the famous *Woman's Home Companion* Child Labor issue of September, 1906. It was a story based on his own experiences in the jute mills of Oakland, and it became a major weapon in the fight for the abolition of child labor in the United States.

The Iron Heel was started on August 29. It was a difficult novel to write, and at the time all Jack could think about was how to make sea-anchors and oil drags, how to make ice, how to make electricity, and how to make gasoline engines go. With only a few short weeks before sailing, he had had no time in which to learn navigation. *The Iron Heel* was worked on intermittently during one of his most hectic periods. Barn, boat, ranch, and *The Iron*

Heel! Jack had a terrible time keeping them all straight, but gave each his undivided attention when necessary. In addition, there was always at least one visitor on the place. Contrary to commonly held beliefs, there were seldom more than four people visiting the ranch at any one period, but the times that Jack and Charmian were alone were few. Most of the visitors were the select few from "the crowd" or Charmian's relatives. Even during later years at the Jack London Ranch this remained true. Other than Xavier and Elsie Martinez, George and Carrie Sterling, Carlton and Lora Bierce, Ed and Ida Winship, Blanche, Dick and Gertrude Partington, Johannes and Elida Reimers, and Jim and Alyse Whitaker, the only ones who visited often were Senator James Duval Phelan, Henry Meade Bland, and George Wharton James. These were all family to Jack and Charmian. Hundreds of others from tramps to ambassadors made their one-day pilgrimages to visit Jack. Harry Houdini, Richard Harding Davis, Harry Leon Wilson, Rex Beach, Arnold Genthe, Jimmy Hopper, Fred Bechdolt, Cloudesley Johns, Bob Fitzsimmons, Jimmy Britt, and many others could be counted on to drop by when possible. On only three or four occasions were there as many as twelve people for dinner at any one time.

From 1906 until 1911 the Londons lived in the annex of Wake Robin. Their visitors were housed in small tent-cabins on the three and a half acres of the Lodge. There simply was no room for the grand entertaining normally attributed to the Londons. From 1911 until his death, Jack and Charmian lived in the old Kohler-Frohling Winery cottage. An attached winery building had been renovated for additional living space while guests were usually put up in one of the six guest rooms of the carriage house. The rooms on the other side of the carriage building housed ranch workers. Everyone ate together in the small dining room.

It was this limited space that caused Jack's gregarious soul to dream of the new stone house that would seat fifty in the dining room, and where he could house all his books—now kept in boxes wherever he could find space. Whenever he needed a reference the book was usually in a box in the loft of a distant barn. But all of this would have to wait until he got back from the cruise around the world. The house he was building now had only three cabins, a very small head, a small crew's quarters,

an engine room, and an extremely compact galley. But even while building the little one he was dreaming of the big one.

The summer was equally busy in many other ways. Johannes Reimers had spent a lot of time with them and supervised the landscaping for the future stone house. A number of varieties of fruit trees, several different varieties of table grapes, and a hedge of pyracantha were planted.

The barn was completed and is still the most beautiful one in the valley. Its walls were done right this time—Jack made sure of it. The concrete foundations for the walls were two feet thick and nine feet high. Upon them rested the great beams designed to carry the weight of hay and the forty tons of tile roof. The first building had been constructed on the Jack London Ranch and was worthy of the honor.

Curiously, one of the highlights of the summer was the two-week visit of Jack's mother and Johnny Miller beginning July 2. On the Fourth of July they played games and Flora had a ball. After a thoroughly enjoyable visit to her son's new ranch, Flora took Johnny with her as she returned to Oakland. As far as we know, this was the last time either she or Johnny ever set foot on the ranch.

Jack and Johnny were never close. As much as Jack wanted a son it is strange that he didn't grasp onto Johnny, but there was a gulf that neither ever crossed—Flora sat in the middle and made sure there was no crossing. Johnny was hers and that was that. Jack didn't understand children since he had never had a normal childhood of his own. By the time he was twelve, he was working long hours before and after school to add his share to the family struggle for survival. He simply couldn't understand that little Johnny thought only of pranks and play. To Jack this was a sign of weakness. He had the same problem with his oldest daughter. He tried to reason with Joan and Johnny as though they were adults and only succeeded in creating an impossible situation in which normal father-daughter and close uncle-nephew relations couldn't survive. In later years Johnny Miller was extremely eager to let any or all family skeletons out of the closet for one of Jack's biographers. Joan revealed the same bitterness in her book *Jack London and His Times.*

In November Jack and Charmian moved into their "townhouse" room at 490 Twenty-seventh in

The grocery store, post office, and the Pioneer Saloon in Glen Ellen. On occasion Jack visited all three.

Xavier Martinez. "Marty" was a renowned painter and Bohemian in California art circles in the early 1900s. He was born and raised in Guadalajara, Mexico. He studied at the Paris Ecole de Beaux Arts. Whistler and Carriere became close friends. The last forty years of his life were spent teaching art at the California School of Arts and Crafts in Oakland. "Marty" married Elsie, daughter of Jack London's close friend Herman "Jim" Whitaker.

A caricature of Xavier Martinez in his studio

Ed Winship picked up Jack and friends for an outing in his big car.

Jack and Charmian in front of the Kohler-Frohling Wine cottage on the Jack London ranch

170

Luther Burbank helped Jack raise spineless cactus on his ranch. This picture was taken on Burbank's place. From left to right: Edgar Lucius Larkin, Luther Burbank, and Jack London.

The Kohler-Frohling Winery building was destroyed in the 1906 earthquake. Jack built the carriage house on top of the old foundation. The cottage is on the right.

Jack and Johannes Reimers

This barn was built on the Hill Ranch. It was the first building Jack built on his ranch.

The barn under construction

Little Johnny Miller. Johnny was the son of Jack's stepsister Ida. Flora London raised him from the age of five.

Oakland so Jack could keep an eye on construction of the *Snark*. From then until sailing day in April, life was routine. Mornings Jack worked on *The Iron Heel*, completing it in December, and then finished the year by writing "Confession" and "Holding Her Down"—two episodes from his tramping experiences of 1894. After lunch at the Saddle Rock, Jack spent much of the afternoons at the dentist and taking care of *Snark* and other business. Charmian shopped or visited relatives.

There were several parties with "the crowd" in Piedmont; football at the University of California, and concerts in its Greek Theatre; plays and concerts at the Macdonough and Orpheum theatres or the Bishop Playhouse; and fun-filled dinner parties at the Oakland restaurants—the Forum, the Saddle Rock, and the Pabst Cafe. Jack's favorite restaurant was the Saddle Rock and his favorite on their menu was "ten-minute" wild duck, washed down with his favorite imported Liebfraumilch wine. Jack loved either canvas-back, mallard, or teal cooked excessively rare and accompanied by po-

tatoes au gratin. He usually made the best of any situation, finding most bad things to have something good in them. The *Snark* was delayed, but now, at least, he could feast on his favorite dish for the whole season and that almost made the whole miserable business worthwhile.

Jack sent his favorite recipe for roast duck to the editor of the *Suffrage Cook Book:*

The only way in the world to serve a canvas-back or a mallard, or a sprig, or even the toothsome teal, is as follows: The plucked bird should be stuffed with a tight handful of plain raw celery and, in a piping hot oven, roasted variously 8, 9, 10, or even 11 minutes, according to size of bird and heat of oven. The blood-rare breast is carved with the leg and the carcass then thoroughly squeezed in a press. The resultant liquid is seasoned with salt, pepper, lemon and paprika, and poured hot over the meat. This method of roasting insures the maximum tenderness and flavor in the bird. The longer the wild duck is roasted, the dryer and tougher it becomes.

As the year ended, *White Fang* was still getting excellent reviews and was selling extremely well. It had first appeared as a serial from May through October in *Outing* Magazine; Macmillan published it in October. It was a companion novel to *The Call of the Wild*. Jack thought it a better work than *The Call of the Wild*, but very few have agreed with him. Today *The Call of the Wild* is still considered not only an American classic, but many also consider it the greatest dog story ever written. *White Fang* is just an excellent dog book that doesn't quite make the classic category. Millions of copies of the companion novels have been sold, and they are still available in paperback on book dealers' shelves.

White Fang created a sensation when it first appeared in 1906. The *New York Independent* on November 24, 1906 remarked:

In sheer force of delineation, passionate feeling for the wilderness and for the things that live in it, *The Call of the Wild* is quite unsurpassed in American writing. It is fully matched in both these respects by *White Fang;* in which Mr. London reverses the process of retrogression traced in *The Call of the Wild,* and follows the fortunes of the wolf-dog until it becomes a human-dog. There are in the story touches of the brutality which Mr. London never quite escapes; but from the beginning to the end the experience of *White*

The Orpheum, Oakland, Cal.

The Orpheum Theatre

Fang is dramatized with striking effectiveness. The psychology is, of course, guesswork, but it is wonderfully convincing. No stronger piece of work in this field has appeared.

Not everyone, however, was impressed with *White Fang*. There were the usual politically oriented newspapers that could never say anything good about Jack London or his works. And the top politician of the country also had a few negative remarks to make. President Theodore Roosevelt told a reporter for the *New York Tribune*, "London describes a great wolf-dog being torn in pieces by a lucivee, a northern lynx. This is about as sensible as to describe a tom cat tearing in pieces a thirty-pound fighting bull terrier. Nobody who really knew anything about either a lynx or a wolf would write such nonsense."

Jack's rebuttal from Honolulu on June 8 said in part, "The President is evidently a careless reader of my stories. He has rushed into this criticism all twisted around. Look here, he says that the lynx in my story killed the dog-wolf. That certainly does not tend to show that he is as careful an observer as the magazine article seeks to indicate. My story was about the dog-wolf killing the lynx and eating the body."

Actually, it was Jack London's fault that *White Fang* could never become a classic. He had written *The Call of the Wild* himself and even he couldn't write a book comparable to it.

The delays with the *Snark* were driving Jack to distraction. Newspapers were having a lot of fun at

A NEW NATIONAL ISSUE.

—St. Louis Republic.

A contemporary cartoonist satirizes London's knowledge of nature

his expense, and his friends were making money betting with him on the date of sailing. His publishers were asking why he delayed sailing, but Jack could only shake his head and wonder how he could explain to them when he couldn't even explain to himself. Roscoe was better at promising a final date of completion than he was at finishing the boat. As Martin Johnson put it in *Through the South Seas with Jack London,* "Even the newspapers began a gentle ridicule, giving wide publicity to a poem written by Kelley, the Sailor-Poet, in which the *Snark* was described as setting out on her long voyage—not yet, but soon—and meeting with all sorts of strange adventures on the deep—not yet, but soon; and it recounted somewhat of the things that befell the voyageurs in the various countries they landed at—not yet, but soon."

Yet, with all the *Snark* worries, and the time needed to finish *The Iron Heel,* Jack was still willing to take time out for lectures on socialism. The *Socialist Voice* on December 15, 1906, reported, "The largest crowds possible listened to Jack London last Sunday, both in Oakland and San Francisco. Both meetings were packed to the doors. And while some may have come because it was the popular thing to do, they stayed to listen spellbound to one of the finest expositions of Socialism ever delivered."

On New Year's Eve Charmian and Jack had dinner at the Saddle Rock and then went to the Mac-donough Theatre to see George Thompson in *Yon Yonson.* After the theatre they returned to the Saddle Rock, where they joined Jim Whitaker and Porter Garnett. Arm in arm, the four good friends participated in the festivities and revelry of the night until the wee hours of the morning. Charmian noted that it was "a fantastic night."

On February 10, after an eternity of delays, the *Snark* pushed her beautiful bow through the Golden Gate and twelve miles out into the stormy Pacific Ocean on her first trial. Everybody was seasick, but Jack was elated with the way the boat handled. She was worth all the time and trouble. He decided to sail as soon as she was near enough to completion for a safe passage to Honolulu, where she would be made thoroughly seaworthy while he and the crew took in the sights of the Islands.

Early on the morning of April 23 Jimmy Hopper's old blue and gold University of California sweater was hoisted to the top of the mast and preparations for sailing were completed. Thousands of well-wishers thronged the docks for the memorable event. With hundreds of whistles tooting farewell, the trim little craft sailed out past the **Farallones Islands and** turned her bow **southward.** On this leg of the trip Jack studied navigation until they were well off the coast of Baja California. When he was satisfied with his newly found navigational expertise he set his course for Honolulu.

The MacDonough Theater

This was Jack and Charmian's favorite picture. It was taken in the studio of Annie Brigman prior to the sailing of the Snark

Jack and Charmian on the Snark

The Snark

The first trial run of the Snark, *February 10, 1907*

Jimmy Hopper's University of California football sweater

The passage from Oakland to Hawaii was the worst part of the cruise. The *Snark* was unfinished and leaking badly. A boat that had cost thirty thousand dollars, that supposedly had been built of the finest materials obtainable and by competent shipbuilders, leaked! The sides leaked and the bottom leaked, even the self-bailing cockpit was filled with water. Gasoline began to filter out through the nonleakable tanks and worked its way through the watertight bulkheads, creating a health and fire hazard. The water ruined the tools in the engine room and spoiled most of the three months' food supply in the galley. Martin Johnson said later, "Our box of oranges had been frozen; our box of apples was mostly spoiled; the carrots tasted of kerosene; the turnips and beets were worthless; and last, but not least, our crate of cabbages was so far gone in decay that it had to be thrown overboard. As for our coal, it had been delivered in rotten potato-sacks, and in the swinging and thrashing of the ship had escaped, and was washing through the scuppers into the ocean. We found that the engine in the launch was out of order, and that our cherished life-boat leaked as badly as did the *Snark*."

Before leaving Oakland, Jack knew that a lot of repair work would have to be done in Hawaii. The main engine had broken her bedplates and was lashed, useless, to the deck. The boat hadn't been painted below decks and her expensive copper sheathing would have to be removed and replaced. The shipbuilder has been unjustly accused of causing all these problems. Actually, they were caused by an accident in Oakland. One night after the first trial run the boat had been badly damaged. Two large lumber-scows had dragged their anchors and laid up against the sides of the *Snark*, nearly crushing her between them. They bumped away all night and by morning the rail of the *Snark* was flattened two inches on one side and bulged out by the same amount on the other side. Jack didn't discover how badly the scows had damaged his boat until they were well at sea.

The extensive itinerary of the cruise was planned for a leisurely seven years. The *Snark* had been designed small to permit inland trips. When it entered the rivers, the masts would be lowered and the engine would take over. There would be the canals of China, and the Yang-tse River. They would go up the Nile, to Vienna by the Danube, up the Thames to London, and up the Seine to Paris, where they would moor opposite the Latin Quarter with a bow-line out to Notre Dame and a stern-line fast to the Morgue. Leaving the Mediterranean, they would go up the Rhone to Lyons, there enter the Saône, cross from the Saône to the Marne through the Canal de Bourgoyne, and from the

Photo taken April 22, 1907, the day before the Snark *left Oakland on her "around the world" trip*

Jack's cabin on the Snark

Marne enter the Seine and go out the Seine at Le Havre. After crossing the Atlantic, they would go up the Hudson, pass through the Erie Canal, cross the Great Lakes, leave Lake Michigan at Chicago, gain the Mississippi by way of the Illinois River and the connecting canal, and go down the Mississippi to the Gulf of Mexico.

Jack quickly learned the basics of navigation and brought his boat safely to Honolulu. Later he said, "Any young fellow with ordinary gray matter, ordinary education, and with the slightest trace of the student-mind, can get the books and charts, and instruments and teach himself navigation. Now I must not be misunderstood. Seamanship is an entirely different matter. It is not learned in a day, nor in many days; it requires years. Also, navigation by dead reckoning requires long study and practice. But navigation by observations of the sun, moon and stars, thanks to the astronomers and mathematicians, is child's play. Any average young fellow can teach himself in a week. And yet again I must not be misunderstood. I do not mean to say that at the end of a week a young fellow could take charge of a fifteen-thousand-ton steamer, driving twenty knots an hour through the brine, racing from land to land, fair weather and foul, clear sky or cloudy, steering by degrees on the compass card and making landfalls with most amazing precision. But what I do mean is just this: the average young fellow I have described can get into a staunch sailboat and put out across the ocean, without knowing anything about navigation, and at the end of the week he will know enough to know where he is on the chart. He will be able to take a meridian observation with fair accuracy, and from that observation, with ten minutes of figuring, work out his latitude and longitude."

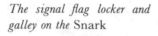

The signal flag locker and galley on the Snark

The galley aboard the Snark

The cabin plan of the Snark

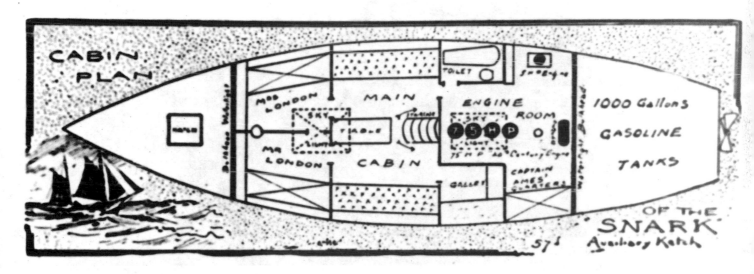

Jack made it sound simple, but he decided when he reached Hawaii that he would hire a captain who knew navigation so he could learn its finer points. A good captain could also relieve him of responsibilities that took vital time so badly needed for his writing.

The crew fell apart in Hawaii. Roscoe Eames, having proven to be absolutely worthless in every way, was sent home. Herbert Stolz, a young Stanford athlete who had gone along as engineer, decided to return to his studies in Palo Alto rather than wait seven years. Tochigi was well liked by everybody and was willing and eager to do his share of work, but couldn't cope with seasickness and left the crew with regrets all around. Martin Johnson proved to be an excellent choice and even his cooking turned out to be satisfactory. George Sterling suggested that Jack hire his friend Gene Fenelon, which Jack did to his sorrow. After paying his way to Honolulu, Jack found him to be worse than Eames and sent him back to California. Andrew A. Rosehill was hired as Captain and Dunn as bos'n. Neither lasted two months. Captain James Langhorne Warren took over the boat from

Tent-house at Seaside Hotel, Hono-lulu

Yoshimatsu Nakata

Jack getting acquainted with a sextant

Rosehill. Just a few weeks before leaving for the Marquesas Islands, Yoshimatsu Nakata was hired to replace Paul Tochigi. It was a fortunate decision, since Nakata turned out to be a nearly perfect servant, and wherever Jack went Nakata was with him for the next several years, becoming more a son than servant, and always treated as one of the family.

The nearly five months spent in the Islands were happy ones. Wherever the Londons went, the people went out of their way to entertain them. When in Honolulu, they stayed in a four-room tent-house at the Seaside Hotel, later the site of the Outrigger Club. Jack could reminisce about his Klondike days since the manager of the hotel, Fred Church, had been a friend during that period in Dawson City. Temporary quarters were in a small cottage in Pearl Locks near Pearl Harbor loaned to them by Thomas W. Hobron, an artist and Honolulu merchant. The *Snark* was anchored just offshore.

Hobron's cottage at Pearl Locks near Pearl Harbor

Meanwhile back home, Bessie took the girls on a vacation in the Santa Cruz Mountains. With them is Glenn, son of their father's dog Brown Wolf.

With a captain to look after the *Snark's* rebuilding Jack and Charmian enjoyed a delightful vacation. Jack still reserved the mornings for his writing stint and other business. Ninetta Eames was his legal and literary agent, but usually she received explicit directions in coded telegrams and in letters. Letters to his ranch foreman reveal Jack's interest even in minute items—when to breed a particular mare or plant a crop.

Prior to leaving Oakland, Jack wrote the articles dealing with his tramp experiences for *Cosmopolitan,* which were gathered later in *The Road.* He also finished "Goliah," "The Passing of Marcus O'Brien," "The Unparalleled Invasion," "The Enemy of All the World," "The Dream of Debs," and "A Curious Fragment."

Before leaving Hawaii, he also finished "Flush of Gold," "To Build a Fire," "Make Westing," "That Spot," "Trust," and "The House of Pride." While staying with Lorrin Thurston, owner of Honolulu's morning *Advertiser,* he started his partially autobiographical novel *Martin Eden,* which would be acclaimed by many critics as his best book. The early struggles of the young writer, Martin Eden, to succeed in spite of nearly insurmountable obstacles are almost exactly those of Jack's own early years. The love affair with Ruth Morse is based on a similar one that Jack had with Mabel Applegarth, except that the Ruth Morse version is so exaggerated and fictionalized that it is hardly recognizable. After achieving success, Martin Eden becomes disillusioned with life and commits suicide by crawling through a porthole of his cabin and dropping unnoticed into the sea. The book has one of the finest endings of any American novel:

Down, down, he swam till his arms and legs grew tired and hardly moved. He knew that he was deep. The pressure on his ear-drums was a pain, and there was a buzzing in his head. His endurance was faltering, but he compelled his arms and legs to drive him deeper until his will snapped and the air drove from his lungs in a great explosive rush. The bubbles rubbed and bounded like tiny balloons against his cheeks and eyes as they took their upward flight. Then came pain and strangulation. This hurt was not death, was the thought that oscillated through his reeling consciousness. Death did not hurt. It

was life, the pangs of life, this awful, suffocating feeling; it was the last blow life could deal him.

His willful hands and feet began to beat and churn about, spasmodically and feebly. But he had fooled them and the will to live that made them beat and churn. He was too deep down. They could never bring him to the surface. He seemed floating languidly in a sea of dreamy vision. Colors and radiances surrounded him and bathed him and pervaded him. What was that? It seemed a lighthouse; but it was inside his brain—a flashing, bright white light. It flashed swifter and swifter. There was a long rumble of sound, and it seemed to him that he was falling down a vast and interminable stairway. And somewhere at the bottom he fell into darkness. That much he knew. He had fallen into darkness. And at the instant he knew, he ceased to know.

Jack's theme in Martin Eden completely misfired. In a copy of the book given to Upton Sinclair he wrote, "One of my motifs, in this book, was an attack on individualism (in the person of the hero). I must have bungled for not a single reviewer has discovered it." It was a protest against the Nietzschean philosophy expounding strength and individualism, even to the extent of war and destruction, against cooperation, democracy, and socialism. Jack's reason for Eden's suicide is clearly stated in a letter to Blanche Partington, "But the point of Martin Eden is this. He was an individualist. He was unaware of the needs of others. Brissenden warned him that he would need socialism to handcuff him to life in the bad time coming. But Martin did not, and so he died. He worked, strove, fought for himself alone. And when disillusionment came, when love, fame, the worthwhileness of the bourgeoisie—all things—failed, why there was nothing left for him to live for."

Jack never knew of one powerful contribution his book made to the literary world. Had it not been for *Martin Eden,* the world could not have read *Lust for Life, Sailor on Horseback, Immortal Wife, Men to Match My Mountains, The Agony and the Ecstasy, An Adversary in the House, Passions of the Mind, The Greek Treasure* and all the other great books given to us by that dean of the biographical novel, Irving Stone. For it was the reading of *Martin Eden* that gave

Frank Strawn-Hamilton, socialist friend of Jack London, was one of the most learned socialist philosophers of his day. Jack said he was the best philosophical speaker he ever heard and that his brain put Macaulay's to shame. Strawn-Hamilton was a teacher—a free-lance educator without tenure, classroom, or degrees. He was a hobo who served at least twenty-nine terms for vagrancy and cared more for study than bathing, according to Charmian. His teaching of philosophy to Jack was better than any series of classes at the University.

Stone the courage to overcome a background in many respects like that of Jack London himself. Stone is but one example of the scores of artists and writers who gained strength and inspiration from reading this near literal account of a young man who climbed from poverty, unaided, to world acclaim before he was twenty-seven years old.

Incidentally, *Martin Eden* was named after a woodchopper who lived on the Thompson ranch in Glen Ellen. Brissenden, the poet, is a composite of London's friends Sterling, Whitaker, and Frank Strawn-Hamilton. "Ephemera," Brissenden's great poem, was in reality George Sterling's "The Testi-

mony of the Suns." The ending of *Martin Eden* reveals Jack's extensive reading of Longfellow, for in the latter's *Golden Legend* we read,

> A single step and all is o'er.
> A plunge, a bubble, and no more.

In California Jack rarely accepted social invitations. Actually, he was seldom asked, since he made his feelings on the subject so clear. Frequently a church brotherhood or a writers' club would invite him to speak, but nearly all invitations came either from his socialist comrades or from a member of his small "crowd." Hawaii was another matter. The people there were less disturbed by his controversial opinions. Jack Atkinson, acting Governor of the Islands, spent so much time with London that they were called the "two Jacks." Lorrin Thurston, Alexander Hume Ford, Joseph P. Cook, William T. Balding, Bruce Cartwright, the Castles, Albert Waterhouse, Dr. E. S. Goodhue and his brother Will, L. G. Kellogg, and Harry Strange were just a few of the people who worked overtime to make the Londons' Hawaiian visit a memorable one.

On June 2 Alexander Hume Ford taught Jack the fine art of surfing. When the day was over, Jack was a much better surfer but in terrible physical condition. The Hawaiian sun was too much for him. Dr. Charles B. Cooper told Charmian that he had never seen a worse case of sunburn. For four days Jack suffered in bed, and eleven days later he still had several huge blisters.

Jack London had an extremely analytical mind and nearly always delved deeply into anything that interested him, and he was interested in nearly everything with which he came in contact. Surfboarding is a good example. He finally succeeded in becoming almost as proficient in the art as were the natives themselves, but he also dug into the books to see how the thing worked. Charmian records his study in *Our Hawaii:*

"A wave is a communicated agitation," he says. "The water that composes a wave really does not move. If it moved, when you drop a stone in a pool and the ripples widen in an increasing circle, there should be at the center an increasing hole. So the water in the body of a wave is stationary. If you observe a portion of the ocean's surface, you will see that the same water rises and falls endlessly to the agitation communicated by endless successive waves. Pic-

The parade of the "horribles," July 4, 1907

Haleakala Ranch, managed by Armine von Tempski's father, Louis von Tempsky.

ture this communicated agitation moving toward shore. As the land shoals, the bottom of the wave hits first and is stopped. Water is fluid, and the upper part of the wave, not having been stopped, keeps on communicating its agitation, and moves on shoreward. Ergo," says he, "something is bound to be doing, when the top of a wave keeps on after the bottom has stopped, dropped out from under. Of course, the wave-top starts to fall forward, down, cresting, over-curling and crashing. So, don't you see? don't you see?" He warms to his illustration, "It is actually the bottom of the wave striking against the rising land that causes the surf! And, where the land shoals gradually, as inside this barrier reef at Waikiki, the rising of the undulating wa-

ter is as gradual, and a ride of a quarter of a mile or more can be made shoreward on the cascading face of a wave."

The sport of surfing was nearly unknown when Jack discovered it. In fact, most of Hawaii's charms were still a mystery to most of the world. Jack would shake his head and say to Charmian, "They don't know what they've got." But, thanks to his enthusiastic writing about the Islands and Alexander Hume Ford's unflagging efforts, the world soon knew much more. With Jack's help, Ford's dream came true as surfing grew in popularity, hotels sprang up, and Hawaii as the mainlander's haven came into being. London's writing pictured Hawaii as one of the world's great sport centers and challenged athletes to join the native Hawaiians in a revival of their native sports, not as spectators but as participants. Jack also worked with Ford in the planning of the popular Outrigger Canoe Club. Immediately after Jack's death in 1916, the Hawaiian Promotion Committee issued this statement: "In the past we have referred in terms of endearment to Charles Warren Stoddard, to Robert Louis Stevenson, to Mark Twain and now the Promotion Committee desires to add to that trio the name of Jack London."

Lucius E. Pinkham, president of the Board of Health, was concerned with the distorted views of the leper colony on Molokai. Irrational fears were prevalent in the Islands concerning leprosy simply because the people didn't understand the disease. Leprosy was mysterious in that nobody knew how it was acquired. One "clean" woman who had married five leper husbands and had children by them never became its victim. Bulletins had been issued to assuage the unreasonable dread of leprosy contact, but few believed. The newspapers only printed sensational items that made things even worse. Maybe people would listen to Jack London! Pinkham was an old fan of Jack's and knew that he always told the truth as he saw it, so he asked him if he would go over to Molokai and live with the lepers for a week and write about his experiences. The only one more eager to go than Jack was Charmian. On July 1 they boarded the *Noeau* and arrived on the following day at Kalaupapa, Molokai.

The self-sustaining colony occupied a small town controlled by the Board of Health but operated by the lepers. Those who wanted to work did and those who didn't or couldn't were cared for. The people were happy and content. On occasion an inmate's leprosy test would be negative and he would be returned to his home, but this was rare.

Jack and Charmian mixed freely. The first day they went to the rifle range, where they used guns still warm from leper hands. On the Fourth of July Molokai had a traditional all-day celebration. At six o'clock in the morning the "horribles" were out, dressed in bright-colored costumes, astride horses, mules, and donkeys (their own property) and cutting capers all over the settlement. Two brass bands provided music for the parade. It was a day of races, horsemanship competitions, and whatever merriment somebody thought of. Jack was everywhere with his Kodak. He read every book on leprosy available in the settlement and talked for hours with the doctors. Then he wrote "The Lepers of Molokai" and mailed it to *The Woman's Home Companion.*

A few days after their return from Molokai, the Londons were taken to the Haleakala Ranch managed by Louis von Tempsky. Jack Atkinson, as usual, made the arrangements. This cattle ranch consisted of some fifty thousand acres on the slopes of Mount Haleakala at about the two-thousand-foot level. The next day Jack and his host mounted horses and rode up another thirty-five hundred feet to a mountain ranch house where they spent the day in leisurely fashion. Jack even had a hearty raspberry fight with von Tempsky's two daughters,

Armine von Tempsky. She used von Tempski in her books.

Armine and Gwen von Tempsky on the Haleakala Ranch

Armine and Gwen. The raspberries were the size of hen's eggs and larger; their ripeness made quite a splatter on contact.

The next morning the party continued on to the crater. Far above them was the distant horizon, and far beneath the great crater, the House of the Sun. Twenty-three miles around stretched the walls of the crater. Jack and Charmian stood on the edge of the nearly vertical western wall and looked down on the floor of the crater nearly half a mile below.

The night was spent at the lower end of the crater, in a small grove of Olapa and Kolea trees, tucked away in a corner of the crater at the base of the walls that rose perpendicularly fifteen hundred feet. Jerked beef, hard *poi*, and freshly killed broiled kid was the evening meal. After examining the crater for two days, the party rode twenty-eight miles to Hana. The next two days of riding brought them through the marvelous "ditch country" on the windward slope of Haleakala. The windward side of the mountain is serried by a thousand precipitous gorges, down which rushes many torrents, each torrent creating a score of cascades and waterfalls before it reaches the sea. More rain falls here than in any other region in the world. Three years before the visit by the Londons the year's rainfall was four hundred and twenty inches. Water means sugar, and sugar was one of the most valuable products of the Territory of Hawaii. The water traveled underground, appearing only at intervals to leap a gorge, rushed onward via a high flume and then plunged through the mountains. Jack said, "This magnificent waterway is called a 'ditch,' and with equal appropriateness can Cleopatra's barge be called a box-car."

The horse trail through the ditch country was very narrow and treacherous. It gouged its way out of walls, dodged around waterfalls, or passed under them where they thundered down in white fury. The party's marvelous mountain horses were unconcerned. They trotted along as a matter of course, though the footing was slippery with rain, and they would gallop with their hind feet slipping over the edge if they were allowed to do so. Only those with steady nerves and cool heads tackled the Nahiku Ditch Trail.

One of the cowboys in their party that day was noted as the strongest and bravest on the Haleakala Ranch. He had ridden mountain horses all his life on the rugged western slopes of Haleakala. He was the best horse breaker on the ranch and had no fear in meeting a wild bull in the cattle pen. But he had never ridden over the Nahiku Ditch. It was there he discovered fear when he faced the first flume, spanning a narrow gorge without railings, with a bellowing waterfall above. He dismounted from his horse, explained briefly that he had a wife and two children, and crossed over on foot, leading the horse behind him.

For a few days after returning to the Haleakala Ranch they attended a great festival of cattle driving, branding, and horse breaking. Jack and Charmian were especially taken with the von Tempsky girls, and in later years Armine von Tempsky wrote about her days with the Londons in her book *Born in Paradise*. When Louis von Tempsky died, the children were sent to live on the Jack London Ranch for a short period.

From Maui the Londons went back to Honolulu for another round of parties, luaus, and sightseeing. In August they were the guests of Dr. E. S. Goodhue in Holualoa, Kona, at the Doctorage. While there, Jack's morning writing stint was devoted to *Martin Eden*. On August 22 and again on the 23rd Jack and Charmian were riding over the countryside, where they could watch the *Snark* making her way to Hilo under the expert guidance of Captain Warren. At Hilo final preparations would be made and stores brought aboard for the traverse from Hilo to the Marquesas Islands.

Saying aloha to Dr. Goodhue, the Londons motored to the one-hundred-fifty-thousand-acre Parker Ranch in Waimea. Here they stayed with the ranch manager, John Maguire. Relaxing in the beautiful weather, surrounded by the easygoing customs of the native Hawaiians, Jack and Charmian loved to take a short nap in the late afternoons. On one of these occasions Jack told Charmian, "You must simply hate me for the way I can sleep, anytime and anywhere," thinking of Charmian's terrible lifelong bouts with insomnia. Another time he told her, "Why, once when I was a boy, I got to thinking how awful it would be to have insomnia, and I stayed awake all of one night. It was awful. But it never happened again to me."

On September 1 Jack was driven to Hilo to lecture in Spreckels' Hall. On the next day the Londons mounted horses for a tour of the vast Parker Ranch. Jack was given a big, stolid, perfectly safe gray horse. He was in the saddle, and turning to speak to Mrs. Maguire at the gate, when his horse rose in the air and came down in a violent bucking maneuver. He had never ridden a bucking horse in his life, but he managed to stay in the saddle until, after a short plunging run, the beast twisted violently. The horse went one way and Jack the other, landing on his left shoulder and the back of his head. Another horse was trotted out and the tour resumed. That night Jack was in severe pain and nearly delirious with fever. The following day was spent in bed recuperating.

On September 5 they toured the Louisson Brothers Coffee Plantation and then returned to Hilo for final sailing preparations. Jack had called Martin Johnson to inform him that he was promoted to Chief Engineer and to ask Captain Warren to hire a new cabin boy and a new sailor. Hermann de Visser was hired to fill the sailor berth; Tsunekichi Wada, a Japanese, was hired to replace Martin as cook; and Nakata, who couldn't speak a word of English, took over as cabin boy at that time. An extra month in Hilo resulted from another broken bedplate on the main engine. It was much like all engines built in 1906—requiring more hours in repair than in running.

During this extended vacation period Jack and Charmian stayed with the Shipmans in their Volcano Home and visited the famous Volcano House and the Kilauea Volcano. After a short stay the

Londons were guests of the Baldings at Wainaku, where they were able to try the dangerous sport of riding the cane-flumes. Cane gathered in the fields was tied in bundles and tossed in a wooden trough filled with fast-running water. The bundles traveled for miles down these flumes across deep ravines to the mill. Jack, Charmian, Martin Johnson, and the rest of their party stripped down to their bathing suits, climbed on a bundle of cane, and shot away. Once on there was no turning back so they went down the flumes at breakneck speeds and over spidery trestles as high as two hundred feet in the air en route to the mill, where they dismounted in a hurry to keep from going on into the cutters with the bundles of cane.

On October 3 Jack answered "the call of the wild" and went on a "pirooting" trip into town, becoming involved in a saloon brawl that caused quite a furor in the small community. Jack explained that he had only had a couple of cocktails, but that on an empty stomach they were too much for him. His explanation was too much for Charmian but she did understand that the delay of their cruise had begun to get on Jack's nerves. The brawl was poor public relations, but it did vent his frustration.

Jack's drinking has been terribly exaggerated, and his "pirooting" periods were few and infrequent. When things went wrong to the point where

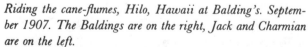

Riding the cane-flumes, Hilo, Hawaii at Balding's. September 1907. The Baldings are on the right, Jack and Charmian are on the left.

The cane-flume crosses a gulch.

he was disgusted enough, he would revert back to his waterfront need for a few drinks. This only happened on a few occasions during his life, after marriage with Bessie and later with Charmian. This brawl in Hilo was the only time when it appears he actually drank more than he could handle. In a later brawl, in Muldowney's tavern in Oakland, it is nearly certain that he didn't even have one drink. In the Solomon Islands Jack indulged far more than he should have, but was never seen in a drunken condition. Actually, there is no reliable record that anyone ever saw Jack drunk after his Fish Patrol days when he was sixteen years old. In Sydney in 1909 Jack was drinking too much wine to suit Charmian and in New York City in 1912 he went "pirooting" several nights. An in-depth study of Jack London's drinking reveals that he did drink enough to injure his health, but that he was never known to be drunk. This seeming paradox comes about because of his unusual ability to drink far more than the average man without showing it.

One reason for Jack's restraint was that Charmian seldom drank and he never drank excessively when he was with her. And there were very few nights, from the day they were married until his death, that they were apart. It would be reasonable to speculate that Jack London could have easily become an alcoholic had it not been for Charmian. This is but one of the many contributions she made to the man she worshipped.

That Jack flirted with alcoholism at times is undeniable, but to call him an alcoholic would be an injustice of major proportion. Martin Johnson stated after Jack's death, "I have known him intimately for ten years, I have never seen him show the slightest effects of liquor." It must be remembered that Johnson was with Jack every day during the cruise of the *Snark*—the period in which one biographer erroneously reports his excessive drinking.

People who spent a great deal of time on the ranch—Janet Winship, Carrie Burlingame, and many others—said that they never saw Jack intoxicated, that he had cocktails along with the rest of his guests and had two or three cocktails at dinner, but no more.

In *The People of the Pueblo*, Celeste Murphy said, "London loved the cup that cheers, as he acknowledged, but if he ever drank to excess it was unknown to his Sonoma neighbors." In New York City, after attending the Columbia Theatre with him, Fred McCloy stated, "Jack, who was abstemious, took one highball which lasted him till about four in the morning." In 1907 a one-month bill at the Seaside Hotel, from whom Jack and Charmian rented their tent-cabin, ran $174.50 for room and board plus an extra $5.25 for bar chits.

The best source for information on Jack's drinking is a look through Charmian's diaries at the Huntington Library in San Marino, California. During their eleven years of marriage Charmian never failed to make her nightly entries. She was extremely candid in her daily entries, even to the point of using the code word *lolly* whenever they made love. The following entries in Charmian's diaries are very revealing: On February 2, 1907, she wrote "Mate not looking well. Drinks cocktails—takes no exercise." On February 15, 1907, "Mate takes three cocktails before dinner, all by himself. I cry!" On February 16, 1907, "Mate came home very late, full." On the trip from Papeete on the *Mariposa* in 1908 she wrote that Jack had been drinking too much. On May 15, 1912, on board the *Dirigo* from Baltimore to Seattle, Charmian entered, "I feel blue. The uncertainty of the alcohol future depresses me unspeakably." After brooding over the thought all night, she and Jack discussed his drinking. His response was, "I have learned, to my absolute satisfaction, that I am not an alcoholic in any sense of the word. Therefore, when I am on land again, I shall drink, as you drink, occasionally, deliberately, not because I have to have alcohol in the economy of my physical system, but because I want to, we'll say for social purposes."

After Jack's death Charmian quoted this last passage from her diary and said, "Although I knew he was giving me the honest content of his best conclusions in the matter, I also felt that I knew he would fail of the perfection of the plan. He did. But what counts in the end—is the end, and near that end he drank but little." These are the only entries in her diaries that mention Jack's drinking.

AN IMPOSSIBLE TRAVERSE

Jack realized that the traverse from Hilo to the Marquesas Islands would be a long, hazardous voyage, but he had complete faith in his new captain's knowledge of navigation, and in the seaworthiness of the *Snark*.

The boat was provisioned and fuel put aboard for the anticipated two-month voyage. On October 7 the trim little *Snark* set her sails for further adventure. The element of uncertainty was ever present, since the crew could expect both storm and calm. Now that they had discovered how to make the boat heave-to perfectly, the storms were not too much of a worry and the calms could be conquered by their seventy-horsepower engine, which was finally working.

Their worries would have been real indeed had they thoroughly read one passage in a copy of Jack's sailing directions for the South Pacific Ocean, in which the author warned that it was very difficult to sail from the Hawaiian Islands to Tahiti across the prevailing trade winds. In fact, most authorities claimed that it was an impossible traverse. But the impossible didn't deter the *Snark*, principally because Jack didn't read this information until they were well on their journey. They were hard at sea when the launch engine, the five-horsepower engine, and the seventy-horsepower main engine had all broken down. The *Snark* was now only a sailing vessel with no auxiliary power of any kind.

Jack reasoned that even though his source stated that he had found no variables on his traverse, and that he "never could make easting on either tack," their only hope was in the variables. The region of variable winds lay between the trades and the doldrums, and were thought to be the draughts of heated air that rose in the doldrums, flowed high in the air counter to the trades, and gradually sank down again.

He finally discovered the variables at 11° north latitude, and he hugged this latitude jealously. To the south lay the doldrums. To the north lay the northeast trades that never blew from the northeast. The days came and went, but the *Snark* couldn't get away from the eleventh parallel.

They found themselves in the midst of one of the loneliest of Pacific solitudes. In the sixty days of the traverse they sighted no vessel of any kind. A disabled vessel could have drifted helpless for years and there would be no rescue.

Yet Jack was enjoying the respite from reporters and the clamor of fans. As he put it, "Our bell rang the hours, but no caller ever rang it. There were no guests to dinner, no telegrams, no insistent telephone jangles invading our privacy. We had no engagements to keep, no trains to catch, and there were no morning newspapers over which to waste time in learning what was happening to our fifteen hundred million other fellow-creatures."

But it wasn't dull. The affairs of their own little world had to be regulated, and, unlike the great world, this world had to be steered in its journey through space. They never knew, from moment to moment, what was going to happen next. There was spice and variety enough to spare.

On November 26 the wind suddenly shifted to the southeast. They had caught the trades at last. There were no more squalls, nothing but fine weather and a fair wind. With sheets slacked off and with spinnaker and mainsail swaying and bellying on either side, they were speeding through the water. On December 6 they passed to leeward of Ua-huka, sailed along the southern edge of Nukahiva, and that night, in driving squalls and inky darkness, finally anchored in Taiohae Bay, Marquesas Islands.

MELVILLE'S TYPEE

When Jack was a little boy, he read Melville's *Typee* and dreamed over its pages. He resolved there and then, come what would, that when he was old enough he, too, would voyage to Typee Valley in the Marquesas Islands. The years passed, but Typee was never forgotten. When he returned from his seven-month sealing trip on the *Sophia Sutherland* in 1893, he decided the time had come. The brig *Galilee* was sailing for the Marquesas, but her crew was complete. He was proud of being an able seaman, but was willing to sign on as cabin boy in order to make his pilgrimage to Typee. Alas, even that berth was filled.

When Jack arrived, the local agents for the Société Commerciale de l'Oceanie, Mr. Kreiech and Mr. Rawlings, hastily volunteered to be the Londons' guides while on the Island. Mr. Kreiech secured horses and a guide to take them to Typee Valley. Early the next morning Jack and Charmian, Martin, Captain Warren, the native guide, and two young native girls set out for the valley. The girls were the daughters of the Chief of the Typee tribe and were sent along by Kreiech to assure them a welcome in their valley.

The way led up an ancient road through a jungle of hau trees. On every side were the vestiges of a onetime dense and proud population. Wherever they looked they saw stone walls and stone foundations, six to eight feet in height, built solidly throughout, and many yards in width and depth. They were great stone platforms on which houses had formerly been built. But the houses and the people were no longer there.

The Typeans of 1907 no longer hoisted and placed such huge stones; they no longer had the incentive. There were plenty of unoccupied dwellings left over. Jack explained, "Once or twice as we ascended the valley, we saw magnificent pae-paes bearing on their generous surface pitiful little straw huts, the proportions being similar to a voting booth perched on the broad foundation of the pyramid of Cheops."

The Typeans were a perishing race. The climate was such that asthma, consumption, and tuberculosis were slowly destroying the population. Melville had lived in the Valley of Typee, in the early 1840s, as a prisoner of the cannibal inhabitants. His "experiences of living with these primitive people as both honored guest and possible 'puerkee' or porker for a ceremonial feast," impressed him vividly and in *Typee* he described the Typeans as a strong, warlike tribe who were feared by all the other tribes. A generation after Melville's escape there were but two hundred warriors left— white men had brought germs to the valley to which the natives were not immune. The greatest destroyer of all was galloping consumption, which could destroy a man's health in two months.

Sadly Jack thought about the magnificent specimens he had read about in Melville's book. They had been described as being of lofty stature and the mightiest warriors of the Marquesas Islands and now all their strength and beauty were gone. The present residents of the Valley of Typee consisted of about a dozen wretched creatures afflicted by leprosy, elephantiasis, and tuberculosis. London gives us a vivid picture of these conditions in his article "Typee" in *The Cruise of the Snark*.

The rest of the Marquesas Islanders were saved by interbreeding with other races. Martin Johnson was not as concerned with the condition of the people as he was with the beauty of the island and the friendliness of the people. He said it had "a climate so perfect that no words can describe it,

The Victor phonograph entertains natives of the Marquesas Islands.

other than to call it a Garden of Eden. The natives are like big happy children. They do not steal, gossip about one another, nor carry grudges. Instead, they sing, dance, hunt, fish, and live together as brothers in a life of perfect peace."

Jack was a little boy visiting all the haunts of his revered Melville. To add to his pleasure, he and Charmian stayed in the very house in which Robert Louis Stevenson lived while he was on the island. Each night their front yard was full of natives listening to the Victor phonograph Jack had had the foresight to bring along. The natives were convinced, despite all explanations, that the talkbox was full of midgets. They didn't dare try to figure out where the instruments were. Throughout their island-hopping cruise the Victor phonograph proved to be their strongest asset in getting acquainted with the natives.

FROM THE MARQUESAS ISLANDS TO TAHITI

On December 18 the *Snark* made her way out of Taiohae headed for Tahiti. Christmas Eve found it sailing in continuous squalls through the dangerous archipelago trying to locate Rangiroa, Society Islands. All that night and Christmas Day all hands were kept on deck. The barometer was falling rapidly as the little vessel entered the most dangerous part of the world in typhoon season. Jack wanted to put in at Rangiroa, but in the storm it was impossible to see. Giving up, they sailed on toward Tahiti. On the ninth day out of Taiohae they anchored in Papeete.

Once more they faced a long delay while the engine was overhauled. Three months' mail had accumulated and in the pile Jack discovered that his business affairs were in chaos. Much of it was Aunt Netta's fault. She had doubled her salary as Jack's agent and was charging him forty dollars a month rent for space at Wake Robin that he wasn't going to use for another six years. As he looked further through the bills, he found that she had spent a thousand dollars to fix up an old building on the property so Wiget could live there with his family.

The newspapers were partly to blame. They reported Jack overdue and some had even reported that the *Snark* had gone down with all hands. A few papers even accused Jack of staying lost for publicity purposes. When his Oakland bank read that Jack was lost, it promptly foreclosed his 490 Twenty-seventh Street property where his mother lived. Several checks he had written in Hilo were marked "Insufficient Funds" and returned by another Oakland bank. Ninetta Eames had changed banks without Jack's knowledge. He had written several checks before he learned of this.

He had taken in well over seven thousand dollars since leaving Oakland, but some quick arithmetic revealed that his total cash assets only amounted to a little over sixty dollars. There was nothing left to do but go back, straighten out his business affairs, raise money, and return.

Jack and Charmian left on the S.S. *Mariposa* on January 13 for San Francisco, arriving on January 25. George and Carrie Sterling and Johannes and Alide Reimers met them at the dock. From there all went to the Saddle Rock Cafe for lunch. Jack organized his business affairs, raised funds, discussed problems between himself and Bessie, saw his children, enjoyed several more lunches and dinners with members of "the crowd" at the Saddle Rock, and attended the Macdonough or Liberty Theatre each night. On February 2 he and Char-

mian boarded the *Mariposa* for the return trip. They were back in Papeete on the 14th, and three days later *Martin Eden* was finished and ready to mail.

The crew was still a problem. Captain Warren was caught grafting on the *Snark* repair bills. He confessed that he had been pardoned for murder and asked for another chance. After talking it over with Charmian, Jack forgave him and left him in command. Hermann de Visser had gone sour and was paid off. Jack was also having problems in getting the engine repaired, but during it all he kept on writing and Charmian kept banging away at the old No. 7 Remington. They finished "The Other Animals," Jack's answer to charges of "Nature-Faking" by Theodore Roosevelt and John Burroughs, and started a series of short stories set in Hawaii.

The engine was finally repaired and on the trial run March 19 the *Snark* did twelve knots at full speed. The following week they sailed to Moorea in the Society Islands. A casting gave way on the engine, causing them to return to Papeete on the 28th for further engine work.

Where Jack and Charmian stayed in Papeete

Charmian poses for picture during the week they were back in California.

Jack gets help from Rollo in answering President Roosevelt's charge of "Nature-Faking."

While in Oakland, Jack took his two girls to Idora Park for an afternoon of fun. Becky is on the left.

"Reason!"

Mr. London to his amanuensis: "Simple reflex action, compound reflex action, memory, habit, rudimentary reason, and abstract reason."

"Instinct!"

The President and Mr. Burroughs observing carefully the antics of tomtits and snipe. Theodore and John together: "Instinct, sheer instinct!"

President Roosevelt collaborates with John Burroughs in denouncing Jack London as a "Nature-Faker."

PAPEETE TO BORA BORA VIA RAIATEA AND TAHAA

The *Snark* weighed anchor on April 4 and her course was set for Raiatea, where they stayed four days. On leaving the harbor, a tiny outrigger canoe with a huge sail came into sight. In it was a big, almost naked native of the little island of Tahaa named Tehei, who invited the Londons to ride with him across the seven-mile channel to visit his home. Accepting the invitation, they stayed for two days of fishing and hunting. After their return to the *Snark* they cruised back to Tahaa to pick up Tehei and his wife, Bihaura, who would be their guests on the twenty-five-mile run to Bora Bora. When they sailed out of Tahaa, the boat was loaded to the gunnels with fruit, produce, and even a pig that were forced on them by the friendly islanders.

Prior to leaving Raiatea Jack finished "The House of Mapuhi" and began "The Chinago" in Bora Bora. The trip was smooth and comfortable, with Tehei and Bihaura sleeping on the deck, Jack and Charmian grinding out reading matter for the American public, most of the crew asleep in their bunks, and Martin Johnson sitting on the edge of the open skylight with one eye on the engine and the other admiring the beauty of the dozens of small islands they passed.

On arrival at Bora Bora, it seemed the entire island population rose up to entertain them and continued to do so for ten full days. Much of the welcome and entertainment was due to Bihaura's royal blood. Though the *Snark* anchored a half-mile from shore, canoeloads of natives bearing gifts of

Part of the Bora-Bora stone fishing fleet

food of every description plied their way to the tiny vessel. On the morning of the third day Tehei announced that he had planned a mammoth stone fishing party, which was to be the biggest in the history of the island.

Over one hundred canoes paddled out three miles. When the signal was given, the long line of canoes slowly moved toward the shore, one man paddling while the other beat the waves with a stone attached to a rope. Beating in rhythm, the men maintained a constant concussion while those on the shore added to the bedlam with yells of every description.

Before the event started, Allicot, a half-caste trader, told Jack, "The natives usually make a big catch. At the finish of the drive the water is fairly alive with fish. It's lots of fun. Of course, you know all the fish will be yours."

Jack let out a groan, for already the *Snark* was loaded down with lavish presents of fruits, vegetables, pigs, and chickens. "Yes," continued Allicot, "every last fish. You see, when the surround is completed, you, being the guest of honor, must take a harpoon and impale the first one. It is the custom. Then everybody goes in with their hands to throw the catch upon the sand. There will be a mountain

of them. Then one of the chiefs will make a speech in which he presents you with the whole kit and boodle. But you don't have to take them all. You get up and make a speech, selecting what fish you want for yourself and presenting all the rest back again. Then everybody says you are very generous."

Letting out a huge sigh of relief, Jack turned to watch the fun. Pandemonium reigned as the stone throwers moved in and all those on the beach ran out and formed a dam with their legs to trap the fish. But no fish broke surface or swam into the wall of legs. There were no fish! There wasn't even a sardine or a minnow! Allicot shrugged his shoulders and said that one in five of these drives is a failure. But everybody had a ton of fun anyway.

Reluctantly, on April 15, 1908, the crew of the *Snark* left Bora Bora. Martin called it the happy paradise and all agreed that its inhabitants were the most thoughtful and generous people alive. Tehei had convinced Jack that he should go on as a member of the *Snark's* crew, but Jack insisted that he could go only if he were paid. Tehei finally agreed to accept twelve dollars a month, but no more. Jack agreed and Tehei joined the crew.

BORA BORA TO PAGO PAGO

Jack finished "The Chinago" and started "The High Seat of Abundance," and on April 24 he read "The Seed of McCoy" to the crew. The weather was hot and all hands slept on deck, Jack and Charmian on the starboard side, Ernest, Nakata, Wada, and Tehei on the port side. Captain Warren slept aft of

the cockpit, and Martin did his snoozing in the bow. There was little to do at sea except lounge around the deck, eat fruit, or play cards. Charmian played her ukulele and sang in the evenings, while Tehei, Wada, or Nakata performed their native dances. Sometimes Jack read aloud his day's work.

Anticipating boredom, Jack had brought along tops, skipping ropes, boxing gloves, and other items to keep the crew occupied. Martin said, "I have seen Jack squat down and spin his tops by the hour, thoroughly absorbed in the fun. He said that this, like his cigarettes, soothed his nerves."

Thirteen days out of Bora Bora, the Manua Islands appeared over the horizon. By noon the adventurers were gliding along a tropical bay, just close enough to see the small grass villages and the dense jungles behind. After a stay of several days in the Manua Islands, they moved on across another ninety miles of tropical ocean to Pago Pago. On

May 3 the Londons moved into quarters in Governor Moore's house, set high on a little ridge that projected out into the bay. The following day Charmian typed Jack's newly finished Klondike story, "Lost Face." Tehei, who could speak little English and no Samoan, preferred to stay aboard. A few days later a big Tahitian named Henry, a native of Rapa Island, came aboard to visit Tehei. He asked for a job and Jack jumped at the chance to hire a sailor who knew the islands so well. For some time he had wanted to get rid of Ernest, the French sailor. Jack bought Ernest a ticket to Auckland, New Zealand, and paid him off.

Governor Moore's residence, where Jack and Charmian stayed in Pago Pago

PAGO PAGO TO PENDUFFRYN VIA APIA

The crew hoisted anchor on May 6 to go to Apia, with Henry at the wheel. He stayed at the wheel all night and most of the next day until around sunset when the anchor dropped in Apia, Samoa, the largest city in Polynesia. The Londons moved into the highly recommended International Hotel. On

the 8th they toured the island on rented horses, and on the 9th they traveled three miles up the slope from Apia to Stevenson's Vailima. After examining the closed house through every available window, they hiked to the writer's tomb at the summit of the mountain. Jack turned to Charmian and said,

The Snark *lies at anchor in Apia, Samoa, May 8, 1908.*

The Snark *anchored at Apia, Samoa, May 1908.*

Where Robert Louis Stevenson lived and died—Vailima, or Five Streams, the former estate of the great writer

"I wouldn't have gone out of my way to visit the grave of any other man in the world." On their ninth day here Jack gave his famous lecture on Revolution in Apia's Central Hotel.

Moving on to Savaii, all hands were thrilled at the sight of huge flames of fire issuing from the big crater as they watched the small red-hot streams of lava flowing down to the ocean. For miles and miles they could see the boiling lava as it rolled into the sea and sent up huge clouds of vapor. The air was sultry and became hotter and hotter as they drew closer. Jack stationed Wada at the bow with a thermometer, and every few minutes he would yell back the temperature, until finally they had to draw back for fear of igniting the gasoline aboard. Henry, their new Kanaka sailor, knew the coast well and steered them to a native village, which they found destroyed by the lava flow. There was total destruction everywhere. After hunting all night for an unharmed village, they found Matautu and anchored nearby. The next day Governor Dick Williams invited the crew to stay with him; he took them with him on his tour of inspection. The devastation was unbelievable. After four days of doing what they could to help, the crew went back aboard the *Snark* and up anchored to go to Suva via the Nanuku Islets, through the Koro Sea, and then into port. The trip was treacherous due to a tremendous gale. The wind was so bad that they remained hove-to throughout one night. While they were passing close to one island in the Koro Sea, a cutter came to meet them nearly five miles out. A voice yelled, "What ship is that?" They responded, "The *Snark* out of San Francisco." "Is that Jack London's boat?" When they told him yes, he yelled, "Heave-to, I'm coming aboard." It was Frank Whitcomb, who had been trading nearly all his life in the Fiji Islands. "And to think that I should ever see Jack London, and on his own boat, too! Why, I have every one of your books aboard my ship, and all your magazine articles." He was so happy he nearly cried. Whitcomb loaded them down with fresh fruit, onions, and potatoes. In exchange the Londons presented him with several bottles of wine. As he went back to his cutter he was muttering, "And to think that I should live to shake hands with Jack London, and on his own boat, too!" He was the only person who boarded the *Snark* at sea during the entire cruise.

En route Jack decided to fire Warren on arrival

Robert Louis Stevenson's resting place. Upon his death in 1894, his body was carried by Samoan chiefs to this spot—1,300 feet above Vailima.

in Suva. Warren's navigation was almost as bad as his personality, and he had broken Wada's nose in a fit of temper. Jack had hoped to find a congenial, efficient captain so he could devote his own time to writing. A captain's salary was far less than the money he could earn with the time saved, but he was tired of trying to find a suitable man. Qualified men already had good berths and were unlikely to forsake a large ship for the ten-ton *Snark*, which left only the inefficients to cull from. He would be his own captain. After all, every time Warren got them lost Jack had to fall back on his own navigational skill to get them back on course. If he was going to spend so much of his time keeping his captain straight he may as well be the captain himself and save the expense and the problems.

The anchor was dropped in Suva under the supervision of Captain Wooley, the harbor inspector, and that night Jack and Charmian moved into Mrs. McDonald's hotel, the most famous hotel in Oceania. Captain Warren was paid off and sailed away from Suva as an ordinary seaman on a windjammer. When the *Snark* sailed out of Suva on June 6, the boat was in excellent condition. The crew that remained stayed intact for the rest of the *Snark's* cruise. It consisted of Captain Jack London and Charmian; Martin Johnson, engineer; Wada, ship's cook and Nakata, cabin boy; and the two Tahitians, Tehei and Henry. Things were different now. The constant turmoil among the crew over the past several months was gone. It was a merry group that was now wandering through the islands of the South Seas.

They sailed past Futuna and anchored at Tanna, then, after a five-day visit, the now happy ship nosed out of the harbor headed for Efate, sailing near land by day and heaving to at night for fear of running into land in the dark. Martin Johnson was deeply impressed by a deed of Jack London on this trip. He said:

As we were cruising in a general westerly direction through the New Hebrides, a little incident occurred which throws a side-light on the man, Jack London. One day, when weather conditions were perfect and everyone was on deck enjoying himself, an animated ball of variegated colours dropped slowly down into the cockpit at the feet of Mrs. London who was at the wheel. She eagerly picked it up, calling out, "Lookie, lookie, what I've got!" It proved to be the pret-

The crew of the Snark *at Penduffryn. From left to right: Tehei, Wada, Charmian, Jack, Martin, Ernest, and Henry.*

tiest little bird we had ever seen. Jack got out his book on ornithology, and proceeded to study book and bird, but nowhere was such a bird described. It was evidently a land-bird that had gotten too far from shore and had fallen exhausted on the deck of the *Snark*. We all stood around looking at it as it lay in Mrs. London's hand, while she chirped and tried to talk bird-talk to it. At last Jack said: "If it's a land-bird you are, to the land you go," and changing the course, we sailed for the island of Mallicollo, just barely visible ten miles out of the way. We sailed as close to the shore as possible, and the little multi-coloured pigeon-like bird, having regained its strength, flew in among the coconut trees. Then we headed out and continued our cruise through the score of small islands comprising the Western New Hebrides.

Critics of the man, Jack London, may call him an infidel. Colonel Roosevelt may call him a "nature faker." Others have not agreed with his ideas of life, but I have little doubt that this is the only time a captain ever went twenty miles out of his way when his fuel was low (our gasoline tanks were fast emptying), just to put a poor little bird ashore to go back to its mate and its young.

Martin and Henry sat eagerly at Jack's feet for their daily lesson in navigation as the *Snark* sailed past the last islands of the New Hebrides and on past the Banks Islands and the Santa Cruz Islands en route to Port Mary. Nakata, Wada, and Tehei were desperately trying to learn English. Nakata was at the top of the class, while poor Tehei was at the bottom. On June 28 the anchor was dropped into the warm waters of Port Mary.

By this time the *Snark* was a hospital ship. Jack had been suffering from yaws, a tropical disease, and the sores in his rectum were very painful. Later these were diagnosed as a double fistula, requiring an operation in Sydney. Acting as ship's doctor, Jack hunted through the medical books and asked the opinion of every man he saw. Most agreed that corrosive sublimate (mercury chloride) would help the yaws. Jack decided to use it, and it proved the only thing that did any good, but he never knew that this substance would cut his life span by many years. It was the worst possible medicine he could have used with his bad kidneys. But he had no idea

that his kidneys were anything but healthy. However, at the time these troubles were minor. His hands were his big worry. The flesh was peeling, giving them every appearance of leprosy. Every time he looked at them he remembered that week with the lepers at Molokai. He never voiced his fear except to Charmian. Yaws, ulcers, malaria, and such could eventually be cured, and the crew could take that, but leprosy was another matter.

The several days at Port Mary were busy with curio collecting, and grappling with the local speech. From Port Mary the wanderers went to Ugi for a short visit and then on to Guadalcanal. Meanwhile the thousand-words-a-day pace of writing went steadily on with seldom a day off. Ready for mailing were "The Amateur Navigator," "Goodbye, Jack," "Chun Ah Chun," and "The Heathen." On July 17 Jack started "Whale Tooth."

AT PENDUFFRYN ON THE ISLAND OF GUADALCANAL

Penduffryn was the largest plantation in the Solomons, on the Island of Guadalcanar (Guadalcanal). The reception for Jack and Charmian went on for one full week. Among the festivities was a masquerade ball with Charmian furnishing the music on her ukulele. After several days of merrymaking, someone suggested that everybody try hashish.

Darbishire, one of the plantation owners, was first, and for several days he wandered around in a half-dazed state. One after another took his turn at hashish until the night Jack tried it. He went clear out of his head and acted so wild that Charmian was frightened. That was the end of the hashish experiment. Nobody else would touch it.

The yaws drove the crew crazy. They dosed themselves daily with corrosive sublimate in larger and larger quantities. Martin said, "This much I learned, however, from our tribulations: Anyone coming to the Solomons should first purchase a barrel of quinine for the fever and a barrel of corrosive sublimate for yaws, and leave an order for more to follow."

Jack had just completed "The Heathen," based on his Tahitian crew member Tehei. On August 8

the ketch *Minota* dropped anchor, and Captain Jansen, its skipper, renewed his invitation to Jack and Charmian to go along on a trip to recruit black natives for work on the plantation. Jack's love for adventure and excitement overcame his dislike for blackbirding and all the evils associated with it. He also smelled plots for future stories. It was definitely raw adventure, with all its danger and excitement thrown in, as the door to their quarters on the *Minota* testified. Its tomahawk marks had been made by a group of Malaitian cannibals at Langa Langa a few months before when they broke in to steal rifles and ammunition after slaughtering Jansen's predecessor, Captain Mackenzie. Captain Jansen warned them, with a roguish smile, that the same tribe still needed two more heads from the *Minota* to square up for deaths on the Ysabel plantation. Not very reassuring, but this news did add to the spirit of excitement.

When Charmian explored her dimly lighted cabin, she met the shy, half-wild eyes of a kinky-haired young girl peering from a dark cubbyhole under the deck. Captain Jansen explained that a Malaitian chief, in return for some favors, or to curry one, had honored him with the gift of his

"Jack, the Pirate" poses with a friend at the masquerade ball in Penduffryn.

DARBISHIRE & HARDING,
BRITISH SOLOMON
ISLANDS.

PENDUFFRYN,
GUADALCANAR.

WE, GEORGE DARBISHIRE, King of Malaita and Grand Duke of Bina,
Mallu, and Sio Harbour, hereby do made *Jack London*
Knight of the Grand Cross of Bina and Sio Harbour on account of
Services rendered to the State.
Granted this day *19, Oto, 08*., and hereunto WE set our seal.

George Darbishire.
H.I.M. King of Malaita.

Jack becomes a Knight of the Grand Cross of Bina and Sio Harbor.

daughter Tésema. "She's a very embarrassing parcel," Jansen said, "but I thought too much of my neck to refuse her." The Captain was taking her to a mission at the end of the trip. The boat also acquired a mascot, an Irish Terrier known as Peggy, who charmed Charmian no end.

As soon as they cleared port, the *Minota* crew rigged a fence of barbed wire above the yacht's six-inch rail, the only break being at the narrow gangway, which would be heavily guarded. The first stop was at Su'u to drop off a group of natives, and then they went to Langa Langa for the first trip there since the Mackenzie slaying—dangerous but necessary. At Langa Langa the Londons saw their first reef village. The great island of Mala was garlanded with palm-plumed little Venices, tiny sea cities built upon outlying coral by the weaker natives of the bush who long ago were driven beyond the beaches of their own land. Charmian wrote, "Very curious and beautiful are these snug strongholds against man and nature, close-walled with firm masonry of coral blocks to resist the smashing sea, the straight lines of walls broken by thatched village roofs and the graceful bendings and sketchy angles of coconut palms. The openings for canoe landings are narrow and rough and steep, as if cannon had tumbled in a thick section of wall, the sides waving with ferns."

Jack and Charmian went ashore to the little vil-

lage of Sio, and to Jack's amusement and Charmian's embarrassment, only he could walk over the tree trunk bridge into the village, for it was taboo for women even if they were white. Charmian had to be taken across by canoe. As she stepped ashore everything went black and she commenced to shake uncontrollably. "Fever," said Jansen, and she was taken back to the boat, where Jack turned to with blankets and hot-water bottles and steaming hot drinks, brought by Nakata, to induce the sweat that brought relief. On August 13 Charmian recovered and joined the rest of the crew in their daily dosings of corrosive sublimate.

On August 19 the *Minota* set sail for the final lap of the blackbirding trip. The wind was baffling and the current drove them toward an ugly reef. Just as they were about to clear it, the wind changed direction and they struck the reef.

The instant she struck, the boat's crew sprang to their rifles and stood guard. In just a few minutes the bay was alive with boats of eager headhunters, with rifles, spears, and clubs sticking out in all directions, waiting patiently for the *Minota* to break up and yield her loot of tobacco, stores, and meat in the form of Jack, Charmian, and Captain Jansen.

Missionary J. St. George Caulfeild came out as fast as possible. He and Jack bribed a native to go to the *Eugénie* for help. On board the *Minota* bedlam

Jack and Charmian joined a recruiting cruise on the Minota *with Captain Jansen.*

Peggy, ship's mascot after Penduffryn.

The Minota *aground on a reef off Malu, August 19, 1908*

reigned. As the tide ebbed and the wind increased in ugly squalls, the swelling breakers lifted the helpless hull repeatedly, crashing it back down with terrific shocks. Then it would roll until the deck was almost perpendicular to the sea. Charmian and Nakata fought their way below to the stateroom, where they packed manuscripts, clothes, money, and the typewriter, in case they had to abandon the yacht.

Captain Keller and the *Eugénie* arrived on the scene and the crews of both boats fought for hours to free the *Minota*. Charmian spent the night in Missionary Caulfeild's house while the battle to free the boat went on. In twenty-four hours the crew had parted two anchor chains and eight sturdy hawsers. The next evening Jack and Charmian were taken aboard the *Eugénie* and delivered to the *Snark,* which was now at Gubutu. On the afternoon of the 21st the *Minota* slid free of the reef and was towed out to a safe anchorage. Jack and Charmian took Peggy with them and were to leave her at Meringe for Captain Jansen.

Returning from the blackbirding expedition, Jack decided his ailments required professional attention not available in the Solomons. He would leave the *Snark* with her crew at Aola, near the Penduffryn Plantation on Guadalcanal, while he, Charmian, and Martin went to the hospital in Sydney, Australia aboard the S.S. *Makambo.*

Since the *Makambo* wouldn't leave Guadalcanal until November 4, Jack and his crew cruised up to Maringe Lagoon on Ysabel, with a run north to Ontong Java Atoll and Tasman, their course taking them in and out of other interesting places in a leisurely fashion.

The weeks at Penduffryn had been adventurous and fun. Besides their steady work, Jack and Charmian boxed, rode horseback, and swam at sunset, sometimes in tropical showers with the stately palms waving in the gentle breezes. Always they had to watch for alligators and unfriendly bushmen.

One delightful diversion was a large jet-black mongrel terrier who gaily answered to Satan whenever he was called to show off or to act as bodyguard. "Made of coil springs," Charmian said, "he could jump straight into the air to impossible heights for food or sticks, or unhusked coconuts, which he incredibly stripped with his teeth and claws in a flash." Satan was the terror of the blacks, and in a moment he could clear the compound of an unruly crowd. Jack put him and certain tales of his valor in *Adventure,* his novel set at Penduffryn Plantation.

In Meringe Jack ran the *Snark* aground on a sloping section of the beach. As the tide went out and the hull lay exposed, all hands and the cook went about removing an astounding accumulation of barnacles, working until ten at night. Jack went through some rough moments when the tide came in, for the *Snark* didn't right and the water crept over the rail and up the vertical deck until it lapped against the edge of the skylight. It was nip and tuck for a time, but at last the heavy hull slowly righted and all was well again.

The crew of the *Snark* relaxed as much as possible during the two weeks at Meringe Lagoon. Henry and Tehei were down with island fever. Nakata was suffering the torments of ngari-ngari (a terrible rash caused by bush poisoning resulting in severe itching) Jack had several yaws, and Charmian, along with the rest, had intermittent bouts of fever. Yet everybody from the Captain down was nearly always able to carry out his full responsibilities.

Jack, Charmian, and Martin took a side trip to Kiaba, where all came down with ngari-ngari. Nakata had already caught it on Guadalcanal. Now they added a generous dosing of Lysol to the daily medication. By this time they were putting just about anything that even looked like medicine on their yaws. Jack finished his article "Cruising in the Solomons" in which he described his amateur medical practice from pulling teeth at Nuka-hiva to prescribing medicine for relief of ngari-ngari on Ysabel.

Wada went completely out of his head and ran away to live in a village of coast natives. When they left Kiaba, Wada was no longer aboard but Peggy was. Charmian had fallen for the dog and left a note for Captain Jansen telling him she would bring her to him on their return to Penduffryn. The *Snark* was now on its way to Lord Howe Atoll (Ontong Java). Jack took a morning sighting and went to his cabin to find their position, only to discover he had left the corrected tables at Penduffryn.

They were hopelessly lost. Everything seemed all right with the chronometer, but something was badly wrong. Naturally, Jack was worried. However, Charmian tells us, "With the worry of this unaccountable situation, with fever threatening, and a new crop of small sores eating into his nerves, I don't see how my husband can be so merry—except that he relished a set-to with adventure and the unknown." Martin was fighting malaria, so Charmian volunteered to take his watch—the first time she had been at the wheel for months except when making harbor entrances and departures.

For days the *Snark* wandered nobody knew where, but the crew refused to worry. Jack was always able to come up with the correct position. On the morning of September 14 Charmian on waking heard an inexcusable pun from Martin: "Lord! Howe did we miss that island."

This pun started a competition. Even Nakata, sick as he was due to malarial fever, came up with "Lord, Howe I wish there was no fever in the Sol-

The Snark *careened at Meringe for removal of barnacles*

Jack's first dental patient at Nuka-Hiva

Charmian takes her turn at the wheel.

omon Islands." While the fun went on, Jack was poring over his charts in an effort to locate his position. On September 16 he shot a perfect noon observation and steered for Lord Howe. At six in the afternoon he proudly announced that they were about seventeen miles from the atoll.

The next day Tehei went aloft and yelled out, "Lan' ho!" Charmian said, "We could not see it from the deck, but Henry climbed up and verified the glorious find, while Jack noted the bearings, west by south, one-half south." The *Snark* hove to beautifully that night. Jack glowed at the excellent performance. The *Snark* had cost a small fortune, but outside a balky engine she was everything he had hoped for, and under Martin's expert handling even the engine worked most of the time.

At Lord Howe they met Harold Markham, a trader, but Jack was most intrigued by Markham's Solomon Island cook, who was serving several sentences for murders, escapes in handcuffs, thefts of whaleboats—a history of bloodcurdling crimes and reprisals. Jack decided immediately to build a short story around his many escapades, calling it "Mauki."

Jack was beginning to worry more and more about his health. For the past week his hands had been swelling as with dropsy and to close them was painful. Pulling on a rope brought excruciating pain. On top of that, his skin was peeling off both hands at an alarming rate and the new skin underneath was growing hard and thick.

After a short stay the *Snark* got underway for Penduffryn, where they found a French motion picture company, sent by Pathé Frères of Paris, making movies of the cannibals. One of the scenes called for an attack on the plantation. Jack was asked to play the part of a plantation owner who is killed by a spear. The director noted that Jack did a great job of acting.

Jack thought he had straightened out matters with Bessie when he went back on the *Mariposa*, but this proved to be an illusion. From ignorance, Jack London has been accused of hundreds of things of which he was innocent. One biographer has stated that Bessie was on the point of marrying again to escape his dominance. In the same passage this biographer also states that Jack sailed on the *Snark* to escape his responsibilities. This is childish and untrue. At no time did Jack try to dominate Bessie—nobody dominated her. She was a shallow person

Bob, the hero of Jack's story "Mauki."

with set ways. Jack's sense of responsibility caused him to do everything in his power to keep Bessie from ruining the lives of their daughters.

Here are a few excerpts from a letter Jack wrote to Bessie just prior to leaving the Penduffryn Plantation:

Now I have pointed out clearly to you that I do not want to make a profit out of you and Charley. And, furthermore, if your marriage should prove a happy one, so that you and Charley are living together twenty years after your marriage, the increased value of the property from the day I bought it and improved it, to the day of your marriage, which said increased price is the cause of the present trouble, will go to you and Charley. That certainly shows that I am not trying to make a profit out of you. I flatter myself, what of the household furniture at which you sneer, plus the increased value aforementioned, that will go to the two of you when you have been married twenty years, is a pretty nice wedding present to a man's first wife upon marrying her second husband.

Then comes the funniest thing in all your letter. You threaten, that if I do not accede to the dragging out of me of aforementioned sums of money for the benefit of you and your second husband, that you will be danged if you will get married. Why, my dear child, I don't care a whoop in high water whether you get married a second time or not. I should like to see you happily married for your sake, but I regret that I cannot genially contribute money to finance that second marriage.

Very few men have met their responsibilities as faithfully as Jack London. Going aboard the *Snark*, Jack took on added responsibility, not less. During his entire career, he carried on most of his business by correspondence. A study of the letters to his ranch foreman reveals an amazing control of even the smallest detail by mail.

A simple reading of Charmian's *Book of Jack London*, Volume Two, gives a clear explanation of the reason for the cruise of the *Snark*:

"Our friends cannot understand why we make this voyage," Jack elucidates his and my "I like," which, he always contended, is the ultimate, obvious reason for all human decision. "They shudder, and moan, and raise their hands," somewhat, he might have added, as did the Lily Maid's mother upon his departure for Alaska. "No amount of explanation can make them comprehend that we are moving along the line of least resistance; that it is easier for us to go down to the sea in a small ship than to remain on dry land, just as it is easier for them to remain on dry land than to go down to the sea in a small ship. . . . They cannot come out of themselves long enough to see that their line of resistance is not necessarily everybody else's line of resistance. . . . They think I am crazy. In return, I am sympathetic. . . . The things I like constitute my set of values. The thing I like most of all is personal achievement—not achievement for the world's applause, but achievement for my own delight. It is the old 'I did it! I did it! With my own hands I did it!' But personal achievement, with me, must be concrete. I'd rather win a water-fight in the swimming-pool, or remain astride a horse that is trying to get out from under me, than write the great American novel. . . . Some other fellow would prefer writing the

great American novel. . . . That is why I am building the *Snark*. . . . I am so made. I like it, that is all. The trip around the world means big moments of living. . . . Here is the sea, the wind, and the wave. Here are the seas, the winds and the waves of the world. . . . Here is difficult adjustment, the achievement of which is delight to the small quivering vanity that is I. . . . It is my own particular form of vanity, that is all."

"The ultimate word," Jack said elsewhere, "is I LIKE. It lies beneath philosophy and is trained about the heart of life. When philosophy has maundered ponderously for a month, telling the individual what he must do, the individual says in an instant I LIKE—and does something else and philosophy goes glimmering. Philosophy is very often a man's way of explaining his own I LIKE." He also said, "There is also another side to the voyage of the *Snark*. Being alive, I want to see, and all the world is a bigger thing to see than one small town or valley." When the voyage of the *Snark* was over Jack said, "It is hard to hammer it into the human understanding that the whole voyage was done for the fun of it."

On October 25, 1908, Jack told Brett that the following were for sale: *Lost Face, Revolution and Other Essays, When God Laughs, South Sea Tales,* and *The Cruise of the Snark*. In addition he had completed thirty thousand words of *House of Pride* and twenty thousand words of his novel *Adventure*.

Plans at this time were to regain their health in Sydney and then return to Penduffryn for resumption of the *Snark* cruise. When the doctors in Sydney advised Jack to forsake the cruise and return to California, he and Charmian were heartbroken. Nobody has ever realized just how much Jack and Charmian loved that cruise. They were extremely disappointed by the turn of events. But the trip certainly was no failure. Several books, short stories, and articles had been written, and their experiences were invaluable to his and Charmian's literary future.

When the decision was made in Sydney, Jack, in his always candid way, wrote a letter, had it duplicated, and sent it to everyone he knew, explaining the breakdown of his health as the reason for the termination of the cruise, one more proof that Jack London never tried to make a myth of his "perfect health" or anything else. Many myths have developed over the years regarding Jack London, but any knowledgeable person knows that none of them were started knowingly by Jack London himself. He was probably the most candid author in history. He knew his morals were far above average and he had nothing to hide, and so hid nothing. It was impossible for him to be humiliated because he knew who he was, and it was up to the public to like him or not. He acknowledged his failures and received a great deal of personal satisfaction from his accomplishments and successes without a trace of conceit—as has been testified over and over by nearly everyone who knew him.

Henry, Tehei, Nakata, and Wada, who had been brought back to the *Snark* by Captain Jansen, had nearly recovered from their ailments; but Jack, Charmian, and Martin eagerly waited for the *Makambo* to put in. Finally on November 3 she dropped anchor at Penduffryn. That night Jack and Charmian gave a big champagne dinner for the Penduffrynites and then went aboard to sail the next day. Thursday at noon they steamed out of the Solomons headed for Sydney and the hospital.

SYDNEY, AUSTRALIA

On November 14 the *Makambo* arrived in Sydney. Dr. Read eased Jack's worry about leprosy when he came aboard and diagnosed his skin problem as psoriasis. Going ashore, the Londons and Martin registered at the Metropole Hotel. On the 16th Jack and Charmian went into St. Malo Hospital on Ridge Street. Dr. Clarence Read operated on Jack on November 30 for a double fistula. On December 8 the decision to call off the rest of the *Snark* cruise was made. Jack hired a Captain Reed to go with Martin to bring the *Snark* down to Australia.

Late in December Jack, though not fully recovered, reported the Johnson-Burns heavyweight championship fight in Sydney for *The Australian Star* and *The New York Herald*. Charmian was given special permission to attend the fight—she was the only woman in a crowd of twenty thousand spectators. In January Jack started writing weekly articles for *The Australian Star*. Thinking a cooler climate would be beneficial, the Londons went to Hobart, Tasmania, to sightsee and recuperate. Their trip lasted from January 9 through February 8, 1909.

Immediately on their return to Sydney, Jack ordered a tailor-made suit and a half dozen silk shirts. Though he would seldom wear a regular tie, preferring a Windsor type, he was always well dressed. While in Sydney he fell for the Panama hats available there and bought several. Charmian, of course, was always dressed in the best fashion of the day. They were considered a handsome couple wherever they went. At the zoo in Sydney they

weighed in at one hundred seventy and one hundred eighteen pounds.

On March 8 Charmian noted in her diary, "Martin is planning to write a book 'Through the

Sydney, Australia, 1909

Photo taken on a motor trip to the National Park in Tasmania in March 1909.

Jack, Charmian, and Frank Strawn-Hamilton in Sydney, Australia, 1909

Jack and Charmian sailed from Newcastle, N.S.W. to Guayaquil, Ecuador, aboard the Tymeric.

South Seas with Jack London.' Haw! Haw!" He did, and the book, published in 1913, is in most ways superior to Charmian's *The Log of the Snark*. Martin went on to become famous for his safaris in Africa and his many books on the subject. Martin and Osa Johnson were lifelong close friends of the Londons. After Martin brought the *Snark* back to Sydney with Captain Reed, Jack advanced him money to continue his trip around the world before returning home to Independence, Kansas.

When the *Snark* returned to Sydney on March 3, it brought Charmian the sad news that her devoted Irish terrier, Peggy, had died en route. She was grief-stricken. Later Jack immortalized the little terrier in *Jerry of the Islands* and *Michael, Brother of Jerry*. The Snark was stripped of most of her instruments and put in the hands of Justus Scharff, Ltd., who finally sold her for forty-five hundred dollars in October 1910.

On April 8, 1909, the Londons boarded the collier *Tymeric* for passage to Ecuador. Charmian signed on as stewardess, Jack as purser, and Nakata as cabin boy. During the trip Jack finished his novel *Adventure* and "The Sea-Farmer," and started "A Piece of Steak." On May 19 the *Tymeric* steamed into Guayaquil, Ecuador. From Guayaquil they crossed the Andes to Quito. On May 30 they attended a bullfight. Jack, thoroughly disgusted with the lack of sportsmanship in the fight, wrote "The Madness of John Harned," in which he registered that disgust forever. After the usual sightseeing they went back to Guayaquil and boarded the S.S. *Erica* for passage to Panama, where they went into quarantine on Culebra Is-

land. On July 6 Jack paid his bill of $187 for their ten-day stay at the Tivoli Hotel in Panama, only to discover he didn't have enough money to buy tickets home. He arranged to pay their transportation on the S.S. *Turrialba* from Colon on arrival in New Orleans and sent a telegram to Eliza in Glen Ellen to telegraph money there.

On arrival in New Orleans, Nakata was detained by the immigration authorities until Jack's wired request to the Secretary of Commerce and Labor brought his release. A five-hundred-dollar bond had to be secured so he could enter the United States on a temporary permit pending a decision on Jack's appeal.

The Londons and Nakata departed by train for Oakland with a short stop at the Grand Canyon. They arrived in Oakland on July 21 unrecognized. During the next two days they had a grand time with "the crowd," taking all their meals at the Saddle Rock. On the 23rd they bought two carriages, a two-seater and a runabout, both bright black and yellow. The following day they ran into Captain McIlwaine, their Captain on the *Tymeric* from Sydney to Guayaquil, and took him to Glen Ellen with them.

Steadily, rapidly, Jack regained his health in the California climate. In a few months all traces of his curious maladies disappeared. And his analytical mind was finally put at ease when he came across a book by Lieutenant Colonel Charles E. Woodruff of the United States Army, entitled *Effects of Tropical Light on White Men,* in which the author had the same medical problem. The ultraviolet rays had simply torn them to pieces.

Jack and Charmian in one of the two black and yellow carriages they bought on their return from the Snark *cruise*

THE HILL RANCH EXPANDS

During the twenty-seven months Jack and Charmian were away, Netta had a fairly good record as manager of Jack's affairs. She did a few stupid things but compensated with a few shrewd dealings. She sold *Martin Eden* for the princely sum of **seven thousand dollars** at a time when the money was sorely needed to catch up on ranch debts and to cover the doctor and hospital bills in Australia. But her crowning achievements were the purchases of the La Motte Ranch of one hundred twenty-seven acres, the small Fish Ranch of nine acres, and the Caroline M. Kohler property of twenty-four acres. Now Jack's ranch, or more correctly his two ranches, totalled three hundred ninety acres. He had to continue the supply of clay to the Glen Ellen brick kiln by granting an easement to the clay pits located on his new property. All in all it was a very wise investment, since Jack now had enough acreage to operate the type of ranch he had in mind. The next step would hopefully be the purchase of the 700-acre Kohler-Frohling Tokay Ranch, which would give him an unbroken stretch of land from Asbury Creek on the west to Graham Creek and Netta's Wake Robin property on the east.

With the added acreage Jack's dream of becoming a full-fledged farmer was accomplished. Work would soon start on their dream home, to be called Wolf House—so dubbed by George Sterling. It would be built on a precipitous bank of Asbury Creek on the extreme western and northern borders of the original Hill Ranch, landscaped before the *Snark* trip by the Londons' very close friend, Johannes Reimers.

Feeling better daily, Jack set out in his highly professional way to write himself out of debt again and to keep the money coming in. The purchase of the ranches had given him a new glow of pride in his agricultural ideas, as well as the setting for the novel he was working on—*Burning Daylight*. The book was started in Quito, Ecuador, set aside to write the bullfight story, resumed in June, set aside again to write "That Dead Men Rise Up Never" for the *Delineator*, and resumed again in earnest on August 14. By December 11 he had seventy thousand words completed. The novel was to be an indictment of individualism, based on experiences of Charmian and himself and using George Sterling's uncle, Frank C. Havens, for the stateside part of the book. The Yukon material was based on the exploits of Jack's old Klondike friend Elam Harnish.

Burning Daylight is an excellent example of how Jack acquired his material from actual events in his own life or the lives of people he knew. For instance, Cloudesley Johns told Jack the story of how Collis P. Huntington and his railroad carefully figured freight rates for his station at Harold, California, to allow a man to earn only two dollars a day. The name Jones was substituted for Johns. Cloudesley didn't burn the shed, however; that part is fiction.

In *Burning Daylight,* Jack reveals much of the force that made his own success possible as he describes Elam Harnish:

> Desire for mastery was strong in him, and it was all one whether wrestling with the elements themselves, with men, or with luck in a gambling game.... Deep in his life processes Life itself sang the siren song of its own majesty, ever awhisper and urgent, counselling him that he could achieve more than other men, win out where they failed, ride to success where they perished. It was the urge of Life healthy and strong, unaware of frailty and decay, drunken and sub-

lime complacence, ego-mad, enchanted by its own mighty optimism.

Burning Daylight is the story of a Northland superman who leaves the Klondike to seek like successes in the business world. He discovers that the jungles of big business are far more savage than all the wilds of the Yukon. After being swindled out of eleven million dollars by a few Wall Street tycoons, he ruthlessly turns the tables and recoups. But in the process he becomes hardened. His consideration of others is destroyed. He falls in love with his secretary, Dede Mason, who refuses to marry him as long as she has to compete with his money, which so totally owns him. When he renounces his wealth, she marries him and they settle down in the midst of the pastoral beauty of the Valley of the Moon. Love has conquered avarice.

When the novel appeared in 1910, it was extremely popular and ranked as one of the best novels of the year. It was also a strong factor in London's return to popular acclaim, which had been partially lost due to his lecture tour of 1905–06 and his absence for two and a half years on the *Snark*.

START OF A BIG YEAR

Jack started the year 1910 at home in bed. On December 31 he, Charmian, and their house guest, Ernest Unterman, were out riding. On their return a gate was sideswiped. In the accident Jack's ankle was crushed by the buggy wheel.

By January 7 he could walk a little. On the 16th he and Charmian went to Oakland. That night they attended the First Congregational Church to hear Rev. Charles Brown's sermon based on *Martin Eden.* The sermon turned out to be a diatribe against Jack London, with a strong emphasis on his having two living wives. Among other things, he called Jack a dangerous agitator.

The next day Jack was quoted, "Since hearing the Rev. Charles Brown's sermon last night on *Martin Eden,* I can understand why for two thousand years the church has been rent with dissention over the interpretation of the Scriptures. Mr. Brown gave last night a splendid sample of the churchman's capacity for misinterpretation." Jack

went on to explain his book, and in so doing gives an excellent pen sketch of himself:

> Mr. Brown interpreted Martin Eden as a man who failed because of lack of faith in God. I wrote *Martin Eden,* not as an autobiography nor as a parable of what dire end awaits an unbeliever in God, but as an indictment of that wild-beast struggle of individualism of which Mr. Brown is not among the least of the protagonists.
> Contrary to Mr. Brown's misinterpretation last night, Martin Eden was not a socialist. Mr. Brown, in order to effect a parallel with my own life, said that Martin Eden was a socialist. On the contrary, I drew him as a temperamental and, later on, an intellectual Individualist. So much so was he an Individualist, that he characterized Mr. Brown's kind of ethics as ghetto-ethics and Mr. Brown's kind of Individualism as half-baked Socialism. Martin Eden was a proper Individualist of the extreme Nietzschean type.
> Now to my parable, which I thought I had

expounded lucidly in the pages of this novel. Being an Individualist, being unaware of the needs of others, of the whole human collective need, Martin Eden lived only for himself, fought only for himself, and, if you please, died only for himself. He fought for entrance into the bourgeois circles where he expected to find refinement, culture, high-living and high-thinking. He won his way into those circles and was appalled by the colossal, unlovely mediocrity of the bourgeois. He fought for a woman he loved and had idealized. He found that love had tricked him and failed him, and that he loved his idealization more than the woman herself. Those were the things he had found life worth living in order to fight for. When they failed him, being a consistent Individualist, being unaware of the collective human need, there remained nothing for which to live and fight. And so he died.

Martin Eden failed and died, in my parable, not because of his lack of faith in God, but because of his lack of faith in man. Even Mr. Brown will agree that he cannot get to God except through man. Martin Eden failed because he did not get even to man. He got only as far as himself, and the rest of humanity did not count.

Unfortunately, Mr. Brown's sermon was not on Martin Eden, but on Jack London, and Mr. Brown was woefully unacquainted with the subject. He said that I was Martin Eden. Let me point out the vital weakness of his parallel—Martin Eden killed himself; I am still alive.

Why am I alive? Because of my faith in man, a faith which Martin Eden never achieved, and a faith which Mr. Brown evidently did not know appertained to his subject, namely, Jack London. Yet my faith is most readily accessible to all men; my books are in the Public Library. Mr. Brown should have read up on the subject before he expounded it. Let me here quote some of my faith from the preface of my *War of the Classes.*

"He must learn that Socialism deals with what is, not what ought to be; and that the material with which it deals is the 'clay of the common road,' the warm human, fallible and frail, sordid and petty, absurd and contradictory, even grotesque, and yet, withal, shot through with flashes and glimmerings of something finer and God-like, with here and there sweetnesses of service and unselfishness, desires for goodness, for renunciation and sacrifice, and with conscience, stern and awful, at times blazing imperious, demanding the right,—the right, nothing more nor less than the right."

Few men ever lived who exemplified that last line more than did Jack London. He always demanded the right—the right, nothing more nor less than the right, from himself. He sincerely believed that socialism was vital to social reform, and he was a completely dedicated social reformer. Sadly, few persons on earth returned to him what he gave to others; only Charmian and Eliza could always be counted on. Almost everybody else wanted something, and seldom gave anything in return.

Jack and Charmian went to the Macdonough Theatre in January to see Olga Nethersole in *Writing on the Wall.* After the play the three went to the Saddle Rock. During the course of the evening, Miss Nethersole asked Jack to write a play for her. Later he wrote *Theft,* which she had to decline because she had signed a two-year contract with the Schuberts. Fate plays strange antics. *Theft* was never wanted by anybody during Jack's lifetime, but now it is one of the books most sought after by Jack London collectors.

Early in January Jack ordered fifteen thousand *E. Tereticornis* eucalyptus trees for his ranch. In February the planting began on the La Motte section. The planting of eucalyptus trees wasn't a rash move on Jack's part. The La Motte place was ideal for the purpose, being unsuitable for anything else except pasture land. Before ordering the trees, he studied everything he could find about the viability of the eucalyptus as a cash crop. Certainly he didn't fall under the spell of the eucalyptus promoters. He checked every government bulletin on the subject and went up to the University of California at Davis to talk with the agricultural experts there. Every possible piece of information was digested.

When it turned out that the eucalyptus tree was worthless, the critics berated London for foolishly planting them, forgetting to mention that nobody knew of their uselessness at the time. Actually, a careful study reveals that Jack London was an excellent businessman, but an unlucky investor. Another of Jack's investments, the Millergraph, a printing process, had an excellent potential, but Joseph Noel, not Jack, was the cause of the loss in this venture. A block of stock in the Oakland Fidelity Loan and Mortgage Company, highly recommended by Jack's lawyer, kept Jack in court for years. Twenty-five shares of stock in the Weaver Patent Power and Pump Company proved to be a loser, but Jack bought this as a gamble. Another gamble with Mr. William Lee in a Wickenberg, Arizona, gold mine was equally unsuccessful. However, each of these investments looked worthwhile at the time and each was checked out thoroughly. Had any of these gambles made Jack a millionaire, his critics would have called him a genius.

Carmel-by-the-Sea intrigued Jack and Charmian into visiting George and Carrie Sterling during the first two weeks of March. Jack was having a wonderful time with the old "crowd"—Arnold Genthe, Harry Leon Wilson, George Sterling, Sinclair Lewis, Mary Austin, Jimmy Hopper, Fred Bechdolt, and many others. For Charmian it was a mixed blessing. She got tired of seeing drunks, but was thankful that Jack wasn't one of them—though she did think he was drinking too much.

On their return to Glen Ellen, Jack went over to the Fish Ranch to see how Eliza and her son, Irving, were doing at getting settled. With the growth of the ranch to three hundred ninety acres and the imminent purchase of another seven hundred acres, Jack had talked his stepsister, now separated from her husband, Captain James Shepard, into moving to the ranch as his business manager. This was one of the wisest decisions Jack ever made. Eliza proved to be a near perfect ranch superintendent. When Jack died in 1916, Charmian kept her on in the same job. When Eliza died in 1939, her son, Irving, took over; and when Charmian died in 1955, the ranch and the literary estate went into the hands of Irving Shepard. Upon the latter's death in 1975, it was left to his wife and children. Today the ranch and the Jack London literary estate are in the capable administrative hands of Irving's son, Milo Shepard.

On May 14, 1910, Jack London was finally able to purchase the Kohler-Frohling Tokay Ranch for twenty-six thousand dollars plus cost of livestock and equipment. The Jack London Ranch now had a total of one thousand ninety acres, making it one of the largest in the Valley of the Moon.

Over two hundred acres of the Tokay addition were suitable for growing wine grapes. With seven distinct soils in the alluvial deposits at the foot of Sonoma Mountain, with its cool mountain breezes at night and warm sunny days, in an area that had never seen frost during the growing season, a crop of premium wine grapes was almost a certainty every year. But at the time Jack bought the ranch, grapes were selling for eleven dollars a ton. Since it cost more than that to raise them, he reluctantly plowed most of the vines under, leaving enough for his own use.

Jack's purchase of the Tokay Ranch didn't include the buildings—the twelve acres containing the ruins of the old winery destroyed in the 1906 earthquake, or the old six-room cottage, the two small stone buildings, and the stone sherry house which were owned by the California Wine Association. Jack's goal now was to buy these twelve acres and the five hundred-acre Freund Ranch above his property, which was vital to his water needs. When, and if, those purchases were made, the Jack London Ranch, as he envisioned it, would be complete.

DISAPPOINTMENT AND MORE NOTORIETY

Charmian entered Fabiola Hospital in Oakland on June 13 to deliver her first child. On the 19th she was put under ether and the baby was taken from her. The birth was extremely difficult, and thirty-eight hours later the baby girl Jack and Charmian had named Joy died—probably due to the severity of the birth. The Londons were devastated. They had made so many plans that the baby was already a vital part of their future, and now in less than two days she was gone. The whole thing was impossible. Charmian was put under sedation, and Jack, still in partial shock and deep in grief, walked toward the waterfront.

As he passed the Tribune building, he noticed some booklets for sale. They were autobiographies of Jim Jeffries, the prizefighter who was challenging Jack Johnson for the world's boxing title. Thinking they would be good gifts for some of the other reporters at the upcoming Johnson-Jeffries prizefight in Reno, he went in and bought several

Charmian, Jack, Carrie, and George Sterling at the Sterling bungalow in Carmel

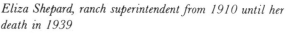

Eliza Shepard, ranch superintendent from 1910 until her death in 1939

April 15th. Ritz Hotel Piccadilly London. W.

The book I like best of any I have read lately is Jack London's "White Fang". A masterpiece I think in its analyses of emotions, human & canine. — In the vast knowledge it shows of the evolution which goes on in all breathing things. "White Fang" & this author's other work "The call of the wild" are my two favourite books of the twentieth Century. — Elinor Glyn

Jack was an admirer of the work of Elinor Glyn. Here she returns the compliment.

Martin and Osa Johnson spent part of their honeymoon at the Jack London ranch.

and continued down the street toward the water-front. Near Seventh and Broadway he walked into a bar owned by Timothy Muldowney, where he was to meet his friend Joseph Noel for a drink.

Muldowney, spotting the colorful booklets Jack carried and evidently thinking he was going to put up some kind of advertising on the walls, yelled at him. Jack probably yelled back and Muldowney started a fight. He and his friends threw Jack out of the bar. Both Jack and Muldowney were taken to court and released for trial on July 8. The first time Charmian saw Jack after losing their baby he was sporting a huge black eye. He insisted that he hadn't had a single drink and that Muldowney attacked him without provocation.

The Johnson-Jeffries world championship fight had originally been scheduled to be fought in San Francisco on July 4. *The New York Herald* had asked Jack to report the bout and to write articles gleaned from the training camps for ten days prior to the fight. Realizing that he would be staying in Oakland, since their baby would be born about that time, he accepted the commission. Later, due to legal problems in California, the match was moved to Reno. Knowing how much it meant to

Jack, Charmian insisted that he go on to Reno and fulfill his assignment.

Jack wrote some excellent articles for the *Herald* before the fight and another great one on the fight itself. He wanted the "white hope" to beat the black Jack Johnson so much that he was goaded into betting more than he should and lost a sizeable amount.

Ed Winship, a very close friend from Napa, drove him back to Oakland. Jack felt as though the bottom of the world had dropped out. The lost bet and the lost fight were of little consequence. But loss of his daughter would become stark reality again when he saw Charmian.

Two days later, on July 8, Jack had to appear in Judge Samuels' court on the assault charges. In court the Judge claimed he was giving both defendants the benefit of the doubt and dismissed the case. Furious, Jack undertook a personal vendetta.

It was childish, irrational, and uncharacteristic of him. Normally he would have laughed and gone arm in arm with Muldowney for a drink at his bar to celebrate, but this time it was different. Blind with rage, he wanted revenge. It was a chance for a one-to-one encounter with injustice. In Buffalo, af-

A group of reporters who covered the July 4, 1910, Johnson-Jeffries heavyweight championship bout. Jack is seated fifth from the right in the second row.

HEARD THE CALL OF THE WILD

YES-QUICK!-GIMME SACRAMENTO-YES-YES-HELLO-YES-THE GOVENOR-HELLO-

THAT FRACAS

JUST BEFORE THE MILITIA ARRIVED

DO I UNDERSTAND YOU CORRECTLY? YOU STATE THAT THIS MAN BUTTED YOU, WHEREUPON YOU ANNEXED HIS GOAT

MR LONDON AT WORK ON HIS "LIFE AND BATTLES" WHILE CRUISING ON THE OAKLAND ESTUARY

GOOD MORNIN' JUDGE, POOR JOHN.

SNARK

TOO LATE! AND I WOULD HAVE SLIPPED HIM $50,000 FOR HIS END OF THE PICTURES

Café

SPECIAL ANNOUNCEMENT
NOW IN THE HANDS OF THE PUBLISHERS, "JACK LONDON, HIS LIFE AND BATTLES" WAIT FOR IT!
THE McMILLION CO

MOVING PICTURE CO

CONTRACT

JOHNSON'S JACK LONDON
CHALLENGE
SHOULD JEFF TAKE THE COUNT —

LONDON-MULDOWNEY CASE IS POSTPONED

Hearing of Author and Saloon-keeper Who Fought Will Follow Reno Battle.

And Jeffries was at the bottom of the whole affair after all.

If the former pugilistic champion hadn't written his autobiography Jack London wouldn't be nursing a swollen optic, nor would his name appear on the Oakland police blotter, nor would he be complainant against one Timothy Moldowney, proprietor of a saloon in Oakland's tenderloin district.

"The whole affair was the result of my having bought four copies of the autobiography of Jim Jeffries," said London yesterday. "I am to report the big fight for an Eastern newspaper and I wanted to read the book. I had the books under my arm when I entered Muldowney's place. He suspected me of being a quack doctor bent on posting some placards. He saw the pasteboard-covered books and believed them to be a package of posters."

Then the fight started. The aftermath came yesterday when London appeared against Muldowney in Police Judge Samuel's court at 10 a. m. The climax was reached fifteen minutes later when London was asked to step outside the courtroom and was formally arrested on complaint of Muldowney, who charged the author with battery. He was arraigned with Muldowney. Each pleaded not guilty to the charge.

The author of "The Call of the Wild," "The Sea Wolf" and other stories appeared in court dressed in a light gray suit, soft white negligee shirt, black flowing knotted tie and Panama hat. Outside of a badly swollen right eye, a puffed nose and other discolorations on the face he looked well.

Muldowney's face told plainly a story of conflict. It was red and swollen, the skin was lacerated in places. London says, however, that his time was spent in trying to get away from Muldowney, whom he didn't want to fight.

The Judge inquired whether the men wished to be tried at once or after July 4th; then before either could answer he continued: "From the appearance of both gentlemen they will be in a better condition to stand trial after July 4th."

And so the decision will be given after Tex Rickard has given the count to one of the two gladiators who meet in Reno July 4th.

London is determined to prosecute Muldowney. In further explanation of the affair, which occurred at the Tavern, as Muldowney's resort at 362 Seventh street is known, London said yesterday:

"I would not care so much about the affair but for the fact that the bartenders and waiters in the place kept shoving me back at Muldowney every time I tried to get away. It was most unfair and it is that feature of the matter that I most resent."

Muldowney says London started the trouble and that when he took him by the arm to escort him out the author "wheeled around and rushed him like a wild bull."

DIVORCE CASE DISMISSED

Stockton Couple Settle Domestic Differences and Agree to Live Together.

[Special Dispatch to "The Examiner."]

STOCKTON, June 22.—The divorce troubles of Theresa Gularte and Joseph Gularte came to a happy ending this morning, when Judge C. W. Norton was requested to dismiss the case on the grounds that the contestants had adjusted their difference.

The wife filed the complaint and it was answered by the husband. Mrs. Gularte alleged that he was disrespectful to her, that he heaped undeserved abuse upon her and otherwise acted in such a manner as to make her unhappy. She said that he frequently ...

3,000 Bankers to Be Entertained in Fall

San Francisco Artist Awarded Medal in Paris

The London-Muldowney bout received more press coverage than the Johnson-Jeffries fight.

ter being unjustly put in prison, he had to slink away and say nothing. Once more he knew he was innocent. Judge Samuels had sufficient evidence to convict Muldowney of unprovoked assault. Why didn't he? There must be a reason. He wrote letters to all the local papers regarding the incident. He asked his reporter friend, Joseph Noel, to look into the ownership of Muldowney's bar. It turned out that the land the bar was on was owned by Judge Samuels. No wonder he turned Muldowney loose! More letters were written and the vendetta was on in earnest. Jack swore he had enough friends to make Samuels lose at the next election and that is exactly what happened. To complete the vendetta, however, Jack wrote a short story called "The Benefit of the Doubt" in which Judge Samuels was given the bad-guy role.

The only logical reason for Jack's unusual reaction in the Muldowney affair was that he was unconsciously venting his frustration over the loss of the baby, coupled with the strain of writing eleven articles in as many days for the *Herald*. Whatever the reason, it was a thoroughly successful vendetta and the only one Jack conducted.

BOHEMIAN CLUB HIGH JINKS

Back in 1904 Jack had become an honorary member of the prestigious Bohemian Club in San Francisco. The club was founded in 1872 to promote the arts on the West Coast, and to provide a place where artists and writers could meet with the prominent men of the city in a convivial atmosphere.

Knowing how much Jack loved the camaraderie at the annual Bohemian Club High Jinks on the Russian River, Charmian insisted that she could recuperate with friends and that he attend the summer camp. He especially wanted to go because, at last, he might meet the old caustic himself, Ambrose Bierce.

George Sterling had been a protégé of Bierce for several years before George and Jack became close friends. Their friendship grew to the point where Bierce's influence on Sterling was nearly gone. The cynic blamed London for ruining the future of the man he thought to be America's greatest poet, and this time Bierce was even more bitter than usual.

In a letter to Charmian on July 29, 1910, Jack spoke of the impending meeting: "Damn Ambrose Bierce. I won't look for trouble, but if he jumps me, I'll go him a few at his own game. I can play act and abuse just for the pure fun of it. If we meet, and he's introduced, I shall wait and watch for his hand to go out first. If it doesn't, hostilities begin right there."

According to Arnold Genthe they did meet at the Jinks. One night after nearly everyone had retired, Bierce, London, Sterling, and Genthe sat around the campfire talking. Just before dawn Bierce remembered that he was staying on the other side of the river with his brother Albert. Afraid his brother would be alarmed if he awoke to find him missing, Ambrose decided he had better go home. It was still quite dark, so Sterling suggested they all escort him safely home.

Bierce's ubiquitous derby was set at a jaunty angle, indicating that he had been imbibing rather freely. Sterling, leading the way, promptly put the lantern out of commission when he fell on it. Undaunted, the group made its way through the forest, deposited Ambrose at his brother's house, and stumbled back to camp. Genthe never disclosed whether Jack and Ambrose shook hands, or, if they did, who put out his hand first. Like many other historical events, this remains a mystery.

FALL OF 1910 IN GLEN ELLEN

Returning to Wake Robin Lodge, Jack sat down and poured forth his thousand words daily. The California Home for the Feeble Minded adjoined Jack's Hill Ranch. When out riding, he often stopped by to talk with the kids. His story "Told in the Drooling Ward," based on one of these converstations, is the finest piece of psychological work Jack did and a perceptive journey into the mind of a mentally handicapped child.

With plots still a major problem for Jack he turned again to Sinclair Lewis:

Glen Ellen, Oct. 4, 1910

Dear Sinclair Lewis:

Your plots came in last night, and I have promptly taken nine (9) of them, for which same, according to invoice, I am remitting you herewith check for $52.50.

Some of the rejected ones were not suited to my temperament; others did not suit because I am too damn lazy to dig up requisite data or atmosphere.

I didn't care to tackle the World Police (which is a splendid series), because I am long on novel motifs of my own, which require only time and relaxed financial pressure for me to put through.

I'll let you know whenever one of your plots is published.

"Winged Blackmail" was published in Sept. number of the *Lever,* a monthly magazine issued in Chicago.

I have 20,000 words done on *The Assassination Bureau,* and for the first time am stuck and disgusted. I haven't done my best by it, and cannot make up my mind whether or not to go ahead with it.

Be sure to send me plots from time to time, with prices attached, and for heaven's sake, remember the ones I take, so that you won't make the mistake of writing them up yourself some time.

> In a wild rush,
> Sincerely yours,
> Jack London

The Assassination Bureau was not completed until Robert Fish, a detective mystery writer, finished it in 1963 from Jack's notes. "The wild rush" was to get everything in order for a cruise on the *Roamer.*

THE *ROAMER* CRUISE

Sailing was always the best medicine for Jack's periods of depression. His problems always disappeared once he was on water again. Now he knew what the term *like a fish out of water* meant. He couldn't exist without a boat. He asked Bessie's brother-in-law, Ernest Matthews, to keep an eye out for a bargain. Several weeks later Matthews happily informed Jack that he had found the ideal boat, the *Roamer.* Together Jack and Ernest met owner William H. Craig. "Yes, the boat is for sale; the price is $175." Jack bought it on the spot. She was forty years old and a beauty—thirty feet long, an extra-wide beam, and an unusually large cabin for such a small boat made it perfect for the Londons. Huge sails gave her a majestic look and caused her to move through the water with the slightest breeze—an ideal boat for the San Francisco Bay waters.

In *The Valley of the Moon* Jack presents a vivid picture of life on the *Roamer:*

Hastings decided to eat dinner—he called the midday meal by its old fashioned name—before sailing; and down below Saxon was surprised and delighted by the measure of comfort in so tiny a cabin. There was just room for Billy to stand upright. A centerboard-case divided the room in half longitudinally, and to this was attached the hinged table from which they ate. Low bunks that ran the full cabin length, upholstered in cheerful green, served as seats. A curtain, easily attached by hooks between the centerboard-case and the roof, at night, screened Mrs. Hastings' sleeping quarters. On the opposite side the two Japanese bunked, while for'ard, under the deck, was a galley. So small was it that there was just room beside it for the cook, who was compelled by the low deck to squat on his hams.

The Londons never grew tired of the *Roamer* and spent months at a time aboard her. Jack's writing stint and Charmian's typing still occupied their mornings. In the afternoon they fished, swam, lounged on deck, played cards, or talked. A favorite pastime was Jack's reading aloud to Charmian and many an hour was whiled away in this manner. Their love grew stronger each year, both loving to do things for the other. Jack was to depend more and more on Charmian during the next few years, a responsibility she never avoided, as though fate had prepared her for that role. Actually Charmian was nearly a hypochondriac, recording her ail-

The Roamer

ments in her diary nightly. But seldom did Jack hear a complaint or see her in anything but a cheerful mood. Her role was to be his mate, companion, lover, or anything else he needed. She played this role simply because she wanted to and because she was so thoroughly in love with Jack.

Charmian and Jack set out on the *Roamer* on October 17 for a cruise up the Sacramento River—their first trip on the new boat. A better galley had been built and a little stove for warmth and cooking was installed in the main cabin. A few months later Jack wrote of his love for boating:

Once a sailor, always a sailor. The savour of the salt water never stales. The sailor never grows so old that he does not care to go back for one more wrestling bout with wind and wave. I live beyond sight of the sea, yet I can stay away from it only so long. After several months have passed, I begin to grow restless. I find myself day-dreaming over incidents of the last cruise, or wondering if the striped bass are running on Wingo Slough, or eagerly reading the newspapers for reports of the first northern flight of ducks. And thus, suddenly, there is a hurried packing of suitcases and overhauling of gear, and we are off for Vallejo where the little *Roamer* lies, waiting, always waiting for the skiff to come alongside, for the lighting of the fire in the galley-stove, for the pulling off of gaskets, the swinging up of the mainsail, and the rat-tat-tat of the reef points, for the heaving short and the breaking out, and for the twirling of the wheel as she fills out and heads up Bay or down.

As they cruised up the river and through the delta waters, Charmian said, "Jack looked much like his piratical early self in blue dungarees, his time honored 'tam' pulled down, with a handful of curls, over his sailor-blue eyes."

Near the Vallejo Yacht Club they ran into Charley LeGrant, so often mentioned in *Tales of the Fish Patrol.* On another cruise up Sonoma Creek's delta, they came upon French Frank, former owner of Jack's *Razzle Dazzle,* of oyster pirate fame. Charmian found Frank debonair and gallant. He now lived as keeper of a shack for a local duck-hunting club.

Since so much of the Londons' time was to be spent on the *Roamer*, it may be best to let Charmian tell what it was like:

What a blissful passage it was, this first *Roamer* voyage, only to be surpassed by the second and

After many years, Jack meets his old friend of oyster pirate days, French Frank

the third, and so on. "Snarking once more," Jack named it; honeymooning up on the face of the winding waters; fanning into Benicia to the sweet melody of birds in the rushes; running across that large, draughty, variegated piece of water, Suisun Bay, where the great scows we had both learned to respect came charging down, grain-laden; picking our way in the "Middle Ground" channels, and gliding close-hauled into Black Diamond in the fires of sunset, where the Sacramento and the San Joaquin tumble their muddy flood together—to port the hazy, Aztec unreality of the tawny-rose Montezuma Hills, palpitating in the westering sunlight; to starboard the low brown banks with green upstanding fringes of rustling tules; all about red-sailed fishing boats homing for the night; and old Black Diamond's lazy waterfront and lazier streets sloping upward toward the Contra Costa Hills; and, in the morning Mt. Diablo crumpled against an azure dome.

Much of the time, after disposing of his morning's work, Jack read through the usual mountain of agricultural pamphlets and then devoured countless numbers of books brought aboard each cruise. Charmian loved to watch her man at the wheel as the little *Roamer* sailed her way from slough to slough. She said, "He was an unfailing wonder to me, my Jack London—my mentor—his continuous cerebration to every impact, mental, physical, awake, and asleep; always young, always old, always wise, and with 'a bigness of heart that kept conscience with itself,' efficient dreamer, har-

Jack at wheel of the Roamer

fort." Words of a loving wife? Yes, but no exaggeration here. This was Jack London as described by everyone who knew him.

After a run down to Escondido, the Menlo Park home of Charmian's cousin, Willard Growall and his wife, Emma, to attend the November 10 wedding of recently divorced Ninetta Eames and Edward Biron Payne, the Londons brought the cruise to an end and returned to Glen Ellen. There Jack finished *The Abysmal Brute,* an opportune event, for on November 16 he noted that he had twelve hundred dollars in the bank and owed nine hundred dollars on a life insurance policy, five hundred dollars for taxes, and had a pressing mortgage payment of a thousand dollars. But this was nothing new. Debt had become a way of life. He knew his steady output would always bring in the money when it was needed. And it never failed. One thousand words a day at ten cents a word equalled one hundred dollars and everything was usually sold before it was written. Add this income to steady royalty payments and foreign sales and the result was a healthy, steady stream of incoming capital—always enough to meet his needs. Eliza never ceased to be amazed at how his "Monthly Miracle" kept on happening.

December found Jack and Charmian poring over Wolf House drawings while twenty men were planting another twenty thousand eucalyptus trees on the LaMotte place. Jack was busy on the Smoke Bellew stories. Hack work he called them, all except "Wonder of Woman." But they turned out to be extremely popular with the reading public when published in 1911. *Cosmopolitan* begged him to continue the series, but he refused, saying, "I'm tired of writing pot-boilers! I won't do another one unless I have to."

As 1910 drew to a close, the Londons were packing for a trip to Los Angeles for a visit with Jack's old friend Felix Peano, the sculptor.

nessed to his work for the sake of Heart's Desire, which included the discharge of so many responsibilities—penalties of patriarchy. How vivid he rises, standing on his handsome legs at the wheel, those robust muscle-rounded shoulders leaning back upon a howling norther before which we fled, tense, caution on hair-trigger, uncapturable thoughts behind his deep, wise eyes, lips parted, and that great chest expanding to breeze and ef-

THE GAME

Boxing was Jack London's favorite sport. His interest began in the early years when he and Jim Whitaker were sharing talents—Whitaker's expertise in boxing and Jack's knowledge of how to get stories sold. Jack's interest never waned. Wherever

he went, boxing gloves always went along, and he was ever ready to put them on with anyone. His favorite sparring partner was Charmian. They boxed nearly every day. They boxed at home, all the way to the Solomon Islands on the *Snark,* from

Sydney, Australia to Ecuador on the *Tymeric,* and from Baltimore to Seattle on the *Dirigo* in 1912. It was on the *Snark* that they had the most fun. In the morning they put on their bathing suits, boxed for a full hour, threw buckets of salt water on one another, and went below to dress for a day of work and sailing. This constant boxing with Charmian gave Jack an excellent defense, for he couldn't strike back as with a man. However, he would box any man, in deadly earnest or for a few rounds of sparring.

His interest didn't stop with his own boxing. He was an avid spectator at every professional boxing match he could get to, preferring to be there as a reporter so he could be assured of a ringside seat. And it wasn't for the brutality of the fights either. He enjoyed the science of boxing, where man was pitted against man, but he hated bullfights, where man's superior intellect destined the slaughter of the poor bull, and he hated hunting with a rifle, which negated any possible sport that could be involved.

Jack's first major boxing assignment was the Jeffries-Ruhlin fight of November 16, 1901. James J. Jeffries was defending the title he had won in the heavyweight championship bout with Bob Fitzsimmons, an eleven-round affair at Coney Island, New York, on June 9, 1899.

The *San Francisco Examiner* paid Jack one hundred dollars to cover the Britt-Nelson championship battle on September 10, 1905.

His work as a boxing reporter continued at the West Oakland Athletic Club late in 1906, when he started attending fights there. One night Fred Goodcell found him standing dejectedly by the box office staring at the sold-out sign and asked him to share his press pass. Alex Lopez, the "Rat" in *Martin Eden,* was on the card that night; Jack thought him a perfect specimen of manliness. Goodcell was astonished since in his opinion Lopez was anything but. Goodcell asked Jack to write a brief account of the matches. Almost the entire article was on Lopez. After this item was published in the *Oakland Herald,* Jack was offered a ringside pass anytime he would write an article on the bouts. This arrangement lasted several months, according to Goodcell.

While in Sydney at the end of the *Snark* cruise, the *New York Herald* paid Jack two hundred and seventy-five dollars to report the world's championship match between Tommy Burns and Jack Johnson. His report of the fight was also published in the *Australian Star.* As mentioned before, he reported the Johnson-Jeffries fight in Reno on July 4, 1910. While in Los Angeles he attended the Dundee-Kilbane bout and reported the fight in the *Los Angeles Examiner* on May 1, 1913.

When Century published *The Abysmal Brute* in 1913, James Barr said in "Is the Prize-Ring Doomed?":

> *The Abysmal Brute* is by Jack London, than whom no man on earth is more entitled to write of prize-fighting. He has seen the biggest big fights that have been waged these last two decades, he has the penetrating brain, the knowledge of the world, and the tense, vivid vocabulary best suited to write a true picture of the ring. And a truly tremendous tale he has made of it. In his own picturesque Western style Jack London hustles the reader through the whole process of preparing for the winning of a world's heavyweight championship. And when you have finished reading through *The Abysmal Brute,* you will realize that the soul of prizefighting, with all its gallantry and sordidness, its heroic points and drab grossness has been laid bare.

Not only was Jack an excellent boxer and an even better fight reporter, but he was also a pioneer in the use of the boxing ring in fiction. His works were exceptionally well received by professional boxers and were also influential in keeping the boxing game clean. *The Abysmal Brute* was a brief for the purification of the sport. His own cleanliness, manliness, and exceptional sense of fair play is readily discernible in his fictional works.

Another illustration of the power of London's pen was Gene Tunney's decision to quit boxing after reading *The Game,* Jack's boxing novel published in 1905. Later, when Tunney felt Rocky Marciano should retire, he gave him a copy of the same book and asked him to read it very carefully.

The *Pittsburgh Labor Tribune* on August 4, 1910, published an article by Jack London that tells why we have the sport of boxing:

Pugilism is an Instinctive Passion of Our Race:

> This contest of men with padded gloves on their hands is a great sport that belongs unequivocally to the English speaking race and that has taken centuries for the race to develop.
>
> Pugilism is no superficial thing, a fad of the

moment or a generation. No genius or philosopher devised it and persuaded the race to adopt it as their racial sport of sports. It is as deep as our consciousness, and it is woven into the fibers of our being. It grew as our language grew. It is an instinctive passion of our race.

And as men today thrill to short Saxon words, just so do they thrill to the thud of blows of a prizefight, to the onslaught and the repulse, and to the exhibition of gameness and courage.

This is the ape and tiger in us, granted. But, like the men in jail, it is in us, isn't it? We can't get away from it. It is the fact, the irrefragable fact. We like fighting. It's our nature.

We are realities in a real world, and we must accept the reality of our nature and all its thrill-ableness if we are to live in accord with the real world, and those who try to get away from these realities, who by ukase of the will deny their existence, succeed only in living in a world of illusion and misunderstanding.

These are the people who compose theater panics, fire panics and wreck panics.

When Jack reported the Britt-Nelson fight, he called Nelson an abysmal brute. Nelson was furious and demanded apologies. Jack said of the incident, "I like Nelson. I named him the 'Abysmal Brute' after his seventeen-round fight with Britt at Colma several years ago. Bat didn't like it at first, but we got together and talked it over, and he began to appreciate the term. I called him that as a compliment. He has the primitive thing in his nerves and fibre and soul that goes ahead; that knows no quitting—primitive."

An article in the *Medford Sun* on Friday, August 18, 1911, best sums up Jack's feeling toward the boxing game:

I would rather be heavyweight champion of the world—which I never can be—than King of

An autographed picture of "Battling" Nelson

England, or President of the United States, or Kaiser of Germany.

Of all the games it is the only one I really like. Yes, the game is going. But I hope that there will remain some arena to which I may go during the remaining days of my life.

1911—A GOOD YEAR LITERARILY

Leaving Oakland on January 5 with their guests, the newly married Netta and Edward Payne, Jack and Charmian were en route to Los Angeles to take advantage of Felix Peano's offer of the use of his home. Peano was the sculptor Jack and Bessie stayed with in his home, Villa La Capriccioso, in Oakland. Peano's offer to Jack and Charmian was the same one he extended earlier—if Jack would furnish the food, Felix would supply the living quarters.

Jack had always admired Barney Oldfield, who held the world's speed record for automobiles. While in Los Angeles, the Londons saw him beat his old record. They then took a two-day trip to Catalina Island after visiting Charmian's Wilmington birthplace, and visited all their Southern California friends. After a relaxing and thoroughly enjoyable visit of a month they returned to Oakland.

Jack and Charmian stayed at 490 Twenty-seventh Street in Oakland for several days. The day after arriving from Los Angeles Jack went to see Bessie and the girls. He hated to go because his visit was bound to end in a fight. Bessie had written, "Could you let me have the one hundred again. Then I would be able to set aside a little for those extras that happen along. Also then I could meet the dancing school bill."

Jack answered her letter on January 8 from Los Angeles, "First of all, let me tell you that I am in the thick of hard times. I have mortgages of over $30,000.00 upon which I am paying interest. In addition to this I have something like $10,000.00 in debts. When you figure repairs of house, painting, taxes, etc., dancing lessons, music lessons, railroad passes (I work for them), etc. you will discover that you are getting more than $100.00 a month, in addition to the free rent of a house."

In his letter Jack went on to explain that he wasn't making the money he had been making a few years before. His socialism, his going out of vogue, and his natural and inevitable deterioration as a writer had reduced the prices he was getting from the magazines and had reduced the sale of his books. He went on to say further, "I am making the effort of my life at the present moment to provide for the future. I am planting eucalyptus trees. My laborer's wages for the month of January will amount to over $1,000.00 and this does not include my horses, my wagons, my harnesses, plows and harrows, and expenses of repairing same; nor does it include a thousand and one other expenses. Do you think this is for myself? I can live on $20.00 a month. Do you think this is for Charmian? She can do the same. This is for all of us. This means Grandma, Jennie, Johnnie, doctor bills, houses, taxes, life-insurances, etc., and all in addition to you, Joan and Bess."

On the way over to see her he knew that he had wasted his words. Bessie cared only for herself and

An Arnold Genthe picture of Charmian

the girls. She was selfish, cold, and jealous, and cared little for anybody else. But she was the mother of his two girls, and it wasn't their fault that their father and mother were so thoroughly incompatible that staying together had been impossible. Yes, there would be a fight. Bessie would see that Jack couldn't enjoy a moment of his visit to his daughters unless he agreed to the added allowance, and he was damned if he would let her get away with it.

He was right. There was a confrontation, a major one. At the height of the argument an incident occurred that has been retold and embellished through the years. Joan London, in her lectures for many years, related the story of how her father was always drunk when he came to their house and that on one occasion he was so drunk that he threw her sister, Becky, through a glass window.

Becky remembers the episode as if it were yesterday. Here is her firsthand report of that incident:

About the "foot through the window" episode. Any other versions must have come from Joan. No one else knew about it. We disagreed greatly about many things we recalled about Daddy. Since I was the recipient, I think my memory is the more accurate.

Uncle Ernest Matthews (Calvin's father) told Joan and me, after Daddy's death, that Daddy had told him he had never written a word that his daughters might be ashamed of (which is absolutely true). Also he had never visited us with alcohol on his breath (again true). When we were old enough to go to dinner with him, he never ordered a cocktail or had wine with his dinner. When Joan read me the draft of this happening, she had written that Daddy was drunk the day it happened. I disagreed, and we had one of our worst fights, and I told her I would never give my permission to have such a thing published. It was weeks before she spoke to me.

I believe I was six or seven when it happened, and old enough to remember it clearly. One would—it was something that didn't happen to a little girl every day.

Daddy, Mother, Joan and I were in the sitting room. It was early afternoon and I guess Daddy had come to take Joan and me out—maybe to a movie.

What had started it I don't know, but Mother and Daddy were very angry and saying terrible things to each other. Joan had gone over to stand beside Mother. I was sitting on the floor beside Daddy. Suddenly Daddy said, "You know I wouldn't hurt either of my daughters. They trust me to take care of them. Don't you Joan?" And Joan said, "Well, I don't know."

Becky (on left) and Joan around 1911

Daddy turned to me and said, "If I told you to put out your hands in mine and I would throw you through the window (which was closed) would you believe me?" I said, "Yes, Daddy, and I know you wouldn't hurt me. I trust you." Then I put my hands in his. He was so angry I'm sure he didn't know what he was doing. He picked me up from the floor and swung me toward the window. One foot crashed through, there was a loud noise and he pulled me back instantly. He was contrite and after examination thought it was just a slight cut. He carried me across the street to the hospital and had it bandaged.

He never knew there was a piece of glass in the wound which gave me a lot of pain and trouble. We never told him. He referred to it in his inscription of *When God Laughs*. He wrote, "Dear Bessie: God often laughs, especially at glass windows."

It was only logical that the two daughters would be nearly as incompatible as their mother and father, since Joan was a carbon copy of her mother, and talking with Becky is like having a chat with her father.

Joan's cynicism and lack of warmth is very evident in her biography of her father, *Jack London and His Times.* Though it is still the best biography to date on Jack London, readers are left with the feeling that they have met a famous man but failed to catch the tremendous personality that lay behind his genius. Joan and her mother were both completely devoid of humor, a terrific handicap to a good relationship with Jack. Someone asked Becky one time what her mother did after the divorce. Her ready response was "She became a professional martyr." Joan, likewise, went through life feeling sorry for herself and bemoaning the fact that her father's estate and genius didn't fall on her like the mantle of Elijah.

Becky, on the other hand, is Jack London all over again. Even her letters read like a Jack London story. One of the tragedies of Jack's life was his unsuccessful attempt to capture Joan's loyalty and affection, not realizing that she was incapable of either. Too bad that he didn't turn to Becky, who would have returned measure for measure and given him the father-daughter relationship he so desperately sought in Joan.

In April, after an overnight horseback ride to Napa for a visit with the Winships, Jack and Charmian boarded the *Roamer* in Vallejo for a three-week cruise. During the cruise, one day was spent in conference with the architect of Wolf House, Mr. Albert Farr. On the 26th a phone call to Eliza brought the good news that she had purchased the twelve acres in the center of the Kohler-Frohling Ranch from the California Wine Association for fifteen hundred dollars. Preparations were made on return from the cruise for a four-horse trip up into Oregon. Before leaving, plans were made for an addition to Wake Robin Lodge, another fifty thousand eucalyptus trees were planted, and a new will was made, providing for the care of Eliza, Irving, Bessie, Joan, Bess, Flora, Aunt Jennie, and Johnny Miller, but leaving the ranch and the literary estate to Charmian.

NAVIGATING FOUR HORSES

Jack hitched four horses to his Studebaker wagon on June 12, 1911. Then he, Charmian, and Nakata began their trip from Glen Ellen to Oregon and back—fifteen hundred miles up the coast and through the mountains. Jack describes how things got started in the September 1911 *Sunset* magazine:

Having selected Sonoma Valley for our abiding place, Charmian and I decided it was about time we knew what we had in our own county and the neighboring ones. How to do it, was the first question. Among our many weaknesses is the one of being old-fashioned. We don't mix with gasoline very well. And, as true sailors should, we naturally gravitate toward horses. Being one of those lucky individuals who carries his office under his hat, I should have to take a typewriter and a load of books along. This put saddle-horses out of the running. Charmian suggested driving a span. She had faith in me; besides, she could drive a span herself. But when I thought of the many mountains to cross, and of crossing them for three months with a poor tired span, I vetoed the proposition and said we'd have to come back to gasoline after all. This she vetoed just as emphatically and a deadlock obtained until I received inspiration.

"Why not drive four horses?" I said.

"But you don't know how to drive four horses," was her objection.

I threw my chest out and my shoulders back. "What man has done, I can do," I proclaimed grandly. "And please don't forget that when we sailed on the *Snark* I knew nothing of navigation, and that I taught myself as I sailed."

"Very well," she said. (And there's faith for you!) "They shall be four saddle-horses, and we'll strap our saddles on behind the rig."

It was my turn to object. "Our saddle-horses are not broken to harness."

"Then break them."

And what I know about horses, much less about breaking them, was just about as much as any sailor knows. Having been kicked, bucked off, fallen over backward upon, and thrown out and run over, on very numerous occasions, I had a mighty vigorous respect for horses, but a wife's faith must be lived up to, and I went at it.

Once Jack's morning writing stint was over, he

drove through the middle of the day and the afternoon to the next stop. But, the irregular occurrence of hotels, coupled with widely varying road conditions, made it necessary to plan each day's drive the day before. He had to know when he was to leave in order to start writing in time to finish the daily quota. Several times, when the drive was too long, he would be up and writing by five in the morning. When the day's journey was short, he might not begin writing until nine o'clock.

Planning was the problem. On arrival in each town, he put up the horses and then went to a local saloon, where he promptly ordered a drink for himself and one for the barkeeper. As they drank, Jack asked about road conditions and stopping places ahead. Often the barkeeper would call for a conference with other customers, and while they talked Jack bought them drinks, too. This way he learned the best road to take, where the best stopping place would be, what running time he could expect, where to find a good trout stream, and so forth. By the time he left the saloon, he knew about everybody in town and had his next day's trip all mapped out. The saloon was not only the poor man's social club; it was also the horse-age information bureau.

The trio spent their first night at Fort Ross, an old Russian colony. Fortunately Jack took many pictures of the old fort, which was destroyed by fire many years after his death. The executor of the Jack London Estate, Mr. Irving Shepard, loaned these pictures to the State for use in the Fort's restoration. This brings to mind the fact that during World War II, the Navy sent a representative to the Jack London Ranch to make copies of the charts Jack had made while cruising on the *Snark*. The Navy used these charts to plan an invasion of the Solomon Islands.

By the end of the first week, the Londons had passed Fort Bragg, and on July 1 they wheeled into Eureka, where they spent a restful ten days on a luxurious houseboat loaned by Mr. H. L. Ricks. However, they were kept busy here and in every other small town in Northern California and Oregon by the local reporters.

In Crescent City Jack and Charmian attended a reception in their honor at the Masonic Hall, where it was announced, unbeknown to Jack, that Mr. London would give an impromptu speech. To the relief of some and the disappointment of others,

On the road

Jack didn't give his fiery Revolution speech, choosing instead to talk about the differences in the climates in various areas of the world and how Northern California could be proud of its weather.

The Oregon border was crossed on July 25 en route to Colgrove's Mountain Ranch. The trip to Port Orford brought them through some of Oregon's most beautiful dairy country, where the Londons paused for fishing and to put the finishing touches on "The Turtles of Tasman."

The issue of the *Port Orford Tribune* after their departure said, "No one ever visited Port Orford and made a better impression, or left warmer hearts behind them, than Jack London and his charming wife."

It was the same story throughout the trip. Every town opened its heart to the popular young couple and received theirs in exchange. Jack's boyish smile and unpretentious spirit even won over his worst critics.

A few years later George Wharton James described an experience in an *Overland Monthly* article entitled "A Study of Jack London in His Prime":

London, like Joaquin Miller, was the victim of much and persistent misrepresentation. He is an avowed Socialist. Many newspapers do not like Socialists, and they seize every possible opportunity to spread unpleasant news about those who are known to profess that faith. Sometimes they

Ten days on Mr. Rick's houseboat while the four horses rest

The reception in Crescent City for the Londons, July 20, 1911

Ready to depart from Crescent City heading north for Oregon

Jack goes fishing at Port Orford. From left to right: T. L. Carey, Jack London, W. H. Meredith, and H. T. Stewart.

are not very particular as to whether their assertions are true or not. In speaking of this several times, and then giving my personal impressions of London, people have said to me: "Why do you not make these things known?"

In order to help make them known, let me tell an experience I had a few months ago with a distinguished and well known Eastern writer on one of the foremost Boston dailies of high standing, was a university man of high ideals and academic standards, who a year or so before had become transplanted to the Pacific Coast and was then doing special editorial writing on one of the San Francisco papers. We dined together several times, and on one occasion the name of London came up. Naturally, I spoke of the things in London that pleased and interested me. To my amazement, my Boston friend opened up with a tirade, denouncing London from every possible standpoint. There was nothing good about him in any way.

Seeing that he was rabid, I decided to let him have his talk out and then quietly informed him that his tirade was nothing but a mass of prejudice, for, said I, "I refuse to accept this unjust and untruthful tirade as your judgment. Judgments imply knowledge. You have no knowledge, but simply a mass of erroneous beliefs gained from mendacious newspapers and other unreliable sources."

I happened to be planning to go up to Sacramento to see the Governor and thence to London's home at Glen Ellen the following day, and asked my editorial friend if he would not like to meet me and accompany me to see London and

his wife. In his finest Bostonese he exclaimed: "But, my dear fellow, I have received no invitation."

Heartily laughing, I replied: "I have given you an invitation!"

"But," said he, "what about Mr. and Mrs. London?"

Again I laughed and said: "Let your New England conscience be perfectly at rest. I have invited you, and that is enough."

James met his friend the next day and together they went to Glen Ellen. On the following day Jack set aside his usual stint and devoted the morning to a horseback tour of the ranch with his guests.

James continues:

Returned to the house, we had music from voice, piano and Victrola, and Jack related a number of interesting stories in connection with his trip on the *Snark*. But more than all, I wanted my friend to see the intellectual workings of London's mind, so I started arguments with him on sociological questions. I aroused him enough by antagonism to stimulate his natural eloquence. Naturally my friend prodded him also, for he prided himself upon his wide reading of all the schools of sociology. When I had got the two head over heels into red-hot debate, I let them "go it," hammer and tongs, for I knew what the result would be. London's memory seldom fails him, and his reading was as four to one compared with the Eastern scholar. The result was the latter found himself utterly unable to hold his own, and yet in his defeat felt that peculiar consciousness of pride that only a well educated man can feel, viz.; that it has taken a man wonderfully well equipped with natural endowment and extraordinary reading to be able to cope with him.

The day was gone all too soon. After a tasty dinner the cart was brought and as we rode out to the train I turned and asked: "Well, how is it?" And then, for an hour, I listened to the Boston man's superlative expressions of the situation, the gist of which was as follows:

"Why, sir, that man's life is the most ideal life of any literary man I know. His home is as near to perfection as I have ever seen a home and his companionship with his wife is something wonderful. It does not require any intelligence to discover the secret of his immense capacity for work. He is living in an artistic atmosphere, every element of which is perfectly congenial. And think of that ride! What a joy and privilege to have been able to take it with him! I never heard anyone who so thoroughly entered into the spirit of Nature and the beauty of things as did this man who has always been described to me as so rude and primitive as to be absolutely brutal."

Jack's fiction has the charisma and intellectual character of the man himself. Both Jack and his work are representative of his times. To millions of Europeans, Jack was America. When they thought of the United States it was usually coupled to an image of Jack London. His fiction has been a better ambassador abroad during the last seventy years than any man the United States could possibly appoint. It would take a full volume to tell the story of his contributions to American popularity among the people of foreign lands.

The *Montreal Gazette,* on June 11, 1910, said, "When the editor of the *Bookman* was asked the other day to name the leading American novelist, he replied that there were only two—William D. Howells and Jack London." The *New York Tribune,* on May 14, 1914, said that Jack London had captured the sympathy and admiration of the city. In 1929 one million of Jack's books were sold in one day in Germany. UNESCO, the United Nations agency, held a worldwide survey in 1952 and discovered that Jack London was the most popular and the most translated American author in Europe and Russia. In 1972 *Hispanoamericano* in Mexico City said, "Jack London was the most read non-Polish writer in Poland." Between 1944 and 1970, 3,300,000 copies of his works were published there.

Mauno Oitinin at the University of Helsinki said in a letter to Joan London, "All of Europe plus the Scandinavian countries are reading Jack London. I also use his books for my English students."

Crown Prince Frederick Wilhelm of Germany said, "London is one of my favorite American authors. I would like to meet him." In 1922 the Prince of Wales declared that he had loved Jack London's works ever since David Lloyd George introduced him to them.

In Russia Jack London is a revered name. Phillip S. Foner in *Jack London: American Rebel* says, "Jack London's popularity in the Soviet Union has frequently amazed American visitors. Other than Russian writers, he is the most popular of all ages, and of all countries, with a lead of many million volumes in print. His nearest rival as a novelist is Victor Hugo, who in 1956 has a total printing of

Jack London, the favorite author of our generation. By the first of September, 1929, one million Jack London books were sold in Germany.

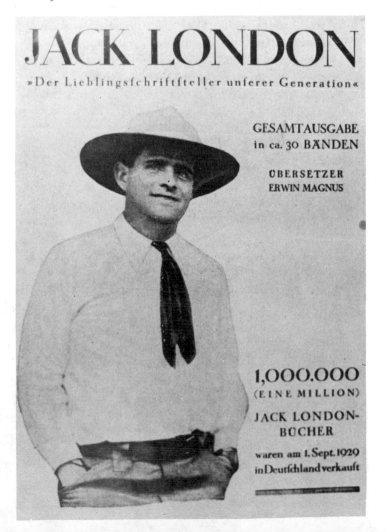

eight and one-half millions compared with London's thirteen millions. No other novelist reached even half of this total." It is now claimed that over thirty million volumes by Jack London have been sold in Russia. It is interesting to note that Russians have little interest in Jack's political beliefs, but are intrigued by his theme of the "struggle for survival."

Now, getting back to the four-horse trip, we find the Londons have reached Medford, Oregon, where the *Sun* reported that when Jack was requested to lecture he said, "A lead horse is not a wheel horse nor a wheel horse a lead horse. Neither is a speaker a writer, nor a writer a speaker." Evidently the Medfordites didn't believe this, finally convincing him to speak on "Why I Became a Socialist." He warned them again before speaking by stating that if he was a tolerable writer he was an intolerable speaker. A local critic described the speech as a huge success, never mentioning whether it was tolerable or intolerable.

At last the Studebaker wagon was headed for Glen Ellen. From Ashland, Oregon, it reentered California. Jack and Charmian made their way through Montague, Weed, Dunsmuir, Le Moyne, Kennett, Reading, Red Bluff, Orland, Williams, Maxwell, and into Leesville. Here they had to arrange for Charmian's thoroughbred, Maid, to be sent home because of a bad shoulder. After buying

a new horse, Cricket, to replace Maid, they rested the night and set out for Lower Lake, Middletown, and Calistoga. On September 5 they rolled through Glen Ellen and up the hill to sleep for the first time on their own ranch. While they were on the trip, Eliza had managed to get the old Kohler-Frohling Winery cottage livable for them until completion of Wolf House.

The fall of 1911 was hectic—arranging for rock for Wolf House, running a busy ranch, writing one thousand words a day, answering nearly one hundred business and fan letters daily, making numerous business trips to Oakland and San Francisco, and entertaining the ever present guests. Though the entertainment on the ranch has been terribly exaggerated, it was far more than Charmian wanted but less than Jack liked. Rarely did more than eight or nine sit down for dinner at one time, probably because the dining room was too small to accommodate more. Although someone was usually visiting, there were seldom more than four at any one time. Tramps found their way to the ranch, but it is unlikely that more than half a dozen did so during the five years Jack lived on it. Glen Ellen was not an easy place for a tramp to get to, or for anybody else.

It has also been stated that the ranch was loaded with paroled prisoners. The records reveal only two—a Mr. Stryber and Ed Morrell. When Jack

Charmian takes her turn at the reins.

The dining room in the Kohler-Frohling cottage, which Jack and Charmian used from 1911 to his death.

Jack and A-No. 1, the famous tramp. A-No. 1, Leon R. Livingston, wrote From Coast to Coast with Jack London. *Jack met and knew A-No.1 on his 1894 tramping trip, but about 98 percent of his book is pure fiction. In a letter to A-No.1 Jack said, ". . . you are making a mistake in telling folks this fairy tale, for some of them have read, or will some time read, my entirely different version of why I quit the road."*

Ed Morrell, author of The 25th Man *and on whose prison experience Jack based his book* The Star Rover

said, "The latch string is always out," he meant it. There were several guest accommodations on the ranch. The carriage house had six rooms on one side and seven on the other, but six of these were used by the hired hands. There were also four guest rooms in the cottage. Jack was at his happiest when all the rooms were filled. On one occasion a young Japanese girl walked up to the ranch from Glen Ellen, over a mile uphill, just hoping to get a fleeting glimpse of her hero. The Londons opened their generous arms to her; she didn't go back down the hill until two weeks later. For Jack this wasn't the least bit unusual.

The year 1911 was also one of exceptional literary output. Even though his office had been in Los Angeles, out on the *Roamer,* or in a different town nearly every night from June 12 until September 5, Jack was able to keep to his schedule. In somebody's home as a guest, in a rickety hotel, or in a luxurious one, camped out under the stars or wherever he happened to be, he managed to do his one-thousand-word stint. His discipline was absolutely amazing.

In 1911 four books and twenty-four short stories by Jack London were published. In addition, he submitted "Small Boat Sailing," "The Prodigal Father," "The Feathers of the Sun," "The Hanging of Cultus George," "The Mistake of Creation," "A Flutter in Eggs," "The Townsite of Tra-Lee," and "Wonder of Woman." Financially his star was rising also. In 1911 he was receiving from eight hundred fifty to one thousand dollars for each short story and sold every single item he submitted. Rejection slips were now almost a thing of the past.

When Jack wrote Bessie in January, he sincerely believed he faced a year of retrenchment, but the public had more faith in him than he had in himself. They proved to be better critics of his value to the world of literature than he ever dared dream himself to be.

Jack and Charmian boarded a Western Pacific train on Christmas Eve, 1911, at Oakland en route to New York City. On the way they would layover in Salt Lake City to visit Charmian's artist friend, Harry Culmer. On December 27 Jack went to the fights. On the following day they were back in their compartment on the last leg of the trip East.

On arriving in New York January 2, 1912, they were met by F. G. Hancock, who shared his apartment at 40 Morningside Park East with them. The reason for the trip was twofold—to finalize arrangements with the Century Company to take over publication of his books, and to arrange passage on a sailing ship around Cape Horn to gain background material for his sea novel, *The Mutiny of the Elsinore.* There were many other items of business for him to take care of while in New York, but these were the primary ones.

Charmian has been accused of whitewashing Jack and their life together as lovers. Actually, her *Book of Jack London* is quite accurate, but she tried so hard to share their great love with the world that she overdid it, and instead of accepting her portrayal the average reader is left skeptical and wondering if she were trying to cover something up. Due to her aversion to drinking, she actually exaggerated his indiscretions in New York on this occasion. She writes:

Almost any passage in our companionship I contemplate with more pleasure than that 1912 Winter in "Gotham." The trip had been one of our happiest; but, once off the train, and his enthusiasm expressed over the new Pennsylvania Station, it was the old story. The City reached into him and plucked to light the least admirable of his qualities. Out of the wholesome blisses of his Western life, he plunged into a condition that negated his accustomed personality. Nine-tenths of the two months that we made our headquarters in Morningside Park East, he was not his usual self. During the other tenth, cropping up in unexpected moments, the manifestation of his dearest self and his love were never warmer nor more illuminating.

Coincident with our arrival, he warned that he was going to invite one last, thorough-going bout with alcohol, and that when he should sail on the Cape Horn voyage, it was to be "Goodbye, forever to John Barleycorn." To me, the promised end was worth the threatened means; and my comprehension and acceptance of his intentions were appreciated. But I could not fail to regret that our new friends should know and base their judgment of Jack London upon this unfortunate phenomenon of him.

In that Jack London, drunken, was not as other drunken men, the majority of those who contacted with him during a period of what he termed his 'white logic' deemed they knew the true, sober Jack London in all his panoply of normal brilliance. Never, in all my years with him, did I see him tipsy.

Except in rare cases when a single drink acutely poisoned his stomach, upon him the effect of alcoholic stimulus was to render preternaturally active an already superactive mind. Keen, hair-splitting in controversy, reckless of mind and body, sweeping all before him, passionately intolerant of man and woman who challenged his way—all this and more was he in his "white logic" extreme. This unnatural state, combined with the depression New York invariably put upon him, was dangerous. And there was wanting—and how were others to know?—the splendid, healthy charm of the big man he was, the fine potency of his moral integrities, the square truth of his fundamental faiths and their observances. But I knew my man, and, content or not, waited, remembering that I had never yet waited in vain to welcome back the sane and lovable boy. More and more deeply am I convinced that it is not the irks of the wayside that should count in one's valuation of events and individuals. I knew my man. I could only wish that some others had had such a vision for crises like these in Jack London's contact with his kind.

Actually, the situation wasn't nearly as bad as Charmian pictured it. Jack spent most of the evenings with Charmian visiting Ella Wheeler Wilcox, Emma Goldman, Commodore Benedict, Arnold Genthe, Anna Strunsky Walling, and many other friends. They also went to the theatre, the grand opera, the Follies, and to several dinners given in nights from January 4 through January 10, but usually arrived home early.

Michael Monohan and Richard Le Gallienne were two New York writers with whom Jack spent much time in the city. Alexander Berkman came by the apartment to talk Jack into writing a preface to his *Prison Memoirs of an Anarchist.* Jack did write the preface, but not being in sympathy with Anarchism, what he wrote was not satisfactory to Berkman and wasn't used.

The business with Century was successful. On February 2 he wrote Eliza to expect one thousand dollars per month from Century for the next six months. On February 8 they signed on the *Dirigo* at the Custom House—Jack as Third Mate, Charmian as Stewardess, and Nakata as Assistant Steward.

The following day Charmian was furious when Jack arrived home with a clipped head, leaving him as bald as a billiard ball. While in Baltimore waiting departure of the *Dirigo,* their picture was taken at a ceremony in front of Edgar Allen Poe's grave. Jack wanted to go to the theatre, but Charmian flatly refused to go anywhere with him that required the removal of his hat and the exposure of his bald dome.

The day they boarded the ship, a pet shop delivered a two-month-old fox terrier, Possum, that they had purchased for ten dollars. Possum turned out to be the best ten-dollar investment they ever made. Both grew to love the dog, and Possum was always their favorite pet at the ranch in Glen Ellen.

The *Dirigo,* a three-thousand ton, four-masted barque, sailed from Baltimore on March 2 bound for Seattle via Cape Horn. Outside of a scary experience in rounding the Horn in a bad storm, the trip was smooth and uneventful. Jack mingled with the crew and drew from them many valuable yarns to enhance his future sea novel. The passage also gave Jack and Charmian a lot of wonderful time together. He loved to read to her as they lay foot to foot in the long bunk in his cabin. Another favorite spot for reading was high up on the mizzen mast.

For nearly three weeks Charmian had a severe case of hives and almost drowned in cream of tartar taken in lemonade as a cure. Nothing helped, and she was almost driven to suicide before it was discovered, to her horror and relief, that her hives were caused by a bunk full of bed bugs. When her cabin was cleared of them, the "hives" went also.

On the voyage Jack made copious notes for *John Barleycorn,* wrote "The Princess," "The Captain of the Susan Drew" ("The Tar Pot") and with Seattle in sight completed his most extensive project of the cruise, *The Valley of the Moon.*

In addition to typing Jack's work, Charmian wrote her one and only short story, "The Wheel," which was later published by a newspaper syndicate in the semimonthly magazine section of several newspapers on December 8, 1912. Charmian received $125 for her story and used the money to pay for Joan's nurse during her bout with typhoid late in October.

Their writing was done separately, but together they put in an order for another baby. Once more they looked for a child to make their Wolf House dream home even more meaningful.

Osa and Martin Johnson greeted the Londons on their arrival in Seattle on July 26. That evening the foursome went to the theatre. On July 30 the Londons boarded the *City of Puebla,* bound for California. Arriving in Oakland on August 2, they dropped their baggage at 490 Twenty-seventh and rushed to the Saddle Rock for dinner followed by a play at the Orpheum.

The ranch looked better than ever to them when they pulled into the little Glen Ellen station on August 5. Jack tackled a mountain of mail in order to get away on the 8th for the Bohemian Club High Jinks. Four days after Jack left, Charmian had a miscarriage and their dream of a son was gone forever.

In November Charmian went to the hospital in Oakland for corrective surgery resulting from the miscarriage. Meanwhile pianist Laurie Godfrey-Smith came for a visit from Australia. While Charmian convalesced, Jack and Laurie went cruising on the *Roamer.* Christmas was observed at the home of Charmian's cousin, Willard Growal, in Menlo Park.

By 1912 Jack was writing fewer short stories and concentrating on longer works. This year was not as productive as the previous one, but even so it was still prodigious. Ten short stories were published, as were *The House of Pride, A Son of the Sun,* and *Smoke Bellew. The Scarlet Plague* was placed on the market in England. "The Captain of the Susan Drew" and "The Princess" were the only short works completed in 1912, but two very sought-after books were finished—his extremely popular *John Barleycorn* and his excellent agrarian novel, *The Valley of the Moon.*

In Baltimore a few days before Jack had his head shaved

UNLUCKY '13

Jack London was never known to be superstitious, but by the end of 1913 he could have easily been convinced. Just about everything that could go wrong went wrong in 1913. Irving Shepard, Eliza's son, was nearly electrocuted while climbing a tree during school recess and was in bed recuperating in the London's cottage for several months. Jack was stricken with appendicitis. One of his most valuable mares was mistakenly killed by a hunter. Captain Shepard went berserk and tried to kill his estranged wife, Eliza, and then had Jack arrested for stopping him too energetically. In addition, a false spring and late frost ruined the fruit

crop, a plague of locusts attacked the young eucalyptus trees, the cornfield was scorched by unusually hot winds, the Balboa Amusement Company brought suit to wrest all of Jack's copyrights away from him for their motion picture company, and the crowning blow came in August when his beautiful Wolf House was destroyed by fire.

Fortunately all was not a total loss. Irving recovered and regained his strength. With the backing of the Author's League of America, Jack won the suit brought against him by the Balboa Amusement Company and retained his copyrights.

In April Jack signed an agreement with H. M.

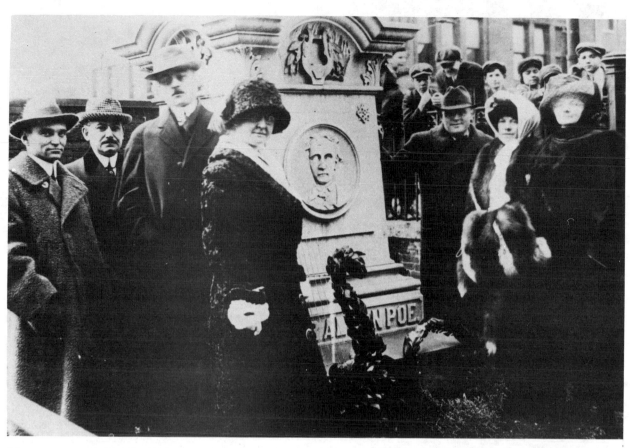

The ceremony at Edgar Allan Poe's monument in Baltimore

The Dirigo

Joan (left) and Becky around 1912

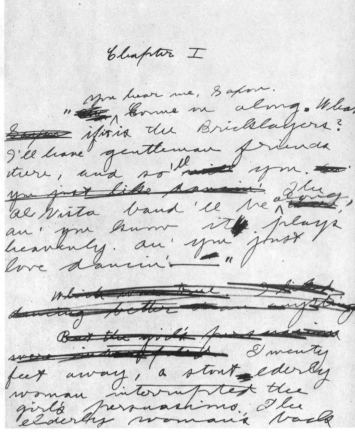

The first page of The Valley of the Moon *manuscript*

Horkheimer and Daniel Sydney Ayres of the Balboa Amusement Company to produce films from his works. A garbled report was published: "I have just completed a deal by which I shall appear as the leading actor in all my own short stories and novels characterized into motion pictures. I am going into the pictures to give them the punch that is almost impossible to communicate to another." It may have been one of Horkheimer's publicity releases.

The following day Jack set the record straight, "I am not an actor and I never plan to be. My connection with the motion pictures will be solely as author and advisor for their production, although I may pose at my desk."

Jack did appear riding across the ranch on his horse in one scene of *The Valley of the Moon*. He also appears in several takes in the documentary *A House Is Burning*. He also appeared in the French film taken when they were at Guadacanal. On August 13, 1915, motion pictures were taken for the *Santa Rosa Press Democrat*. Some of the scenes were taken on the Jack London Ranch, and Jack appeared in several of them.

Twenty books by Jack London have been made into motion pictures, some of them several times. Twenty-eight other movies have been based on his short stories, articles, or plays, and three films have been made of his life—*Prince of the Oyster Pirates*, *The Story of Jack London*, and *A House is Burning*.

Finding it impossible to deal with the Balboa Amusement Company, Jack decided that Hobart Bosworth should do his films. Bosworth had a small motion picture company and played the lead in his own films. Bosworth was an excellent choice. When *The Sea Wolf* was filmed, Jack eagerly told everyone that Hobart Bosworth was the perfect Wolf Larsen.

Though the Balboa Amusement Company had lost its suit against Jack, the court guaranteed it the

240

a long tender silence.

...Billy's finger laid warningly on her lips. Guided by this board, she turned her head back, and together they gazed far up the side of the knoll where a doe and a spotted fawn looked down upon them from a tiny open space between the trees.

END

Jack London

On Board Sailing Ship Dirigo,
48 N. Lat.
144 W. Long.
July 17, 1912.

The last page of The Valley of the Moon *manuscript. It was written on the* Dirigo *just off Seattle.*

Jack, Charmian, and Laurie Smith. This picture was taken a few days after Charmian left the hospital.

A British advertisement for The Valley of the Moon

right to produce *The Sea Wolf,* but only if it used a different name. As a result, Balboa's *Hellship* ran on one side of Hollywood Boulevard at the same time that Bosworth's *Sea Wolf* ran on the other.

When *John Barleycorn* was serialized in the *Saturday Evening Post* in March, it was a sensation. The Women's Christian Temperance Union of California immediately used excerpts from it for their campaign for statewide prohibition in California, and Alcoholics Anonymous groups have been recommending it to their membership ever since. Thomas T. Horton of the U.S.S. *Wyoming* wrote Jack on April 5, "We are all reading your *John Barleycorn* on board this battle-wagon and I guess all the other crews of the fleet are doing the same."

The book was written as an appeal for prohibition. Jack wanted to stop the sale of alcoholic beverages of every kind so youth, being deprived, might never acquire a taste for it. Jack said, "*John Barleycorn* is frankly and truthfully autobiographical. There is no poetic license in it. It is a straight, true narrative of my personal experiences, and is toned *down,* not up." However, when the public began to classify him as drunkard and alcoholic, he clarified his position: "I shall not go so far as to say that *John Barleycorn* is the story of my life, but I will go so far as to say that *John Barleycorn* is the story of part of my life and that it is a true story of that part of my life."

In later years, Jack London was a staunch prohibitionist. In fact, the Prohibition Party wanted Jack to run for President of the United States on their ticket.

The movie *John Barleycorn* was also a huge success and played to packed audiences in nearly every theatre in the United States. A headline in the *Rochester Union* said, JOHN BARLEYCORN DECLARED TO BE THE MOST POWERFUL TEMPERANCE ARGUMENT EVER BROUGHT FORTH.

By March 14 Jack had completed sixty-five thousand words of *The Mutiny of the Elsinore* and was anxiously waiting publication of *The Valley of the Moon* in *Cosmopolitan* magazine. His relationship with Century had been thoroughly unsatisfactory, causing him to return to Macmillan. Century agreed to release him from his contract after publication of *John Barleycorn,* and Macmillan published every book he wrote from that date to his death. Brett wired him twenty-five hundred dollars to give to Century in return for the rights to publish *The Mutiny of the Elsinore.* Century had given Jack this amount in advances.

Being the most popular author of his day was very satisfying and flattering, but it also brought with it an almost unbearable responsibility. The fame meant nothing to Jack and changed his life style very little. He was still the same gentle, unaffected person he always had been. Bombastic, energetic, dominant, the central figure in any gathering, but never a trace of conceit. Fame meant a better market for his prodigious output, and that was all it amounted to. A letter to Fred Barry gives us a glimpse into the cost of fame:

Glen Ellen, Calif.
June 26, 1913

My Dear Friend—
Please remember:
I average a receipt of 100 gold mine propositions a year.
I average a receipt of at least 100 perpetual motion and other inventors devices per year, including all sorts of disease cures.

I average, per year, at least 300 manuscripts, novels, short stories, and plays, which I am supposed to correct, and most of the writers of which desire me to rewrite said manuscript and to sell and publish over my name, and divide up with the writers thereof.

I average at least 300 propositions a year to take care of people, furnish college educations to orphan boys, endow old ladies' homes with libraries, muck-rake the powers that be from one end of the world to the other, and contribute to every bazaar that ever was got up by a ladies' aid society.

I have endless applications to assist struggling geniuses such as painters, sculptors, writers, musicians, composers, and singers; such as men who want to leave on my land their mothers, wives, children, grandparents, etc., while they pursue their own favorite phantoms.

I have had men by the score who wanted to die on my ranch from tuberculosis of the lungs, of leprosy, and of cancer. I have had on my hands men by the score who wanted to send their wives here on my ranch to be confined while they should muzzle into their own favorite lard-pail.

Oh hell! I have no time to enumerate further the flotsam and the jetsam that swamp this ranch ten-deep year in and year out and all the time.

I am sending you a Le Gallienne letter. He, too, has had some sort of experience in the game. Let it burn its way into your appreciation; and try for a moment to appreciate my situation and the penalty I pay for being decent to the tens of thousands of persons who write to me all the time. Each one pursuing his favorite phantoms. Each one with his muzzle in his particular lard-pail.

All sorts of love to you and Ray,
Jack London

None of the above letter is exaggeration. His daily output of mail was staggering. No letter went unanswered. Few worthy requests for money or literary help were refused. He usually scaled the requests for money down to half. There were many occasions when he borrowed money to loan to friends or even perfect strangers when their need was desperate.

His generosity was almost beyond belief. During the Londons' last visit to the Islands, Jack and

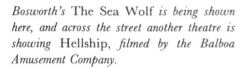

Bosworth's The Sea Wolf *is being shown here, and across the street another theatre is showing* Hellship, *filmed by the Balboa Amusement Company.*

Harry Strange had become close friends. Harry, a brilliant young Englishman, gave up his job to go back to England for service with his country in World War I. To some harsh criticism in Honolulu that Harry had no right to leave his dependents, Jack responded with fervor: "You do not seem to understand. He *had* to go. He walked the floor night after night trying to see the way out—the right way. There was no other way out, for him, than the one he took; he could not have done other than he did. . . . As well criticize the flame that burns, as criticize this royal thing of the spirit within him that drew him from success, and love for children, and fat security, half across the world to fling himself into the maelstrom of battle—all for an Idea."

After returning to Glen Ellen, Jack read a newspaper article telling about the desperate circumstances Strange's mother and children were facing. He turned to his secretary, Jack Byrne, and told him to send a fifty-dollar check every month to Mrs. Emma Strange in care of the Pacific Sanitarium, 1451 Kewalo St., Honolulu. After his death Charmian kept on with the payments until Harry returned home.

July of 1913 was a turning point in Jack's health. He was at the very height of his physical stamina and recuperative powers when he suffered an attack of appendicitis. Today fast recoveries from this operation are common, but in 1913 a minimum of two weeks in bed was considered a necessity. Here is a report by a local newspaper at the time of Jack's operation:

London's recovery is one of the most remarkable in the history of appendicitis operations in this city. On Monday, July 7, he was operated on by Dr. W. S. Porter at the Merritt Hospital, and last Thursday, nine days later, he was able to be dressed and to go to the home of his mother, Mrs. Flora London, on Twenty-seventh Street, where he has been since that time. He was prevented from going to a prize fight Thursday evening only by the fact that the house was sold out, and since leaving the hospital has been to the theater every evening with Mrs. London, who is his constant companion.

On his arrival in Los Angeles shortly after the operation, the papers were full of his remarkable recovery and excellent physical condition. What nobody knew, because Jack didn't tell them, was that his doctor had informed him after the operation that his kidneys were in terrible condition. He informed Jack further that he must go on a bland diet with no alcohol or expect an early death. Since kidney transplants and dialysis machines were unknown, he and his doctor knew he had only a few years to live. But nobody else knew! From this time until his death three years later, uremia gradually took its toll.

The newspapers, naturally, had a bit of fun with Jack's operation. The *Boston Transcript* said, "Jack London is such an egoist that no doubt his next novel will be a romance with an appendix for a hero." The *Jackson Ledger* said, "There's no extent that man won't go to get local color." The *New York Herald* reported, "The doctors may take Jack London's appendix but it won't affect his overwhelming impudence a bit."

Though *The Abysmal Brute* had been published in 1911 in *Popular Magazine,* it was an immediate hit in 1913 when published in book form by Macmillan. The book was written to expose the evils of the fight game with a strong emphasis on the exploitation of boxers by their promoters. The *Boston Post* in October of 1913 said, "Few authors living today have the force and directness, the rugged strength and vitality of style of Jack London. This novel shows Sunday *Post* readers London at his best. It is

a story of the prize ring, big and vigorous and thrilling. Behind the tense life, the excitement of the fight itself, one can see in reading it the crookedness, the devious ways of the keen-witted men who stage the big fight and reap the profits. More than this, one can see the soul of the Abysmal Brute himself, one of the strangest, most human and fascinating characters London had ever drawn, a bruiser who is a scholar as well, who is honest and clean—and innocent up to the point of his disillusionment. A veritable cross-section of a strange phase of American life."

At different times Jack was asked which of his books was his favorite. Early in his career it was *The People of the Abyss,* later it was *Martin Eden,* and at the State Fair in Sacramento in 1914 he told a reporter that *The Abysmal Brute* was the one he liked best, though he thought *Martin Eden* was his best work.

The other two books published in 1913 were also very well received by the reading public around the world. *The Night Born* is a collection of stories and contains two of his finest, "War" and "The Mexican." Due to the popularity of *John Barleycorn* and *The Valley of the Moon, The Night Born,* though an excellent collection, was to a large extent ignored.

The Valley of the Moon caught the public's imagination and received rave critical comments throughout this country and abroad. The book is about the heroic odyssey of Billy and Saxon Roberts from their working-class ghetto life in Oakland through the devastating teamster strike to the discovery of their idyllic Glen Ellen ranch in the "Valley of the Moon." The book is an excellent source of information regarding the early years of labor strife in the San Francisco Bay Area. With his masterful descriptive touch, Jack deals with the displacement of the old Anglo-Saxon pioneers by the new immigrants of various nationalities, and the beastlike existence of the exploited workers in Oakland's emerging industrial complex. It also gives us an intimate glimpse into the carefree escapades of the artist colony at Carmel-by-the-Sea, where George Sterling, Mary Austin, Harry Leon Wilson, Jack London, Jimmy Hopper, Sinclair Lewis, Grace MacGowan Cooke, Nora May French, and others of their "crowd" cavorted to the tune of their famous "Abalone Song" and spent their leisure hours in clean, generally wholesome, and thoroughly enjoyable ways, with here and there a bit of sexual intrigue and booze for spice.

The *Rochester Chronicle*'s review of *The Valley of the Moon* is typical of most:

Jack London has written another novel that bears all of the marks of his best work in fiction. It is entitled *The Valley of the Moon* and it is one of the best illustrations of his admirable blending of realism and romance. From the first page to the last, it pulses strongly with almost desperate human life in many phases, and it is crowded with characters that stand out so distinctly that the reader can see them in all dimensions and act so naturally that he can feel their emotions. Around all is a sensible atmosphere of actualities. Yet, no matter how grimly he pictures hard or sordid life conditions, no matter how relentlessly he portrays human character with all its flaws as well as its virtues, he softens all with the light of his broad sympathies and conveys to those who view his vigorous, vivid canvasses a sense of mystery, of the spiritual, behind all. This is a compelling tale of the various stirrings and sordid life and love experiences of a girl with imagination who is first seen in the drudgery of a laundry, and of a determined, composed young prize-fighter and wagon-driver. They marry and leave the big city for the country. On their odyssey they meet many hardships and then they go into the mountains, to the Valley of the Moon, where they find peace and contentment.

The first cabin boy of the Snark—*Paul H. Murakami*

A trusted friend left the ranch with a dozen pair of Jack's pajamas. This is the way a newspaper reported it.

Part of "the crowd" at Carmel. From left to right: George Sterling, Jimmy Hopper, Charmian, Jack, Alice Mac-Gowan, Grace MacGowan Cooke, and Carrie Sterling.

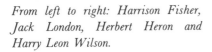

From left to right: Harrison Fisher, Jack London, Herbert Heron and Harry Leon Wilson.

THE WOLF HOUSE

Jack and Charmian's dream home was planned before their marriage and landscaped prior to their *Snark* voyage. Actual work on it, however, didn't begin until April of 1911. The first indication of actual construction on the house is found in a letter to Herbert Forder on February 3, 1911, in which Jack states that he was beginning his feeble at-

tempt to build a house for himself and was chopping some redwood trees and leaving them in the woods to season so that two or three years hence they could be used in building the house. On March 2 Jack and Charmian rode to Bocca's quarry across the valley to arrange for the rock.

Albert Farr of San Francisco was the architect

who transferred Jack's ideas into blueprints. For earthquake protection, the building was put on a huge floating slab large enough to support a forty-story building. Redwood trees, fully clothed in their own bark, deep chocolate-maroon volcanic rocks, blue slate, boulders and cement were chosen for prime building materials. The roof was of Spanish tile and came from the N. Clark and Sons Pottery, built on the old Davenport place in Alameda. Large redwood trees, with bark still intact, formed the carriage entrance, the pergolas, and porches. The rafters were of rough-hewn, natural logs. Tree trunks in the gables and balconies were interlaced with fruit twigs for a beautiful effect.

Wolf House was not a castle in any sense of the term, though Jack and others referred to it as that. It was big, unpretentious, open, natural, and inviting, just like its builder. It was designed as a busy author's workshop, and as a home big enough for the many needs of the Londons, and for the entertainment of their friends. Everyone was welcome to put his legs under Jack's dining table, which was often full. While in Hawaii a friend asked him why he always had exactly twelve guests to dinner every night. If he was expecting some exotic explanation, he was disappointed; for the answer was a simple, "Because that is all the table will seat." Jack's small wooden cottage on the ranch couldn't accommodate many guests, thus the pressing need for Wolf House.

Jack's workshop was to be 19 by 40 feet with a library of the same size directly under it on the second floor, connected by a spiral staircase. Here he would have room to work and house his huge library. At the time his books were stored inaccessibly in every building on the ranch. The work area was completely secluded from the rest of the house. High on the fourth floor and directly above Charmian's apartment Jack's sleeping quarters perched like an eagle's nest.

The 18 by 58 foot living room was two stories high with rough redwood balconies extending three-fourths of the way around. A huge stone fireplace and open ceiling rafters made a cozy nook of the huge room. One large alcove in the room was designed for Charmian's beautiful Steinway grand.

A large breezeway and courtyard, entered between two gigantic redwoods, extended all the way through the house. Three large guest rooms, the patio, a huge reflection pool, and the library

Wolf House under construction. Jack's sleeping quarters were on the fourth floor.

opened off to the left. On the right was the living room, a gun room, and stairs. Excellent servants' quarters, a magnificent 18-by-58-foot stag party room, kitchen, a dining room capable of seating fifty, and the utility room were on the first floor.

Wolf House had its own hot water, laundry, heating, electric lighting, vacuum and refrigerating plants, a milk room, storeroom, root cellar, and wine cellar.

The house, built of stone, bark-encased redwood logs, and concrete and heavy timbers, was thought to be fireproof. But around midnight on August 22, 1913, a few weeks before occupation, the house was a blazing inferno. The next day Jack said, "It was a very quick fire. We can't tell whether it was incendiary or not. The walls are standing, and I shall rebuild."

Later he believed the fire was the result of arson, because the building was so far gone when the fire was discovered. He felt that some disgruntled socialist, upset over his building a castle, set the fire. The building superintendent, Mr. Forni, believed it was a simple case of spontaneous combustion started by oily rags carelessly thrown in a corner by one of the workmen.

Through the years many stories have grown up about the fire. Somebody even added the story that a wood pile near the house had also been set afire—the incongruity of somebody's setting the big house on fire and then taking time to run over to set a pile of lumber afire never occurred to him. Actually, Mr. Forni was probably correct. Naturally the house was an inferno when discovered; it was in a hollow where nobody could see it until the roof fell in and let the fire blaze into the sky. Smoke would

247

Jack checks plans during construction of Wolf House.

The ruins of Wolf House have become a unique memorial to Jack, a symbol of all his unrealized dreams.

Jack and Charmian on the porch of the cottage at Christmas time in 1913

An architect's rendering of Wolf House

have been unobserved since the house burned around midnight. The tile roof was supported by massive, roughly hewn redwoods, so the building would have been an inferno before the roof could fall in.

Spontaneous combustion is the most logical explanation. The floors were being laid and panelling installed. That day, according to Forni, the men were wiping everything down with turpentine. It is also logical to assume that they were using linseed oil. The workmen were careless, for they too believed the building to be fireproof. Despite Forni's pleading, they were throwing their oily rags on the floor to be used again the next day. Only there was no next day this time. From close of work to midnight was enough time for an oily rag to develop enough internal heat to burst into flame. Conditions were ideal for this to happen, since the fire was during the excessively dry California August.

Exactly one month after his own home burned Jack was instrumental in saving those of his neighbors. On September 23, 1913, the *San Francisco Examiner* reported: "JACK LONDON IS HERO OF FIRE—SAVES GLEN ELLEN WHEN TOWN IS MENACED BY FLAMES SWEEPING DOWN SONOMA CREEK. Jack London was the hero of the day at Glen Ellen. His presence of mind, his direction of an army of firefighters whom he rushed from his ranch in the hills overlooking the Sonoma Valley, and his own hard work as a fireman, saved the town from destruction."

Though the burning of Wolf House was undoubtedly not arson, those who thought it was made a pastime of accusing their favorite suspects. Finn Frolich thought Eliza's estranged husband was the culprit. A workman discharged that day was under suspicion. The I.W.W. was considered a prime target, and even Charmian has been accused. In fact, one authority is convinced that she did set the fire. His reason was that Jack wouldn't talk to Charmian after the fire. This authority evidently failed to see the entry in Charmian's diary on August 27, four days after the fire: "Love is the order of the day, and in some ways we never were happier." Nor did he know that from September 11 through 21 they had a virtual honeymoon at the Hotel Sacramento during the State Fair. He also failed to read Jack's statement on October 2, "Mrs. London and I are running away just now for Los Angeles, and after that we are going out for a two months cruise on the Bay, along with our work."

New Year's Eve, 1913, was another of Charmian's "fantastic" evenings with "the crowd," first at the Saddle Rock Restaurant, the Pantages Theatre, then back to the Saddle Rock. From there they went to a party at the Hotel Oakland and then back to the Saddle Rock again. Finally, tired but happy, Jack and Charmian returned to their Oakland "townhouse" at 490 Twenty-seventh Street and tumbled into bed at 4 A.M.

JACK
LONDON
*Royal
Tailored
Man*

JACK LONDON—
Able Seaman

COPYRIGHT 1913. THE ROYAL TAILORS

"It's funny what a difference a few Clothes make!"

When Jack London picked out a Royal Fabric for a 2 piece Fall suit a few weeks ago, the fancy took him that he wanted a hat made of the same material. "Nothing easier!" said the local Royal dealer. And straightway he measured the London head and the London crown—sending those measurements to us along with the London body dimensions.

We cut and tailored the hat just as we did the suit, to exactly dovetail the specifications given us. Perhaps it may, or it may not be to your taste to wear a hat that matches your suit. But the point is:

Royal Service gives you exactly what you want—exactly as you order it. There is no such thing as "partial satisfaction" in a Royal Tailor transaction. A Royal deal means *complete* satisfaction or no sale.

You select the fabric you want. You pick out the style and cut you want—and if any little individualities are wanted, not shown in the fashion plate you select, you dictate the desired changes to your local dealer—and we edit them into your suit! The Royal Tailored Man is the type of man who appreciates exact perfection—and gets it in his clothes.

SIX BIG FEATURES of ROYAL TAILOR CLOTHES
- Made to Your Measure
- All Pure Wool
- A Legal Guarantee With Each Garment
- 100% Process Shrunk
- Cost No More Than Ready Mades
- Six Day Schedule Deliveries

We pay $1 A Day For every Day of Delay When A Royal Garment isn't Finished on time

This Guarantee comes buttoned onto the Garment.

"Get that Royal Tailored Look"
The Royal Tailors

Royal Tailored-To-Your-Order Clothes

Chicago   *Joseph Nelson* President   New York

The Clothes That Real Men Wear

Contrary to many reports, Jack London was usually very well dressed.

The new year started beautifully and serenely as Jack and Charmian went back aboard the *Roamer* to continue their cruise. Less than a week later, on January 6, Jack received news that Joseph Noel, a friend to whom he had assigned the dramatization rights of *The Sea Wolf,* had bungled his job so badly that the motion picture rights were in jeopardy. Jack grabbed the first train for New York. It was a hard decision to make. It was vital that Jack go, but he couldn't afford to take Charmian along.

The agent involved in the deal with Noel had bought the rights for dramatization. Claiming that he also held the motion picture rights, he did everything in his power to prove it in court. He finally offered to release these rights for forty thousand dollars. This was ridiculous to Jack, and the talks went on. Days turned into weeks and finally the deal was closed, with Jack paying $3,835 for the release. He left for Glen Ellen on February 16.

While Jack was in New York, the newspapers missed the headline of the year. The manager of a burlesque show invited Jack to see a performance. As the show unfolded Jack was amazed. This wasn't the kind of burlesque he had known. From first to last there wasn't an objectionable word uttered nor the slightest approach to vulgarity. It rated with the best of Broadway shows. After the performance the manager escorted three of the actresses to their hotel and invited Jack to go, promising to drop him off at his hotel on the way. The following day the *New York Journal* ran this story: "3 WOMEN HURT IN AUTO WRECK REFUSE SURGICAL ATTENTION—Fearful that they would have to tell their names to police three stylishly gowned young women, all painfully cut and bruised about the face and hands in a three cornered automobile crash on upper Broadway today, refused medical attention from Dr. Labaree of Polyclinic Hospital. With two men who were with them, the women, bleeding from lacerations and contusions, entered a taxicab and sped away."

If the press had only known that the man in the wrecked cab, his mouth full of glass splinters, was the famous Jack London, headlines across the country would have been interesting and varied.

Jack wrote Charmian about the incident: "I'd have looked well with the report flashing all over the country that I'd been 'joy-riding' with a bunch of actresses!—I've never been joy-riding in my life," he teased her, "but I'm going to sometime, for I'll never be satisfied until I come home to you with a pink-satin slipper in my pocket."

It is difficult for most people to realize that, as little as Jack was on the ranch, he was still responsible for all that was done. Jack and Eliza were an unbeatable combination. Loyal to the very heart of her being, Eliza faithfully carried out everything that Jack planned with amazing ability. Letters and coded telegrams told her exactly what he wanted done. Whenever he returned to the ranch, he found things exactly as he had instructed. She never failed in even the smallest details. For instance, during the 1911 four-horse trip he had told her by letter to put up their own poles and have the telephone company use them in installing a five-party line to the ranch. On his return he found his cottage ready to move into with the phone where he wanted it.

He decided to make a carriage house out of the old Kohler-Frohling building behind the cottage. He showed Eliza a rough sketch. When he returned from his next trip, there it rested, exactly as he had visualized it. They worked in perfect harmony, with the exception of one slight source of irritation. Eliza told Jack he would have to let her do all the hiring and firing, since he never turned down anybody who asked for a job, and she had to fire all the incompetents he had hired. Jack agreed to leave all personnel matters in her hands and full harmony was restored.

While in New York, Jack made tentative arrangements with a weekly publication to write a series of articles from interesting tourist spots around the world. The first of the series was planned for Japan. Late in March Jack and Charmian were getting ready to leave. Work on the ranch was going on schedule. Needing water for irrigation, Jack and Eliza decided to build a dam on the side of the mountain and create a lake large enough for water storage and recreation. In March the dam was nearly finished and Jack ordered fifteen hundred live catfish for the lake. He mentioned to Eliza that he would like to have a bathhouse at the lake. The next day she had workmen on the site and a few days later a rustic boathouse with six dressing rooms and space at each end to store a boat was ready for use.

The most popular picture of Jack. It was taken on the Roamer *in 1914 by Charmian.*

The "carriage house" nestles on the ruins of the old Kohler-Frohling Winery. Jack and Charmian's cottage is on the right.

On April 16, 1914 Jack and Charmian's plans to go to Japan were abruptly changed when *Collier's* offered him eleven hundred dollars a week plus expenses for himself and Nakata to go to Mexico to cover the Mexican Revolution. When the magazine agreed to pay Charmian's expenses as well, Jack accepted. They left on the 17th of April for Los Angeles. From there they rode the *Sunset Limited* to El Paso and Galveston.

In Galveston Jack was refused transportation by General Funston because of a canard he thought London had written degrading the life of a soldier. After Jack convinced the General's aide that he had not written "The Good Soldier," Funston approved his credentials. Meanwhile, Secretary of the Navy Josephus Daniels had wired Jack permission to go on a destroyer, if Funston didn't relent. On April 24 Jack left for Vera Cruz on the transport *Kilpatrick,* while Charmian followed on the *Atlantis.* Since there was no war, he was once more deprived of the opportunity to show his ability as a war correspondent, but he did write seven excellent articles.

Jack's major accomplishment in Mexico was to alienate himself from the Socialist Party. In 1911 he had written glowing tributes to the Mexican revolutionaries, but now that he was seeing the problem in person, he reversed his opinions.

At first Jack thought that the United States was spending millions of dollars and many lives to save the life of the dictator Huerta. But American residents in Mexico convinced Jack that 80 percent of educated middle-class Mexicans welcomed intervention. They were tired of revolution. He also came to believe that it was American ingenuity that had developed Mexico industrially. About the revolutionaries, Jack said, "These 'breeds' do politics, issue pronunciamentos, raise revolutions or are revolutionized against by others of them, write bombastic unveracity that is accepted as journalism in this sad, rich land, steal payrolls of companies and eat out hacienda after hacienda as they picnic along on what they are pleased to call wars for liberty, justice and the square deal."

The socialists at home thought the Mexican Revolution was a genuine revolution of the working class. According to Jack, they simply didn't realize the truth. He tried to explain it to them when he said, "The stay-at-home American listens to the slogans uttered by the various leaders of this anarchy and makes the mistake of conceiving the leaders in his own image and of thinking that 'Liberty,' 'Justice,' and a 'Square Deal' means the same to them that they mean to him.

"Nothing of the sort. In the four centuries of Spanish and Mexican rule, liberty, justice and the square deal have never existed. Mexico is a republic in which nobody votes. Its liberty has ever been construed as license. Its justice had consisted in an effort at equitable division of the spoils of an exploited people. That even thieves' honor did not obtain among these thieves is shown by the numerous revolutions and dictatorships. In a country where a man is legally considered guilty of a crime until he proves himself innocent, justice must mean an entirely different thing from what it means to an American. And so it is with all the rest of the bombastic and valorous phrases in the vocabulary of the Mexican."

Back home the socialists were of a different mind and felt that Jack London had betrayed their cause in Mexico. A fellow journalist, John Kenneth Turner, even accused him of having been won over to the capitalists by the flattering good fellowship of the oilmen of Mexico. This misunderstanding between London and the socialist movement, and an even bigger rift caused by divergence of opin-

Jack is on his way to the Mexican Revolution on the U.S. Army Transport Kilpatrick.

Old war correspondent friends in the Russo-Japanese War meet again in Mexico. From left to right: Jimmy Hare, Jack London, Frederick Palmer, and Richard Harding Davis.

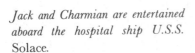

Jack and Charmian are entertained aboard the hospital ship U.S.S. Solace.

ions over the role of socialism in World War I, led to his later decision to resign from the Socialist Party.

While in Mexico, Jack was able to introduce Charmian to Jimmy Hare, Robert Dunn, Richard Harding Davis, and Frederick Palmer—old war correspondent friends from the Russo-Japanese War. The Londons also made a host of new friends. They completely captivated the U.S. Navy and were lavishly entertained on the hospital ship

U.S.S. *Solace*, the repair ship U.S.S. *Vestal*, and the battleships *New York, Arkansas,* and *Mississippi*.

In Mexico Jack suffered severely because of a case of acute dysentery. At one point Dr. Goodman reported him to be in an extremely serious condition. After several days of a rice, cocoa, and malted milk diet, plus medication, Jack was able to leave on the transport *Ossabow* for Galveston, where he left for Oakland. Jack's personal physician, Dr. William S. Porter, met the couple at the depot, and

Jack London in 1914

Charmian and Jack have a good laugh on board the battleship U.S.S. Arkansas *with Captain Gulick and two of his officers.*

the three went to the Saddle Rock for lunch.

An excellent example of Jack's careful approach to business ventures is seen in a letter to Eliza from Galveston. Two of his good friends had proposed to set up a grape juice company and offered him 26 percent of the stock for the use of his name. Here is the letter:

April 21, 1914

Dearest Eliza:

Inclosed telegram and telegraph advice speak for themselves.

When these papers are sent to you to sign, please be sure, even though you have to consult a lawyer, that in no way am I to be financially responsible for any losses, damages or bills the Grape Juice Company may incur. If the papers do not make me clear in every way of such financial responsibility, have them make out new papers that will make me clear.

Also pledge no grapes from our ranch to the Company, unless said grapes are paid for in cash in just the same way that you sell grapes to a winery.

Also, note that in my conversation with Beatley and Wilkinson, it was understood that we three reserved fifty-one (51%) percent of the stock for ourselves; that this stock was to be put in escrow, or in some similar fashion, so that no one of us could sell without the consent of the

other two; that I was to receive, for my share, twenty-six (26%) percent of the capital stock, and that Beatley and Wilkinson were to receive twenty-five (25%) of the capital stock for their share, thus totaling for the three of us the fifty-one (51%) percent.

It looks as if I shall be sailing tomorrow for Vera Cruz.

In a rush,
Lots of love,

Jack London

Eliza did her consistently thorough job, for when the company went bankrupt and Jack was sued for a large amount of money, the case was thrown out of court.

In September Jack and Charmian rejoined the *Roamer* in San Rafael and spent the rest of the year on board resting, working, and sailing.

The year 1914 had been good financially, with *The Saturday Evening Post* offering seven hundred fifty dollars for all the stories he could supply. He signed a contract with *Cosmopolitan* that brought in two thousand dollars a month in advances. *Collier's* had paid eleven hundred dollars per week for his time in Mexico, and royalties for books and motion pictures were coming in steadily.

Jack's fame was at its peak. Motion pictures of his books and stories were showing all over the

The letterhead of the Jack London Grape Juice Co.

country, and his name was probably in more newspapers in 1914 than any other author's had been before or since. *The Strength of the Strong* and his Cape Horn novel, *The Mutiny of the Elsinore,* had been extremely well received. *The Star Rover,* considered by many to be his finest book, was serialized in *The American Sunday Monthly Magazine* in many newspapers throughout the country, and *The Little Lady of the Big House* was off to the publishers. This was the first year in his writing career in which he had not written a single short story.

The steady progress on the ranch gave Jack the most pleasure that year. Now complete, the ranch had a total of 1,439 acres and was a full working ranch—no rich man's toy. Terraces were in, eucalyptus trees were growing taller, a fine herd of Angora goats was roaming the brush, the herd of purebred Jersey cattle was healthy, the lake was stocked full with fish, Forni was building a beauti-

ful, fully modern stone piggery capable of housing three hundred Duroc hogs, orchards and grapes were thriving, and concrete blocks were being made on the ranch with which two silos would be built. The horses were sleek and healthy; crops were good. All the buildings were complete except for the silos and the rebuilding of Wolf House. Now all he had to do was keep writing to pay the bills until in a few years the place would begin to pay its own way. But he knew he wouldn't live to see it.

The last years were productive and happy ones, even though the "noseless one," Jack's euphemism for death, was always close by. The year 1915 began as it should—sailing on the *Roamer.* Jack finished *The Acorn Planter* for the Bohemian Club High Jinks. It was never performed because of difficulties in staging and musical arranging. However, Macmillan published it in 1916. It is a play using Indian myths and legends to show the effects of war

The lake on the Jack London Ranch was used for irrigation and recreation.

Blacksmith shop on the ranch

Jack's friend Finn Haakan Frolich examines the bust he did of Jack.

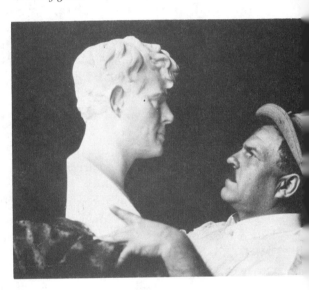

One of the two silos. This was the first concrete block silo in California.

Jack, Charmian, and Miss Young cavort in the snow at Truckee.

Jack loved to ride over his ranch.

on the human race. *The Acorn Planter* is just beginning to receive its long awaited recognition.

To a casual observer, Jack's charisma and brilliance were undiminished. He was the highest-paid author in America, and his fame was unequalled by any other in history. However, he knew the vagaries of fame—overnight it and his income could fall unless he kept up the pace. He was tired of hack work and longed for the time when he could write what he chose. Still needing money, he decided that since *The Call of the Wild* and *White Fang* were still popular, he would write two more dog

stories when he got to Hawaii on their upcoming visit there.

The *Roamer* sailed into Stockton, where Jack and Charmian joined an excursion group for a trip to Truckee on January 15. Then they returned to the *Roamer* and completed the cruise. Then followed the usual rush to get everything in shape for an extended trip. With their affairs in order, they attended the Panama-Pacific Exposition in San Francisco on opening day. On the following day they sailed for Hawaii on the *Matsonia*.

He spent three-fourths of the remainder of his

life in the Islands, hoping that the climate and the easygoing life would help him to regain his health. Here he found a near paradise. Life was quiet, and serene, but full of friendliness and enjoyment.

Jack was now free of socialist bickering, intrigue, and harassment. The patriarchal system of the Islands seemed to be satisfactory to worker and employer. Labor problems were few; everybody appeared to be happy and contented. The owners of the huge sugar and pineapple plantations were charitable and generous with their workers, and there was little poverty.

Surfboarding, thanks to Jack London and Alexander Hume Ford, had been revived. The Outrigger Club, now standing on the site of Jack's tenthouse of his 1907 visit, was full of vigorous, happy surfers. Hospitality was so genuine and warm that Jack's depression over how little people were concerned with others was somewhat alleviated. Racial relationships were beautiful and convivial; he began to believe that a utopian society might come to pass without socialism. The lack of racial friction was a wonder to him.

Jack and Charmian cavorting in Hawaii—1915

Jack and Charmian in Honolulu—1915

Honolulu—1915

Jack and Charmian in Honolulu—1915

Waikiki Beach in 1915

The two dog books *Jerry of the Islands* and *Michael, Brother of Jerry* kept Jack on his thousand-word-a-day schedule. Though the entertainment he had enjoyed so much in the past was still available, he was no longer interested in surfing or doing anything that required much energy. Daily life in the pretty cottage on Beach Walk was spent much like the days on the ranch. After his writing stint Jack usually put on his favorite blue kimono, carried a long box full of reading material and cigarettes, and set out for the Outrigger Club. Charmian and Jack spent most of their afternoons there, lying on the shady sand, reading aloud, napping, and talking with friends and passersby. Later in the day they would swim leisurely out beyond the breakers

Jack models his favorite Hawaiian writing attire.

and back. These were happy hours of closeness. Those who question their love relationship through the years should read the inscriptions in the books Jack gave Charmian. On July 16, 1915, he received his copies of *The Scarlet Plague* and wrote this inscription in the copy he handed Charmian:

My Mate-Woman:

And here, in blessed Hawaii eight years after our voyage here in our own speck boat, we find ourselves, not merely again, but more bound to each other than then or than ever.

Mate Man

Jack's health was fairly good that summer, though Charmian noted he was more tense than normal and was prone to argue too long and too intensely. In April he had a bad bout with uremia. He was sick all night with vomiting, gripes, and diarrhea, spending the next day in bed from weakness.

The war in Europe depressed and worried him. He was thoroughly disgusted that the heads of states were so inept that war could occur, and he was worried about what it would do to his book sales. His expenses would continue and, if his sales were off badly, he could be in deep financial trouble. Up to this point his deficit spending was safe because he knew his market, but now there might be no market.

On July 16 the Londons said Aloha to Hawaii and sailed for home on the S.S. *Sonoma*.

The popularity Jack and Charmian enjoyed in Hawaii continued at home. Summer and fall at Glen Ellen saw a constant flow of guests. Charmian made this note in her diary on October 11: "First time alone in three months since our return from Honolulu."

Jack was enjoying the ranch more than ever. The new lake was an excellent place to take his guests, and the new buildings he had added made it possible to expand his scientific agricultural experiments. He was still trying to find the ideal crops and livestock for his particular needs. It was still a working ranch, but it was also one of the best experiments in modern, scientific ranching in the state. He enjoyed every minute of it.

JACK LONDON

As a cartoonist saw Jack's two novels Jerry of the Islands *and* Michael, Brother of Jerry

Hawaiian Bred

Jack always had an enjoyable experience at the annual Bohemian Club's High Jinks at their Russian River campgrounds. Here he could renew friendships and make new ones. The play in 1915 was Apollo, *written by Frank Pixley. Jack is shown here with a group of friends. Edwin Markham is at his left; George Sterling is the one seated on the ground.*

At the 1915 High Jinks. From left to right: George Sterling, Jimmy Hopper, Harry Leon Wilson, and Jack.

The famous "pig palace"

George Sterling and Jack London study nature at the 1915 High Jin

Jack loved every animal on the ranch, including the pigs.

264

Guests inspect Jack's "pig palace."

At the 1915 High Jinks. Porter Garnett holds the tent up while George Sterling and Jack relax.

George Sterling, Stewart Edward White, and Jack London pose in front of one of the redwood trees at the Russian River Bohemian Club campground in 1915 during the High Jinks

Jack loved to hitch up four horses and take his guests sightseeing on the ranch and through his beloved Valley of the Moon. Now he could also show them his piggery, which had been completed in February. It was the showplace of the country; there had never been anything like it before. The two-room "suites" were arranged in a circle surrounding a two-story cylindrical feed building. One man could easily feed all the hogs, even when filled to its capacity of over two hundred. He simply let the feed down a chute from the second floor into a mixing vat. From there it was only a few feet out either door to a trough in each enclosure. Each unit had a water trough that was filled simultaneously by the turning of a single valve. It was a magnificent stone structure with every possible convenience. Nobody called it a pigpen; it was known throughout the valley as the "Pig Palace."

After Jack had completed the business that had necessitated his coming home, he and Charmian returned to Honolulu on December 16. On New Year's Eve, 1915, they attended a reception in the throne room of the old Palace, with both Queen Liliuokalani and Governor Pinkham present.

LOOKING INTO A BRIGHT NEW WORLD

By 1916 Jack was a prematurely aging man with ever-increasing symptoms of terminal uremia, but his spirit was still undaunted. The project he was now engaged in gave him a boost mentally and financially. In October *Cosmopolitan* had asked him to novelize *Hearts of Three*, a movie scenario being written by Charles Goddard. Not only did the magazine offer the munificent sum of twenty-five thousand dollars, but it also let him take a hiatus from his contract to do the work.

A pensive mood

For the first time in his life he could actually see himself solvent in a few years. With the money from *Hearts of Three* he was able to pay off almost every mortgage on the ranch and on the houses in Oakland. Now that he was earning in the neighborhood of seventy thousand dollars a year, the ranch and all his dependents were no longer eating up his earnings faster than he could bring them in. He was still writing his thousand words and everything was already sold at a minimum of twenty cents a word. Royalties were coming in from nearly forty books, both in the United States and from several foreign countries. The royalties from motion pictures were also adding their share.

The only thing that marred his perfect happiness was the ever present company of the "noseless one." The medical books told him people could live thirty years after the discovery of bad kidneys. But his worsening condition told him otherwise. In March he woke during the night in terrible pain. Jack had Charmian call in Doctors Herbert and Walters, for he had been seized with the agonies of kidney stones. His body was filling with poison from pyorrhea. His kidneys could no longer perform their function. He was ordered to stop eating *aku*, raw bonita, and he actually gave in and went on a strict bland diet.

He wasn't the same Jack London. He was bloated, pale, and nervous, and irritable with friends. His boyish laughter was seldom heard. He had grown old and tired. Most of his friends in the Islands thought he was overworking, but never guessed that the invincible Jack London was suffering greatly and facing terminal illness.

Most of that spring and summer the Londons entertained with luncheons, dinners, dances, card parties, teas, and swimming parties in a lavish effort to let their friends in Hawaii know how much they were appreciated. Obviously Charmian realized that this could be Jack's last opportunity. No longer did he want to go riding or swimming, being content to sleep in his hammock most of the afternoon.

Before leaving the Hawaiian Islands on July 26 to attend the Bohemian Club High Jinks in August, Jack not only kept up his pace on *Hearts of*

A rare picture of Jack and Charmian London

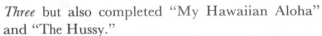

Jack, Charmian, and Possum on the ranch in 1916

Three but also completed "My Hawaiian Aloha" and "The Hussy."

While in Hawaii, Jack had been influenced by his reading of Carl Jung. It caused him to reevaluate his writing. He looked back over his literary efforts and realized that he had been highly successful with his books, but that his underlying motif had not been effective. His attempts to preach socialism and evolution had seldom succeeded. The world read and reread his books, and still these things escaped them.

In March Jack resigned from the Socialist Party. Petty quarrels and squabbling among socialists had robbed the party of its fire and its emphasis on the class struggle. Some of the choicest issues peculiar to socialist doctrines had been siphoned off by the other parties and were now being promoted by them to the detriment of the Socialist Party's strength. The fight to abolish child labor, to gain better working conditions, for public ownership of utilities, etc., were no longer issues monopolized by

the socialists. The only thing left to them exclusively, other than total socialism, was their attempt to gain public ownership of essential industries.

Now Jack could see that in Honolulu democracy and capitalism were working and bringing happiness to the majority without the poverty and suffering of exploited masses. He still believed in socialism, but he no longer had faith in the ability of the workingman to achieve it. Socialism was utopian. He had tried his best to inspire the working class into a cohesive force that would insure victory in the class struggle, but he had failed—the workers had not responded.

On September 21, 1916, he wrote a letter to the Secretary of the Socialist Party of the United States:

I gave a quarter of a century of the flower of my life to the revolutionary movement, only to find that it was as supine under the heel as it was

Charmian always rode astride. She was one of the first in the Bay Area to do so.

a thousand centuries before Christ was born. Will the proletariat save itself? If it won't, it is unsavable.

Jack had said in his letter of resignation: "Liberty, Freedom and Independence are royal things that cannot be presented to, nor thrust upon, races or classes."

Because of its fear of socialism, the capitalist class had thrown enough sops at the working class to satisfy their basic demands, and the workers were no longer willing to fight for equality. They weren't willing to take a chance on losing what they had gained. Jack was thoroughly disgusted and felt free to pursue a few of his own goals and aspirations. No longer tied to socialism, he also was free of Alaska, the primitive, the survival of the fittest, evolutionary concepts, and raw red-blooded tales; now he could look into new worlds. And as he looked he found Carl Jung and the *Psychology of the Unconscious*. He was enraptured and enlightened.

He turned to Charmian and said, "Mate Woman, I tell you I am standing on the edge of a world so new, so terrible, so wonderful, that I am almost afraid to look over into it."

When Jack's *Star Rover* appeared in serial form in 1914, a careful London student would have noticed two things—first, that he knew his years were numbered; second, that he was reaching out for a different writing theme. His use of astral projection was new and exciting. The book is a curious mixture of idealism and mysticism designed to expose the corrupt and brutalizing penal system of his day. The story is based on the actual experiences of Ed Morrell and Jake Oppenheimer as they suffered all the indignities and horrors of the straitjacket—a diabolical device for punishing incorrigible prisoners in the dungeons of San Quentin prison.

Earle Labor in *Jack London* described the astral projections:

If the *Star Rover* is not "the staggering punch"

that London wanted, it is not a dull book. Taking Morrell's story as the basis for his main narrative, London added a series of soul-flight adventures, any one of which would have made a marketable short story: Darrell Standing, the narrator, through astral projection relives parts of former lives as (1) the French Count Guillaume Sainte-Maure, who loves and fences during the late Renaissance in the best Dumas style; (2) the youth Jesse Fancher, who, traveling with a wagon from Arkansas, is killed by the Mormons and Indians in the notorious Mountain Meadow Massacre; (3) a fourth-century Christian ascetic who inhabits a tiny cave in the Egyptian desert; (4) Adam Strang, a blond superman who fights nobly against the 'yellow peril' in the sixteenth-century Orient; (5) the herculean Dane, Ragnar Lodbrog, who is captured in a battle with the Roman Army and subsequently becomes a legionary officer under Pilate during the time of the Crucifixion; (6) Daniel Foss, a castaway who lives for eight years on a desert island during the early nineteenth century. In addition to these major projections, other fragmentary reincarnations take Darrell Standing back to prehistoric existences.

Neither *The Star Rover,* which marked an abrupt change in London's literary style, nor *On the Makaloa Mat,* which contains some of the finest short stories written after his literary life was turned around by Jungian psychology, received the place it deserves in American literature. The war in Europe was too much in the minds of the reading public for these books to be adequately promoted by the publishers, and Jack's vast European market was in shambles.

The last story Jack London ever wrote was "The Water Baby." This frame story is full of the same lyrical beauty that is found in his earlier Northland tales. It employs Oedipal symbolism and other Jungian concepts. According to James McClintock in *White Logic,* "Lakana discusses with Kohokumu Christian and Polynesian mythologies, their basis in scientific theories of evolution, the nature of dreams, and ultimately, the meaning of life and death." Kamaaina was the name given by Hawaiians to those nonnatives of Hawaii who had been accepted as one of them. It was very rarely bestowed. It was a title that Jack coveted most. When, late in 1916, the Hawaiian people began to accept Jack, he was elated and humbled to know that he was thought of in terms of Kamaaina; a distinction that even Hawaiian-born Americans seldom achieved.

In *Our Hawaii* Charmian says:

Kamaaina, desire of his heart, he became, until, in the end, the Hawaiians offered him the most honored name in their gift, which is my pride forever. In Hawaiian historical events, Kamehameha I was the only hero ever designated:
"Ka Olali o Hawaii nui Kuaulii ka moa mahi i ku i ka moku," which is to say, "The excellent genius who excelled at the point of the spear all the warriors of the Hawaiian Islands, and became the consolidator of the group." And to Jack London, this is their gift: "Ka Olali o kapeni maka kila."

"By the point of his pen his genius conquered all prejudice and gave out to the world at large true facts concerning the Hawaiian people and other nations of the South Seas."

LAST DAYS ON THE RANCH

Jack and Charmian attended the State Fair in Sacramento after his annual participation in the Bohemian High Jinks. Immediately after arrival on September 4 Jack went to bed with extremely painful "rheumatism" in his left foot. Unable to even stand on the foot, he spent the entire week in bed. On the 13th Dr. Martin Van Buren Turley of Portland, Oregon, who had known Jack in the South Seas, visited him in his hotel room. Finding him in bed, the doctor sent his traveling companion, R. H. L. Davis, for a prescription. By the following day Jack was on his feet again and returned to the ranch with Dr. Turley and Davis, who spent several days as ranch guests.

By late September Jack was getting his work shipshape in preparation for a business trip to New

Jack loved to work outdoors.

York, with a stopover in Chicago. He planned to leave in the middle of November and return after Christmas, but the trip was delayed by a legal battle with his neighbors concerning riparian rights over his new lake, which was fed by Graham Creek. Landowners below the ranch, with property on Graham Creek, felt Jack would siphon off too much water and stop the flow past their land.

His beloved horse Neuadd Hillside, "The Great Gentleman," was found dead in the pasture the morning of October 22. The news hit Jack harder than the burning of Wolf House. He broke the news to Charmian, looking like a lost child, with tears streaming down his face. The next day Jack announced that he was putting aside the novel *Cherry* to write a novel based on Neuadd. Charmian said that the death of Jack's Shire stallion weighed heavily on him, and he gave way to a listlessness she had never seen before.

Charmian was getting more and more alarmed over Jack's health. From October 15, when the duck hunting season opened, Jack threw caution to the four winds and with gusto consumed two large ducks, canvasback or mallard, each day. Charmian said later, "Poisoned as he already was with uremia, this richest of diets was nothing less than suicidal, and put him out of the world of human affairs in less than six weeks."

On the afternoon of his second court hearing in the riparian suit, Jack was threatened with another severe attack like the one suffered in Hawaii. Worrying that the pain might get beyond him, he instructed Charmian in the use of the hypodermic needle to administer morphine. Though extremely painful, the attack passed without the need for the needle. On November 10, the day of his fourth appearance in court, he came home complaining of what felt like ptomaine poisoning. However, after taking an antidote for stomach upset he felt better.

"I've never been quite right since my sickness and operation in Australia—and Mexico didn't help matters any. But don't worry, don't bother, I'll be all right, my dear," he confided to Charmian that evening.

On November 16 Ernest Hopkins, *San Francisco Bulletin* reporter, and a Mr. Wood and a Mr. Moissant spent most of the day taking motion pictures of Jack on the ranch, which were shown in a Gaumont News Reel in theatres across the nation in December of 1916.

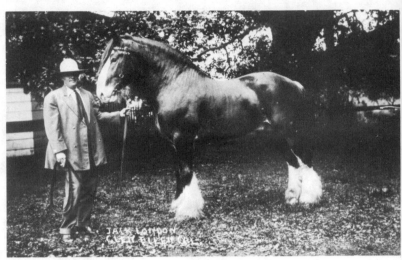

G. L. Parslow exercises Neuadd Hillside.

Jack and his favorite shire stallion, Neuadd Hillside

The following day Jack invited all the neighbors who had lost their riparian suit against him to a big dinner at the ranch. He wanted them to see what the water from Graham Creek could do for agriculture and to explain his moral and legal rights in the matter. After the tour and Jack's explanation, his neighbors agreed they should have talked the matter over with him before bringing suit.

After his usual morning writing stint on November 20, Jack rode Fritz to the top of Sonoma Mountain to look at land he wanted to buy. He was feeling good. That night, however, he barely slept. On the morning of the 21st he was melancholy, fatigued, and complained of dysentery. He lost his breakfast, worked but a short period in the morning, and slept all afternoon. He was hard to wake up and after dinner complained of indigestion. That night he went over plans with Eliza for things he wanted done on the ranch while he was away on business in New York. Now that the water suit was settled, he would leave November 29 and return to the ranch in February. Charmian noted that Jack didn't frolic with Possum as usual. He went to his room about eight. When she returned from a short walk around nine, his light was on. Peeping across from her own quarters (her bedroom was a few feet from Jack's, with the front porch between the win-

dows of their sleeping porches), Charmian saw that his head had fallen upon his chest, the eyeshade down. As she looked, he made a slight movement, as if settling to sleep. Knowing his sore need of rest, she didn't venture waking him. The book he fell asleep over was *Around Cape Horn, Maine to California in 1852* by James W. Paige.

On November 22 Sekine, Jack's house boy, tried to awaken Jack at 7:45. Failing to get a response, Sekine rushed up to Eliza's house to get her to come, it being an ironclad rule that Charmian never be awakened because of her terrible insomnia. At 8:10 Charmian was called. Since the telephone was out of order, Jack's secretary, Jack Byrne, rushed to Sonoma to get a doctor. He returned with Dr. A. M. Thomson, who diagnosed Jack's condition as an overdose of morphine. Phone service restored, Dr. Thomson called his assistant, Dr. W. B. Hayes, for an antidote for morphine poisoning and a stomach pump. The Sonoma druggist, Mr. Simmons, prepared the antidote.

Jack's personal physician was called to come from Oakland. Jack's friend, Dr. J. W. Shiels, was summoned from San Francisco. Dr. Shiels arrived at noon, and Dr. Porter in midafternoon.

The four doctors tried to arouse Jack from his coma. They lifted him to his feet, walking him

This picture, taken on November 16, 1916, was the last Jack ever posed for.

throughout the day. They yelled that the dam had burst in hopes that something alarming would break through to him. Nothing worked. Once or twice during the day Jack seemed to respond, but soon lapsed back into coma.

In a letter to Irving Stone in 1936, Thomson said that he reached the ranch around eight o'clock and found Jack lying doubled up in bed with his head thrown forward. Propped up on pillows, he breathed stertorously, his face bluish black. He was totally unconscious. Dr. Thomson had found a morphine bottle and counted the number of grains of morphine that Jack might have taken. "If he had taken 12½ grains early in the evening, he would have been dead. If he had been accustomed to morphine, had a tolerance for it," said Dr. Thomson, "he might have lasted; but if he had not been taking it, he wouldn't have lasted more than four hours."

Dr. Thomson went on to say that he knew immediately it was morphine poisoning, and went to work with artificial respiration. He gave Jack 50cc of atropine.

When Dr. Porter arrived, he immediately changed the diagnosis and treated Jack for what he had expected would be the terminal situation of the ravaging uremia for which he had been treating Jack for the last three years. Jack had taken morphine as any patient would who had renal colic. It was highly possible that in the throes of his terrible suffering he had taken extra doses of the morphine prescription given him by Dr. Porter to ease his agony. It was possible that the extra morphine was a contributory factor, but the coma was induced by retention of bodily poisons his inoperative kidneys could no longer release.

It is understandable that Dr. Thomson erred in his diagnosis. Seeing Jack in a coma and a morphine vial on the floor with only four tablets remaining, he concluded that Jack had taken an overdose, an opinion based on circumstances rather than medical evidence. He had no knowledge of Jack's kidney trouble and made the only decision possible at the time. After Dr. Porter explained Jack's medical history, Thomson revised his diagnosis and signed the joint press release with the other three doctors.

HE SOLVED THE MYSTERY

When Jack discovered in 1898 that Fred Jacobs had died en route to the Spanish-American War in the Philippines, he told his friend Ted Applegarth, "He solved the mystery a little sooner." Death was never one of Jack's worries. In fact, he had always been intrigued by it. His "dream of rest" had often been associated with death itself. He who was so much alive looked upon the "solving of the mystery of death" as one of man's greatest experiences. This probably accounted for his complete lack of fear. Complete, that is, except for his lifelong fear of being hit in the back of the head by some accident that would damage him mentally.

He once mentioned to Charmian, "To me the idea of death is sweet. Think of it—to lie down and go into the dark out of all the struggle and pain of living—to go to sleep and rest, always to be resting. Oh, I do not want to die now—I'd fight like the devil to keep alive. . . . But when I come to die, I will be smiling at death, I promise you."

When Jack was told of his diseased kidneys by Dr. Porter in 1913, it is reasonable to assume that he knew "the noseless one" was only a few years away. The *Oakland Tribune* reported on November 23, 1916, "According to Dr. Shiel, since London was operated on four years ago by Dr. William S. Porter, his family physician, he has suffered from weak kidneys. Despite the fact that his physician warned him of this, he did not seem to agree with him and continued his work as usual."

Jack knew that Dr. Porter had given him good sound medical advice and it wasn't that he disagreed with him; but he decided to continue to live according to his own credo:

I would rather be ashes than dust!
I would rather
     that my spark should burn out in a brilliant blaze
     than it should be stifled by dry rot.

I would rather be a superb meteor,
     every atom of me in magnificent glow,
     than a sleepy and permanent planet.
The proper function of man is to live, not to exist.
I shall not waste my days in trying to prolong them.
I shall use my time.

An article written by Dr. William Brady reveals the extent of the knowledge of uremia in 1916. The article, published in the *San Francisco Examiner* on December 14, 1916, was entitled "The Mysterious Disease that Killed Jack London."

Jack London, the most original and forceful novelist of our day, who has just died suddenly and prematurely at the age of forty, is stated to have been the victim of uremic poisoning. When both kidneys are diseased an individual is always in danger of various sudden but not unforseeable attacks involving the nervous system or the circulatory system, and known as uremia. . . . Perhaps the most common warning signal of uremia are headaches which persist for several days or weeks without relief, unusual drowsiness in the daytime, sudden nausea or vomiting or great distress in stomach, insomnia, sudden onset of watery diarrhea which resists ordinary treatment, and a peculiar odor, resembling ammonia on the breath and about the skin and clothing of the patient. Uremia is often misinterpreted as "dyspepsia," "asthma" and even drunkenness. . . . Delirium or maniacal outbursts sometimes develop suddenly in an individual who is uremic . . . Kidney stone is usually a concretion of uric acid salts and other material. It is capable of causing uremia . . . if kidney stone does produce uremia it is by causing serious disease of the kidney. . . . There is falling off in general health, a "run down condition," a shortness of breath on moderate exertion, insomnia, loss of weight, digestive disturbances. . . . Jack London, according to his own written word, drank tremendously for some years. He had will power such as not one drinker in thousands commands, and he managed to break the habit, he told us. But not before it had broken him. . . ."

During his last two years Jack's health declined rapidly. Stomach disturbances, rheumatic edema in his ankles, sporadic melancholia, dysentery, and dull headaches were not uncommon. At times he became argumentative and he would debate to win rather than for debate's sake alone.

Very few people noticed the change. One of them who did was Finn Frolich, who noted, "He didn't do the sporting things he used to do, wrestle, play, didn't want to go up into the mountains riding horseback anymore. The gleam was gone from his eyes." George Sterling and other close friends were aware that he was not the same Jack London. They erroneously attributed this to excessive drinking. Actually Jack was drinking less and less. His condition was caused by the ravages of uremia. And the death certificate signed by Dr. William S. Porter in the presence of Dr. A. M. Thomson, Dr. W. B. Hayes, and Dr. J. Wilson Shiels stated that the cause of Jack London's death was "Uraemia following renal colic. Duration one plus days. Contributor chronic Interstitial Nephritis. Duration three years."

Jack died on Wednesday, November 22, 1916. The next day his body lay in state in a small gray casket in the tiny study of his home. On Friday Eliza accompanied his body through hundreds of tearful neighbors to the station in Glen Ellen, en route to Oakland for cremation. Waiting at the station in Oakland was Yoshimatsu Nakata, Bessie London and their two daughters, Joan and Bess, most of "the crowd," and scores of friends.

The funeral was simple, in accordance with Jack's wishes. Services started shortly after twelve o'clock. Rev. Edward B. Payne delivered a short oration and read this memorial poem by George Sterling:

Oh, was there ever face of all the dead
In which too late the living could not read
A mute appeal for all the love unsaid—
A mute reproach for careless word and deed?

And now, dear friend of friends, we look on thine,
To whom we could not give a last farewell—

On whom without a whisper or a sign,
The deep unfathomable Darkness fell.

On! gone beyond us, who shall say how far?
Gone swiftly to the dim Eternity,
Leaving us silence, or the words that are
To sorrow as the foam is to the sea.

Unfearing heart, whose patience was so long!
Unresting mind, so hungry for the truth!
Now hast thou rest, gentle one and strong,
Dead like a lordly lion in its youth.

Farewell! Although thou know not, there alone,
Farewell! Although thou hear not in our cry
The love we would have given had we known,
Ah! and a soul like thine how shall it die.

Mrs. John Layne, at whose husband's funeral years before London had read Bryant's "Thanatopsis," did a like service for the old friend of her family. In the casket with Jack at the funeral, tucked neatly in a breast pocket of his coat, was the note written by Tokinosuke Sekine in a last farewell to his beloved employer, "Your Speech was silver, now your Silence is golden."

Among those present at the funeral service, other than his family, were George Sterling, Frederick Irons Bamford, members of the Ruskin Club, and other intimate friends. Charmian, feeling that the Oakland funeral service was for his first family, remained in Glen Ellen; her farewell would be when Jack's ashes were buried on the ranch. On Sunday, November 26, George Sterling and Ernest Matthews brought the urn containing Jack's ashes to the ranch in Glen Ellen.

Once when Jack and Charmian rode up to the knoll where the little Greenlaw children were buried, he said, "They seem so lonesome up here." Jack was touched by the fact that little David had died the year he was born. Later he told Charmian, "If I should beat you to it, I wouldn't mind if you laid my ashes on the knoll where the Greenlaw children are buried. And roll over me a red boulder from the ruins of the Big House. I wouldn't want many to come. You might ask George."

And that's the way it was on Sunday, November 26, 1916, when Charmian, Eliza and her son Irving, George Sterling, Ernest Matthews, and a few ranch hands gathered on the little knoll. Charmian wreathed the urn with ferns and yellow primroses from their own garden and wound into them the withered rust-colored leis of ilima given Jack in Hawaii by Frank Unger and Col. Sam Parker. A concrete tile, manufactured on the ranch, had been cemented in place; G. L. Parslow, the elder ranch hand, put the urn and flowers in the tile and filled it with cement. A huge boulder from Wolf House was rolled over the grave. There were no prayers, for Jack prayed only to humanity. No words were spoken; the eternal silence of the universe claimed him as he returned to the realm of his beloved Nature.

In November, 1960, the *Greenwich Village Lantern* published Anna Strunsky's "Memories of Jack London." Her article closes with this beautiful tribute:

I see him lying down among the poppies and following with his eyes his kites soaring against the high blue of the California skies, past the tops of the giant sequoias and eucalyptus which he so dearly loved.

I see him becalmed on the *Spray*, the moon rising behind us, and hear him rehearse his generalizations made from his studies in the watches of the night before of Spencer and Darwin. His personality invested his every movement and every detail of his life with an alluring charm. One took his genius for granted, even in those early years when he was struggling with all his unequalled energies to impress himself upon the world.

I see him seated at his work when the night is hardly over, and it seems to me that the dawn greets and embraces him, and that he is part of the elements as other less generic natures are not. I see him on a May morning leaning from the balustrade of a veranda, sweet with honeysuckle, to watch two humming birds circling each other in their love ecstacy. He was a captive of beauty—the beauty of bird and flower, of sea and sky and the icy vastness of the Arctic world. No one could echo more truthfully the 'Behold, I have lived' of Richard Hovey, with which he closed the essay which sums up his world philosophy, "Human Drift,"

"Behold, I have lived!"

He lived not only in the wide spaces of the earth, under her tropic suns and in her white frozen silences, with her children of happiness and with her miserable ones, but he lived in the thought always of life and death, and in the great struggle for justice for all mankind.

The beautiful little knoll where Jack and the little Greenlaw children lie together is now a shrine for the millions of admirers from around the world who come day after day to pay homage to the man who is still one of the most popular authors in the world.

A huge boulder, rejected because of its size by the builders of Wolf House, was rolled over the grave.

BOOKS BY JACK LONDON

COLLECTIONS OF ESSAYS

The War of the Classes. New York: The Macmillan Co., 1905.

The Road. New York: The Macmillan Co., 1907.

Revolution, and Other Essays. New York: The Macmillan Co., 1910.

The Cruise of the Snark. New York: The Macmillan Co., 1911.

The Human Drift. New York: The Macmillan Co., 1917.

Jack London Reports. New York: Doubleday & Co., 1970.

COLLECTIONS OF LETTERS

The Kempton-Wace Letters. New York: The Macmillan Co., 1903. A correspondence on love. Herbert Wace was Jack London. Dane Kempton was Anna Strunsky. The book was co-authored by London and Strunsky.

Letters from Jack London, ed. King Hendricks and Irving Shepard. New York: Odyssey Press, 1965. Contains 486 pages of letters from Jack London, a sampling of the thousands of letters he wrote in a nineteen-year period.

COLLECTIONS OF SHORT STORIES

The Son of the Wolf. New York: Houghton Mifflin & Co., 1900.

The God of His Fathers. New York: McClure, Phillips & Co., 1901.

Children of the Frost. New York: The Macmillan Co., 1902.

The Faith of Men. New York: The Macmillan Co., 1904.

Moon Face. New York: The Macmillan Co., 1906.

Love of Life. New York: The Macmillan Co., 1907.

Lost Face. New York: The Macmillan Co., 1910.

When God Laughs. New York: The Macmillan Co., 1911.

South Sea Tales. New York: The Macmillan Co., 1911.

The House of Pride. New York: The Macmillan Co., 1912.

A Son of the Sun. New York: Doubleday, Page & Co., 1912.

The Night Born. New York: The Century Co., 1913.

Strength of the Strong. New York: The Macmillan Co., 1914.

The Turtles of Tasman. New York: The Macmillan Co., 1916.

The Red One. New York: The Macmillan Co., 1918.

On the Makaloa Mat. New York: The Macmillan Co., 1919.

Dutch Courage. New York: The Macmillan Co., 1922.

JUVENILES

The Cruise of the Dazzler. New York: The Century Co., 1902.

Tales of the Fish Patrol. New York: The Macmillan Co., 1905.

NOVELS

A Daughter of the Snows. Philadelphia: J. B. Lippincott Co., 1902.

The Call of the Wild. New York: The Macmillan Co., 1903.

The Sea-Wolf. New York: The Macmillan Co., 1904.

The Game. New York: The Macmillan Co., 1905.

White Fang. New York: The Macmillan Co., 1906.

Before Adam. New York: The Macmillan Co., 1907.

The Iron Heel. New York: The Macmillan Co., 1908.

Martin Eden. New York: The Macmillan Co., 1909.

Burning Daylight. New York: The Macmillan Co., 1910.

Adventure. New York: The Macmillan Co., 1911.

Smoke Bellew. New York: The Century Co., 1912.

The Abysmal Brute. New York: The Century Co., 1913.

The Valley of the Moon. New York: The Macmillan Co., 1913.

The Mutiny of the Elsinore. New York: The Macmillan Co., 1914.

The Scarlet Plague. New York: The Macmillan Co., 1915.

The Star Rover. New York: The Macmillan Co., 1915.

The Little Lady of the Big House. New York: The Macmillan Co., 1916.

Jerry of the Islands. New York: The Macmillan Co., 1917.

Michael, Brother of Jerry. New York: The Macmillan Co., 1917.

Hearts of Three. New York: The Macmillan Co., 1920. A motion picture scenario written by Charles Goddard and serialized by Jack London for Hearst's *New York Evening Journal.*

The Assassination Bureau, Ltd. New York: McGraw-Hill Book Co., 1963. This suspense novel was half-completed at the time of Jack London's death. It was completed by Robert L. Fish.

PLAYS

Scorn of Women. New York: The Macmillan Co., 1906.

Theft. New York: The Macmillan Co., 1910.

The Acorn Planter. New York: The Macmillan Co., 1916.

SOCIOLOGICAL STUDIES

The People of the Abyss. New York: The Macmillan Co., 1903. A study of the East End slums of London, England.

John Barleycorn. New York: The Century Co., 1913. Written as an indictment of alcohol as a beverage. Jack said, "John Barleycorn is the story of part of my life and it is a true story of that part of my life."

BIOGRAPHIES

Bamford, Georgia Loring. *The Mystery of Jack London.* Oakland, CA: The Piedmont Press, 1931.

Barltrop, Robert. *Jack London, the Man, the Writer, the Rebel.* London: Pluto Press, 1976.

Calder-Marshall, Arthur. *Lone Wolf: The Story of Jack London.* New York: Duell, Sloan & Pearce, 1962.

Day, A. Grove. *Jack London in the South Seas.* New York: Four Winds Press, 1971.

Foner, Philip S. *Jack London/American Rebel.* New York: The Citadel Press, 1947.

Franchere, Ruth. *Jack London: The Pursuit of a Dream.* New York: Thomas Y. Crowell Co., 1962.

Garst, Doris Shannon. *Jack London, Magnet for Adventure.* New York: J. Messner, 1944.

Johnson, Martin. *Through the South Seas with Jack London.* Cedar Springs, MI: Wolf House Books, 1972.

Lane, Frederick A. *The Greatest Adventure; A Story of Jack London.* American Heritage Series. New York: Aladdin Books, 1954.

Lane, Rose Wilder. *He Was a Man.* New York: Harper, 1925.

London, Charmian. *The Book of Jack London.* 2 vols. New York: The Century Co., 1921.

———. *The Log of the Snark.* New York: The Macmillan Co., 1915.

———. *Our Hawaii.* New York: The Macmillan Co., 1917.

London, Joan. *Jack London and His Times.* Garden City, NY: Doubleday & Co., 1939.

O'Connor, Richard. *Jack London: A Biography.* Boston: Little, Brown and Co., 1964.

Recknagel, Rolf. *Jack London.* Berlin: Verlag Neues Leben, 1975.

Sinclair, Andrew. *Jack: A Biography of Jack London.* New York: Harper & Row, 1977.

Stone, Irving. *Sailor on Horseback.* Cambridge, MA: Houghton Mifflin Co., 1938.

———. *Irving Stone's Jack London.* Garden City, NY: Doubleday & Co., Inc. 1977.

BIBLIOGRAPHIES

Blanck, Jacob. *Bibliography of American Literature.* vol. 5. New Haven, CT: Yale University Press, 1969.

Bubka, Tony. "A Jack London Bibliography: A Selection of Reports Printed in the San Francisco Bay Area Newspapers: 1896–1967." M. A. Thesis, San Jose State College, 1968.

Walker, Dale L., and Sisson, James E. III. *The Fiction of Jack London: A Chronological Bibliography.* El Paso, TX: Texas Western Press, 1972.

Woodbridge, Hensley C.; London, John; Tweney, George H. *Jack London: A Bibliography.* Georgetown, CA: Talisman Press, 1966.

BOOKS WITH SIGNIFICANT MATERIAL ABOUT JACK LONDON

Austin, Mary. *Earth Horizon.* Boston: Houghton Mifflin, 1932.

Etulain, Richard W. *Jack London on the Road.* Logan, UT: Utah State University Press, 1979.

Geismar, Maxwell. *Rebels and Ancestors: The American Novel, 1890–1915.* New York: Hill and Wang, 1963.

Genthe, Arnold. *As I Remember.* New York: Reynal & Hitchcock, 1936.

Guerin, Labor, Morgan, and Willingham. *Mandala: Literature for Critical Analysis.* New York: Harper & Row, 1970.

Hendricks, King. *Jack London: Master Craftsman of the Short Story.* Logan, UT: The Faculty Association, Utah State University, 1966.

James, George Wharton. *California Scrapbook.* Los Angeles: N. A. Kovach, 1945.

Johnson, Osa. *I Married Adventure.* Philadelphia: J. B. Lippincott Co., 1940.

———. *Four Years in Paradise.* Philadelphia. J. B. Lippincott Co., 1941.

Kellogg, B. W., ed. *The Singing Years.* Santa Rosa, CA: The Press Democrat Publishing Co., 1933.

Labor, Earle. *Jack London.* New York: Twayne Publishers, 1974.

Lynn, Kenneth S. *The Dream of Success, A Study of the Modern American Imagination.* Boston: Little, Brown and Co., 1955.

McClintock, James I. *White Logic.* Cedar Springs, MI: Wolf House Books, 1975.

McDevitt, William. *Jack London as Poet and as Platform Man* (pamphlet). San Francisco: Recorder-Sunset Press, 1947.

———. *Jack London's First* (pamphlet). San Francisco: Recorder-Sunset Press, 1946.

Markham, Edwin. *California the Wonderful.* New York: Hearst's International Library, 1914.

Mighels, Ella Sterling. *Literary California.* San Francisco: John J. Newbegin, 1918.

Murphy, Celeste G. *The People of the Pueblo.* Sonoma, CA: W. L. and C. G. Murphy, 1937.

Noel, Joseph. *Footloose in Arcadia.* New York: Carrick & Evans, 1940.

Payne, Edward B. *The Soul of Jack London.* Kingsport, TN: Southern Publishers, 1933.

Rather, Lois. *Jack London, 1905.* Oakland, CA: The Rather Press, 1974.

Shepard, Irving, ed. *Jack London's Tales of Adventure.* New York: Doubleday & Co., 1956.

von Tempski, Armine. *Born in Paradise.* New York: Duell, Sloan and Pearce, 1940.

Walcutt, Charles Child. *Jack London.* Minneapolis: University of Minnesota, 1966.

Walker, Dale. *The Alien Worlds of Jack London.* Grand Rapids, MI: Wolf House Books, 1973.

Walker, Franklin. *Jack London and the Klondike.* San Marino, CA: The Huntington Library, 1972.

———. *The Seacoast of Bohemia.* San Francisco: The Book Club of California, 1966.

Ware, Wallace L. *The Unforgettables.* San Francisco: Hesperian Press, 1964.

Weiderman, Richard, ed. *Selected Science Fiction & Fantasy Stories.* Lakemont, GA: Fictioneer Book, Ltd., 1978.

SIGNIFICANT ARTICLES ABOUT JACK LONDON

Baggs, Mae Lucy. "The Real Jack London in Hawaii." *Overland Monthly,* May 1917.

Bashford, Herbert. "The Literary Development of the Pacific Coast." *Atlantic Monthly,* July 1903.

Baskett, Sam S., "A Brace for London Criticism: An Essay Review." *Modern Fiction Studies,* Spring 1976.

———. "Jack London on the Oakland Waterfront." *American Literature,* November 1955.

Bland, Henry Meade. "Making of Jack London." *Wilshire's Magazine,* December 1905.

———. "Hail and Farewell to Jack London." *California Writer's Club Bulletin,* December 1916.

———. "Jack London." *Overland Monthly,* May 1904.

———. "John Barleycorn at the Plow." *Sunset,* August 1914.

———. "Jack London, Traveler, Novelist and Social Reformer." *The Craftsman,* February 1906.

Briggs, J. E. "Tramping with Kelly Through Iowa: A Jack London Diary." *Palimpsest,* May 1926.

Buchanan, Agnes Foster. "The Story of a Famous

Fraternity of Writers and Artists." *Pacific. Monthly,* January 1907.

Bykov, Vil. "Jack London in the USSR." *American Book Collector,* November 1966.

Connell, S. "Jack London Wooed Fame Through the *Overland Monthly*." *Overland Monthly,* October 1920.

Darling, Ernest W. "Jack London's Visit to Papeete, Tahiti." *The International Socialist Review,* September 1908.

Debs, Eugene V. "Eugene V. Debs on Death of Jack London." *The National Rip-Saw,* February 1917.

Dickson, D. H. "A Note on Jack London and David Starr Jordan." *Indiana Magazine of History,* December 1942.

Dunn, R. L. "Jack London Knows not Fear." *San Francisco Examiner,* 26 June 1904.

Eames, Ninetta. "Jack London." *Overland Monthly,* May 1900.

Emerson, Edwin, Jr. "When West Met East." *Sunset,* October 1905.

Fiske, Minnie Maddern. "Mrs. Fiske Endorses Jack London Club." *Our Animals,* July 1918.

Flink, Andrew. "Call of the Wild—Parental Metaphor." *The Jack London Newsletter,* Carbondale, IL, May-August 1974.

Ford, Alexander Hume. "Jack London in Hawaii, Rambling Reminiscences of the Editor." *Mid-Pacific Magazine,* February 1917.

Francoeur, Jeanne. "Jack London Is Dead? There Is No Death for Such as He!" *Everywoman,* December 1916.

Friedland, L. S. "Jack London as Titan." *Dial,* 25 January 1917.

Garnett, Porter. "Attempt to Place Jack London." *Current Literature,* May 1907.

————. "Jack London—His Relation to Literary Art." *Pacific Monthly,* April 1907.

Goodhue, E. S. "Jack London and Martin Eden." *Mid-Pacific Magazine,* October 1913.

Haldeman-Julius, E. "Jack London." *The Western Comrade,* June 1913.

Hamilton, Fannie K. "Jack London: An Interview." *The Reader,* August 1903.

Hawthorne, Julian. "Jack London in Literature." *Los Angeles Examiner,* 12 January 1905.

Hopper, James. "Tribute to London Is Paid by James Hopper, California, 1898." *Alumni Fortnightly* (University of California), December 1916.

James, George Wharton. "The Influence of California Upon Literature." *National Magazine,* April 1912.

————. "Jack London: Cub of the Slums, Hero of Adventure, Literary Master and Social Philosopher." *National Magazine,* December 1912.

————. "A Study of Jack London in His Prime." *Overland Monthly,* May 1917.

Kendall, Carleton W. "Jack London." *The Occident* (University of California), January 1917.

Kingman, Russ. "Author Jack London Bought Glen Ellen Ranch with $7000 Advance Royalties on 'The Sea-Wolf.'" *Sonoma Index-Tribune,* 26 September 1974.

————. "Author Jack London Was Also a Farmer." *Sonoma Index-Tribune,* 22 September 1977.

————. "Becky London Fleming." *What's New About London, Jack?,* 16 October 1976.

————. "High Jinks at the Sea Wolf." *The Wolf '73,* January 1973.

————. "How Jack London Planned and Made the Cruise on the 'Snark.'" *Sonoma Index-Tribune,* 21 September 1978.

————. "Introduction," *Jack London's Tales of the North.* Secaucus, NJ: Book Sales, Inc., 1979.

————. "Introduction," *The Valley of the Moon.* Salt Lake City: Peregrine Smith, Inc., 1975.

————. "Jack London Had Vision of a Better Era for All." *Sonoma Index-Tribune,* 15 January 1976.

————. "Jack London in the Valley of the Moon." *Action,* October 1974.

————. "Jack London, Neighbor." *Sonoma Index-Tribune,* September 1975.

————. "Jack London, Playwright." *World Premier Performance of "Scorn of Women."* (Booklet), Jackson, CA: The Jackson High School Drama Class, 1979.

————. "Jack London, the Man Who Lived His Dreams." *North of San Francsico,* 1977.

————. "Jack's Jinks Number Four." *The Wolf '73,* January 1973.

————. "The Kritic Looks at 1979." *The Wolf '79,* January 1979.

————. "London Lived Here." *Metroakland,* September 1970.

————. "London's Yukon Cabin Now at Jack London Square in Oakland, California." *Jack London Newsletter,* September-December 1970.

————. "Moving on in the '70's." *The Wolf '78,* January 1978.

———. "The Search . . . The Mystery of Jack London's *Snark*." *Bay and Delta Yachtsman*, October 1972.

———. "Somewhere the *Snark* Lives." *Pacific Islands Monthly*, January 1971.

———. "Topping the Centennial" *The Wolf '77*. January 1977.

———. "What About the Second Hundred Years?" *Jack London Centennial Pieces* (Booklet). Olympia, WN: London Northwest, 1976.

Labor, Earle, "Jack London: 1876–1976: A Centennial Recognition." *Modern Fiction Studies*, Spring 1976.

———. "Jack London: A Writer for All Ages." *Shreveport Journal*, 5 May 1978.

Lachtman, Howard. "Jack and George [Sterling]. Notes on a Literary Friendship." *The Pacific Historian*, Stockton, CA, Summer 1978.

Larkin, Edgar Lucien. "Recollections of the Late Jack London." *Overland Monthly*, May 1917.

McClintock, James I. "Jack London's Use of Carl Jung's Psychology of the Unconscious." *American Literature*, November 1970.

McNamara, Sue. "Jack London at Home." *The Writer's Magazine*, August 1913.

Millard, Bailey. "Hard Labor Made Jack London Succeed." *San Francsico Examiner*, 26 November 1916.

———. "Jack London, Farmer," *The Bookman*, October 1916.

Murphy, Celeste G. "Library Collected by Jack London Reveals Thirst for Knowledge." *Overland Monthly*, May 1932.

North, Dick. "Diary of Jack London's Trip to the Klondike." *Yukon News* Magazine, November-December 1966.

Pease, Frank. "Impressions of Jack London." *Current Opinion*, April 1917.

Shivers, Alfred. "Jack London: Not a Suicide." *The Dalhousie Review*, Spring 1969.

Sinclair, Upton. "A Sad Loss to American Literature." *California Writer's Club Quarterly Bulletin*, December 1916.

———. "About Jack London." *New Masses*, November-December 1917.

Stellman, Louis J. "Jack London, the Man." *Overland Monthly*, October 1917.

Sterling, George. "Farewell, Farewell." *California Writer's Club Quarterly Bulletin*, December 1916.

Stevens, Louis. "Jack London, As I Knew Him." *Book News*, March 1948.

Strunsky, Anna. "The Meaning of Jack London." *New York Call*, 28 November 1920.

———. "He Was Youth Incarnate." *San Francisco Labor Unity*, 27 November 1924.

Thomson, Allan. "Doctors Deny Jack London Killed Self." *San Francisco Call*, 15 February 1929.

Tully, Jim. "Writers I Have Known." *Storyworld and Photo Dramatist*, October 1923.

Tunney, Gene. "Gene Tunney Tells of His Quitting Because of Jack London's *The Game*." *The Ring* Magazine, November 1971.

Unterman, Elsa C. "London's Achievements." *The Progressive Woman*, February 1910.

Walker, Dale. "Jack London: A Writer's Writer." *Art Form*, Issue 25 (n.d.)

———. "Jack London (1876–1916)." *American Literary Realism*, Fall 1967.

Walker, Franklin. "Frank Norris and Jack London." *Mills College Magazine*, Spring 1966.

———. "Jack London's Use of Sinclair Lewis Plots, Together with a Printing of Three of the Plots." *Huntington Library Quarterly*, November 1953.

Walling, Anna Strunsky. "Memories of Jack London." *Greenwich Village Lantern*, December 1940.

NEWSPAPER CONTRIBUTIONS ABOUT JACK LONDON

"Chaney Discards Flora." *San Francisco Chronicle*, 4 June 1875.

"The Death of Jack London." *Santa Rosa Republican* 23 November 1916.

"Fear Jack London Is Lost in Pacific." *New York Times*, 10 January 1908.

"'Get a Gun,' says London, Writer Talks About War." *San Francisco Bulletin*, 31 August 1915.

"Hawaii to Unveil Jack London Bust." *New York Times*, 20 August 1917.

"Heinold's First Encounter with Jack London, As Told by Himself." *San Francisco Chronicle*, 24 November 1916.

"Jack London's Appeal for Lepers Is Heeded." *Philadelphia Public Ledger*, 11 February 1917.

"Jack London and Fire Fighters Save Glen Ellen."

Santa Rosa Press Democrat, 23 September 1913.

"Jack London and Wife Are Going to Japan." *Santa Rosa Press Democrat,* 8 April 1914.

"Jack London Involved in Tenderloin Brawl." *Oakland Times,* 22 June 1910.

"Jack London the Socialist . . . A Character Study, When and Why the Author of *The Call of the Wild* Became a Convert and Propagandist. His Literary Methods and Aims." *New York Times,* 28 January 1906.

"Kipling Lauds Jack London." *Sonoma Index-Tribune,* 23 September 1905.

"Last Rites for Jack London." *San Francisco Bulletin,* 24 November 1916.

" 'A Little Debate,' Comrade Armstrong Holds that Jack London Was Socialist. L. Manly said London Was Not Socialist." *Seattle Socialist,* 28 May 1910.

"Little Vessel to be Ready for Sea." *San Francisco Examiner,* 14 January 1907.

"The Mysterious Disease that Killed Jack London." *San Francisco Examiner,* 24 December 1916.

"Nation Mourns London's Death." *Berkeley Daily Gazette,* 24 November 1916.

"Naval Cadet's Favorite Author Is Jack London." *San Francisco Examiner,* 27 January 1918.

"Russians Name Siberian Lake for Jack London." *San Francisco Chronicle,* 13 November 1976.

MAGAZINE ARTICLES ABOUT
JACK LONDON

"About Jack London." *The Masses,* November-December 1917.

"Adventurous Jack London." *Human Life,* September 1907.

"Debs Praises *The Strength of the Strong.*" *International Socialist Review,* March 1912.

"Eastern Estimates of London's Genius." *California Writer's Club Quarterly Bulletin,* December 1916.

"John Barleycorn and the Drink Traffic." *Current Opinion,* October 1913.

"Jack London." *Overland Monthly,* May 1900.

"Jack London at Harvard." *The Arena,* February 1906.

"Jack London at Yale." *Yale Alumni Weekly,* 31 January 1906.

"The Jack London Club." *Our Dumb Animals,* November 1918.

"Jack London Films." *Films in Review,* March 1967.

"Jack London in Demark." *Jack London Newsletter,* September-December 1975.

"Jack London in Hawaii." *Mid-Pacific,* February 1917.

"Jack London in Mexico." *The New Review,* July 1914.

"Jack London in Tahiti." *Otahiti,* September 1972.

"Jack London in Yosemite." *Yosemite Tourist,* 3 August 1895.

"Jack London Invited to Pitcairn Island." *Town Talk,* 20 June 1908.

"Jack London Lived Adventure." *Boy's Life,* September 1952.

"Jack London News." *The CEA Critic,* May 1972.

"Jack London's Literary Habits." *Writer's Weekly,* July 1915.

"Jack London's New Haven Speech." *The Arena,* April 1906.

"Jack London's Place in American Literature." *The Nation,* 30 November 1916.

"London Leads All Authors, Native and Foreign, in Sweden." *The Publisher's Weekly,* 3 September 1932.

"London on Socialism." *The Advance,* 8 February 1906.

"London Slumming." *Sunset,* June 1903.

"Notes on Upton Sinclair and Jack London." *Courier—Once a Week,* 20 May 1906.

"Oakland's First and Last Chance." *Air California Magazine,* vol. 2, no. 10, n.d.

"Oakland's Jack London Square." *The Searchlight,* March-April 1951.

"Turned Down in Bohemia." *Town Talk,* 3 July 1915.

"The Valley of the Moon Remembers Jack London." *California Highway Patrolman,* January 1961.

"W. H. Chaney: A Reappraisal." *American Book Collector,* November 1966.

"The Year in Letters." *Town Talk,* 23 December 1911.

MAGAZINE AND NEWSPAPER
CONTRIBUTIONS BY JACK LONDON

"Again the Literary Aspirant." *The Critic,* September 1902.

"Ape and Tiger in Us Demand Fight." *New York Herald,* 28 June 1910.

"Are There Any Thrills Left in Life." *Overland Monthly,* May 1917.

"Describes Hawaii's Lure." *New York American,* September 1916.

"Each Record Broken Adds to Country's War Strength." *San Francisco Examiner,* 21 July 1901.

"The Economics of the Klondike." *Review of Reviews,* January 1900.

"Editorial Crimes." *Dilettante,* March 1901.

"From Dawson to the Sea." *Buffalo Express,* 4 June 1899.

"Housekeeping in the Klondike." *Harper's Bazaar,* 15 September 1900.

"The Joy of Small-Boat Sailing." *Country Life in America,* 1 August 1912.

"The Joy of the Surf Rider." *Pall Mall,* September 1908.

"On the Fights." *Oakland Herald,* 30 January 1907.

"Phenomena of Literary Evolution." *The Bookman,* October 1900.

"Plea for the Square Deal." *Overland Monthly,* May 1917.

"The Psychology of the Surfboard." *Mid-Pacific,* May 1915.

"Pugilism Is an Instinctive Passion of Our Race." *Pittsburgh Labor Tribune,* 4 August 1910.

"A Reminiscence of Boston." *Boston Transcript,* 26 May 1900.

"Resignation from the Socialist Party." *Overland Monthly,* May 1917.

"Riding the South Sea Surf." *Woman's Home Companion,* October 1907.

"Ruhling-Jeffries Fight." *San Francisco Examiner* 16 November 1901.

"Running a Newspaper." *Australia Star,* 4 February 1909.

"The Social Revolution." *Australia Star,* 16 November 1908.

"Socialist VS Capitalist." *Yale Alumni Weekly,* 31 January 1906.

"Socialist Views." *Oakland Times,* 12 August 1896.

"Something Rotten in Idaho: The Tale of the Conspiracy Against Moyer, Pettibone and Haywood." *Chicago Sunday Socialist,* 4 November 1906.

"Strange Verbs." *Journal of Education,* 14 July 1899.

"Stranger than Fiction." *The Critic,* August 1903.

"Strike Methods—American and Australian." *Australia Star,* 14 January 1909.

"Their Alcove." *Woman's Home Companion,* September 1900.

"The Voter's Voice—a Plea for the Initiative and Referendum." *Oakland Times,* 9 May 1896.

"The Walking Delegate." (A Review.) *San Francisco Examiner,* 28 May 1905.

"Washoe Indians Resolve to Be White Men." *San Francisco Examiner,* 16 June 1901.

"What Are We to Say." *American Journal of Education,* 13 July 1899.

"What Communities Lose by the Competitive System." *Cosmopolitan,* November 1900.

"What Life Means to Me." *Cosmopolitan,* March 1906.

"What Shall be Done with This Boy." *San Francisco Examiner,* 21 June 1903.

"What Socialism Is." *San Francisco Examiner,* 25 December 1895.

"What We Will Lose When the Japs Take Hawaii." *San Francisco Examiner,* 20 August 1916.

"Wheatland Hop-Field Riot." *San Francisco Bulletin,* 12 December 1913.

"Why I Voted for Equal Suffrage." *New York Independent,* 11 September 1913.

"The Writer's Philosophy of Life." *Occident,* 8 December 1916.

"The Yankee Myth." *Australia Star,* 2 November 1909.

"Young Author's Endowment." *New York Independent,* 28 July 1910.

MAJOR SOURCES FOR FURTHER
STUDY OF JACK LONDON

Henry E. Huntington Library, San Marino, CA.

Jack London Research Center, Jack London Bookstore, Glen Ellen, CA.

Jack London State Historical Park (Holman Collection), Glen Ellen, CA.

Oakland Public Library, Oakland, CA.

Stanford University Library, Stanford, CA.

University of California Library, Berkeley, CA.

University of California Library (Irving Stone Collection), Los Angeles, CA.

University of Southern California (Cresmer Collection), Los Angeles, CA.

Utah State University Library, Logan, UT.